Sanitary Commission United States, Lydia Minturn ed Post

Soldiers' Letters

From Camp, Battlefield and Prison

Sanitary Commission United States, Lydia Minturn ed Post

Soldiers' Letters
From Camp, Battlefield and Prison

ISBN/EAN: 9783744760980

Printed in Europe, USA, Canada, Australia, Japan

Cover: Foto ©ninafisch / pixelio.de

More available books at **www.hansebooks.com**

Soldiers' Letters

SOLDIERS' LETTERS.

FROM

CAMP, BATTLE-FIELD AND PRISON.

> "To thee, O dear, dear country!
>   Mine eyes their vigils keep:
> For very love, beholding
>   Thy happy name, they weep!
> The mention of thy glory,
>   And thy noble martyr throng,
> Is life, and love, and power!
>   Thine is the victor's laurel,
> And thine the golden dower!"

EDITED BY

LYDIA MINTURN POST.

Published for the U. S. Sanitary Commission.

NEW YORK:
BUNCE & HUNTINGTON, PUBLISHERS,
540 BROADWAY.
1865.

Entered according to Act of Congress, in the year one thousand eight hundred and sixty-five,

By BUNCE & HUNTINGTON,

In the Clerk's Office of the District Court of the United States for the Southern District of New York.

ALVORD, PRINTER.

RENNIE, SHEA & LINDSAY,
STEREOTYPERS & ELECTROTYPERS,
81, 83 & 85 Centre-st.,
NEW YORK.

TO THE

SOLDIERS OF THE UNION,

THE

NOBLE ARMY

OF BRAVE DEFENDERS OF FREEDOM AND THE RIGHT,

Living and Fallen,

TO WHOM

EVERY NON-COMBATANT IN THE LAND,

MAN, WOMAN, OR CHILD,

OWES A DEBT OF GRATITUDE, LIFE-LONG AND PROFOUND,

THIS VOLUME

IS

IN PRIDE AND PLEASURE

DEDICATED.

PREFACE.

THE events of the past four years are fresh in the minds of all. Who has forgotten the thrill of horror experienced when the news came of the attack upon Sumter, confirming the truth he was so slow to believe, that sacrilegious hand had been laid upon the sacred Ark of the Union, and the terrible alternative forced upon the Government of war, dismemberment, or complicity with an evil which would rear its hydra-head, and spread blight over our fair territories and sister States yet to be?

And we remember, too, that when the grievous necessity of war was accepted, each one felt that the lion had but to shake off his lethargy, put forth his strength, and go forward—the Army of the North—in a grand triumphal march, to quell and intimidate, by its *presence*, our rebellious, misguided brethren, and bring them with contrition back into the fold—back into the once United compact, those who had inconsiderately stricken a blow at the great Magna Charta of Union and Liberty.

Nor have we forgotten that instead of erring repentant *brethren*, we found a foe powerful, persistent, implacable—nor the dark days months, and years of gloom, disaster, and defeat—the times when the "heavens seemed as brass," and sympathy was shut against us from abroad, and the powerful nations of the earth—saving the great Empire of the North, which was *breaking* chains, while our Southern insurgents sought perpetually to *rivet* them—appeared to rejoice in our discomfiture, and take satisfaction in the design of the building up of a great Confederacy, to be founded upon the cornerstone of human slavery.

But we will not dwell upon the mournful picture—for surely the white-winged Angel of Peace is hovering near, and rays of hope and joy are breaking through the dark cloud so long resting upon our beloved country, and we shall ere long hear the sweet music of the glad tidings sung on the Judean plains,

"Peace on earth, good-will towards men."

In looking back upon this sad history, upon the times when the gray-haired—the middle-aged—the heads of families—the only sons of widowed mothers—and ofttimes *all* the sons of aged parents—members of a peace-loving, industrious community, who had known of war but as a dream of the past—all rushed to arms in their country's defence; a gleam of comfort pierces the gloom overspreading every home and fireside of the North, the East, the West: it is the welcome thought of the blessed ministrations, never to be forgotten—the efficient, far-reaching, provident, beneficent, Sanitary Commission.

In its behalf, this collection of soldiers' letters is made, published —letters sent in response to the following appeal:

"SOLDIERS' LETTERS.

"A collection of extracts from the letters and diaries of soldiers, both officers and privates, is being made for publication in aid of the Sanitary Commission. It is believed that much material of interest may thus be brought to light, viz.: Thrilling incidents of heroic conduct and self-sacrificing patriotism, and noble sentiments, expressed to mothers, sisters, wives, friends—from camp and field, fort and outpost, ship and gunboat. Persons possessing such records are earnestly invited to respond to this appeal."

The letters are, with few exceptions, printed from manuscript letters, never before published.

CONTENTS.

	LETTER
ABRAHAM LINCOLN TO MRS. BIXBY. A Loyal Family.	
G. H. WESTON, Chaplain. March of the Seventh Regiment	1
ABIGAIL GRANT. Letter of '76 Patriotism	2
BYRON WILSON. Army of the Potomac	3, 4
DWIGHT LINCOLN. Spiking a Rebel Battery	5, 6
" "	7
RICHARD DERBY, Captain	8, 9
ANONYMOUS	10
RICHARD DERBY. Ball's Bluff	11
" " Poolesville	12
" " Ball's Bluff	13
ANONYMOUS. Duties of an Army-Officer	14, 15
ARTHUR BUCKMINSTER FULLER. A Memorial and Letters	16
RICHARD DERBY. Ball's Bluff	17
WALTON GRINNELL, Acting-Master. Naval Engagement	18
A. DAVENPORT, Lieutenant. Army of the Potomac	19
STAFF-OFFICER. Knoxville	20
W. H. TIMBERLAKE, Lieutenant. General Sherman's Division	21
" " Expedition to Port Royal	22
" "	23
" " Hampton Roads	24
" " Hilton Head	25
" " Flight of the Chivalry	26
W. M. McLAIN, Lieutenant. Memorial of T. A. Rollins	27
CHARLIE H. WHITE. Expedition to Newbern	28
" " Battle of Roanoke Island	29
" "	30
A. DAVENPORT. Battle of Yorktown	31
" " Battle of Chickahominy	32
ANONYMOUS. A Bloodhound Chase	33
JOHN WHIPPLE. Seven Pines	34
JOHN SWARTZ. Falmouth	35
BYRON WILSON, Lieutenant	36
" " Lines	37
S. P. KEELER, Sergeant. Army of the Potomac	88
A. CLARKE, Lieutenant. Gettysburg	39
" "	40
LEWIS BENEDICT, Col. A Memorial	41, 42
ANONYMOUS. The Brave Tars	43
S. D. GREENE, Lieutenant. The Monitor—Naval Fight	44
RICHARD DERBY, Captain. Poolesville	45
J. T. SMITH, Chaplain	46
THOS. McCABE. Lines—Pat. Dregan's Effects	47
R. G. MITCHELL. Merrimac and Cumberland	48
GEORGE T. McGILL. Yorktown	49
A. T. McGILL	50

CONTENTS.

	LETTER
BYRON WILSON. Camp before Richmond	51
ANONYMOUS. Shippen Point	51
RICHARD DERBY, Captain. Yorktown	53
ANONYMOUS	54
" Lines	55
JOHN E. WHIPPLE. Lieutenant. Seven Pines	56
REUBEN S. POTTER. Seven Pines	57, 58
RICHARD DERBY, Captain. Harrison's Landing	59
A. DAVENPORT. Battle of Gaines' Hill	60
" " Malvern Hill	61
" " Bull Run	62
RICHARD DERBY, Captain. Battle of Bull Run	63, 64
" " " " Frederick City	65
GEORGE J. FENNO. Battle of Antietam	66
W. H. TIMBERLAKE. John Morgan, Guerrilla	67
JAMES LOUIS. David's Island	68
T. W. HEENAN, Captain. Newbern	69
A. M. LEWIS. Vicksburg	70
M. G. CHRISTIE	71
W. H. TIMBERLAKE, Adjutant. Perrysville	72
ANONYMOUS. Perrysville	73
" Just Enlisted	74
" Shiloh	75
A. DAVENPORT. Falmouth	76
W. H. TIMBERLAKE, Adjutant. Murfreesboro	77
ANONYMOUS	78, 79
" Fall of Vicksburg	80, 81
" Lines	82
EDMUND EVARTS, Sergeant. Federal Hill	83
" " " Fort McHenry	84-88
" " " Eastville	89
" " " Federal Hill	90
JOHN WHIPPLE, Lieutenant. Battle of Newbern	91
H. H. PENNIMAN, M.D. Lake Providence, La.	92
E. H. KETCHUM. Falmouth	93
ANONYMOUS. Algiers	94
" A Western Soldier to a N. E. Woman	95
ROBERT HORAN. Vicksburg	96
JOHN WHIPPLE. Fort Anderson	97, 98
S. A. ROLLINS, Sergeant.	99
JOHN WHIPPLE. Fort Anderson	100
H. H. PENNIMAN, M.D. Vicksburg	101-104
HUTCHINSON. Fredericksburg	105
" Forlorn Hope	106
S. A. ROLLINS, Sergeant. Vicksburg	107
J. G. GOODMAN. Resting after Battle	108
CHARLES E. HOOVER	109
LLOYD KNIGHT	110
CORNELIUS HARRIS. Camp Parapet	111
FRANK NICHOLS. " "	112, 113
GEORGE O'MALLEY. " "	114
H. P. MITCHELL. " "	115
H. H. PENNIMAN, M.D. Vicksburg	116
JOHN WHIPPLE. Snuff-Eaters	117

CONTENTS.

	LETTER
CHARLES A. HAITSTOCK...............................	118
BENJ. A. WILLIS, Major...............................	129
ROBERT GOULD SHAW. The First Colored Regiment........	120
ROBERT GOULD SHAW. Darien...........................	121
" " " St. Helena's Island............	122
S. A. ROLLINS. Vicksburg............................	123
O. M. MITCHELL, Major-General. Bowling-Green.........	124
ROLAND G. MITCHELL. Baltimore Club-House.............	125
C. F. WAKEMAN, Corporal. Newbern.....................	126
LLOYD KNIGHT..	129
GEORGE M. FRANKLIN, Captain and Aide-de-Camp. Sabine Expedition....	130
HENRY WASHBURN. Vicksburg............................	131
W. M. McLAIN. Vicksburg..............................	132
J. G. NIND...	133
S. A. ROLLINS. Vicksburg.............................	134
HAZELTINE DUNTEN. Vicksburg..........................	135
HARVEY F. MUNSELL, Lieutenant. The Spy...............	136
W. M. McLAIN. "Comfort Bags."........................	137
GEORGE M. DOFF. Culpepper............................	138
EDGAR WADHAMS.......................................	139
STAFF-OFFICER. Knoxville............................	140
ROWLAND M. HALL, Captain. Advance on Goldsboro.......	141
S. A. ROLLINS, Sergeant. A Soldier's Prophecy........	142
WARD B. FROTHINGHAM, Lieutenant.....................	143
" " " Vicksburg.......................	144
ANONYMOUS. Sanitary Fairs............................	145
"	146
W. M. McLAIN, Lieut. Greenhouse.....................	147
W. S. HUBBELL. The Raid.............................	148
W. M. McLAIN..	149
S. A. ROLLINS, Sergeant. The Emancipation Proclamation..	150
JOHN E. WHIPPLE. Elmira Prison......................	151
JAMES C. GOODMAN....................................	152
THOMAS SULLY..	153
OSGOOD J. NOYES. Alexandria.........................	154
W. M. McLAIN..	155
W. S. HUBBELL. On Furlough..........................	156
ANONYMOUS...	157, 158
D. McCALL, Lieutenant. Vicksburg....................	159, 160
S. A. ROLLINS, Sergeant. Surrender of Vicksburg.....	161, 162
W. M. McLAIN, Lieutenant. Huntsville................	163
" " " Contrabands.....................	164
S. A. ROLLINS, Sergeant. Red River Expedition.......	165
C. HUTCHISON. Fort Morton...........................	166
R. A. TALBOT..	167
W. M. McLAIN. A Rainy Day in Camp...................	168
J. R. PILLINGS. Before Petersburg...................	169
J R. AYRES. Spottsylvania Court-House...............	170
BYRON B. WILSON. The Women of the North.............	171
J. R. PILLINGS......................................	172
CHARLES DE MOTT, Lieutenant. Brandy Station.........	173
" " " " Battle of the Wilderness.	174
" " " " In the Camp, on the Field.	175
S. A. ROLLINS, Sergeant. Red River Expedition.......	176

CONTENTS.

LETTER

D. McCALL, Lieutenant	177
ANSON HEMINGWAY. Vidalia	178
J. R. PILLINGS. Pamunkey River	179
" Army of the Potomac	180
JOHN WHIPPLE. The Prison Camp	181
WARD B. FROTHINGHAM, Lieutenant. Patriotism and Hard-Tack	182
JOHN R. PILLINGS. Near the Chickahominy	183
S. A. ROLLINS. Red River Expedition	184, 186
CHESTER HUTCHINSON. Fredericksburg	187
J R. PILLINGS. Army of the Potomac	188
ANONYMOUS. Guntown Expedition	189
WILL. M. McLAIN. Headquarters in the Trenches	190
JOHN R. PILLINGS. Before Petersburg	191, 193
JOHN W. STARKINS, Lieutenant	194
F. W. MILLER	195
W. M. McLAIN. Atlanta	196
" " Preaching an Abolition Sermon	197
W. B. FRANKLIN, Major-General. Capture and Escape	198
EDWIN G. MARSH. Army of the Cumberland	199
C. P. PARKER. Campbell Hospital, Washington, D. C.	200
C. C. CONE. Chicago Convention	201
W. H. TIMBERLAKE. The Hero of Chickamauga	202
ISAAC STOKELEY. Hart's Island, N. Y.	203
J. R. PILLINGS. The Mine	204
JOHN H. COOK. "	205
W. M. McLAIN. Compromise	206
OSCAR BENNETT, Drummer-Boy. David's Island	207
DOUGAL McCALL. A View from a Soldier's Watch-tower	208
S. R. KEENAN, Captain. A Happy New Year	209
STAFF-OFFICER. The Mine	210
J. E	211
W. M. McLAIN. Exodus of the Nineteenth Century	212
J. S. CONOLLY, Colonel, A.D.C. Battle of the Wilderness	213
W. S. HUBBELL. Lost Mountain	215
JOHN ENGLAND. Prison at Andersonville	216
W. R. SNOOK. General McPherson	217
CHARLES H. WHITE. Before Petersburg	218
W. M. McLAIN, Lieutenant	219
WARD B. FROTHINGHAM	220
E. G. MARSH. Lee's Surrender	221
DOUGAL McCALL, Lieutenant. Our Loss	222
T. R. KEENAN. Joy and Grief	223

Letter of Abraham Lincoln,

COMMANDER-IN-CHIEF OF THE UNITED STATES ARMY.

The Record of a Loyal Family.

The names of the sons of Mrs. Bixby, of Boston, Mass., soldiers in the army, are as follows:

Sergeant Charles N. Bixby, 20th Massachusetts, killed at Fredericksburg, May 3d, 1863; Henry Bixby, corporal, 32d regiment, killed at Gettysburg, July 3d, 1863; Edward Bixby, private, died of wounds in hospital at Folly Island, South Carolina; Oliver Cromwell Bixby, 58th regiment, private, killed before Petersburg, July 30th, 1864; George Way Bixby, killed before Petersburg, July 30th, 1864.

A sixth son, who was wounded in one of the recent battles, and who belongs to a Massachusetts regiment, is at present in the hospital at Readville, under treatment.

Executive Mansion,
WASHINGTON, November 21st, 1864.

Dear Madam — I have been shown in the files of the War Department, a statement of the adjutant-general of Massachusetts that you are the mother of five sons who have died gloriously on the field of battle.

I feel how weak and fruitless must be any words of mine which should attempt to beguile you from the grief of a loss so overwhelming. But I cannot refrain from tendering to you the consolation that may be found in the thanks of the Republic they died to save.

I pray that our Heavenly Father may assuage the anguish of your bereavement, and leave you only the cherished memory of the loved and lost, and the solemn pride that must be yours to have laid so costly a sacrifice upon the altar of freedom.

Yours very sincerely and respectfully,

A. Lincoln.

Mrs. Bixby.

SOLDIERS' LETTERS.

MARCH OF THE SEVENTH REGIMENT.

"In reading the account of the march of the 7th regiment, it seems *tame* after the baptism of fire and blood through which our beloved country has since passed; but as an exponent of the temper of the people at the *beginning*, it may possess interest.

"G. H. WESTON, Chaplain 7th regiment."

LETTER I.

"THE regiment left New York April 19th, 1861, with the intention of passing through Baltimore. I believe it was known to the officers and to most of the men, though not to the public generally, that a terrible riot had just taken place in that city. In a few hours the regiment expected to arrive there, and if the faces of the soldiers looked pale as they marched down Broadway, as was remarked by friends, it was the pallor of determination, and not of fear. It was only on arriving at Philadelphia that we learned that the communication was cut off by the destruction of bridges and the tearing up of rails, and that it was impossible to reach Baltimore, except by marching, which would have consumed too much valuable time.

"The insurgent city was in a terrible ferment; exasperated to madness by what had just transpired—expecting their houses to be laid in ashes by the next body of advancing troops. Even Union men united with rebels and fanatics in the resolution to dispute our passage, to the bitter end.

"On the streets through which we would have to march, every house was converted into a fortress filled with armed men, and even howitzers hoisted into the second stories to sweep the avenues with grapeshot. Under such circumstances, we should have been at their mercy; and had we attempted the passage, as would have most certainly been done had not the communication been destroyed, the regiment would have been received with a storm of fire they could but very imperfectly have returned. Had we been able then to reach the city, the startling reports that convulsed all New York would have proved too true, and it was no doubt in 'the anticipation' of such a bloody catastrophe that they originated—'the wish was father to the thought.'

"On the 20th, in Philadelphia, the regiment was placed in a most embarrassing position. No orders could be obtained from Washington; the wires were in possession of our enemies; our colonel was doubtful how to act. A council of war was held: it was determined to proceed by sea. Accordingly, at half-past 4, P. M., we embarked on the steamer Boston, the best that could be procured, and resolved to be guided by circumstances. From this moment, until our arrival at the junction, I believe we were in constant peril, and I confess my heart bled as the young ardent faces filed by me to take their places on board. I acknowledge I had serious misgivings as to the issue. The boat was old and small, and even in smooth water careened so that the men had to be moved from side to side to keep her on an even keel. How so many could be crowded into such narrow quarters is still to me a mystery; and a gentleman, familiar with such operations, declared to me, on our return, that he could not have conceived it possible to convey so large a body of troops with such a transport. Fortunately we had calm weather and a smooth sea, the like of which, the pilot declared, he had rarely seen. The lower hold, filled with men, was almost unendurable; with the hatches on, it would have been a "Black Hole." But He who measureth the waters in the hollow of his hand was our protector and guide.

"Another danger to which we were exposed was, we had no convoy. The enemy knew we were coming. We were, no doubt, under their glasses almost from the hour of leaving, and a steam-tug, with a single gun, might have captured or destroyed us. One shot would have disabled our machinery, and then it would have remained either to surrender or sink. In the crowded state of our vessel, every ball that passed through her must have caused fearful loss of life.

"Arriving off the mouth of the Potomac, we looked eagerly around for a man-of-war to convoy us to Washington; nor do I yet understand how, in so fearful an emergency, such a precaution was neglected. Every boat we hailed reported every thing in the hands of the secessionists; and if the enemy meditated an attack on the capital, it was not likely they would permit a thousand men to go to its relief, when a single gun on the banks of the river could have barred our passage. Could we have ascertained the position of the batteries, we could have perhaps landed and stormed them; but it would have been an easy task to mask them until we were under their fire, and then resistance, at the best, would have been madness. I retired to rest that night with the expectation of being awakened by the crash of a cannon-ball through our bulwarks, and the cries of wounded men.

"During the night our course was altered, and the dawn of day disclosed the distant city of Annapolis. Even here our approach was cautious, for the city might be in the possession of the enemy, and a swift steamer lurking there ready to dart out on its prey. But the sight of the "brave old flag" streaming from the mast-head of the Constitution frigate, which the 8th Massachusetts had towed out as she was about to be seized by a party of rebels from Baltimore (their fathers, they said, had built her, and they were determined to preserve her), this flag reassured us. Never did the stars and stripes seem so dear to us. We never before realized how much we loved them, and at the sight there went up a cheer from our gallant men that made the welkin ring.

"The 8th Massachusetts regiment left Philadelphia a few hours before us, and at Havre-de-Grace had seized the steamer Maryland, and arrived in advance. In towing out the Constitution they grounded, and when we arrived, these brave men had been confined on their steamer for twenty-four hours, without food or drink; some, in their agony, drank salt-water, and became delirious. We consumed half a day in attempting to tow them off, and were at last compelled to land our own regiment and send back the Boston to land the 8th.

"We found the Naval School of Annapolis in hourly expectation of an attack, as the whole country round was in possession of secessionists. But we were once more on land, where the Seventh, if attacked, could defend themselves, and thus were we mercifully brought to the haven where we would be; and never did I utter a more hearty 'thanksgiving for a safe return from sea.' We all realized the fulfilment of the promise, 'When thou passest through the waters, I will be with thee; and through the rivers, they shall not overflow thee.'

"But in Annapolis we were yet a weary way off from our destination. Still not a word from Government—the telegraph torn down—the locomotive disabled—the rails displaced—the bridges demolished—and the road reported in possession of the enemy. Our position was still critical and trying. It was the original intention to march for Washington immediately on landing, as the capital, if not already captured, was supposed to be in great peril; and here, for a third time, there seems to have been an interposition of God in our behalf.

"It was finally concluded to hold Annapolis, to make it the basis of military operations, and open the road to Washington. The rails had been torn up for miles, but the '8th Massachusetts,' a noble body of men, commanded by General Butler, a brave man, commenced to lay them down and repair the engine. Intimidated by numbers, the rebels did not molest them.

"Late on the evening of the 23d inst., the discharge of a rocket from the Constitution, followed by the report of a cannon, gave the signal of unfriendly visitors in the bay. The drums immediately beat to quarters, and in *just seven minutes* from the first tap, the Cadets, the 8th Massachusetts, and the National were in line of battle, ready for action. It proved a false alarm; but I am convinced, from what I subsequently learned, that it saved us from molestation, if not from a battle, on the next day's march.

"The vessels proved to be friendly, loaded with troops. They came to take our place and hold the city.

"On the 24th of April, the 6th and 7th companies and the engineer corps, marched as an advanced guard: the 8th

Massachusetts followed, and the main body of the National Guard moved forward. The morning was one of the most sultry I can remember, and the men suffered terribly, marching, as they did, on the railroad, often between high banks; not a breath of air could reach them, while the sun was intensely warm, and they loaded with heavy knapsacks.

"By dark, the Seventh was in advance of the Eighth, after having rebuilt a large bridge which had been destroyed. Of the sufferings of that night's march, I need not speak. A shower had drenched the men and changed the atmosphere: it was cold, and the men could not walk fast enough to keep themselves warm, it being necessary, every few minutes, to halt the whole body to lay rails.

"Hungry, thirsty, cold, weary, in constant expectation of an attack, the Seventh toiled on without a murmur, dragging the two howitzers by hand; and as fast as the poor fellows fell from exhaustion, often insensible, they were put on the surgeon's car, and dragged by hand also, this having become necessary, as we were now cut off from our locomotive by a break we could not repair. Three times did I lift a soldier of the Massachusetts regiment after he had fallen, and at last left him on the ground in the care of his companions; and when, at last, the dawn broke on our weary line, I could scarcely recognize my intimate friends, so pale, haggard, and altered did they look in the cold morning light.

"Fires were now built along the line, to warm the men. The adjoining fences furnished the fuel, but the proprietor was sent for and amply remunerated at war prices. The men rummaged their knapsacks for any remaining piece of raw meat, and scoured the neighborhood for food; and under other circumstances it would have been amusing to see the tired soldiers drop asleep while conveying it to their mouths. Sleep was even more imperative and exacting than hunger.

"We found the Junction in possession of the Federal troops, and were soon on our way to Washington by rail. It was there I saw and heard read a mass of captured telegraphic dispatches, in which was disclosed the plan for cutting off the Seventh, by destroying the bridges, removing the rails, and charging with cavalry through every crossroad they were to pass. The plan was admirable, and I afterwards learned why it was abandoned.

"It seems the colonel of the body of the enemy's horse (some 500 strong) had been sent in disguise to Annapolis to watch our movements. He was there on the eve of our march, and saw the rapid formation of the troops in order of battle, when the alarm was given to which I have before alluded. He returned and reported it was inexpedient to attack.

"Hence the reported destruction of the Seventh, from the Charleston papers. They reported as done what was so well planned and confidently anticipated.

"The wisdom and prudence of our delay at Annapolis were now apparent. Had the National Guard been cut to pieces, as they might have been, not only would New York have been clothed in mourning, but a severe blow would have been given to our cause throughout the land, and Washington would have probably fallen into the hands of the insurgents. Again and again was I informed by high military authority, that our capital could have been captured by a thousand resolute men. The authorities knew not whom to trust—men sworn in and furnished with arms would desert—and the city was filled with traitors; and, aside from the enemy in Virginia, there were foes in their midst sufficient to take possession of the place.

"I cannot describe to you the raptures of joy with which we were received at Washington. Old men hailed us as deliverers, and wept like children. They had been long looking for us, and 'hope deferred had made the heart sick,' but when the Seventh wheeled into Pennsylvania avenue there was one long sigh of relief. The inhabitants felt (for the time, at least) they were safe, and that night slept soundly, who had not done so for many anxious days.

"Of the importance of the march to Washington, perhaps it does not become me to speak; I might be a partial narrator. But sober history will assign it its proper place in its future pages. The Seventh marched at a few hours' notice—marched with one day's rations—marched expecting battle—marched at a moment when the executive arm was literally cut off from its body, the North and West—marched when the government were in utter ignorance of the spirit of the loyal States, and did not know whether they were to be supported or not. At this critical moment, when the seat of government was menaced by an unscrupulous foe, they responded to the call made on them, in greater numbers of the original members than ever appeared on any gala day, at any period since their formation. Less than this I cannot say. I might say much more. I might make comparisons, but I forbear. Where all are patriotic—self-sacrificing—brave—let all petty rivalries, mean jealousies, and unmanly detractions be laid, at this solemn hour, as a sacrifice on the altar of our common country. Let the only emulation be, who shall best serve his country. Suffice it to say, the Seventh, aided by the immortal Eighth of Massachusetts (whom the descendants of Bunker Hill well know how to honor), to whom a word in our disparagement would be **very** unsafe, opened a road from the loyal States to their capital, and, as a distinguished citizen of that State remarked to me, 'broke the backbone of secession in Maryland forever.'

"Nor can I forbear saying one word in commendation of our judicious commander. It would have been easy for him to have incurred foolish risk; to have put his regiment in unnecessary peril; to have made daring experiments; to have furnished brilliant paragraphs for the press; to have criminally sacrificed his men, and furnished material for pictorial sheets. But he was intrusted with a higher and more important mission than to create a sensation and minister to a morbid taste. He was to take care that the Republic received no harm. That 'discretion is the better part of valor,' has become a synonym of ridicule; but it is a great truth, and one on which the great captain of this age, and the most humane, too, is conducting probably his last, and, we hope, his most splendid campaign. Our colonel deserves, as he has won, not only the thanks of his superiors, but the gratitude of every father, mother, wife, child, brother, and sister of the members of the National Guard.

"Napoleon Bonaparte once ordered a charge to gratify the caprice of a beautiful lady, who wished to see something of war; and as he gazed on the dead—sacrificed for an idle whim—he declared he regretted that rash order more than any act of his life. When the light brigade—the famous six hundred—made their mad charge at Balaklava, the French, the most dashing soldiers in the world, exclaimed, as they swept by, ' *C'est très magnifique, mais ce n'est la guerre*—this is very splendid, but it is not war.' No, a well-ordered retreat even, may be more serviceable than a barren triumph. Many a rash commander has had reason to exclaim with the ancient captain, 'Alas! another such victory, and I am undone.' 'The true soldier contends not for brilliant momentary success, but for solid and lasting results.' He deserves best of his country, humanity, and religion, who insures success while he spares the effusion of blood.

"I cannot refrain from noticing the mercy of Providence in the preservation of the health of the soldiers.

"At Camp Cameron, for several days and nights the exposure was terrible. Our encampment was called Mount Pleasant; but for a time, this was a palpable misnomer. It rained incessantly; the weather cold; the tents were without floors; the men, without beds, were compelled to lie down (many of them drenched to the skin from being on guard) in wet, rank clover. The hospital was soon filled with invalids, and I can only attribute their rapid recovery to their youth, spirits, temperate habits, and the skill of our excellent medical staff.

"At two o'clock, on the morning of May 25th, we crossed the Long Bridge into Virginia. It was a sublime spectacle. The silent tramp of ten thousand men hardly aroused the sleeping inhabitants of Washington. Three thousand men moved by me like phantoms; not a beat of the drum, not a word exchanged. The profound silence was more emphatic and expressive than the most noisy demonstration. Each man felt he was engaged in the discharge of a stern and solemn duty. Once across, the tired men threw themselves down and slept the deep sleep of the exhausted.

"Though there were twelve hundred and thirty names on our muster-roll, we brought or sent home every man but one alive, and nearly every one in good health. Alas for the exception! A widowed mother, and a fond young wife, mourn to-day their untimely loss,—one gallant spirit that went from them buoyant with health, glowing with patriotic fire, and eager to win an honorable name in the service of his beloved land. But let them be comforted. He fell in the discharge of his duty; his memory is embalmed in the hearts of his comrades that loved him so well; and it is sweet to die for our country.

"At Annapolis, several hundred Testaments (with Psalms) were distributed. They were eagerly sought for, and there were not enough to supply the applicants.

"It was at once touching and gratifying to observe, during a halt, the men reading their Testaments, in some instances by single individuals—in others, groups listening with the most marked attention; and no doubt many a fervent prayer was offered up in silence by the weary soldiers, for danger makes men grave and serious, and they no doubt realized that loved ones at home were praying also. Many had brought their Bibles and Prayer-books with them, but all were anxious to possess another, as a memento of the campaign. One father sent five sons to the war, all in one company: each applied for a Prayer-book, and two additional ones for their parents at home. Throughout the entire period of absence the behavior of the regiment was creditable to them as gentlemen, soldiers, and Christians. The trials and dangers through which they have passed I am sure have chastened their hearts, made them wiser and better men, and produced impressions that will not soon be effaced. If never before, they now realize what it is to pray in earnest.

"How this unnatural contest is to end, Omniscience only knows; unless He interferes to overrule the wrath of man, it threatens to be one of the most disastrous in the annals of time. But we have put our hand to the plough and cannot look back. We hope the government will adopt no narrow or mercenary policy, and accept no dishonorable compromise. The people are ready to do their part, and such a remarkable and unexampled unanimity of sentiment in the North and West, under the circumstances, seems like an augury from God, and an earnest of success. We can afford to expend one hundred—nay, one thousand millions if need be. A grateful posterity will cheerfully pay the debt. A vigorous display of our resources and courage now may be economical in the end, and save us from long dissensions and a future foreign war. Let us stop at no proper sacrifice of money or men, or regard any peril too imminent, or sacrifice too great, to accomplish this glorious result.

"We have for long years been enjoying the benefit of our fathers' toils and sufferings. Let us resolve to bequeath to posterity a similar legacy. We believe God is on our side, and it is a great consolation to know that our great captain, whom, may Heaven preserve, purposes, so far as possible, to make it a humane war. But, under any circumstances, war is a fearful evil—civil war doubly so Let us endeavor, therefore, to banish, as far as possible, all private hate and personal animosity; and while we aim to chastise our mistaken foes, let it be like the correction of a loving parent of an erring child—more in sorrow than in anger—ever praying God to give them repentance and better minds."

NEW YORK, June 9th, 1861.

LETTER II.

Copy of a letter picked up in camp by Colonel John Chester, called in history "the gallant Colonel Chester."

He was present at the siege of Bunker Hill, and was selected to go before the British lines with an exchange of prisoners, on account of himself and his company of men, whom he had *raised* and *equipped*, being the flower of the American army.

In writing home to his wife he sends this, and says:

"I was vastly pleased with the natural simplicity of it, and cutting reflections. I could not but send it to you. What must a man of any feeling undergo at upbraidings of such and so near a friend! Would you not rather be cut inch by inch to pieces? Would you undergo half so much in that way?"

LETTER III.

August 19th, 1776.

Loving Husband—After love to, I would inform you that all are well through God's mercy upon us; and through the same mercy, I hope these lines will find you well also. I keep writing to you again and again, and never can have only one letter from you; though I hear, by Captain ——, news that makes me very sorry, for he says you proved a grand coward when the fight was at Bunker Hill, and in your surprise he reports that you threw away your cartridges, so as to escape going into the battle.

I am loth to believe it—last! Yet I must, unless you will write to me and inform me how it is. And if you are afraid, pray own the truth, and come home and take care of our children, and I will be glad to come and take your place, and never will be called a coward. Neither will I throw away one cartridge, but exert myself bravely in so good a cause. So, hoping you will let me know how it is, and how you do. So, bidding you farewell, wishing you the best of heaven's blessings, and a safe and manlike return, subscribing myself your loving wife until death,

Abigail G——.

"Dear ——: I send this, thinking that as the spirit of the women of '76' still lives in our country, this may not be inappropriate for your book.

"The valorous deeds of our brave and noble men (their descendants) attest it, and will bring us, through God, to victory.

"F. T. W."

LETTER IV.

CAMP, NEAR COOL HARBOR, January 18th, 1861.

THE sentiments of your letter do you credit as a *patriotic* woman, one who appreciates the dangers and hardships of the soldier—his hopes and fears, his struggles and his *agonies* in the efforts to crush this monstrous rebellion. How great and numerous the occasions during this war for heroic deeds, and how many are already recorded for all time! The army and navy furnish examples for the historian, the poet, and the painter, that perhaps in very truth have no parallel in the annals of battles.

The Cumberland fighting so terrible a foe as was the Merrimac, going down freighted with her brave defenders, and the national banner still flying at her mast-head, is one of the brightest and yet most terrible of naval battles! It really *seemed* as if it *could* never have a parallel, and yet we find it in the *Varuna*, which, after having sent *several* of her antagonists to the bottom, and is ready to go down herself, is attacked by a powerful foe, when she, with her decks submerged to her guns, deals him a broadside, sending *him* down with herself, *her* flag still flying, *brave to the last*, and terrible in her agony! Before the record of *our* naval battles those of Europe grow pale. If we have poets, let them sing of these. If we have painters, let them paint, and get a *name* for the reproduction of such glories!

We are now seven miles from Richmond. We have forces within four and a half miles, though not across the river.

BYRON B. WILSON.

LETTER V.

CAMP GRIFFEN, February 18th, 1861.

You are feeling comforted on account of the bad weather, thinking we cannot advance; or, in other words, that *I* shall not as yet be in battle! Now are you as *fully patriotic* as a sister of mine *ought to be?* Are you not willing to give me up, if it *be my lot* to fall in battle? Certainly it is *no harder* for *me* to die than for others; and can it be harder for you to give me up than for others to give up those near and dear to them? If I return at all to Vermont, *it will not* be until the war is over.

BYRON B. WILSON,
4th Vermont Vols., Army of the Potomac.

This noble young soldier fell in the "battles of the Wilderness," May 5th, 1864, after "having been engaged in *fifteen* battles! Antietam, Fredericksburg, Gettysburg, and others equally severe. Fighting bravely, he died at his post," writes one who knew him. "By precept and example, he gave evidence of his soldierly culture. He was a young man of high literary taste and perseverance. In our *Lyceum* he stood always first. As a soldier he was unimpeachable, and as an officer highly beloved." "I could say much in praise of your dear brother," says another friend; "but all would not bring him back to you. He fell in the Wilderness, and was buried as he fell. He was buried in the silence of the night, but a few rods in front of the enemy's lines." The patriotic young Wilson, contemplating the contingencies of life and death, said: "Whatever it may be, I am content, only that the *Union* may be preserved."

LETTER VI.

SPIKING THE REBEL BATTERY.

CAMP IN MISSOURI (fifteen miles from Island No. 10), April 3, 1861.

I WROTE you at Fort Holt, but as I have time, I will inform you of the proceedings of the last week, though nothing of importance has occurred *except* the spiking of a rebel battery of six large guns.

Company A was on picket since I wrote. We could hear the rebels' reveille beating on the island, and we could also hear them mounting guard quite plainly. You have probably not heard of the daring deed executed by Colonel Roberts and company A on Tuesday last. While we were on shore for *dress-parade*, we were ordered on board the *Rob Roy*, and were taken down to the *Benton*, flag gun-boat, on which Commodore Foote stays. We were informed then that our destination was to spike a rebel battery on the Tennessee shore, where there were some big guns, which stopped our gunboat from going down *to play on* the island.

The commodore told the colonel (Roberts) that he would give him five yawls and fifty men to row them, and the colonel accepted them.

Our arms and ammunition were then inspected, and the colonel told us that our object was to spike the rebels' battery, and that "*we must accomplish it or die in the attempt.*" We were ordered to put five loads in before we left the boat. We were then divided off into five squads, and commanders appointed to each squad.

Colonel Roberts and Sergeant Atwater were commanders of the squad I was in—squad No. 1. We were put in the yawl *Benton*, which went ahead. When all was ready, we ran into the edge of the timber and waited for the moon to go down a little. After eleven P. M., when the sky had clouded over with the *appearance* of rain, the colonel gave orders to start our boat with a crew of twenty, colonel included. We took "the lead." We had spike-hammers, hand-grenades, and muffled oars. We kept close to shore, so as not to be seen until close under the fort; *for we knew* that if they saw us *soon enough* they could open fire from their battery, and blow us sky high.

My position was right in the bow of the *Benton*. We sailed along down the river silently and fearlessly, until we were right upon the battery *before we knew it*. We were about a rod from shore. The first notice we had of our nearness to the battery was two shots from the rebel sentinels guarding the guns. The boatmen shoved the boat right in where the shot came from, and we jumped ashore, expecting to find *some* rebels there, but they had fled!

The next thing we did was to spike their guns, which were seven in number. We then jumped into our boats and put back to the *Rob Roy* again. A heavy thunderstorm came on, and we came as near wrecking as I want to be. It frightened all of us *considerably*. We should no doubt have been wrecked if we had gone the upper side of a boat to report to Colonel Buford. The boat dipped water, and one of the deck-hands went overboard and was drowned.

Sergeant Atwater spiked three guns and the colonel one, but as the mail is going right away, I will close with love to all.

Dwight A. Lincoln.

The heroic young patriot who wrote the above was among the first to offer his services in defence of his country. He entered the army at the age of nineteen in the summer of 1861, joining as a private the 42d Illinois Volunteers. He was wounded and fell into the enemy's hands at the battle of "Stone River." At his release he was taken to Nashville, where, in the hospital, he died, January 20th, 1863.

In a letter of June 5th, 1862, he writes to his father these noble, patriotic words: "I am willing to sacrifice my life, if necessary, for my country's good. I hope you will all pray that I may be prepared for whatever awaits me. There is scarcely a day passes but I see men who have died a willing sacrifice for their country, and it has its effect upon me." His last letter is placed here, although not in the order of date.

LETTER VII.

NASHVILLE, Jan. 10th, 1863.

DEAR FATHER—I received your kind letter at Nashville, after having marched all day through cornfields and mud, expecting to have a fight every moment; but lo and behold, the enemy were gone, and we went into camp, wet through and nothing scarcely to eat. But the next day we had an abundance. The next day we started for Murfreesboro, and arrived at night as near there as we thought it healthy to go. But we were not allowed to have any fire, so we had to make a supper of a few pieces of crackers. The next morning we got up all wet, it having rained in the night. We ate what we had left in our haversacks, and started our brigade in advance.

We did not go more than a mile before we were stopped by the enemy. Our regiment was thrown out as skirmishers. We "*skirmished*" most of the day. Night came, and not having had any dinner, we had nothing for supper. A hog made his appearance, and we soon dispatched him. We had no time to cook it before we were called to go on picket. We went; lay on the ground four hours; and liked to have shook ourselves to death with cold; came back to the reserves, cooked some meat and ate it, and then lay down till morning.

In the morning we were relieved, and took our position in line of battle, when some meat and mush were brought up. We had hardly time to eat it before we were called on to make a charge on the enemy. We started, and had only gone a short distance before a man, who stood beside me in the ranks, was shot dead. On we went, the boys cheering, and the enemy peppering us and falling back. We drove them, and regained our old ground, which was covered by dead and wounded. Just at this time the men on our right gave way; so of course we had to retreat. In the charge, which was made across an open field, we had five wounded and one killed. The fighting after this was terrific. Our division was at one time surrounded on three sides. It was about this time that I was wounded. Colonel Roberts was shot dead a few paces behind me. I ran around till my boot was full of blood, and saw it was no use, so I lay down and was taken prisoner. I was held four days, during which time I had *two small biscuits a day to eat,* and it was over a day before my wound was looked to or washed. I am wounded in the left knee, the bone being a little shattered. It is a pretty bad wound, but I guess it will heal if nothing befalls it. If the ball had struck an inch and a half higher, it would have been all day with me. The brigade doctor said it was as narrow an escape as I would ever have.

The rebels forgot to parol the wounded in the tent I was in, so I am not paroled. Much love to all.

From your son,
DWIGHT A. LINCOLN.

LETTER VIII.

ON THE POTOMAC, Sept. 13th, 1861.

FOUR companies of the regiment are stationed on the banks of the Potomac as picket-guards. We are living like Indians or Gipsies, in brush huts in the woods, while watching the rebels on the other side of the river, who have pickets thrown out in the same way. We see them every day, but there is a general agreement not to fire on one another unless an advance is attempted, or reconnoitring parties sent out. The four companies are distributed along for three or four miles. The captain has one platoon and I the other, about a quarter of a mile apart. He has the charge of the whole detachment in place of the major, who is sick. Most of the care of the company comes on me. The men like the duty very much: it is more novel, and they have very little drilling to do, lounging around our bivouacs like Indians. We are not allowed tents, because it would disclose our position too plainly to the enemy. And for the same reason no fire or light after dark. . . . .

I don't know of any thing that I *really* need, though to open a little box of *knicknacks* from home would be very pleasant. . . . . I have written this in great haste, on my knee, just at dark.

From your affectionate son,
RICHARD.

CAPTAIN RICHARD DERBY.

LETTER IX.

HARRISON'S ISLAND, Oct. 6th, 1861.

WE were suddenly ordered day before yesterday to pack our blankets and overcoats and proceed to take possession of this island. The island is half way between Conrad's and Edward's Ferry. Between it and the Maryland shore the stream is two hundred and fifty yards wide. The river has fallen, leaving the steep clay bank softened to the consistency of butter, and overgrown with roots, vines, and weeds as thick as a hedge. We arrived after dark on the canal path, and found only one boat for us to cross on—a metallic lifeboat capable of carrying fifteen men: it was in the canal, from which we had to drag it to the river. The island had been reconnoitred during the day, but we were suspicious that it was occupied during the night by the rebels, and every thing was to be done with the greatest possible silence.

The captain went in the first boat and landed without resistance: I went in the second, and four loads took us all. When we reached the top of the bank, a dirtier ninety men you never saw. Some of my men hoisted *me* bodily over the obstructions.

The only human being we found was an old slave who takes care of his master's plantation. He thought *his time had come*, and falling on his knees began praying fervently. Pickets were posted all along the Virginia side, two miles in length, and the rest of us went to sleep. Our quarters were very comfortable, as they (the Virginians) would keep their cannon out of the way. The channel on their side is quite narrow, and in some places the bank is a bluff one hundred feet high, which gives them the advantage.

After we had "turned in" for the night the lieutenant-colonel arrived with new orders—viz., to withdraw all but thirty men to be left as pickets. We all returned this morning, and now it is night again, and the same process is to go through with again.

RICHARD DERBY.

LETTER X.

WASHINGTON, Sept. 20th, 1861.

I HAVE just been listening to an address to us soldiers by our worthy chaplain. It was a fine thing, worthy the man, the place, and the occasion. I tell you, sister dear, that his allusions to our friends at home, and their prayers for us far away, started tears which I could not—indeed, which I cared not to restrain. I know you will consider it no condemnatory weakness to shed tears at such a time. His advice to us, still to be *men* and *true soldiers*, was well-timed, and I, for one, feel a renewed determination to be worthy the recollections and kind remembrances of those I left among the green hills of my own native State.

RICHARD DERBY.

LETTER XI.

After the battle of Ball's Bluff,
POOLESVILLE, Md., October 22d, 1861.

MY DEAR MOTHER—I hasten to send you, by the first mail, a few lines to relieve you from anxiety about my fate. We have had a terrible fight, but I have come out of it "safe and sound," except the effects of exhaustion and fatigue.

We crossed into Virginia, and were driven back to the river, and had to swim it or be captured; of course I took to the water, but had a hard time over. Ours, Company H, had a fight all by itself before the rest of the regiments were engaged. Everybody acknowledged that we fought nobly, but, after fighting all day, we were repulsed, and I am afraid there isn't half the regiment left.

I suppose the fight will go on to-morrow, but we shall not take part in it. They are burying the dead to-day, it being cold and rainy.

I am ever your affectionate son,
(Capt.) RICHARD DERBY.

LETTER XII.

POOLESVILLE, November 2d, 1861.

I HAVE received your two letters after you heard of my safety. . . . . . You will see the folly of giving much credit to newspaper reports. . . . Captain P——, drove me out of the tent to-day (it stormed furiously), and said I must go in-doors to recruit, after my drenching in the river. I was quite ill for several days after. I lost my sword, pistol, and belt, as did all who swam the river. I put them on a board and tried to push them across, but could not get along with one hand, and had to let them go to the fishes. I came out of it better than some who threw away clothes, money, and all. Captain Philbrick swam across with his money in his mouth. Captain Bowman was a schoolmate of mine in Groton. We are now afraid he was drowned. He could not swim, and made one attempt to cross on a small raft, but returned. Some time after, Captain Watson thought he heard his voice out in the stream crying for help, and is afraid he made another attempt and was drowned. . . . Miss Dix has been up from Washington, and supplied the wounded with all sorts of comforts and luxuries. They are generally getting along finely.

We are looking for great deeds from the "naval expedition." If that succeeds, it will lighten our tasks on the Potomac; if, on the other hand, it fail, we may have trouble with England and France. I hope it is out of reach of this tremendous storm. You must not look on the dark side in regard to the war: affairs are at this time looking better for us than ever before. . . .

Your ever affectionate
RICHARD.

LETTER XIII.

BALL's BLUFF.

THE fight was pronounced by all to have been a very severe one, and the ratio of loss was greater than that of "Bull Run." It is a mystery to me how any man escaped the shower of bullets that was poured in upon us for two hours.

The pieces of artillery seemed to be the especial target of the sharp-shooters, and hardly a man was left standing by them after the second volley. I had always been afraid that the men would become unmanageable, but I was never more disappointed. Through the whole affair, from our embarkation in the miserable little skiffs to the retreat down the bluffs, they obeyed every order as promptly as though they were merely drilling, and fought as coolly as veterans. They showed the real English "pluck," and I think if they had not seen that it was a hopeless and desperate fight, they would have added some of the French "dash," and carried every thing before them.

Early in the forenoon, Company H had a skirmish on its own account, with a company of Mississippi riflemen. We got the better of them, even with our old smooth-bore muskets, but had to fall back to the shelter of the woods on the approach of cavalry. Our loss was seventeen killed and wounded in that affair, and the same in the general battle. I went through the whole of it without a scratch, not even a hole in my clothes. I was very much disappointed, as some officers had three or four bullets through their coats and caps; so I made up for it by nearly drowning myself in the Potomac.

I hadn't a suspicion but what I could swim across with ease, so I pulled off my boots, and laid my sword, pistol, and belt on a small board to push across. I was anxious to save my sword, as it looked too much like surrendering to lose that.

I kept all my clothes on, and my pockets full. I pushed off quite deliberately, although the water was full of drowning soldiers and bullets from the rebels on the top of the bluff. I made slow progress with one hand, and had to abandon my raft and cargo. I got along very well a little more than half way, when I found that every effort I made only pushed my head under water, and it suddenly flashed across me that I should drown.

I did not feel any pain or exhaustion—the sensation was exactly like being overcome with drowsiness. I swallowed water in spite of all I could do, till at last I sank unconscious. There was a small island near Harrison's, against which the current drifted me, and aroused me enough to crawl a step or two, but not enough to know what I was doing, until I dropped just at the edge of the water with my head in the soft clay mud. My good fortune still continued, and Colonel Devens, swimming across on a log, landed right where I laid. He had me taken up and carried over to Harrison's Island, to a good fire, where I soon began to feel quite comfortable, but was afterwards taken ill, and have been till this time recovering.

I feel as if it was in answer to the many prayers of my friends that I was saved at last through so many dangers. . . . Notwithstanding our mutilated condition, we are ready to "try again," but hope they will show a little better generalship on our side.

(LIEUT. DERBY to REV. JAMES MEANS.)

LETTER XIV.

DUTIES OF AN ARMY OFFICER.

If any one attempts to haul down the American flag, shoot him on the spot.

GEN. JOHN A. DIX.

"The following strictures, by a Massachusetts officer of experience in the army of the Potomac, were made in notice of a newspaper article calling the death of Lyon, Baker, and Ellsworth *military suicide*, and in reply to letters from his friends, whom he supposed had feared *he* might be rash.

"Without liberty from the writer of the letter, I would not dare give you his *name*. The letter was written as a reply to the wife of the officer and her father, who, without concert and simultaneously, had begged him not to be rash. It is everywhere believed, where his services and sacrifices have been made known, that he has carried out to the *very letter* all that he has pointed out as being the duty of an army officer, and his severe wounds are an added testimony to this fact.

"Very respectfully, S."

LETTER XV.

To call the death of Lyon and Baker "*military suicide*," as —— has done, is a cruel aspersion upon the dead, against which they cannot defend themselves; and he has no right, sitting safely at home and knowing nothing of the circumstances, and never having seen *active service*, to write and publish such an article as his.

Circumstances must govern in all cases. Our men are not veterans. The fact must never be forgotten. They *must be led*. You cannot order them forward and expect them to go alone. You cannot station them in a heavy fire, and expect them to remain without flinching, unless supported and controlled, *though they be the bravest* men on earth.

Example is every thing. A single word, the turning of a hair, may sway them, so as to make all the difference between a fight and a flight; and this is not from fickleness. They are intelligent and reasoning beings. They are not afraid to do whatever you are not afraid to lead them in yourself; but if they suspect you of flinching, there is something impossible or something going wrong; and then they are like sheep without a shepherd. Thus may one firm man support a whole corps, and that one must be their leader. They absolutely lean on him, relying on his superior judgment; and thus can he control them in time of emergency, after they have learned the *power* of *his* support, and not before. They gradually learn this mesmerically, unerringly. Inexperienced troops must be led; and you see now the vital importance of their having officers reliable and equal to any emergency; who, in all coolness, can judge when it is necessary to be rash and when to be merely courageous, and can act accordingly.

Lyon and Baker appreciated all this. When the occasion arose they were equal to the emergency, and their noble self-forgetfulness was as far removed from suicide as a death by consumption would have been.

Ellsworth, gallant fellow as he was, perished unworthily, as all must feel, doing the work of a corporal. It may be well enough, while we have so large a proportion of young officers in the army, to write some such words of warning against rashness, but it is unnecessary to carry them to the extent of committing foul slander upon the dead.

Thus far I have spoken only of *new* soldiers. But, even after they have learned confidence in their leaders, and still later, even after they have learned full confidence in themselves, you cannot always stay in the rear and expect your men in front to do their thorough work—however much they may feel the power of your presence to back them up. There are times when the toughest veterans will flinch and the best-drilled machines hesitate and stop, although the mighty presence of Napoleon himself be there to force them on! He was a model of cool courage and of caution, and knew well the necessity of guarding his own personal safety. Yet Napoleon in person was obliged to lead his bravest men over the Bridge of Lodi, and again at Arcola; and at Waterloo, in the last grand charge of the Old Guard, he felt the *dire* necessity of leading them himself, and he rushed to their head, but his officers seized him and forced him back. Had they left him to follow his own instinct, he might have turned the fortunes of the day.

Behind all this comes the grandest consideration of all: *God guides the balls;* and a man is really as safe in the front as in the rear. When his earthly mission is fulfilled, the shot will find him as quick as the bayonet. Then it is time for him to go.

All things work together for good. Lyon's death was more useful than his longer life would have been, else Providence would have detained him here. Newspaper critics and some others have lost sight of this.

As for me, when I am shot down let no one put on mourning for me; rather hang out the stars and stripes, and be proud. Say what you will, I am not a rash person —neither am I so brave as one hundred thousand others; I mean naturally and constitutionally brave. What courage I have comes by force of reason, and of faith, and of self-discipline, and of *determination*. I pray Heaven that when

I see the *need of* sacrificing myself, no weakness of nerve shall deter me.

"*Rather hang out the stars and stripes and be proud!*" Proud indeed may be "father and daughter," state and country, of *such a soldier*, living or dead.

LETTER XVII.

A Memorial of Arthur Buckminster Fuller, with Extracts from his Letters.

As a follower of Him "who came not to be ministered unto but to minister," Chaplain Fuller felt that he could no longer remain inactive at home, while so many noble men were yielding up life for country, humanity, and God. Actuated by these feelings, he gladly accepted the chaplaincy of the 16th Massachusetts volunteers. This regiment left Boston in the August of 1861. For a few days they were encamped at Baltimore. The chaplain here visits the spot where, for a short time, our first noble martyrs were interred. He writes: "Touching to me was the sight of the Mausoleum which was opened for my view, that I might see just where our Massachusetts dead lay, when their lifeless remains were borne to the tomb for awhile, after the 19th of April massacre. They were 'cared for tenderly' even here, and now in their green graves in the Old Bay State, 'after life's fitful fever they sleep well.' The memory of the just is blessed, and 'the blood of the martyrs is the seed' whence springeth up the army of liberty." He next writes from Hygeia hospital, where his labors among our sick and wounded soldiers began. "Here I find many wounded soldiers of the Great Bethel fight—some Germans, some Americans, and all so patient, so willing to lose life or limb for their own or adopted country, and only mourning that they did not achieve a victory. It is a privilege to visit and pray with such noble men. God bless the wounded soldiers of our patriotic army, and send them always as good care as they get from the physicians and nurses at this hospital at Old Point Comfort. Once this was *the* hotel of Virginia. In the very room I occupy and whence I write, Senator Mason, only last year, in the summer, was an occupant. These walls have looked on many a nest of rebels, and listened to many a plot of treason. In the beautiful hall with its splendid mirrors, once the ball-room of the Hygeia hotel, we held our religious services yesterday. Your correspondent preached from the text, Isaiah, xxxiii 24 : 'And the inhabitants shall not say, I am sick; the people that dwell therein shall be forgiven their iniquity.' My effort was to point to the heavenly land and its hopes as a solace for the trials of this, and to show the sick and wounded soldiery that if their physical wounds are gained in their country's service and are patiently endured; if, too, they are 'soldiers of the living God,' as well as loyal American soldiers, *all* such shall ultimately be victors,— 'conquerors though they're slain,'—and shall dwell forever in the land, no one of whose inhabitants need to say, 'I am sick.' " He now describes his first experience in tent life, which contrasts strikingly with that which soon followed when encamped on the bloody field of Fair Oaks. "I am trying my first real experience of tent life in Virginia. General Wool is determined that officers and men shall, as far as practicable, fare alike, and in that determination every good officer will cheerfully acquiesce. We relinquished, a few days ago, Mr. Segur's comfortable mansion, making it a hospital for the sick soldiery. With the aid of my two boys who serve me, my tent was soon pitched and ready to occupy. It is very comfortable, with its clean, white, arched roof and walls. I really wonder, after finding how cool it is, and that it can be moved in a half-hour, that most people consent to live in and pay rent for houses of brick and mortar; and after all, when 'the children of Israel dwelt in tents,' they had a pretty good time of it. If, however, the mosquitoes and other insects were any thing like as thick in Judea as in Virginia, I don't see how they got along without some substitute for the capital mosquito-bar, without which the musical enemy would murder sleep every night. Before the tent I have a fly or awning spread, and under that receive my visitors. The soldiers love to come there and tell of their hopes, or indulge in memories of home, and borrow a religious book or a Boston paper, to improve the passing hour. Often they ask religious counsel or solace, when tidings of some bereavement or sickness of their loved ones makes their hearts sad. Every evening, too, they congregate before my tent to hear a few words of advice, sing some religious songs, and listen to a brief prayer, at the conclusion."

Writing from Fair Oaks, after a battle, he says: "I found ample employment during the day, aiding, what little I could, those who were borne wounded and dying from the field. What sickening sights those were! Brave, uncomplaining men, borne out from the woodland, their life-blood ebbing away in its crimson tide. Some smiled sweetly in dying: some of the dead had that set look with which brave men meet a proud, insulting foe. Oh, what death-beds I stood beside yesterday! Almost all died like heroes, with scarce a groan. William C. Bently, of the 2d Rhode Island—can I ever forget his heriosm? Both his legs were broken by a bombshell, his wrist and breast mangled, and yet he was as calm as though he suffered no pain. He refused any stimulating drink that might dim his consciousness; he asked only prayer, and sent a message to his mother. Then, and not till then, opiates were given, and he slept sweetly, and for the last time. Francis Sweetser, of Company E, 16th Massachusetts Regiment, witnessed in death, as he had done uniformly in life, a good confession of Christ: 'Thank God,' he said, 'that I am permitted to die for my country; thank God more yet, that I am prepared to go:' then, after a moment's thought, he added modestly, 'at least I hope I am.' Two houses and the ground beneath 'Fair Oaks' witnessed scenes of heroism unsurpassed in history's annals."

Among his last letters he speaks of the "Sanitary Commission." "This noble agency for the relief of sick, wounded, or destitute soldiers, continues earnestly and faithfully its kind and judicious labors. It has prevented and relieved an untold amount of suffering, and the blessings of those once ready to perish rest upon it. At Manassas Junction it had very properly established a branch, in view of an impending battle. In case the expected contest had taken place, what incalculable good such supplies and stores as this commission can afford, must have accomplished by its timely action! A change of plan makes this storehouse unnecessary here, and it is being removed, but it comforts and cheers the soldiers to see such forethought. When in Washington I passed a day or two in examining the working of the Commission. I have never praised it before, for lack of this previous examination: I desire now to add my hearty and sincere testimony as to the wisdom, energy, and kindness of the action of the Sanitary Commission. After viewing its operations, I hardly see how the army could have existed without it. Its work has been quietly but energetically performed, and in perfect harmony with the Government, who approve its operations more and more, as they are longer continued. .... God bless all who care for the soldier away from his home and its comforts; thrice blessed be those who, when he is sick, or wounded, or just paroled from prison, or hungry, or dying, visit, comfort, and minister unto him. Great shall be their reward in heaven!"

After an absence of several months from his regiment, caused by dangerous illness brought on by the labors and exposure of the Peninsula campaign, he returns to his regiment for a brief period, but his enfeebled frame can no longer endure the hardships and exposure of the camp. In his last letter he describes his farewell of his regiment. He was in a measure reconciled to this course by a promise from the President that either a post or hospital chaplaincy should be granted him. Over the beginning of this last letter he writes, "Home again."

"Once more I have returned to the camp of the 16th Massachusetts regiment. For nearly a year and a half I have been constantly with them, except when absent from sickness, and have learned to regard its noble officers and brave soldiers as brothers, and its camp as a *home*, second only in affection to my own domestic household. I am here once more—not, alas! long to remain; for exposure to the Virginia summer's heat and winter's cold, together with privations and hardships necessarily incident to campaigns such as ours have been, these have done their work, and for years I can scarcely hope to be as well in the future as I have been in the past; but I have no complaints to make or regrets to express. What I have seen is worth all it has cost, and I *thank God* it has *been my high privi lege* to be with our loyal and heroic army during its hours of trial and danger. If any regret were mine, it would be that I am not able to remain with my regiment longer; but this is doubtless, in God's providence, all right, and I am grateful that in some hospital or stationary camp I am still able to labor on for the officers and soldiers of our army, for whom in hours' of sickness, or when wounded and suffering, none of us can do too much. Meanwhile, I am *here home* again for a little while. In a few days my public service closes with this regiment of as brave and noble men as ever left the Old Bay State. Their ranks have been thinned by disease and battle, till those who have gone are far more than those who remain. The history of the glorious 'Sixteenth' is written in blood—their own, and yet more their enemies'; but it is a history which will be read with tears, yet with a smile of holy triumph and joy, when the record of this war is made, and sealed at last with assured victory, to be followed by a peace that shall be perpetual, because based on liberty and righteousness."

"The Sanitary Commission have here—at Aquia Creek—erected a portable house, and stocked it with the needful supplies for sick and wounded men. These supplies are in great demand, and the Elizabeth, the sanitary storeship, plies frequently between the Creek and Washington to satisfy this need and relieve the suffering. The noble work is nobly done. I passed Saturday night in the hospitable precincts of this portable house. The night was very cold, and the ground, white with snow, frozen to a crust; ice formed even within-doors. The next day the creek was frozen near the shore, and many were walking, or sliding, or falling, on its glassy surface. Virginia looked as cold and forbidding to us as did dear New England in 1620, when, in this same month, our pilgrim fathers landed on Plymouth shore.

And indeed the cold has been bitter. The last two nights I have suffered beneath the canvas as I never did from cold before. The poor soldiers, in their wretched little shelter-tents, must have suffered even more. Few of us have slept much, but have ran often out in the night hours to warm almost frozen feet or hands at the camp-fires kept constantly burning. Many deserters find their way to our ranks from across the river. Six of these entered our lines last night. They were barefooted and almost without clothing, and ate voraciously when food was offered them. The suffering, then, is not confined to our side. Much as we endure, the rebels endure more.

"When will they abandon their suicidal course, and seek peace on conditions honorable to both sides and advantageous to the whole country? Never till they are conquered, and their idol—slavery—overthrown. Then shall we have peace—a sweet, blessed, perpetual peace."

"Joining the ranks of the brave men he had aided to gather beneath the folds of the national flag for its defence and perpetuity, Chaplain Fuller left home, and kindred, and innumerable comforts, for the privations and hardships, and the dangers and death that attend the life of a soldier.

"Having accepted the position of chaplain of the 16th regiment of Massachusetts Volunteers, the best and finest motives only were permitted to influence him in the high and holy mission to which he so fully and devoutly consecrated the best powers of his cultivated mind, and the warmest affections of his loving heart."

ARTHUR BUCKMINSTER FULLER.

"He died a soldier! though he preached
The Gospel of the Prince of Peace;
For his great soul the height had reached,
From which true patriots seek release

>From all that can their country's honor stain:
>For this he died; nor has he died in vain!
>The day he prayed for, lived for—gave his life,
>Now breaks upon us, through the closing strife."
>
>   SIDNEY HERBERT.

"The resignation of Chaplain Arthur B. Fuller (he being in feeble health, and totally unfitted for that inclement season in camp) having been duly accepted, he was mustered out of service only the day before our advance-guard crossed the Rappahannock for the purpose of dislodging the rebel sharp-shooters from the houses in Fredericksburg.

"During the day on which this movement took place, as he was seated at the entrance of his tent, preparing for his final departure, a portion of this advance-guard, composed of Massachusetts soldiers, passed by on its way to the river-bank. These men had volunteered for the dangerous service (almost a forlorn hope) which they had thus assumed to perform; and as the patriotic and devoted chaplain, who, from the first, had manifested a deep interest in the proposed movement, saw these noble men from his own beloved State, though not belonging to the regiment he had so long served, moving forward so cheerfully and bravely at the call of duty, he paused not to call to mind the fact that he was mustered out of service, and to let that set aside any sense of his own duty in the matter; nor did he stop to consider the claims of the dear ones at home (and no man loved his own more tenderly); but placing his love of country, and his desire to serve her to the utmost of his ability, above and beyond all these, he in a moment's time assumed the sublime character of the old-time Revolutionary patriots and heroes, who left their ploughs in the furrow, and seizing a musket, he entered the ranks of the advancing party, crossed over the river, and was among the first to fall after entering the streets of the city.

"The officer who commanded the company to which Chaplain Fuller thus attached himself as a volunteer, has given an account of his intercourse with him during the last hour of his earthly career. Being discovered by him in the streets of Fredericksburg with the skirmishers, and with a musket in his hands, he said to that officer, "Captain, I must do something for my country; what shall I do?" Captain Dunn said there never was a better time than the present, and that he could take a place at his left. As he seemed to be perfectly calm and collected, that officer felt that he might be of important service to him in his present emergency.

"Chaplain Fuller at once took the position assigned him by Captain Dunn, who says he has seldom seen a person on the field so calm and self-possessed in his demeanor, though in the midst of great peril; for, in five minutes after, having himself fired but one or two shots, he was made the mark of the unerring aim of the rebel sharpshooters by whom he was surrounded. He was struck by three bullets from their rifles. He was instantly killed.

"Full and spontaneous as were the military and civic honors bestowed upon his burial, they add nothing to the brightness and glory of the fadeless wreath of fidelity to duty, devotion to country, and calmness in death, which the providence of God had placed upon the noble brow of him who had thus fallen in the fore-front of battle. Thus lived and died one of the purest and best types of the old-time American patriots which these latter days have brought to the surface and made conspicuous. His, indeed, was a noble and useful career; but

"Nothing in his life
Became him like the leaving it; he died
As one that had been studied in his death."

LETTER XVIII.

Ball's Bluff, Camp Foster,
Poolesville, Md., December 15th, 1861.

. . . . . I STILL keep possession of my fork—it was in my haversack with my spoon and caseknife, and I put them into my pocket before I took to the water. I will enumerate the articles I had about me while swimming, just for your entertainment, and you will wonder I floated as long as I did. The three items just named, my large jackknife, pocket-comb, about a half pound of gold and silver coin, a package, a large memorandum-book, a package of envelopes, a handful of bullets, a metallic box of caps, a flask of powder, watch, and all my clothes, except my boots. I ought to have saved my canteen as a life-preserver, but I did not think of it, and threw it away. . . . .

Professor Lowe has been up here with his reconnoitring balloon, and made an ascension. I don't know that he made any important discoveries. . . . . I will go up town some day, and see if the artist that keeps a daguerreotype shop on wheels can take a miniature on mailable material. If he can, I will send you one. . . . Ellen is just a little too late for a lock of my hair. I had it cut only a few days ago. . . . . In company K they have an owl in a cage, and that is the latest pet.

You must not expect to see me home on furlough this winter. Officers are not allowed leave of absence except on most urgent occasions. I thought, from the tone of E.'s letter, she was hoping I should come home this winter. . . . .

Your affectionate son and brother,
RICHARD DERBY.

Alas, he came never more to the homestead on earth!

Lines written on hearing that Colonels Creighton and Crane had lost their lives in Hooker's "Battle above the clouds," at Lookout Mountain.

Oh, tell me not that lives are lost
  When spent in Freedom's cause,
When nobly, freely, given up
  For Union and the laws.

When patriots to the contest rush,
  Disdaining every cost,
And by their best blood victory's sent,
  Such lives cannot be lost.

For though the silver cord be loosed
  Amid the cannon's roar,
Yet will the spirit, freed from clay,
  Up to its Maker soar!

Yes! by such lives our country's rights
  Will be restored again;
And surely if they gain the end,
  They are not lost in vain.

That life alone is really lost
  When to no purpose given,
But lives when lost in Freedom's cause
  Are found again in heaven.

Then tell me not that lives are lost,
  Who to the death-shot yield,
But rather write beneath their names,
  "Promoted on the field."

LETTER XVIII.

Engagement between the United States ship-of-war Richmond and a rebel steamer.

Head of the Passes,
Mississippi River, October 11th, 1861.

Day before yesterday our ship had a sharp engagement with the enemy—a naval action! For three hours the shells were bursting and whizzing around us, but only five took effect — wounding three, but killing none, thank Heaven! To explain: At one o'clock a rebel steamer was discovered up the river. An hour afterwards—greatly to our astonishment, I can assure you—she very pluckily opened fire upon us. At first we laughed at what we called her impudence; but as her shells began to fall around us, and as we found our heaviest gun failed to reach her, things looked disagreeable. I will confess, and frankly tell you, that the first five or six shells that came whizzing through our rigging made me tremble all over; my knees knocked together; my mouth was bound; I could hardly speak, hardly breathe; I was frightened. But as soon as we "beat to quarters," and I was ordered to my division, all fear left me. The shells still whizzed, but I neither heard nor cared for them. I was intent upon my duty, and, as my division had all the fighting to do, being the only one bearing upon the enemy, I was too much absorbed in the working of my gun to think of any thing else; and I can assure you I felt as happy and unconcerned as ever in my life. The rebel (who, by the by, was the New York tug-boat William H. Webb, armed with four broadsides and two heavy 32-pound rifles) was our superior, inasmuch as her guns ranged quite a half mile beyond ours. About one hundred shots were exchanged, and I do not think a single one of our shots hit the enemy.

Half-past 12 P. M., October 11th. The "Webb" is again in sight, and we are preparing for action. I wish it was all over, for I am exceedingly doubtful of the result.

Two o'clock P. M. The ship is cleared, and we have given the enemy eight or ten shots, but she does not return them. She is evidently "playing us some trick," but we will never "give up the ship;" and if we only get our rifle 42's (which are expected daily), New Orleans will be ours before Christmas.

Five o'clock. The "Webb" is out of sight, so I will continue my account of the first engagement. After firing from half-past one until four o'clock the enemy retired, leaving us as bewildered as we were relieved. Besides three shots in our hull, our mizen topmast backstays were shot away. We are in a rather critical position: first, our draft has been increased by six additional guns; the water on the bar is low—we cannot cross: second, the enemy can steam two knots to our one—we cannot run: third, the enemy's guns range further than ours—we cannot fight.

These circumstances were communicated to the commodore, who said, "I thoroughly appreciate your position, and will leave myself for 'Pickens,' to obtain some rifle-guns." When these guns arrive, we can defy all secessiondom."

I have read most glowing descriptions of battles, and my imagination has very often presented to me pictures so vivid that I thought they exceeded reality; but I am convinced that the terrible excitement and absorbing interest, the bursting shells and flying splinters, the enthusiasm and huzzas of the men, defy human power to describe. The man that says he felt no fear or trembling for the first few shots in an action, you may stamp as a coward. As for myself, I never had such a sensation—nothing so terrible.

After each discharge from a gun, all the crew (officers included), except the loader, sponger, and powder-man, fell flat on their stomachs, thus avoiding the shell that may happen to strike on deck, for, in bursting, the splinters have a tendency to fly upwards. It is laughable to see them all go down at once; but I can assure you it is a very pleasant sensation to even think one's self out of the way of these terrible splinters; as one would much prefer being shot away with a solid ball, than to be mangled by one of these ugly missiles.

So much for my first sensations in battle. Although I have before been under fire of musketry, yet I can fancy nothing comparable with the whizzing and bursting of rifle-shell.

WALTON GRINNELL,
Acting-master U. S. steamer Nyack.

Mr. Grinnell enlisted in the service of his country at the commencement of the war of the rebellion in the year 1861, at the age of seventeen. He has since taken active and heroic part in numerous engagements; and, but lately, volunteered his service on a perilous embassy within the lines of the enemy, from General Schofield, at Wilmington, to General Sherman, in company with Ensign Colby, which terminated successfully, redounding to the patriotism and heroism of the persons engaged in it.

LETTER XIX.

CAMP BUTLER, FORTRESS MONROE,
5th Regiment N. Y. V., Duryea's Zouaves,
June 11th, 1861.

DEAR MOTHER—I suppose that ere this you have heard of our engagement with the enemy. Sunday evening we were out on parade as usual. After we were dismissed we were called together again, and each man given twenty rounds of ammunition, in addition to what we already had. All was bustle and activity: we knew we were going somewhere, but as to the direction we were completely in the dark. Taps were sounded as usual, and we were ordered to our tents. A few minutes after a man might be seen going to each tent, and whispering the words, "At half-past ten every man will be called; he will immediately, and without noise or light, arise, equip himself, and fall in line in front of the tents. He will be supplied with one day's rations; will also tie his turban around his left arm twice, as a distinguishing mark."

About an hour before the time I was outside of my tent, when I saw a body of men going by : they made so little noise that it seemed to me mysterious where they had come from. I learnt that they were two of our companies, who were to go ahead as skirmishers under the command of Captains Kilpatrick (now major-general of cavalry) and Bartlett. I now understood that we were to surprise a rebel camp about fifteen miles from here. It seems that a negro who had ran away from the rebels, being employed by them to help build their batteries, had given information of it, which led General Butler to determine to attack it. There were several secessionists who came down to Hampton for the purpose of shooting the negro. We were to act in conjunction with a regiment at Newport News, and others were to follow us.

We were finally on the march. Nobody would have thought that a large body of men were on the move, by the stillness that prevailed. After we had gone some five or six miles, we were ordered to halt. I looked through the woods and saw a bright light; it could not be mistaken, it was a rebel signal: it was in a house, and pointed directly in the line of their company. Further on we came in sight of another. Soon after we came to a slight halt, heard a volley of musketry, and were ordered on at a double-quick. Our company being on the right was ahead of the line, and I am near the head, so that I had a chance to see every thing. We halted, and found that we had come upon the extreme outpost. There was a camp-fire burning, and we had taken an officer prisoner. He was well mounted, with a fine revolver and sword, the edge of which was sharpened up to the handle. He was a fine looking man, over six feet high. We then heard rapid firing in the rear. We supposed that the rebels had come in contact with the Newport News regiment under Colonel Bendix. We soon saw that a most lamentable mistake had occurred. Colonel Bendix in the uncertain light of morning had taken Colonel Townsend's 3d N. Y. regiment, who were following after us, for an enemy, and engaged them! The result was that eleven were wounded, some probably mortally!

Our commander now determined to go back and attack the camp. We started, but not before we had burned down a very handsome, well-furnished house, from which one of our men had been shot dead. Further on we burned down a low wooden hut, known as the "Little Bethel," a noted place of meeting for spies and secret orders.

We finally came upon the enemy, tired and exhausted. We learned from negroes that they were very strong and had more men than we had. We were so close to their batteries that we could hear them calling "Turn out!" "Turn out!" and the drums beating the "long roll."

Captain Kilpatrick threw out his skirmishers. We ascertained that there was a strong battery commanding the road, besides others to the left and right. It was a strange sensation standing there, awaiting the approach of the foe for the first time, expecting every moment to receive a volley from the woods into our closed ranks; but every man was firm: to be sure we looked *a shade* paler, but there was but one look, "to do or die."

Our captain said the ball had commenced. Instantaneously another report was heard, and a shell came whizzing through the air: now they came thick and fast.

We were ordered to charge through the wood. On we rushed through the brush, which was raked by grape and canister, bombs and rifled cannon. All the companies got mixed up in squads, and every man was his own officer. It now became too hot; we were obliged to get behind trees and stumps. Some of the boys crept close to a fence nearest the enemy, on the outskirts of the woods, and took advantage of every opportunity to pick off a man. Captain Kilpatrick was shot twice in the legs: he did not seem to mind it, but said, "It won't do to stay here and be shot down without doing any thing." He ordered the men to keep covered as well as they could and to *form*, but the brush was so thick that it was impossible to find captains, or any officers, or companies. Finally some few of us rushed out of the woods and across the road, headed by Lieutenant Jacob Duryea, a son of the colonel, and Captain Kilpatrick, notwithstanding his wounds, who is the most dashing officer in the regiment, and charged across a ploughed field with no cover after leaving the wood. In this charge there were not more than forty, and *all had red breeches*. We laid down often to escape shot. About the same time Colonel Townsend charged further to the left. The colonel was mounted, and sat on his white horse at the head of his men without flinching. We finally got to the cover of two old sheds, and were about four hundred feet from their batteries. We kept up fire for a short time, but it was folly to stay there any longer, as we were not supported. There was no concert of action or anybody to command, and most of the troops were lying behind stone walls, at a good distance to the rear. There were only three officers to be seen on that part of the field. I guess they did not like the fun. *Outside* of their fortifications we fear the rebels in no *way, shape, or manner*. General Price thought that the place could not be taken by storm without too much sacrifice of men.

The hardest part was held by the regulars' battery; they deserve the greatest credit and glory for holding their position on the road in such a raking fire. Lieutenant Greble was killed. The guns would have been spiked and left in the road, but our Colonel Warren, who appeared to be the only officer who knew what he was about, saved the guns, and, if he had had the command, would have taken the batteries. Captain Kilpatrick's company are also deserving of great credit for skirmishing duty.

Major Winthrop, aid to General Butler, and a very superior man, was picked off early by a sharp-shooter. He was showing himself carelessly while reconnoitring their position, and hence his death. Hoping that Providence will prosper our cause and give us the victory, I now close.

Your affectionate son,
A. DAVENPORT,
New York Duryea Zouaves.

LETTER XX.

KNOXVILLE.

My last letter brought the historical narrative up to the point where, some two weeks ago, we mounted our steeds at Henderson's station for an all-night ride. It was a most magnificent night, clear, cold, with a stunning moon, and we trotted on in the best possible spirits for ten or fifteen miles, singing and cracking jokes till bedtime came without the accompanying bed, and we subsided into the regular cavalry jog. About four in the morning we reached Jonesboro, a little village wrapped in slumber.

Ambulances containing our servants and luggage did not arrive, and there was much tribulation. I pegged round and tried to get some information about roads, but the fool crop must have been immensely heavy in that part of the country, for not a man could be found who knew any thing. I managed to get half an hour's sleep, with my head on a table, and then started again. About daylight, overtook the troops, thus shaking themselves after reveille, and they yelled for the space of half an hour at the sight of "old father Burnside," as these Western men call him, riding up through the dawn.

At the end of three hours' sleep, violent shaking aroused us to accompany the general to the front. Rode some few miles—took a cheerful view of some woods filled with rebs—sent in a flag of truce, telling them to get the women and children out of the village hard by, and went home to dinner, and after it resumed the napping until 1 o'clock p. m., with slight lucid intervals, when the general roused me, and I was up and doing the rest of the night.

The assault on the enemy's position was ordered at daybreak, and I pegged around in the darkness to give some additional instructions.

The skirmishers discovered that the rebs had evacuated during the night, burning a long railroad bridge behind them. We concluded to let them alone and turn our steps to aid Rosecrans, so we pulled up stakes and turned round. Reached the station at half-past three in the morning, spread our blankets on the bottom of a freight-car and went to sleep, being dragged the while by a wheezy engine towards Knoxville.

Two divisions of the Ninth corps were slapped up to Morristown by rail; and a cavalry brigade was sent round by way of Rogersville, to intercept the enemy's retreat. On Friday, headquarters went up to Bull's Gap, 14 miles beyond Morristown. Next day started for the front, half a dozen miles off—passed through the troops, who cheered with their caps off, and found the cavalry brigade skirmishing feebly with the enemy. Egged them on, and soon the jolly and familiar boom of cannon saluted our ears as we sat on a hill-side—the general walking to and fro cogitating—we dashing hither and thither, bringing up troops, &c., quite after the fashion of a large battle, though this was only a small fight.

Some contractor, who ought to be hung, had furnished very poor ammunition—just as we got there one of our shells exploded among our own men, killing two. We were all standing out on the hill, when some enterprising rebel sharp-shooters opened on us, and the first thing we knew, bullets were whistling around rather lively. The hill was cleared with great celerity, but Colonel Sanders and myself stayed to finish some observations we were making. We were standing close together talking when a bullet passed between us and struck a gun-carriage behind us. We concluded to take the hint and retire to cover. Just then a shell burst over the place we were going to, causing the liveliest stampede of spectators; two or three negroes never stopped to run, but literally rolled down hill, and I saw an able-bodied cavalryman crouching behind a sapling the size of my wrist. I can't say I felt comfortable—quite the reverse—in fact, I have a suspicion my *body* was somewhat frightened, but my spirit scorned the suggestion: so I remained—especially as a division of the Ninth corps was just advancing, and the sight was worth seeing; it was beautiful. The long dark line advanced from the woods and formed on the edge of a cornfield; beyond was the rebel position. The line of skirmishers moved steadily forward, firing as they went; behind them came the unwavering resistless line of battle. Occasionally a man would go down; and once the colors of a regiment dropped, but the advance never stopped. As they came near the woods they poured in a volley and charged, and the rebels broke and ran like sheep. It was one of the prettiest things I ever saw, and the movement was so rapid that the loss was quite slight, only about seventy. Darkness came on very soon, and the brief engagement was over.

Our cavalry was at once sent in pursuit. I supposed there would be any quantity of fun when the rebs found themselves between the upper and nether millstones of our intercepting and pursuing forces, and was disgusted at the prospect of losing it, so I obtained permission for Sanders and myself to ride ahead; and off we powdered, riding at a fast gallop. "Fighting three miles ahead," said the countrymen we passed—we got only vague information. Posted on like a couple of wild huntsmen. We overtook our advance on the top of a ridge, just as the enemy made a stand on the top of the next one, opening on us with four guns. The colonel commanding the advance regiment, an excitable old gentleman, replied at once with a little mountain howitzer that reached about half way. We sat on our horses and watched the progress of the skrimmage, groaning in spirit to see how the thing was managed.

Instead of taking a couple of regiments and dashing boldly up the road, and right into the rebels, capturing their guns and breaking their force to pieces, the little howitzer thundered valiantly on. Skirmishers went only, and advanced as if treading on eggs—hanging in a field as though glued there. It was the officer's fault, of course: a live man could have taken them right on. Finally a company of skirmishers appeared on the hill where we were, and the rebels, who had disdained to pay any attention to the two "solitary horsemen," now commenced throwing shell and minié balls at us in a highly inspiring and cheerful manner.

We had no business there; but as Sanders didn't run, I thought I wouldn't. He presently went off to get a battery, and I was left to enjoy the thing myself. The rebels grew pointed in their attentions. Hiss—the ball went over my head—thud—into the ground around me. The fun wasn't so perceptible, and I concluded to retire when the line of skirmishers lying in the grass behind me commenced calling out, "Major, they are firing at you!"

I showed my appreciation of the polite remark by retiring to a small hollow in rear of them. Presently a section of a rifled battery came, and we returned the compliment with such success that they speedily withdrew. So we went from ridge to ridge: there was a painful sameness in the operation. Rested while my horse was being shod. The man was a savage Union man, carrying a huge club, wherewith he smote the ground forcibly whenever he spoke of the rebels. Moved back to meet the general. Met him some miles back and went into camp, and thus ended rather a strange Sunday. The main object of the move, bagging the whole lot of rebels, was defeated by the failure to intercept them. So the cavalry pushed on after them, and we with the infantry returned to this place.

LETTER XXI.

"CAMP SHERMAN," Washington, Sept. 27, 1861.

THE rebel flag is now waving in sight of the President's house!

I myself saw it, though unable to distinguish the *colors*. The place is Munson's Hill, three and a half or four miles from the city. Daily skirmishes take place in hearing of the city: even now I can hear the report of musketry in the distance, and perhaps some good soldier has fallen in defence of his country while I have been writing these *three* lines. I believe *in the end* we shall succeed; yet *how soon* that event may come God only knows. I anticipate a much longer war than most at the North, but I mean to fight for the old flag till it is again unfurled and *respected* in all the present rebellious States! I wish you could see how I am managing to write this, sitting on the ground, knapsack in my lap, ink on the ground by my side—you have a slight idea. All the pleasure to be derived from a happy home, and the society of the dear ones there, I am willing, aye *glad*, to lay upon the altar of my country; and until the *Union* is again "one and *undivided*," I shall do all in my power to accomplish this end.

One great reason for the fatal result of the battle at Bull Run was, the positions of *command* in the army were generally held by those who did not look upon their post as one of *honor*, but as one of *pecuniary* benefit! consequently the base desertion of the brave men by the officers elected over them. Now it is generally different, for it is understood that battles are to be fought, and brave men to be subdued, and only at great risk. Yet still there are some, and it may be with us, to whom the clink of dollars is the sole reason for being connected with an army which should be only animated by the love of country, liberty, and democracy. Such men will be tried before a great while, for a battle is not, cannot be far distant, and *it is a refiner's fire* which will consume all such.

Our brigade, composed of 3d New Hampshire volunteers, 46th, 47th, 48th New York, and 8th Maine, is under command of Brigadier-General Viele, and attached to General Sherman's division.

We are encamped about half a mile east of the capital,

near the Bladensburg road. We were to have been sent on a secret expedition south, but the government thought two weeks ago that a battle was to be fought at once, consequently we were ordered here.

Lieut. W. H. Timberlake,
8th Regiment Maine Volunteers.

LETTER XXII.

Annapolis Camp, October 17th, 1861—before joining Sherman's expedition to Port Royal.

To-day has been a great and proud occasion for our regiment. We had a flag presented to us, made by the *wife* of our general, Mrs. Viele. The presentation speech was beautiful; and whom do you think made by? No less a person than his excellency Governor Hicks, of this State. It was a very solemn occasion, and every thing passed off appropriately.

Our colonel made a very happy reply to Governor Hicks, saying that Maine has for him (the governor) the reverence usually given to patriots; that he occupies in their hearts a place second, almost, to none. That no more fitting place could be in which to receive our colors—here, in the capital of the State of Maryland, where Washington resigned his commission as commander-in-chief of the American army, at the close of the first revolution. "We, at the commencement of the second revolution, again unsheath the sword, which has so long rested in quiet, to fight again for a free government." I can't think of half said in that brief hour, so filled to the brim with a sense of our individual responsibility in this crisis.

We are to leave here very shortly, and "they tell us"

are to land beneath the enemy's fire in surf-boats, and a battle is expected immediately on our landing. So *it may be,* when I leave Annapolis, you may not hear from me again. *But it seems to me* as though I should see this war closed, and a *whole Union,* purified *as by fire,* again in North America.

There can be but little doubt that we shall land at or near Charleston, for which we are exceedingly desirous; for it will be *glory enough* to again possess *Fort Sumter,* and to see the glorious old "stars and stripes" waving proudly from her walls! How I wish the brave *General Anderson* was to be with us! It seems almost *wrong* that he is not sent with this "expedition," for he fired the *first gun* for the Union, and fought nobly in her defence.

There are now *twelve* large steamships in the harbor waiting to transport us south. It is a fine sight. The men of our regiment are all anxious *to see the enemy,* as are all the brigade. I think they will do their duty when in battle.

The colonel of the 48th New York was a *clergyman* before entering the army. There are men of all callings in life here, and we can do any thing, from working a telegraph to making pins!

W. H. TIMBERLAKE.

LETTER XXIII.

SPEECH OF GENERAL VIELE.—SOUTHWARD BOUND: "SECRET EXPEDITION."

WE have been delayed here in Hampton Roads, wholly on account of a severe storm which has lasted ever since our first starting from Annapolis. To-day it is blowing more severely than ever, and the ship is rocking so that I can scarcely write.

We are under sailing orders now with steam on, ready for a start the moment the signal is given, which will be *the moment the storm abates.* Our expedition daily assumes more gigantic proportions, transports and *war-ships* continually arriving. When we do sail it will be an imposing sight for an indifferent observer.

General Viele last night addressed the officers of our regiment in his thrilling style. He told us *we were to land* on the enemy's *best fortified coast* and under their fire; that it would demand all the coolness and intrepidity of the *bravest* soldiers to insure success; and that the slightest wavering would be almost certain to cause an inglorious and direful defeat. He appealed to our patriotism and our pride to do *our whole duty* to our country, state, and friends. "When you land," said he, "do not look to see who is killed or wounded, but *fall into line* and fight valiantly with unbroken ranks, and win laurels for all coming time! Some of you must fall, but wait until after the engagement is ended to make your regrets and pay the proper and fitting obsequies to the remains of your comrades and friends. Without this is done we *are all* lost, and I rely on each and every officer to see that this is done."

Of course, we "each and every one" resolved to do our utmost to insure success—for none of us, I presume, desires to spend the next few months (and perhaps years) in a Southern prison.

I visited Fortress Monroe the other day, and enjoyed myself amazingly. For "sights," I saw General Wool, whose *martial spirit* is thoroughly aroused, and whose intellect I should think had failed but little, if any. Also,

I saw the famous " Floyd guns," the largest in the world I suppose ; and last, though not least, numberless legions of " contrabands," which reminded me very much of my residence in Kentucky.

W. H. TIMBERLAKE.

LETTER XXIV.

HAMPTON ROADS, Steamer "Ariel,"
Oct. 27th, 1861.

THIS time I have something to say of importance. I have seen a *naval* engagement! Last night, at 4 o'clock, five rebel gunboats came out from Savannah, which is fifteen miles distant, and made an attack on our fleet, which returned their fire and speedily *drove them.* Shortly after sunrise, this morning, they again returned and attacked our ships, who again drove them, and shelled their batteries on shore. The battle lasted two or three hours, when the rebel batteries ceased firing. There are two batteries yet to be taken before our troops can land, and I suppose they will shortly attack them. We are expecting orders every moment to land, as soon as firing commences.

Nine o'clock, P. M. The war-ships of our fleet are all in line-of-battle, " ready to open fire" on the rebel batteries at daybreak. We anticipate *hot work*. The place where we land is called *Port Royal*, in the miserable State of South Carolina, fifteen miles from Savannah and seventy-five from Charleston.

The objects in taking this point are these. It has one of the finest harbors on the whole Southern coast; and as the blockade is the most effectual arm of the service in the present war, any thing which strengthens it is of great importance. The storms in the winter-time, which on this coast are violent and frequent, would drive our vessels from the coast and destroy the blockade.

Now if we *held* this point and made it a *depot* for all things needed, coal, provisions, &c., in our fleet, it would answer every contingency, as well as being a point from which any operations against Savannah or Charleston could be easily made. It is situated in that portion of South Carolina in which the wealthiest men and largest slaveholders reside. Near here, as the captain of the "Ariel" says, live the *famous* "Secesh *aristocracy*" of this "Secesh" State. We will pay our respects to them in our *best style*. They *shall remember* the visit of the North to the South!

LIEUT. W. H. TIMBERLAKE,
8th Mich. Vols.

LETTER XXV.

THE NAVAL VICTORY AT HILTON HEAD.

PORT ROYAL, S. C., November 9th, 1861.

ON the morning of November 7th our fleet sailed into this harbor and prepared for action. At ten o'clock precisely they commenced, and for *four* hours the shell and shot flew thick I assure you, when the rebels deserted their "impregnable fortifications," and the "stars and stripes" waved *again* over the "sacred soil" of South Carolina!

Our transports were in plain sight of the battle, and *perhaps* there was no excitement among the troops! But, judging from the surging mass of beings upon the decks of the ships, as well as the wild cheering, one would draw a different inference.

There were two forts taken, one on each point, which were three miles distant from each other, and mounted by twenty large cannon of the very best kind. The sailors and officers of the fleet say that Hatteras was not compared to this in strength; and I should have thought, from what I saw of the work yesterday when I went on shore, that *it could not possibly* have been taken by our force. The rebels said, before the engagement, that "with their forts here they could blow the whole Union fleet out of the water;" and in a letter found on shore, a young rebel writes to his lady-love that "after they had *destroyed* the 'Yankee fleet' he would make her a visit!"

On the walls of the fort, written the day before the engagement, were these words: "2,000 *Carolina natives* at Hilton Head, and 75,000 Yankees in sight!"

There were about three thousand rebels in the fort, they being reinforced the night before the fight. Our loss was eleven killed and a few wounded. We have not disembarked yet, and shall not probably here; for the "talk" is now, that the fleet is to make a series of captures of forts and batteries, and to garrison wherever taken: to leave one brigade here, and take the other two with the fleet for some other point. I will send you a letter which I picked up at Hilton Head. You will prize it as a souvenir of American triumph over the slave oligarchy. It is reported that the general commanding the rebel forces, Dayton, was killed in the engagement.

Lieut. W. H. Timberlake.

LETTER XXVI.

The Flight of the Chivalry.

Their flight was even more inglorious than the famous Yankee stampede at Bull Run, over which Southern rebeldom laughs so much. This place is an island, divided from the main land by a body of water about three-fourths of a mile in width. Into this they rushed pell-mell, even those who could not swim, and many were drowned in their endeavor to escape the Yankees, who were six miles behind them and never attempting to pursue!

So the brave South Carolina chivalry lost more lives on that occasion, in "fleeing from a shadow" (as the *wicked* always do), than in any other way.

We captured upwards of fifty cannon of the largest calibre and most approved patterns, two forts here, and Beaufort, a town some fifteen miles from here, at the head of the bay, of which this (Port Royal) is the entrance.

When Beaufort was taken possession of by our fleet, there were found but two *white* persons in the place, and they were in a state of beastly intoxication; not very well fitted to guard the sable sons of Africa placed under their watchful care!

The negroes of the place had broken into the stores and dwelling-houses and plundered them of all valuables. This act will, of course, be ascribed to the "*Yankees*" by our South Carolina friends; and "*vandalism*" will be the string their papers will finger for a long time to come.

Lieut. W. H. Timberlake.
8th Regiment Maine Volunteers.

Hilton Head, S. C., Nov. 14th, 1861.

The eloquent tribute now to be given was written by Lieutenant W. M. McLain to his friend and fellow-soldier, *Stephen Albert Rollins*. It is inserted here in order that the letters which follow, throughout the volume, of the hero, scholar, and patriot, may testify its truthfulness, and the warm appreciation of the writer of his noble lost friend and companion.

The proud satisfaction was his of "placing with his own hands his country's flag on the strongest fortress of his country's foes." Our banner of beauty and glory was flung out to the breeze in the city of Vicksburg, July 4th, 1863. As the first breath of wind came floating up from the Mississippi, and caressingly spread out its silken folds, some one commenced singing, "Rally round the flag, boys." The example was contagious; the entire crowd soon joined in the song, with thrilling effect. The words, "Down with the traitor, and up with the stars," rung through the streets of the conquered city, laden with a meaning they never had before.

LETTER XXVII.

MEMORIAL OF STEPHEN ALBERT ROLLINS.

WHEN the final reveille shall arouse the sleepers bivouacing in the tombs of earth, and the last roll-call shall be read in the light of the Great White Throne; when the scars that disfigure and the dross that defiles shall all be washed away, and man stands erect in the image of God, who shall appear lovelier, fairer, or freer from stain than those who have suffered and died for conscience' sake? All theories, creeds, and systems of religion award a crown of unfading glory to the martyr. Not only

"To the hero, when his sword
Has won the battle for the free,"

and who then falls with his back to the earth and his feet to the foe; not only to him who plans campaigns, and at the head of glittering squadrons charges to the battle shock; not only to these does that crown belong. Nor only to these does Columbia owe what she is to-day, but equally with them to all those

"Unremembered, unrecorded,
Who are sleeping side by side,
While to others is awarded
That for which they, nameless, died."

And although the silver trump of fame sounds not their name or lineage, nor monumental marble marks the spot which their ashes have hallowed, yet their companions know well where they sleep—on the rugged mountain-side, in the dark morass, or in the deep cane-brake. In their comrades' memories their deeds are ever green, and in those comrades' hearts is erected to them *monumentum perennius ære.*

In the church-yard at Brier's Cross-roads, on Tishemingo creek, near the boundary line of Tennessee and Mississippi, was buried one of these heroes, the subject of this sketch.

Stephen Albert Rollins, color-sergeant of the 95th regiment of Illinois infantry, was mortally wounded in what is known as the Guntown fight, on the 10th of June, 1864, and died on the 16th, aged twenty-two years, nine months, and eleven days.

It is as nothing to say how loved and valued he was by his comrades, and how lamented is his down-going to the grave, for these are stereotyped expressions, and have ceased to mean much; but we who held him close and warm in our heart of hearts, can do no less than commune together over this precious dust, and mourn together over our own and (as we believe) our nation's loss.

He had not entered on life's more serious duties, before he entered his country's service, but the vast fund of energy he possessed, no less than the exalted grade of intellect vouchsafed him, gave promise of a position in the very front ranks of men when he should engage in the battle ot life. The writer was only fortunate enough to meet him during the lull of arms in the winter of '63-4, when both their regiments, belonging to McPherson's 17th corps, were stationed at Vicksburg.

Of course the routine duties of camp-life prevented uninterrupted intercourse, but my association with him and other kindred spirits during that winter make me revert to it as a social oasis in the monotony of soldier-life. Of a fine presence and handsome face, with a firm lip, and eye mild, but glittering like a Koh-i-noor when discussion aroused his energies, he could look the whole world in the face unabashed. With a good judgment and keen perception, a fine debatant and a charming *raconteur*, he was the life of all the society he went into. Where *all* were *brave* he was a marked man. The secret of his dauntless courage, I think, will be best explained by an extract from his pastor's (Mr. Eddie's) funeral sermon over his remains, when they were borne to their last resting-place, preached at Belvidere, Ill., his home. He said:

"He was a representative of that noble class of soldiers who offer themselves as intelligent, voluntary, living sacrifices for the good of their country. Comprehending the tremendous interests at stake, and burning with a worthy passion for their preservation, he was willing to endure the hardships of a soldier's life, and risk the chances of battles and of campaigns." And this displayed itself through all his actions,—a firm belief in the justice of his cause and in the God who speeds the right; and it nerved his arm to strike home, and his tongue to cry aloud for freedom. When he enlisted he wrote to his father, then absent in the West, thus: "I have obeyed the call of my country, and on that point I am sure I have done rightly. The cause of the Union is sacred, and calls loudly for defenders. The sacrifice is a great one to me"—he was in the midst of his studies—"but if I can strike one blow towards putting down this unholy rebellion, I shall feel satisfied at the course I have pursued. My heart and hands are in the work, and I expect they ever will be until victory shall have crowned our efforts, or my body lies in the grave."

To his mother he wrote, shortly afterwards: "Dear

mother, I want to say, right here, that I do most deeply feel and appreciate that lofty and holy patriotism that has made you give up your two sons, most deeply loved, to go forth and fight the awful and bloody battles that are taking place. I glory in your patriotism, mother; and I tell you that your words of comfort and loyal cheer have done me much good, for, in spite of my will, sometimes my spirits will sink."

Nowhere nor at any time was his self-sacrificing courage displayed to more advantage than when he lay twice wounded on the battle-field, when his loving comrades flew to aid him. Soon the "retreat" was sounded, and our broken and bleeding ranks were falling back, leaving him to that terrible fate, "wounded, in the hands of the enemy." The foe, Forrest's worse than Tarletonian troopers, their hands yet reeking with the blood of the butchered defenders of Fort Pillow, and their passions inflamed at the stubborn resistance of smaller numbers than their own, were closing in clouds upon the Federal flanks. Now, if ever, selfishness would have been excusable. But though his comrades desire to risk all to serve him and stay with him, he will not have it so, and exhausted and worn out, he yet bids them seek safety with their friends. Even then, when to return to him was certain captivity and possible death, one, with a devotion worthy of any heroic age, James G. Goodman, returned to nurse and comfort him. He was taken prisoner, and to him we are indebted for all we know of the last hours of our dying hero. In a letter written from the rebel prison in Cahawba, Alabama, Goodman writes: "He had the full use of his faculties till the last, and expressed the conviction, two days before his death, that he would reach that better land above—beyond this world" The few days mercifully spared to him proved the harvest-time of his life, during which were garnered up all the increase derived from the hallowed influences of home and the grateful memories of Christian teaching. And our hope is strong that he found that balm for the wounded spirit that shall avail him in the land of the hereafter. Who shall shorten the arm of Jehovah, or say unto God, "What doest thou?" Who shall tell what passes between the soul and its God in the trying hour of dissolution? We *do* know that he answered "Lord, save, or I perish!" from one sinking in deep waters; and who shall say but that His mercy, which endureth forever, first suggests and then answers that prayer! And where shall a fitter place be found for the mortal to put on immortality than on the battle-field, where he gives his life to that to which, next to his God, it belongs—his country?

The last words his passing spirit breathed were, "*My faith in my country has ever been firm!*" Noble heart! Though dead, shall he not "still live" in those words? Shall they not be our watchword in every dark day of the republic? I would I might have stood by him then, when the death-damp was on his brow, and his eye was dimmed with the clouds of approaching dissolution, when his frame was racked with the torture of his wounds, his feet just "brushing the dew on Jordan's banks," and his voice, that was wont to entrance his audience, almost hushed in everlasting silence. I would I might have heard those words: "MY FAITH IN MY COUNTRY HAS EVER BEEN FIRM!" sounding almost from that undiscovered country whither he was speeding. I think it would have nerved me to shout them clarion-voiced in the ears of all who waver or hold back in giving their full confidence to that land for which he fell! I think they are enough to sear the eyeballs of those who read them and still doubt!

And thus he went before his God. Alas! his is not a solitary case. He is a representative of thousands for whom our Northland weeps to-day, who have fallen in martyrdom to a principle. May they all

> Sleep deep! sleep in peace! sleep in memory ever!
> Wrapt, each soul, in the deeds of its deathless endeavor,
> Till that great Final Peace shall be struck through the world,
> Till the stars be recalled and the firmament furled
> In the dawn of a daylight undying; until
> The signal of Zion be seen on the hill
> Of the Lord; when the day of the battle is done,
> And the conflict with time by eternity won!

WILL MOSBY MCLAIN.

January 12th, 1865.

PART SECOND.

1862.

> "Then, Father, lay Thy healing hand
> In mercy on our stricken land;
> Lead all its wanderers to the fold,
> And be their Shepherd as of old."

LETTER XXVIII.

EXPEDITION TO NEWBERN.

THE first of January, 1862, we started with Burnside on his great expedition to North Carolina. We were just four weeks upon the water; and one Sunday afternoon (I shall never forget that day and night) there arose a terrible storm.

The ocean steamer we were on had on board twelve hundred men, besides General Rend, his staff, and horses. We were driven out to sea, off the coast of Hatteras, and the ship became unmanageable. We were fast driving upon the rocks and shoals, and our *only* hope, the *anchor*, was dragging.

Every sea washed the hurricane-deck, and the timbers were strained to their utmost. The engine could not be worked, for the water put out the fires. Our last hope was in one small anchor that yet remained on deck. It was cast into the boiling tide. How anxiously did we watch the great cable *as it snapped* and jerked upon the anchor, which could not find a hold upon the rocky bottom. We were but a ship's length from the rocks when, at last, the anchor caught. The iron cable creaked and groaned with the strain, but it was strong, and we were safe!

In the morning, the storm abated, and we were able to start the fires and work the steamer out to sea. About noon we made Hatteras Inlet, and at four P. M. entered the harbor and cast anchor in its calm waters. Our escape had been witnessed from Fort Clark by hundreds of sailors and soldiers, and as we passed the fort a salute was fired in honor of our gallant General Burnside and his brave boys. There were several of our steamers and ships lost in that fearful storm: the City of New York, loaded with ammunition and tents; another, the Pocahontas, also; she had on board five hundred horses.

General Rend was killed at the battle of South Mountain, Md. He invented the badge now worn by the troops composing the Seventh army corps, and the troops who were in the expedition to Newbern. It is a shield of red, white, and blue, with an anchor and cannon crossing each other at right angles. It is a beautiful badge, and very appropriate for General Burnside's boys, and is worn as a pin.

CHARLIE H. WHITE,
21st Massachusetts Veteran Volunteers.

LETTER XXX.

BATTLE OF ROANOKE ISLAND.

I WILL tell you something more about our "expedition." After stopping at Fort Hatteras about four weeks, crowded upon the steamer, enduring all the dangers of that stormy coast, and the lost vessels and stores had been replaced, we were one morning delighted to hear the order to "weigh anchor at seven A. M." and follow the commodore's boat. The anchors were raised amid the deafening cheers of thousands of soldiers and sailors, who were glad of the prospect of once more stepping on shore, even though it were the soil of our enemies. At eight A. M. of the sixth of February the great expedition started on its way to Roanoke Island. We sailed all that day and night; and nothing occurred to stay our progress until the morning of the seventh, when just at daylight the gunboats, fourteen in number, opened upon the three forts on Roanoke Island, which mounted in all sixty guns. It was a beautiful sight. The forts and gunboats were hardly discernible, and the sun, which was just rising, was obscured by clouds of sulphurous smoke. The transports were a mile distant from the scene of action, but we could hardly hear one another speak, so heavy was the cannonading.

The bombardment lasted till four P. M., when the forts were compelled to surrender to the naval fleet under Commodore Goldsboro. The troops were then landed under cover of the fleet, and that night we lay upon the ground without any shelter, and before morning were wet through, for it rained hard all night. But morning came at last, and at daylight of the eighth of February we opened the great battle of Roanoke Island. The battle lasted all day, and at night we were in possession of the island, sixty-four guns, a large number of small-arms, ammunition, etc., and 3,500 prisoners. We rested there about four weeks, and the eighth of March found us on the way down the Sound towards Newbern. On the morning of March 13th we landed at the mouth of Slocum's creek, eighteen miles from Newbern, and marched all day, proceeding carefully along the line of the Beaufort railroad, and just at night, our regiment in the advance, came upon the fortifications.

We then halted for the night, and prepared for the morrow's conflict. We sheltered ourselves as much as possible from the storm, for it had rained hard all day; but the morning of the fourteenth was bright and beautiful, and every thing seemed to favor our cause.

The battle commenced at once, and in earnest, and lasted, without intermission, till $3\frac{1}{2}$ o'clock P. M., when our boys made a charge, drove the rebels from their works, and the victory was ours!

We captured from the enemy fourteen pieces of artillery, fifty-five pieces heavy ordnance for the river batteries, about five hundred prisoners, and large quantities of commissary and quartermaster's stores.

The rebels were 18,000 strong, and well fortified, while we had but 12,000 men and *no artillery*, and had to advance *in the face* of theirs! But we knew not defeat in such a cause, and overcame every obstacle before us. It was the hardest fought battle I was ever in. Our noble Burnside had taught us there was no such word as "*fail*," and we were bound to conquer.

Our regiment since then has been engaged in many bloody battle-fields in Maryland, Virginia, and Tennessee, and until lately has always been under the command of the brave and gallant Burnside, whom we have learned to love and respect for his many noble qualities and sincere devotion to his country.

CHARLIE H. WHITE,
21st Massachusetts Veteran Volunteers.

LETTER XXXI.

Camp Winfield Scott, near Yorktown, Va.,
5th Reg't N. Y. V., Duryea Zouaves,
April 21st, 1862.

Dear Mother—I received your kind letters of the 11th and 17th inst., and I can assure you was glad to hear from home, and that you were all in good health. We still remain in camp, and are as comfortable, that is for soldiers, as circumstances will admit. Our tents are of good material and keep out the rain, and the camp is situated on rather high ground, therefore the water runs off. To the south of our portion of the ground is a small ravine through which a small stream runs, supplied by pure springs, from which we get plenty of water for drinking and cooking purposes. In the stream itself we wash our clothes and ourselves. On the banks above the ravine there was a thick wood of pine, with their ever-green foliage; elm-trees, which were soon robbed of their bark to satisfy the chewing propensities of the men; sassafras bushes, the roots of which are pleasant to eat, and are therefore pulled up without regard to quantity; but the wood is now getting thinner every day, falling a sacrifice to our axes, and used by the cooks to keep up their fires, and by us as a means to warm ourselves when it is necessary. We can see the balloon make its ascensions every day, and once in a while we hear a report up in the air, look up and see a ball of smoke, resembling a small cloud, which tells us that a shell has burst in the air; but it is of such frequent occurrence that often we do not notice it. A few shells have landed in camp, one of which killed a mule; another was filled with rice, so they say; one fired yesterday cut a man in half—he was in the woods; but we are as safe as can be expected, and might stay here for forty years without being hurt; but about a mile further to the front I can't say the same thing, as there is sharp practice there on picket.

We see very little of Colonel Warren; he is with General McClellan and staff most of his time, making observations, etc., by whom he is highly esteemed. Many of the regulars know him, having seen him out West and other places, before the war. They say that he is a smart officer. We all like him, so far as a man and a soldier is concerned; he is strict, but he knows all the wants of a soldier from experience, and seldom taxes our endurance too much; but he may change—it would not be strange.

Our men are on details, night and day, building batteries and roads in every direction; one cannot tell at what time of night he may be called up to shoulder his musket, and march off on a detail. Saturday night I was on fatigue duty; we marched about three miles to the York river, where they are putting up a battery. Part of the road has been built by our army, leading over a creek through which a solid bridge has been built. As we came out of some woods at one point we could see a rebel fort (deserted, of course) in the middle of a swamp, to the right of the road; it was built square and in a substantial manner, with barracks inside, a ditch nine feet deep all around it, filled with water, and an abatis, bushes and stumps of trees. Near it was an inferior work, partially masked: the place could not have been stormed. Further on we went through the camp of the 1st Connecticut heavy artillery. We were astonished to see the heavy guns that have been sent to this point for the purposes of the siege. We next passed through the largest cornfield that I ever saw or heard of, and came to an extensive peach-orchard, which was in full bloom. Emerging from the latter, we came upon the grounds of one of the first families, on which was built a fine large house, with a water-front on the York river. The battery we are building is a little way from the house.

The owner of this place is said to be a lieutenant in the rebel army now at Yorktown, and owns five thousand acres of land hereabouts. This place is certainly the handsomest one I have yet seen in Virginia. I, with others, was trotted off to the cornfield, to await our time to be called upon to take our turn at the pick and shovel, which was to be in about four hours. We accordingly stacked our arms, and sat down on the soft and yielding soil, to take it easy. In company with some others, I lit my pipe, and we sat there talking, trying to worry through the time, but it was not long before a storm, that had been threatening for some time, burst upon us with all its fury. It was rough enough for us, notwithstanding the joke went around as usual, and all tried to be merry, but it was under poor circumstances: we were all obliged to stand up side of our muskets, and take it all. The furrows between the hills of corn were filled with water, and we were all soaked through, muskets and all: the latter is always a source of anxiety to a soldier, as every one knows that with a wet rusty musket he would stand a poor chance in case of attack. Finally our turn came to work; we fell in, and were soon hard at work in the mud and water, with very little light, so as not to attract the attention of Johnny Reb. We worked about three hours, and were relieved, when I, with some others, succeeded in getting into a sort of kitchen of the mansion; we found a roaring fire in an old-fashioned fireplace, but every place that a human being could squeeze into was occupied. The boys were stowed away on shelves not over six inches wide, snoozing away as if they had no troubles in the world; some were sitting on barrels, asleep, in the cellar which led off from the room; others on the window-sill, and I saw one fellow trying to crawl under a refrigerator: in fact, it would have taken a New York detective to have ferreted them all out. In one corner of the room sat Hough, looking full of mischief; he is one of the leading spirits. Butch, the head devil, was not to be seen; he was stowed somewhere, and I warrant a comfortable place, if there was such a thing. Fuel becoming short, having burnt up several cot-beds, Hough says, "George, just put that mantel-piece on the fire: there are some more of them up stairs, I will bring them down." No sooner said than done; the mantel-piece was blazing away in no time. Just then a crowd of officers of all grades filled the doorway, with alarm on their countenances, saying that the chimney was on fire. The boys looked at each other, as much as to say, we have done it now; at the same time we did not care whether the house burned down or not, as far as the loss of it was concerned, but the truth was, it was a dangerous accident, as the rebels could have shelled us easily by the light; but the chimney was soon all right again, and every thing went on as before. A little while before this, the innocent Hough and the missing Butch had been scouting around on their own hook, to see if any thing was to be made. They came across a pig-sty, the pigs in one end, and a lot of our boys in the other asleep. Hough grabs a grunter, Butch draws his knife across his throat in the dark. Hough lets go of him, and says he is a dead pig, when the pig makes off as fast as four legs can carry him. Butch finds out that in the hurry and darkness he used the back of his knife; they go after the others, but find them all flown. Trotting along, not in a very good humor at the loss of fresh meat, Butch spies a horse in a field: what does he do but drive him in a barn, where a lot of the boys are sleeping in stalls and on the floor; they all wake up, scared out of their seven senses, and it is some time before they will believe that the enemy have not been on them, and that they are all prisoners. This is the way some fellows act, in mischief all the time. When the boys were down on the Eastern Shore expedition, one time on a long march the colonel observed somebody lagging in the rear: he went to see who it was, and found it was the intelligent Hough, driving a nigger along, who was carrying his knapsack, while he carried the nigger's basket, eating therefrom the poor darkey's hoecake, while poor Sambo, utterly unconscious of what was happening to his dinner, was patiently trudging before him.

The battery we were working on is one of great importance; it is called Battery No. 1, and is built of gabions, and will mount two two-hundred-pounders, and four one-hundred-pound parrots, also two thirteen-inch mortars. It was commenced and put up within two or three days; the guns are brought up at night by a large truck, and will be mounted by to-morrow: although it has rained and stormed a cold northeaster for two days, the work has still gone on night and day; in fact, everybody is busy doing something.

A colonel of the rebels was taken the other day in a Maine regiment uniform; he was stopped by some of the very regiment whose clothes he was surreptitiously wearing. In reply to the question what regiment he belonged to, he replied the very one of his captors; they knew different, and marched him off to headquarters. A private of a secesh regiment also came into camp just after we arrived here, and asked for the 5th Virginia; he was forthwith nabbed: he had been away on furlough, and had not heard that Uncle Sam's troops had possession of the former rebel camp-ground.

Once in a while we have a chase through camp after a rabbit, but do not generally succeed in catching it.

The boys are greatly in need of tobacco, but I managed to get a handkerchief full of smoking—you know I don't chew—while out foraging on my own hook; it was a good thing I can assure you. Some of the captains supply the men from company funds, and Captain Partridge buys it himself, and trusts the men until they are paid. Our captain has company funds, but is so mean, he will not use it for any thing. He has never done any thing for the men, by which he would spend a cent of his own money.

I hope that the taking of Yorktown will be the means of stopping the war; and I think if General McClellan's plans succeed, that he will succeed in bagging the whole of the rebs. The Prince de Joineville was addressed the other day by the title of prince, when he immediately corrected the person who spoke to him, saying that he was a captain, and no prince here, in his broken language, and appeared quite angry.

I have had quite a cold for about two weeks past, and I cough some at night—I suppose that it will wear off as soon as warm weather sets in. There have been a number of men discharged already on account of disability—camp-life beginning to tell on them. Give my love to all, and write when you can.

Your affectionate son,
A. DAVENPORT.

P. S.—I forgot to mention the heroic conduct of a young man who for some time mated with me; his name was Walter S. Colby, and he came from Boston, I believe.

He was sick when we left Baltimore for Fortress Monroe to take part in this campaign, and consequently left behind; he had a kind of slow consumption on him, and usually coughed all night. The surgeon, in Baltimore, after he got a little better, offered him his discharge, seeing that he could not live long, but he replied that he would rejoin the regiment and go home with it, or go home in a box. So, one day, who should join us on the march up the Peninsula but Colby; he was thin, but had come to stick it out, he said; and he did as long as he lived, which was up to Gaines' Hill. I never saw a man with a stronger will in my life, that was all that kept him up; he never dropped out on a march, while many a strong man failed to come to camp with the regiment. He was one day changing some of his clothes, and I happened to get a look at his lower limbs. I was horrified at the sight; I could have put one of my hands around either one of them; he was actually a walking skeleton, and how any man could do duty as he did, in such a state, surpassed all my reasoning. Well, at Gaines' Hill, poor Colby, while fighting bravely, was shot in the leg, which was very much shattered; as soon as he fell, he got up on the sound leg, supporting himself as well as he could on the shattered stump, took off his cap, and waving it in the air, gave three cheers for the Union at the top of his voice. He then became weak and flopped down again. One of the boys went to him, and asked him if he could do any thing for him? He thanked him, and said that he would not live a great while anyhow, and he might as well die as he was, and that he had better not mind him, but look out for himself; so he took a drink of water, and we never after heard from him. I could enumerate many instances of presence of mind, and self-sacrifices amidst suffering; but you must wait till I come home, to hear of them, and then I will have much to tell—providing, of course, that God spares my life.

A. D.

LETTER XXXII.

Battle of Hanover Court-house.

Chickahominy River Camp, June 1, 1862.

The last eight days have been trying ones to the regiment. We have been kept constantly moving, and were almost *starved*, sleeping on the road with no covering but an overcoat. We marched over eighty miles. Colonel Warren has command of our regiment (Fifth N. Y. Duryea Zouaves),—1st Connecticut, 1200 men, one of the finest body of men in the service, a Rhode Island battery of six pieces, and a regiment of cavalry were included. We went on an expedition the other day to destroy a bridge over the Pamunkey river, by which the rebels received supplies from the open country. We had a skirmish, and killed and wounded a few of the rebel pickets; the others *skedaddled*, and company H, headed by Col. Hiram Duryea, charged over the bridge after them; but they, being mounted, escaped.

An amusing incident occurred here: at the first shot fired by the rebels, as the ball whistled over our heads, a man in our company named ——, who was detailed in the surgeon's department, and on a march carried the box that contained our medical stores on his back, strapped on like a knapsack, at the first fire dropped on his knees behind a large tree, with his hands clasped in front of him, and his countenance showing every sign of terror. Now, this same fellow, in the seven days' retreat, made himself scarce, apothecary shop and all, and we never saw any thing of him until about a month before our time expired. He had been hanging about hospitals and convalescent camps, and had joined *us* then to get an *honorable discharge*. This is only one of the many specimens of the curs that shirk duty and come to no punishment and receive government pay. There are thousands of them.

We came near being engaged in the Battle of Hanover Court-house. A brigade of North Carolina troops stationed there under General Branch, were surprised by Porter's corps, and after a skirmish retreated. We followed on in the direction of the firing; all of a sudden aids on horseback came flying by us, and we were ordered back again. It appeared that reinforcements had arrived on the cars to the rebels from Richmond, which runs right through the battle-field, and were advancing on our rear, and were actually then on the very place from which our forces had just driven Branch's brigade of rebels.

It was an immense wheat-field, about a mile and a half across. When we came back on it we wondered where all the troops had come from. All was excitement. They were moving on in " quick time" to engage the rebels who had just emerged from the woods which skirted the field of wheat.

Presently the "*music*" commenced just in front of us, in the wood. Our artillery did not get to work until they (the rebels) were on the retreat. General Porter did not send us in directly, and just before we did advance, General Butterfield rode up before, with his hat off, and told us to "do our best," and that he would see us supported.

We were all very tired from our previous expedition, but we advanced at a "double-quick," though some of the boys fell exhausted. We went into the woods and out across the railroad, but the rebels were retreating as fast as they could, and had got into another wood where we could not reach them, but the artillery in the road, *sighted* by General Griffen himself, was firing at them and doing a great amount of damage. At every good shot the general (Griffen) patted the piece and said, "Well done! another shot in the same place." Soon the order came to cease firing, it being near night, and the battle was over, resulting in a complete victory for our side.

The 44th and 25th New York were fighting in the woods and suffered severely, but they said as soon as the rebs saw our red breeches (the Zouaves) coming through the woods they skedaddled. We had marched eighteen miles the day before, and at least thirty that day, and were completely exhausted.

When we came through the woods the sight was sickening and mournful, but we seem to look on these things as if we had been used to them all our lives. I have often read descriptions of great battles, but did not realize or comprehend them until I saw the reality. The rebels were lying in every position along by a fence near a road, most of them dead: many of them when shot dead have a horrible look on their countenances, *as if they had seen something that had scared them to death.* I saw a father and son side by side, wounded; the old man was crying and trying to stop the blood that was flowing from his wound. They were both found dead where they were in the morning. Men get hardened seeing so much misery. In one place there were two or three found dead, that looked as if they had died talking together. All night we heard the moans of the wounded, who were undergoing surgical operations at a house near our bivouac.

The next day Colonel Warren, with "*ours*," the 1st Connecticut, and the Lancers, made a reconnoissance on the same road as the rebels retreated on, to see if he could speak General MacDowell's advance.

It was the object of the battle of Hanover Court-house to open the way for General McDowell, but it seems he was kept back by the authorities at Washington. Had he been permitted to join us, there is little doubt but what Richmond would have been captured—at least it is the general opinion in the Army of the Potomac.

That night we marched back again to camp, sixteen miles—men strewn all along by the road, completely exhausted. Our cheeks were sunk in, and we had *famine* in our countenances. By some neglect of our regimental quartermaster, we ran short of rations, and consequently nature was supported on air.

Our camp is in a dense pine wood—a beautiful spot comparatively. We are liable to be called upon at any moment to go into the contest which is to decide the fate of one army or the other. We are so near the enemy that no drum or bugle-call is allowed to be sounded. The order was read off this afternoon to the effect that we were about to go into battle—that we were to leave knapsacks, wagons, and every thing on this side of the Chickahominy; to carry only haversacks, three days provisions, and canteens.

So you see the ball will open in a day or two. The men will all *fight well*—there is no mistake in that, and we will win; but the loss will be heavy. I will not have a chance to write to you for some time, and, perhaps, may never; but God's will be done. Now good-by, and love to every one: hoping that God will give us the victory, and that we may crush out the rebellion, and that in my next I can say "*Richmond is ours*,"

I remain, &c.,

A. DAVENPORT.

LETTER XXXIII.

A Bloodhound Chase.

Our escaped prisoners are hunted by bloodhounds. These are kept at all the pens for that purpose. To kill one of them is certain death if discovered.

Hundreds of our officers and men have been chased by these dogs. They are kept at all guard-stations and picket-posts throughout the South, especially at the ferries and fords of the rivers, and are used to hunt both our men and deserters from the rebel army.

A party of our men who had escaped from prison were chased by fifteen dogs, in charge of some twenty men.

One man, private Crummel, of the Ninth Illinois cavalry, finding the dogs close upon him, and no chance of escape presenting itself, climbed on the porch of a house, and waited till the party came up. Enraged that their thirst for Yankee blood had not been gratified, they made Crummel come down to them, then knocked him on the head with a musket, formed a ring, put the dogs in it, and threw him to them. He was terribly torn, and soon after died.

Patterson (of the Second New York), who was a mere boy, kneeled down and prayed these human fiends "not to let the dogs tear him," but to no purpose. He was forced down from the roof of the porch whither he too had fled, and on endeavoring to regain it, was kicked in the face, all his front teeth broken out, and he rendered insensible, and in that state thrown into the ring.

The dogs had satiated themselves with blood, and refused to touch him!

LETTER XXXIV.

BATTLE OF SEVEN PINES.

WHITE OAK SWAMP, Va., June 22d, 1862.

DEAR LIZZIE—We are still in camp on the Chickahominy, and in all probability will never be ordered to "the front" again. Casey's division is used up, and will, it is thought, never go into battle again; we got no praise for what we did at Seven Pines, although we held the field against desperate odds for a long time. McClellan gives us no credit for it. The battery which the Ninety-second supported fired 266 rounds of canister shot in less than an hour. A canister is a bag with 100 bullets in it, and 266 such canister shots give the number of bullets fired 26,600. As soon as the canister is fired it bursts, and the bullets spread in all directions; so you can imagine how many they might kill or wound. But this was only one battery; there were others on the ground, and they were all busy I assure you; and another thing, the enemy were so close up to the battery that every shot took effect, piling up their dead in heaps. Besides this were regiments of infantry all firing as fast as they could. There were more dead on that part of the field than on any other. The secesh themselves admit that their greatest loss was there. Casey's division lost far more men than any other in proportion to their number; and yet, because we had to retreat before the superior numbers that threatened to outflank us and take us prisoners, and because that retreat was not conducted in a proper military manner, pacing over the ground in solid columns, with measured steps and military bearing,—while the enemy came surging onward like an ocean flood, threatening us flank and rear, and pouring in a storm of lead and iron hail upon us, before which our men fell like the forest leaves in autumn,—McClellan says we behaved shamefully. The men, in consequence, are discharged, and many swear that they will never fight again, for they do not like to be blamed after suffering what they have for their country.

The Ninety-second is about used up; most of the men are sick, and many of the officers have resigned. Our colonel was wounded in battle, and is not with us yet. Exertions are being made to get the regiment mustered out of service; whether they will succeed remains to be seen.

To give you some idea of our present situation, I will give you company I's report, as made out by your humble servant this very morning. At Potsdam we had one hundred: where are they now?

Absent, sick, 33; wounded in battle, 6; missing, 3; killed, 2; discharged, 18; detached service, 5; present sick, 19; present for duty, 5; died of disease, 9: total, 100.

Thus you see we have only twenty-four in our company here, and only five of those are able to do duty. The other nineteen are not very sick, but are worn out, and with needed rest and quiet they will soon be all right again. Other companies in the regiment are about as bad off. This morning, at inspection and dress-parade, the regiment mustered sixty-six men fit for duty out of nine hundred and fifty-seven that left Potsdam, N. Y. The fact is, we have not been used as we should have been, and the men don't care whether school keeps or not. So when they get on the sick-list they stay on it as long as they can, to get rid of duty. Our company had eight corporals and five sergeants, and not one of them is within a hundred miles of our regiment now except myself, the rest being sick, wounded, or dead. The three new corporals we put in are also used up; so I have all the business (which, in fact, is not very great) to do; and any day when we are ordered out on picket, or fatigue duty, or for drilling, myself as orderly sergeant, as in duty bound, report myself for duty; and, if need be, I get an excuse of the surgeon, and when I wish I report for duty again. I have to keep the company books, make out morning reports, detail the guards, take the sick to the doctor each morning, warn them out to drill, inspections, and parade, and see to things generally; and so, like all orderly sergeants, have to know far more about the company's affairs than the commissioned officers. As for standing guard, I have not done any of that important service for two months, having been acting company commissary when not engaged as orderly: that excuses me.

We have a nice camp; it would do you good to see it. It is in a pine grove, laid out in streets, and beautifully adorned with shade-trees. Our tents are raised on scaffolds of poles, two or three feet from the ground, to allow the air to circulate beneath. The streets are swept clean early each morning, and the dirt carried off in pails. We are not allowed to throw any thing under the tents or in the streets; and take it altogether our camp is very pleasant and healthy. But the mail man is calling, and I must hurry. Dr. Kalt's boys are all well, except Stevens and Loure; but they are not very hard up. I have not heard from Court le Cooper yet. The Third brigade, General Palmer, has gone up. Palmer has gone into Church's division, and we, the Ninety-second, into the Second division. My love to all the friends. Yours as ever,

JOHN.

P. S.—Address C. S., 92d regiment N. Y. S. V., General Casey's division, sergeant 92d regiment N. Y. S.

LETTER XXXV.

Camp near Falmouth, Va.,
Hancock's Division.

It is Sunday—a beautiful, calm, still Sunday. God never smiled more graciously upon our army by the gift of a more serene and lovely day. We have no beautiful flowers to tread upon; no soft green carpet to lighten our tread. No! nothing to walk over but the hard dry ground, hardened almost like the sidewalks of an old city by the tramp of the soldier; still, the sun is shining with all the splendor that urges one from beneath the canvas to taste the sweet breeze, that reanimates us and makes us forget the fatigues and hardships we have undergone in the last ten days. Our regiment now numbers fewer than a *single* company a year ago! We see a few veteran patriots, not *home-staying, talking* patriots, but staunch old veterans of work, of action—in short, *real* patriots. Watch us: silence prevails; orders are given and obeyed with that dexterity that careworn experienced soldiers only can perform. One hears not that careless, boyish laugh; sees no childish playing balls or racing, as new recruits are wont to indulge in, when a good home is left and a change created for a new life; but here we have sober, thinking men—men who realize the situation of our country and feel the great responsibility that rests upon them. Oh, how heartily we wish this war were over! Who knows the thoughts of the bosoms of these brown men? What changes have come over their families and friends at home? The mind here is not centred on the idle wish for pleasure at any expense, that weighs upon us at home; but two thoughts obtain the ascendency: one, of dear parents, or wives, or little ones, left behind (for, mark! a true soldier has the warmest affection for the latter); the other thought is for a speedy end of the war. These are thoughts after a battle.

I have no doubt you wish a description of the great battle. In the first place, I must inform you that I was there. The general (Hancock) gave me a horse some three months ago, with the understanding that I should be always with him. We were under marching orders two weeks. We struck tents on the 28th of April.

At daylight our corps marched to Banks' Ford: were caught in a very severe rain—as you know it usually rains when the Army of the Potomac moves. We slept in the mud that night; and the next day, under a very heavy fog we marched to the U. S. Ford, some ten miles from Falmouth.

Our cavalry got in the rear of the enemy along the river, and caused them to abandon their rifle-pits, and left us to cross without molestation. At the same time the Fifth, Sixth, and Tenth corps were making a demonstration on the left, and succeeded admirably in making a feint, sufficient to put the enemy off guard, and he drew up his whole army right opposite to them, expecting a rich reward; but a dense fog was all we wanted, which came with a vengeance, under covering of which our three corps made a forced march to our support and left the enemy entirely exposed; and so completely was he taken by surprise that our whole army, with the exception of Sedgwick's corps, were across the river, in line-of-battle, on the enemy's *flank*. On the first of May—a fine day—we moved towards Chancellorsville and encountered his pickets. We marched beyond the town, occupied and held the plank-road leading from Gordonsville to Fredericksburg. In the evening, at 5 o'clock, a terrible cannonading commenced on our "right," the same as at Fair Oaks. The corps on that end of the line—the 11th (Sigel's corps), commanded by Howard—broke and ran, leaving every thing behind, and skedaddled all over the country. The First corps came in just in time to save the army. They regained what the 11th corps lost; but the other portion of the army had to fall back about one mile and give up the road, which was the whole point lost! "That was the point."

The next day, however, we attacked the enemy and whipped them all along the lines, except the right, and therefore we could not advance. We worked all that night throwing up works. The next day both seemed to attack at the same time. They were repulsed, but kept the *right* and were throwing up works. They had gained the best position, and were making it impregnable; and as we could not advance, we thought there was no use staying so far from our supplies, so we recrossed again under a severe rain, and occupied our old position. The loss in our brigade was about 140. We have four regiments in our brigade, Fifty-seventh, Sixty-sixth, Fifty-second, One Hundred and Fortieth.

P. V. Brooke has a brigade. Our boys averaged 150 rounds during the fight. The enemy's loss is certainly three to one, if not more. They were the charging party. It was a splendid fight, and the boys are in as good spirits as before the fight: we captured about as many prisoners as we lost. Sedgwick crossed where we did in December last, and took all the heights across the river, but was outflanked by superior numbers, and compelled to fall back.

We are again under marching orders, with eight days' rations; expect to move every moment.

JOHN SCHWARTZ.

LETTER XXXVI.

I SEE that B—— is still earnest in his devotion to the Government, and hearty in his denunciations of the traitors who seek its overthrow. If ever any should be despised of men and cursed of God it is those traitors seeking the destruction of the best and most beneficent Government in the world's history; and their abettors at the North should be doubly despised. There can be no palliation for them.

Many a poor soldier owes his life to the Sanitary Commission, to the comforts furnished by the noble, generous-hearted women of the glorious North. You say I write nothing of the horrors of battle: why should I? It has been written and written as long as the annals of history. Each and all battles are alike in horrors, varying only in magnitude. But our cause is just, and must be victorious. You wish me to live aright, and not yield to the temptations of camp-life. I thank you kindly for your advice, knowing it to be prompted by a love for me. Do not fear for me. I am just the same here as at home. I know one need not lose his manhood in becoming a soldier.

You almost wish I may get a slight wound, so as to come home: I may get a mortal one, and not come at all. There are fearful uncertainties in war. I feel less concern on this account than you do at home. Now, don't worry for me!

BYRON WILSON.

LETTER XXXVII.

ONE need not yield to temptation. Indeed, a true man will never do this. If one has good moral principles established, he will still, in camp or out, be a man, and being a true man, will be his country's best soldier and noblest defender. We have "good reading" and singing in our tent every day, and no swearing or card-playing. These lines are much sung among us:

> " Mother dear, oh, pray for me!
> When pleasure's syren call
> Shall tempt thy child to wander free
> In paths where he may fall.
>
> " Mother dear, oh, pray for me!
> When all looks bright and fair,
> That I may all my danger see,
> For, surely, then 'tis near!"

Wives mourn husbands fallen, fathers mourn sons; but this is their consolation: they have fallen in a glorious cause—the most just cause for which man ever did battle. As much as I desire peace, let it not come until it brings liberty to all; yes, liberty full and complete. I never was in favor of meddling with the institutions of any State before this wicked and causeless rebellion made it a necessity.

BYRON B. WILSON.

LETTER XXXVIII.

ARMY OF THE POTOMAC, October 6th, 1862.

DEAR BROTHER—I was surprised to hear of the death of Henry. I had heard that he was wounded, and got a furlough of two days to go and find him. Starting when your letter came to me, I wandered all day over the field at Antietam. I kept going for miles and miles, looking at every grave I saw, and was about to give up the search from fatigue and hunger (for I had already gone over twenty-five miles), but I kept on till dark, and just as I was about to lie down for the night, I saw a few graves under an apple-tree, a few rods off, and there I found the grave of our dear brother. It was a solemn time for me as I sat by the grave.

I found a person who watched with him, and was present at his burial. He was shot in the early part of the action. He died without a struggle. It will be a hard struggle for mother. To think he was taken away in so short a time after leaving home, while I have been engaged in six or seven battles! But the thought of his dying so peacefully (and no one can doubt his Christian character or fitness to meet his Maker), will lessen the grief of our mother, and brothers, and sisters. We have lost him; but this we know, he was a Christian, and showed a Christian spirit in all his actions. It seems like a dream. As I look from the "Heights" (Bolivar), I can see the rebel army, and a battle is expected in a few days. I am willing to meet them, no matter how hard the battle, or how long and forced the marches are, if we can only finish the war, or make a beginning of the end. I may too, like Henry, be shot down. If I die, I die in the faith of Christ, and have no fears as to what awaits me. I am happy wherever I am. I can lie down with as much ease, and rest for the night within range of the enemy's guns, knowing that at dawn we may meet face to face, as I could at home upon my bed. It is near midnight, and I must close.

Sergeant S. P. Keeler.

"Henry Keeler," writes his sister, "who fell on the bloody field of *Antietam*, enlisted in the 14th Connecticut regiment. He had been gone but five weeks when the sad news that brought mourning to so many homes, brought the intelligence to us that our brother was among the noble slain! His warfare was soon ended. I have now two brothers in the army—both severely wounded. My brother Henry's remains were brought home and interred in the Ridgefield (Conn.) burial-ground."

LETTER XXXIX.
GETTYSBURG.

MARYLAND, August, '62

I WROTE a few days ago in detail of some of our common experience in the exciting and triumphant campaign which has just passed into *history*.

I must say that though we had to endure many hardships; though we had to swing many days in the balance of suspense, and march hot, dusty miles under the lowering cloud of universal gloom, and pass through the fiery ordeal of battle; yet I would not part with what I saw, and heard, and learned, with the joy we felt in the long train of advantages which will follow the pathway of our victorious army, for a mint of what the world calls earthly riches. I may never be able to show forth the profit I have derived; nevertheless it will be one of the richest treasures of my life.

We are now charged with the duty of guarding against Moseby's guerrillas. Moseby, the leader, lives near here whenever our army is absent; he has 1,000 men under him, a small proportion regularly enlisted soldiers; the remainder are citizens without any lawful connection with the army, who have been induced by a fanatic zeal for the unholy cause of rebellion to abandon family and home, and, arrayed in the black coat of outlaws, to lay secret plots against the defenders of our institutions and national honor. Upon the negroes, upon whose word we can always depend, whose fondest hopes are all bound up in the cause of our Union armies, we rely for information. Surely the *Angel of Freedom* follows in our track! How many of God's poor, dejected, despised children has she taken up upon her white wings and borne into the high estate of manhood. In all this region not an able-bodied negro can be found in bondage. Surely the Southern people who let slip the dogs of war upon our once happy land, are suffering most from their envenomed bite.

Whether the war end to-morrow, or in ten years, slavery must perish by its hand. Then who shall say it is an unrighteous war, if it destroys its own authors and trains flowers to grow upon its desolation!

LIEUTENANT A. CLARKE RICE,
121st New York Volunteers.

LETTER XL.

"Hoping," writes the sister of Lieutenant Rice, "that the almost dying words of my dear brother may find a place with the records of thousands who speak to us now in the noble words and deeds which have here found a termination, but the influence of which can never die." Lieutenant Rice died in Seminary Hospital, Georgetown, of typhoid fever, after only a few days illness. "Though dead, he yet speaketh!"

LETTER XLI.

A MEMORIAL OF COLONEL LOUIS BENEDICT.

THE present unhappy war found him enjoying the generous confidence of the people of his native city, with ample means to make life pleasant and to be longed for, surrounded by a family circle of beloved and loving relatives, and possessed of a gentlemanly courtesy and breeding that were a passport to the best society of the land. But full of love for the institutions of his birth, actuated by the purest patriotism, and moved by a controlling sense of duty, he sacrificed all, as the sequel proved, to die for his country. I need not speak of his military career, for his abilities, his patient endurance of hardship and suffering, his devoted patriotism, chivalrous courage, gallant daring, and noble heroism are household words in the city of his birth.

Oh! how I dreaded, when I first heard of the fatal battle in which he fell, that disaster would be his! I knew him so well. I had occasion to know, before the fire of battle proved it, how brave a heart he carried in his bosom. I knew that where duty called, or honors were to be won in the service of his country, he would be no laggard.

He fell as I believed he would fall, if fall he must, with "his back to the field and his feet to the foe."

With a heart as kind, as gentle and loving as a woman's, ever open and responsive to every appeal for charity and sympathy, with a sense of honor as fine as ever found a lodgment in a human bosom, he had a courage as cool, a spirit as chivalrous, a soul as brave, as ever dwelt in mortal tenement.

Is it a wonder that such a man died for his country?

Blessed be his last sleep! Forever cherished among us with whom he lived, and the people in whose cause he died, be his memory!

As an expression of the sentiment that ruled him, an extract from a letter to his mother, written whilst the siege of Yorktown was in progress, is given.

LETTER XLII.

OF COLONEL LEWIS BENEDICT.

"I am pained to learn that so much apprehension for my safety is mingled with the gratification you feel at my being in a position to do service to my country. I know it is impossible for a mother to forget her son; but I would, if I could, inspire you with the pride I feel in devoting my life to the cause of freedom and the Union. Thus far, though I have endeavored to do, as far as my frail nature would permit, my duty to man [and the truth of this his carefulness for the interests of his men most constantly affirms], I know I have not forgotten myself, as I should in many instances have done; but, in the struggle to be soon inaugurated here, the opportunity will be given me to furnish unmistakable evidence that I am animated by the noblest sentiments—that I can resign life, which I love, that my country may again enjoy the blessings of peace and the development of its beneficent principles of government. Politically, I have sought its weal; personally, my life belongs to it in its woe: so that I view the result of the battle with complacency. If I fall, through all the grief which you and our dear ones will feel, will breathe the consolation that I was a soldier fighting in a just cause. Let that feeling, dear mother, console you, as it reconciles me to the chances of war."

"What patriot ever has penned nobler words than these? Who among us has risen to a more illustrious height of patriotic devotion? Above the voices of home and congenial companionship he hears the awful trump of *duty*, and that is the incitement by which he marches—the imperious summons to self-renunciation, and possibly death."

LETTER XLIII.

THE BRAVE TARS.

"As a set-off to our recent disaster in Hampton Roads, our frigates sustain the traditional renown of our *navy*. The *Cumberland* went down with her guns firing and her flag flying. 'Better,' says Lowell, in the Bigelow papers,

> 'That all our ships and all their crews
> Should sink to rot in ocean's dreamless ooze,
> Each torn flag waving challenge as it went,
> And each dumb gun a brave man's monument,
> Than seek such peace as only cowards crave.
> Give *me* the peace *of dead men, or of brave.*'"

LETTER XLIV.

ENGAGEMENT OF THE MONITOR WITH THE MERRIMAC.

U. S. STEAMER MONITOR, Hampton Roads,
March 14th, 1864.

MY DEAR MOTHER AND FATHER—I commence this now, but don't know when I shall finish, as I have to write it at odd moments, when I can find leisure. When I bid C—— good-night on Wednesday, the fifth, I confidently expected to see you the next day, as I then thought it would be impossible to finish our repairs on Thursday. But the mechanics worked all night, and at eleven A. M., Thursday, we started down the harbor, in company with the gunboats Sachem and Currituck. We went along very nicely, and when we arrived at Governor's Island the steamer Seth Low came alongside and took us in tow. We went out, passing the Narrows with a light wind from the west and very smooth water. The weather continued the same all Thursday night. About noon the wind freshened, and the sea was quite rough. In the afternoon the sea was breaking over our decks at a great rate, and coming in our hawse-pipe forward in perfect floods. Our berth-deck hatch leaked in spite of all we could do, and the water came down under the tower like a waterfall. It would strike the pilot-house and go over the tower in most beautiful curves, and came through the narrow eye-holes in the pilot-house with such force as to knock the helmsman completely round from the wheel. At four P. M. the water had gone down our smoke-stacks and blowers to such an extent that the blowers gave out, and the engine-room was filled with gas. Then occurred a scene I shall never forget. Our engineers behaved like heroes, every one of them fighting with the gas, endeavoring to get the blowers to work, until they dropped down, apparently dead. I jumped into the engine-room with my men as soon as I could, and carried them on top of the tower to get fresh air. I was nearly suffocated with the gas myself, but got on deck, after every one was out, just in time to save myself. Three firemen were in the same condition as the engineers. Then times looked rather blue, I can assure you. We had no fear as long as the engine could be kept going to pump the water, but when that stopped the water increased rapidly. I immediately rigged the hand-pumps, on the berth-deck, but we were obliged to lead the hose out over the tower, and there was not force enough in the pump to throw the water out. Our only resource now was to bail; and that was useless, as we had to pass the buckets up through the tower, making it a very long operation. We knew not now what to do, but felt we had done all in our power, and must let things take their own course. Fortunately the wind was off shore, so we hailed the tug-boat and told them to steer directly for the shore, in order to get into smooth water. After five hours of hard steaming we got near the land and in smooth water. At eight P. M. we succeeded in getting the engines to work, and every thing apparently quiet. The captain had been up nearly all the previous night, and as we did not like to leave the deck without one of us being there, I told him I would keep the watch from eight to twelve, he take it from twelve to four, and I relieve him from four to eight.

The first watch passed away nicely; smooth sea, clear sky, the moon out, and the old tank going along at the rate of six knots. All I had to do was to keep awake, and think over the narrow escape we had in the afternoon. At twelve o'clock, things looked so favorable, I told the captain he need not turn out; I would lie down with my clothes on, and if any thing happened, I would attend to it. He said, "very well," and I went to my room, hoping to get a short nap. I had scarcely gone to my berth, when I was startled by the most infernal noise I ever heard. The Merrimac's firing on Sunday last was music to it. We were just passing a shoal, when the sea suddenly became very rough, and right ahead. It came up with tremendous force through our anchor-well, and forced the air through our hawse-pipe, where the chain comes, and then the water would come through in a perfect stream to our berth-deck, and over the ward-room table. The noise resembled the death-groans of twenty men, and certainly was the most dismal sound I ever heard. Of course, the captain and myself were on our feet in a moment, and endeavored to stop the hawse-pipe. We succeeded partially, but now the water commenced to come down the blowers again, and we feared the same accident of the afternoon. We tried to hail the tug-boat, but the wind being directly ahead, they could not hear us; and we had no way of signalling to them, as the steam-whistle, which father re-

commended, had not been put on. We commenced to
think, then, the Monitor would never see daylight. We
watched carefully every drop of water that went down the
blowers, and sent continually to ask the fireman how the
blowers were going. His only answer was, "slowly," but
could not be kept going much longer, unless we could stop
the water from coming down. The sea was washing completely over decks, and it was dangerous for a man to go
on them, so we could do nothing. In the midst of all this,
our wheel-ropes jumped off the steering-wheel (owing to
the pitching of the ship), and became jammed. She now
commenced to sheer about at a fearful rate, and we thought
our hawser must certainly break. Fortunately it was a
new one, and held on well. In the course of half an hour
we fixed the wheel-ropes, and now our blowers were the
only difficulty. About three o'clock on Saturday morning
the sea became a little smoother, though still rough, and
going down our blowers to some extent. The never-fail-
ing answer from the engine-room, "blowers going slowly,
but can't go much longer." From 4 A. M. until daylight
was the longest hour and a half I ever spent. I certainly
thought old "Sol" had stopped at China, and did not intend to visit us again. At last, however, we could see,
and made the tug-boat understand to go nearer in shore,
and get in smooth water, which we did at about 8 A. M.
Things were again a little more quiet, but every thing wet
and uncomfortable below. The decks and air-ports leaked,
and the water still came down the hatches and under the
tower. I was busy all day making out my station bills,
and attending to different things that constantly required
my attention. At 3 P. M. we parted our hawser, but the
sea was quite smooth, so we secured it without difficulty.
At 4 P. M. we passed Cape Henry, and heard heavy firing

in the direction of Fortress Monroe. As we approached it increased, and we immediately cleared ship for action. When about half way between Fortress Monroe and Cape Henry, we spoke the pilot-boat. He told us the Cumberland was sunk, and the Congress was on fire, and had surrendered to the Merrimac. We could not credit it at first, but as we approached Hampton Roads, we could see the fine old Congress burning brightly, and we then knew it must be true. Sadly, indeed, did we feel to think those two fine old vessels had gone to their last homes with so many of their brave crews. Our hearts were very full, and we vowed vengeance on the Merrimac, if it should be our lot to fall in with her. At 9 P. M. we anchored near the frigate Roanoke, the flag-ship, Captain Marston. Captain Worden immediately went on board, and received orders to proceed to Newport News, and protect the Minnesota (then aground) from the Merrimac.

We got under way and arrived at the Minnesota at 11 P. M. I went on board in our cutter, and asked the captain what his prospects were of getting off. He said he should try to get afloat at 2 A. M., when it was high water. I asked him if we could render him any assistance; to which he replied, "No!" I then told him we should do all in our power to protect him from the Merrimac. He thanked me kindly and wished us success. Just as I arrived back to the Monitor, the Congress blew up, and certainly a grander sight was never seen; but it went straight to the marrow of our bones. Not a word was said, but deep did each man think, and wish we were by the side of the Merrimac. At 1 A. M. we anchored near the Minnesota. The captain and myself remained on deck, waiting for the appearance of the Merrimac. At 3 A. M. we thought the Minnesota was afloat, and coming down on us; so we got under way as soon as possible and stood out of the channel. After backing and filling about for an hour, we found we were mistaken, and anchored again. At daylight we discovered the Merrimac at anchor, with several vessels, under Sewall's Point. We immediately made every preparation for battle. At 8 A. M. on Sunday, the Merrimac got under way, accompanied by several steamers, and started direct for the Minnesota. When a mile distant she fired two guns at her. By this time our anchor was up, the men at quarters, the guns loaded, and every thing ready for action. As the Merrimac came close, the captain passed the word to commence firing. I triced up the port, run out the gun, and fired the *first* gun, and thus commenced the great battle between the Monitor and the Merrimac.

Now mark the condition our men and officers were in. Since Friday morning, forty-eight hours, they had had no rest, and very little food, as we could not conveniently cook. They had been hard at work all night, and nothing to eat for breakfast, except hard bread, and were thoroughly worn out. As for myself, I had not slept a wink for fifty-one hours, and had been on my feet almost constantly. But after the first gun was fired we forgot all fatigues, hard work, and every thing else, and fought as hard as men ever fought. We loaded and fired as fast as we could. I pointed and fired the guns myself. Every shot I would ask the captain the effect, and the majority of them were encouraging. The captain was in the pilot-house, directing the movements of the vessel; Acting-master Stodder was stationed at the wheel which turns the tower, but as he could not manage it, was relieved by Steiners. The speaking-trumpet from the tower to the pilot-house was broken, so we passed the word from the captain to myself on the berth-deck by Paymaster Keeler and Captain's Clerk

Toffey. Five times during the engagement we touched each other, and each time I fired a gun at her, and I will vouch the 168 pounds penetrated her sides. Once she tried to run us down with her iron prow, but did no damage whatever. After fighting for two hours we hauled off for half an hour to hoist shot in the tower. At it we went again as hard as we could, the shot, shell, grape, canister, musket and rifle-balls flying in every direction, but doing no damage. Our tower was struck several times, and though the noise was pretty loud it did not affect us any. Stodder and one of the men were carelessly leaning against the tower, when a shot struck it exactly opposite them and disabled them for an hour or two. At about 11.30 A. M. the captain sent for me. I went forward, and there stood as noble a man as lives, at the foot of the ladder to the pilot-house, his face perfectly black with powder and iron, and apparently perfectly blind. I asked him what was the matter. He said a shot had struck the pilot-house exactly opposite his eyes and blinded him, and he thought the pilot-house was damaged. He told me to take charge of the ship and use my own discretion. I led him to his room, laid him on the sofa, and then took his position. On examining the pilot-house, I found the iron hatch on top, on the forward side, was completely cracked through. We still continued firing, the tower being under the direction of Steiners. We were between two fires—the Minnesota on one side, and the Merrimac on the other. The latter was retreating to Sewall's Point, and the Minnesota had struck us twice on the tower. I knew if another shot should strike our pilot-house in the same place, our steering apparatus would be disabled, and we should be at the mercy of the batteries on Sewall's Point. We had *strict* orders to act on the defensive, and protect the Minnesota.

We had evidently finished the Merrimac as far as the Minnesota was concerned. Our pilot-house was damaged, and we had orders *not* to follow the Merrimac up; therefore, after the Merrimac had retreated, I went to the Minnesota and remained by her until she was afloat. General Wool and Secretary Fox both commended me for acting as I did, and said it was the strict military plan to follow. This is the reason we did not sink the Merrimac; and every one here, capable of judging, says we acted perfectly right.

The fight was over now, and we were victorious. My men and myself were perfectly black with smoke and powder. As we ran alongside the Minnesota, Secretary Fox hailed us, and told us we had fought the greatest naval battle on record, and behaved as gallantly as men could. He saw the whole fight. I felt proud and happy, then, mother, and was fully repaid for all I had suffered. When our noble captain heard the Merrimac had retreated, he said he was perfectly happy, and willing to die, since he had saved the Minnesota. Most fortunately for him, his classmate and intimate friend, Lieutenant Wise, saw the fight, and was alongside immediately after the engagement. He took him on board the Baltimore boat, and carried him to Washington that night. I was now captain and first-lieutenant, and had not a soul to help me in the ship, as Stodder was injured. I had been up so long and had so little rest, and been under such a state of excitement, that my nervous system was completely run down. Every bone in my body ached, and my limbs and joints were so sore that I could not stand. My nerves and muscles twitched as though electric shocks were passing through them, and my head ached as though it would burst.

About twelve o'clock, Acting-lieutenant Ely came on board and reported to me for duty. He immediately assumed his duties, and I felt considerably relieved, but no sleep did I get that night, owing to my excitement. The next morning, at eight o'clock, we got under way, and stood through our fleet. Cheer after cheer went up from the frigates and small craft for the glorious little Monitor, and happy indeed did we all feel. I was then captain of the vessel that had saved Newport News, Hampton Roads, Fortress Monroe (as General Wool said), and, perhaps, your Northern ports. I am unable to express the happiness I felt that I had thus served my country and flag at such an important time. At about 10 A. M., General Wool and Mr. Fox came on board, and congratulated us on our victory. At eight o'clock that night, Captain Selfridge came on board and took command, and brought the following letter from Mr. Fox:

"U. S. STEAMER ROANOKE, OLD POINT, March 10th.

. "MY DEAR MR. GREENE—Under the extraordinary circumstances of the contest of yesterday, and the responsibility devolving upon me, and your extreme youth, I have suggested to Captain Marston to send on board the Monitor, as temporarily commanding, Lieutenant Selfridge, until the arrival of Commander Goldsborough, which will be in a few days. I appreciate your position, and you must appreciate mine, and serve with the same zeal and fidelity. With the kindest wishes for you all,

Most truly,
G. A. FOX."

Of course I was surprised at first, but soon saw it was as it should be. You must recollect the immense responsibility resting upon this vessel. We literally hold all the property ashore and afloat in these regions, as the wooden vessels are useless against the Merrimac. At no time during the war, either in the army or navy, has any position been so important as this vessel. You may think I am exaggerating somewhat, because I am in the Monitor, but the President, General Wool, Secretary Fox, all think so, and have telegraphed to that effect. Lieutenant Selfridge was in command for two days, until Lieutenant Jeffers arrived from Roanoke Island. Lieutenant Butts, my old room-mate at the academy, was on board the Merrimac. Little did we think, when there, that we should ever be firing 150 lb. shot at each other, but so goes the world.

Our pilot-house is now nearly completed. We have solid oak extending from three inches below the eye-holes to five feet out on the deck. This makes an angle of 27 degrees from the horizontal. This is to be covered with three inches of iron. We shall now be invulnerable at every point. The deepest indentation on our sides was four inches, tower two inches, and deck half an inch. We were not at all damaged, except the pilot-house. No one was affected by the concussion in the tower, either by our own guns or the shots of the enemy. This is a long letter for me; so, with much love to you all.

Your affectionate son,
S. D. GREENE.

LETTER XLV.

CAMP FOSTER, POOLESVILLE, Md.,
January 24th, 1862.

COLONEL DEVENS is determined to *weed out* his regiment, and he is in a fair way to make it *one* of the best in the army. . . . The victory at Somerset is a cause of great rejoicing. If *we* can't do any thing *here*, we are glad to see *somebody* making progress. We are in daily expectation of *marching orders;* but how it will be possible to move with the face of the country in its present condition I cannot imagine; but the "*natives*" assure us there will be no improvement till late in the spring. We had nothing but storm for nearly a week; to-night, for variety, we have sleet, and the wind drives it like pins and needles! The poor fellows "on guard" have a hard time of it; but that is a part of *their* duty, as much as fighting is. . . We have all donned the "army hat," an elaborate head-gear of lace and feathers, costing ten dollars apiece. Some of our *short* officers look ridiculous enough in them. . . . I have some of my last year's photographs, but I do not like to send them to ———, they look so lean and careworn.

We had a funeral in camp this afternoon, with military honors. It is a very imposing ceremony. The colonel, in absence of the chaplain, reads the Episcopal service. The band and the muffled drums play a dirge as the procession moves to the grave, where three volleys are fired over the body by the escort, which varies in size according to the rank of the deceased.

The inhabitants of Poolesville, who refuse to attend our dress-parades and reviews, seem to take some interest in a funeral! Perhaps it is because there is one more *Union man* dead and out of their way. E—— would not wish me *to try* to grant her request of "a piece of wood from near the spot where I landed when I swam the Potomac!" (so great would the risk be). No troops, either Union or rebel, have occupied Harrison's Island since the second day after the fight at Ball's Bluff, when Captain Phillbrick, with a small party, tried to recover some tools left there, and the rebel cavalry forded the Virginia branch of the river, and would have captured him if he hadn't *retreated* at *double-quick!* I will try to find some little memento of the fight to send E——.

Lieut. Richard Derby.

LETTER XLVI.

The following verses, composed, with other poems, by soldiers in our hospital, are at your disposal. They prove that the brave fellows who are exposing their lives in defence of our country are not, as some vainly imagine, an ignorant and ungrateful set of men, but can, when opportunity offers, express as beautiful sentiments and exhibit as refined feelings as ever emanated from the heart of man.

J. S. Smith, Chaplain U. S. A.

LETTER XLVII.

The following *poem* is given, as being humorous if not sentimental. It was written in accordance with hospital regulations, which require every ward-master, immediately on the death of a patient in his ward, to make returns in writing of the effects of the deceased to the assistant-surgeon in charge of the ward.

Schedule 7th of the late Patrick Dregan's Effects.

Impromptu.

Dregan's *effects*, 'twixt you and me,
  Dear doctor, are but trifling;
And when I name them, you will see
  His pockets I've been rifling;
But not in time, alas! alas!
  Dollars and cents, he gave 'em,
Full quite a pile, for holy Mass,
  From Hades' blue flames to save him!

He left a dress-coat and a pants,
   Likewise a pair of braces,
Lengthened with cord to suit his wants;
   A pair of shoes and laces.
He also *left* a cap, and vest
   With fine combs in the pockets;
An old black pipe, adapted best
   For throwing bombs or rockets.

He left himself at six P. M.,
   The thirtieth of May, sir;
And since that time our good nurse, Jem,
   For him has ceased to pray, sir.
Hoping he'll not come back in haste
   For "pills," "beefsteaks," or "wine," sir;
We've got nothing here to waste.
   Subscribed as ever thine, sir.

                WARD-MASTER THOMAS MCCABE.
U. S. A. GENERAL HOSPITAL, New York City.

LETTER XLVIII.

NAVAL ENGAGEMENT: MERRIMAC AND CUMBERLAND— MONITOR AND MERRIMAC.

                BALTIMORE, March 11th, 1862.

DEAR ——: Taking for granted that ere this you have received my note informing you we had reached Fortress Monroe, I will resume the account of our rambles, and relate what has befallen us since.

On the afternoon of the day of our arrival, you may remember, we intended to visit the fortress, General Wool having promised us a guide. But the Fates decreed it otherwise, and destined us to see something far more imposing than any fortification.

Most fortunate spectators were we of a grand naval drama, the varied scenes of which will be pictured on the page of history. Long, very long, will the audience who looked out on Hampton Roads that afternoon, remember the thrilling play. We were seated at dinner when first the cry was heard, "The Merrimac is coming out!" and in an instant all were running a race for the beach.

The bay, from our point of observation, appeared like a lake, seemingly perfectly land-locked, and the water was sparkling and glistening under a bright, warm sun.

At our right, several miles distant, though in plain view, lay the frigates Congress and Cumberland. To the left, but much nearer, was a vessel with her upper sails set, moving down with stately pace towards the other two.

As we looked admiringly at her, we suddenly were startled by the report of a gun, and the little cloud of smoke that hovered over the far-off shore told us that it was fired from a rebel battery. In answer to the compliment, the vessel, as she glided by, delivered her broadside—the whole affair being so neatly managed that we well could imagine it was but a friendly salute.

But where is the Merrimac? Directly before us we saw something that looked very much like the peaked roof of a house drifting silently across the bay, and this was the famed craft. Its singular appearance—its still progress—its gloomy blackness, impressed one with a feeling of awe, and one forgot that it was fashioned by hands, and thought it some terrible monster, whose dread power none could foretell.

Every eye was now fixed on the strange vessel, and with breathless silence we awaited, expecting each moment an engagement would commence, about the result of which we could not but feel a painful solicitude.

All at once, as we gazed, there shot out from her dark side a puff of downy smoke, and a few seconds after we heard the dull, heavy report; suspense was at end and the action begun.

With what intense interest we watched the ensuing conflict, you well can imagine.

How at first a belt of fire flashed 'long the broadside; then dark sulphurous clouds eddied slowly away; and then, so quickly following, the rumbling roar of the explosion would come booming over the water.

How the balls went skipping over the bay, wide of the mark, sending sparkling jets high into the air.

How, when a better range was obtained, shot aimed point-blank at the Merrimac, glancing from her sloping side, dashed the water into foam at almost a right-angle from the direction in which it was fired.

How, as the firing became more and more rapid, the volume of sound swelled momentarily, until the ground trembled under our feet with the intermingling concussions.

And then how, when the shades of evening gathered round us, the view grew very grand, for at every discharge there issued from the vessel a sheet of flame—a perfect torrent of fire.

Truly it was a gallant sight, once seen never to be forgotten!

As the day wore on, however, the affair became more tragic, and sorrowfully we heard the sinking Cumberland fire her last shot at the foe, and saw the white flag flutter on the mast of the Congress.

Most deeply were we impressed that this was no holiday sport, on hearing men just behind us busily engaged in making coffins, and seeing the many already prepared.

The clang of hammers sounded in our ears with a mournful significance, for sad was the thought that many a brave heart had ceased to beat while we were idly looking on.

The Congress was now in flames, burning at first slowly, and then more and more fiercely. Forked tongues of fire would tower up, writhing like serpents, and again all was dark; only, however, to break out with renewed brilliancy, bringing into sharp outline the spars and rigging.

Thus the night set in with this fit closing scene to the appalling drama of the day.

The "long-roll" was now beaten, summoning the garrison to their posts, and the yellow flag was displayed from the hospital, as it was thought that the enemy would come down to the fortress, and complete the work of destruction.

It having been proved that several wooden vessels were no match for one iron-clad, all hope of staying the progress of the Merrimac lay in the arrival of the Monitor, which we knew had sailed from New York.

Anxiously we looked for it, and well were we rewarded, for it came like a hero in a play, and nobly was the part sustained.

The next morning, when the Merrimac steamed round the point, she met an antagonist worthy of her mettle; but nothing daunted, both moved to the onset, and "Greek met Greek."

For hours the conflict lasted. Sometimes so near were the vessels they appeared in contact, and again three miles apart; but all the while vomiting forth seeming destruction with frightful rapidity, looking, as a gentleman near me observed, like very "hell cats."

At last the Merrimac drew off, and, delivering a parting shot, moved slowly away.

Thus ended an engagement that has no precedent in history, and from which dates a new era in naval warfare. Long will its stirring scenes live in story and in song.

ROLAND GREENE MITCHELL,

"The poor fellows came staggering in at the fort that night, who swam ashore from the Cumberland, when she went down with her living freight, firing her last broadside. They sank down, unable to speak or tell us of the fight; exhausted by the long tramp after the terrible action they had taken part in, they slept where they fell down without eating or drinking."

LETTER XLIX.

CAMP SCOTT, YORKTOWN, May 1st, 1862.

MY DEAR MA—Thy welcome letter found me at this beautiful little camp, surrounded with wild-flowers. But a few days ago we were marching in mud and water six inches deep. The storms have passed away, and we now enjoy the bright sunshine of May in our new little camp, four miles from the memorable Yorktown, which is soon again to be ours.

I have now an opportunity of getting acquainted with rebel lines and breastworks, for I am engaged in building towers for signalling on our lines; and I have seen all their fortifications, a distance of five miles in length, and a perfect survey of the country around, which I can appreciate much better than many who have not pored over those ancient and modern pages, which have taught me that Hannibal was not a McClellan, nor Virginia the sandy deserts beyond the far-off Nile. Neither is our noble Fremont, clad in his armor bright, a despotic Bonaparte, climbing the Alpine hills.

In comparing the two nations, the heroic deeds and valor are no greater than in former times, but the science and prosperity of an enterprising people have made the American domain shine like a star in the firmament, and brought to light the truth that man is capable of self-government: encouraged by that great principle of liberty, planted deep in the hearts of our Union soldiers, we will drive the rebels to despotic lands to enjoy the bitter fruits of tyranny.

The letter given above was written by George T. Magill, who volunteered in the service of his country in the summer of 1861; as sergeant he entered, and bravely fell facing the enemy at Fair Oaks, 1862. "Two days before the brave boy fell mortally wounded," writes his sorrow-stricken yet proud mother, "these last noble lines were written by him:"

LETTER L.

"If I am destined to be wounded, or fall beneath my foes, God wills it to be thus. Have confidence that the future will make all well, and have no fears for your loved boy."

"If these last lines of a true patriot suit your collection, they are at your disposal," continues the writer; "a mother's heart goes with them.

"Yours for the memory of the lonely dead, for the brave who bled for us all.

ANNA S. MAGILL."

Bucks County, Pennsylvania.

LETTER LI.

CAMP BEFORE RICHMOND, 1862.

SISTER DEAR—I thought of you on the seventeenth, the anniversary of the battle of Bunker Hill and of your birth. How I should have liked to be with you on that birthday! but my duties are here, and will be for a long while, I reckon. You are twenty-four—is it possible? Yes, for I am twenty-six. How swiftly have passed these years! How short the time since in childhood we sported together and gambolled gleefully, oblivious of care! Those were happy days, but they are not to return. You express the opinion that your life has been unprofitable. Not so. True, we all see in mature age the follies of our youth, and where we have erred. If we could commence with the knowledge and experience we now have, it would be different; but in our ignorance, youth's years were as well spent as mature age.

When this rebellion broke out, I felt it to be my duty to help put it down. I think you all feel that our family owes some assistance to the Government. Who could better be spared to render it than I? If I fall, remember me as a *patriot* and a *soldier*, though ever so humble.

BYRON B. WILSON,
Veteran Volunteers.

LETTER LII.

8TH ILLINOIS CAVALRY,
Shipping Point, May 3d, 1862.

WE are eight miles from Yorktown, and five from the nearest rebel fortifications. At intervals we hear the booming of artillery, and rather more than usual this afternoon. . . . . . The firing at Yorktown is increasing. The evening is quiet; we can hear the whistling of a ball, the bursting of a shell, occasionally, with the deep boom of the cannon. The fine brass bands of the infantry are playing, some "The Retreat," others "Yankee Doodle," "The Soldier's Dream of Home," etc. It is very pleasant, and the sun, according to my compass, is setting in the northeast; yet I know it must be west by the retiring of old Sol and the direction of Yorktown. Judging by the firing, I think we shall see active times now until the whole thing is over. Our forefathers besieged Yorktown under Washington and Lafayette, while it was held by the British, and were victorious. We cannot be less so when it is held by traitors to the best of governments. If I am wounded, have no fear but that I shall be well cared for; if killed, remember I die honorably, in the glorious cause of defending my country and its constitution against those who have dared to raise a hand to overthrow them. They, the rebels, will be subjugated, and peace will again be enjoyed by the citizens of the United States.

Camp of Williamsburg, 4th.—We were ordered (unexpectedly) to prepare for a march, and I did not mail this letter. To our great surprise, Yorktown was evacuated, and we were detached in pursuit of the rebels. They fled, leaving the best of fortifications.

July 5th.—It has been a long and busy time since I wrote or received a letter. On 26th of June, Jackson's force attacked our pickets three or four miles from Mechanicsville. Our boys fought them with carbines and revolvers, as they fell back to Mechanicsville, holding them in check near four hours after they attacked us ere they reached Mechanicsville. There we fell back in the rear of General Reynolds' brigade of infantry and some artillery. The enemy came on him in such force that he was obliged to fall back across a ravine, when he received reinforcements, and held them in check till night, slaughtering them as they attempted to cross. The general wondered how the 8th Illinois cavalry managed to hold them back so long. During the night the forces all retreated. Our regiment started at daylight, acting as rear-guard, retreating down the Chickahominy to just above the new bridge, where the battle of the twenty-seventh was fought.

July 26th, Harrison's Landing.—We are not having hard times now, only on picket duty thirty-six hours in four days: we invariably have a brisk skirmish every time we go out. The last time we were out, we were within a short distance of the battle-field on Malvern Hill, when we emptied at least one dozen saddles. A contraband who came to our lines the next morning said that they had twenty-eight killed and wounded.

August 24th.—After witnessing something of the horrors of war, we are again in Yorktown, and have received orders for embarkation from here to Alexandria, which was read to the regiment while on dress-parade last; and from General Pleasanton great praise for our conduct since we have been under his command; also, as he expressed it in his order, the approbation and praise of all who witnessed our bearing in the late skirmish on Malvern Hill.

Belle Plain, December 25th.—It has been a long, long time since I mailed a letter, yet I assure you all from home receive a glad welcome. I should have written sooner, but we were very busy around Fredericksburg. I waited until the fighting was over, and when it was over *I could not write.*

January 21st, 1863.—The army moves; we are glad of that. Our brigade is attached to Sumner's division; are doing well and living high; enjoy remarkably pleasant weather—till cold rain last night and to-day. It does not tend to letter-writing to think how our noble State is being disgraced by those left in charge of her; while hundreds and thousands of her citizens, willing to drop party and join hands in crushing this mighty rebellion, volunteered; leaving home, friends, and comforts innumerable; suffering hardships and privations,—the life-blood of many being poured out like water, and their mutilated bodies filling unknown graves: and yet we flinch not a hair's breadth. This is what we expected, and expect to see much more of it before the rebels are subjugated; and this is what we are bound to do, and those at home should support us. . . The blood shed by the volunteers of Illinois will atone for her disgrace.

Feb. 4th.—Am sorry you are willing to think me homesick. No matter where I may be or what my business, providing I think it right, there, for the time being, *is my home:* now the army is my home, and I have never been guilty of wishing for any other as long as war is a necessity, save for a short vacation. Yet it is a pleasure, when a man has leisure, to think over "ye olden times," comparing past and present. In writing to you, I simply noted the difference regarding the one thing needful—soldiers call it grub. And a man who would get sick on poor living should know better than ever to enlist. I would not change places with any man that is at home, able and free to volunteer and has not done so (not that I like the business, for no *amount of money* would hire me to be a soldier were it not for the cause). Were it necessary for me to exchange situation with any man, I should want him to be "a scarred veteran" of the war; and should want his scars, even though minus a leg or an arm. For should I be found at home, I would want the evidence that I had served my country in time of need.

May 4th.—Yours of April 19th and 26th are received and very welcome. We have been very busy, but of course you know what this army has done by hard fighting. We have been victorious; our horses are badly jaded, therefore are resting to-day; will march to-night or to-morrow morning. In skirmishing, one man of our regiment was killed and several horses. Captain Waite's horse was killed, and himself in the hands of the enemy. This company charged—taking him back, and three prisoners. In our perambulations we passed near the old battle-field of Cedar Mountain. In many places the bones of the slain have been rooted from their shallow graves by hogs, and are now bleaching where they gave their life for their country's honor.

July 13th.—I have missed none of your welcome letters, although, we have been so busy and moved around so much, we scarcely get a mail once a week; and when it accumulates in such abundance much is lost. On the 4th inst. we (our regiment) got a three-bushel bag full, and the rain was pouring finely on that day. The army, for the time, isolates a man from any but war matters and military affairs, and that we have enough of, and there is no inducement to write that of which you read and hear so much about. I mailed you a letter 25th of June, giving an account of a heavy cavalry fight at Upperville, in which we had hot work. In Maryland we have not been idle, as paper accounts will show. We are in Buford's division. . . . . . Buford's division arrived at Gettysburg on the 30th June, and on 1st July was attacked by rebel infantry in force. We fought them two hours ere the infantry came up. The rebs had crowded us back slowly, and their lines of battle not more than sixty rods off, and advancing for a charge when the infantry relieved us. They (our infantry) had no idea the rebs were so near. Here General Reynolds was killed. Of the three days' work here you have read. We had another fight with rebel infantry at Williamsport, July 6th. Have had some close calls, but am all right. Fighting, with us, is past being a novelty or a thing to talk about; and after fighting all day go to sleep (unless duty bid us wake), feeling we have done one more good hard day's work for Uncle Sam.

Sept. 28th.—I do not expect to hear of the fall of Charleston till an army from the interior reaches it; but do not see why Gilmore does not give them Greek fire enough to burn them up. What is there in that vipers' nest, which has hatched nothing but treason since it was settled, that we should be tender of? They are only fathers, mothers, and children, aiders, abettors, lovers, and supporters of treason, and as long as we are at war, I wish we would wage it against them as though we meant it, and in earnest.

October 24th.—Since writing last, our army has fallen back from the Rapidan to Fairfax Court-house, and advanced again to Warrenton. We picket the Rappahannock, and have fought the rebel infantry and cavalry combined, losing many valuable men in killed and wounded, and many of our best horses, in severe skirmishing, and I feel refreshed by five days' rest. You speak of my re-enlisting. As long as the war lasts I shall be a soldier; not that I love it, but from duty. I can do Uncle Sam's work better now I am a veteran than when I enlisted a raw recruit; and if he needed me then, he needs me more at the present time, as my capacity for serving him is greater.

November 9th.—Your letters are highly prized; reminiscences from home cheer the soldier. Our army has moved on the enemy, of which you have probably read accounts in papers. Our cavalry division crossed the Rappahannock at Sulphur Springs, and moved in the direction of Culpepper. When within four miles of there, we came upon a body of infantry in strong position (prisoners taken said there was one division of infantry and one brigade of cavalry); we attempted to drive them, but they could not see it in that light, as the woods and rifle-pits were good security for them. The result was, in a few minutes we lost two men killed and twelve wounded, and twenty-four horses killed.

May 22d, 1864.—Our regiment is scattered—four companies in Washington, one in Alexandria, and seven here (Belle Plain). This is at present the base of supplies. It will soon be moved to Acquia Creek. We are kept busily engaged scouting on the left, below King George's Courthouse; on the right, beyond Stafford Court-house. Our being acquainted with every road and path, we are better suited for the service than cavalry unacquainted with this section of country. We gobble many. Got on Moseby's track once, but a little "too late" to overtake him.

July 13.—I have long delayed writing, though I think I miss but few of the kind missives from home and friends; and I can assure you that each one received is prized as a treasure; for a soldier's memory of home and friends is ever green and ever fruitful of pleasant thoughts. We left Washington July 4th, and have had a lively time since, I assure you. Never fear for Washington; the enemy is not strong enough to take it.

November 22d.—Our country is dearer to us than life, and our cause is right: it is the cause of God and the civilized world. In such a cause it would be sweet to die, rather than to live and see traitors triumph; or to live, having saved my life by the slightest flinching from duty at a perilous post. I have been criticized and rebuked for needlessly exposing my life, and of being rash. It was a false charge, for it never was without its object or effect. Was there ever a better regiment of cavalry than our men first organized, and most that now are veteran soldiers? What makes a good regiment? Their officers. Yet how often is raw material wasted for lack of properly knowing how to apply and use it. The officers give or destroy the spirit of their men. Oft have I rode at a walk along and in front of our line of sinuous skirmishers. Was it needless or without good result? No; witness the effect upon the men. Though they watch me, expecting to see me fall from my horse pierced by some of the many bullets hissing by, after I have passed you will see them crouch down again behind their rock, tree, or fence, grasping their carbines with more firmness and confidence. And you cannot panic-strike those men by telling them they are flanked or surrounded! Why? Because they know that their officers are watching every movement of the enemy, and that orders given are for the best; and they never yet flinched to move forward or back, having confidence that their officers knew what they were about—which they would not have had if they knew their officers kept in the rear, or were secreted as themselves for safety, and of course had no better chance for observation than they had. In such a case the trooper would suppose he knew as well what ought to be done as the officer, and would be more readily panic-stricken, not having confidence in commands given by their officers. None who know the results consider it needless exposure or rash, though an officer may ride calmly and slowly along a line in face of the enemy's bullets. It makes every man a host in himself. But I have been more lengthy than I meant to on this point; but it is to show you why good officers are so often the victims of sharp-shooters, as Generals Sedgwick and McPherson, Colonels Baker and Humphrey. Do not think I flatter myself at all by what I have written. What I have said applies to every good officer in the army; and almost every officer in this regiment, I am proud to say, belongs to this class. Colonel Gamble has been appointed brigadier-general, and will, without doubt, be confirmed by the Senate: the third appointment from the 8th Illinois cavalry.

ANONYMOUS.

LETTER LIII.

YORKTOWN, Va., May 6, 1862.

MY DEAR MOTHER AND SISTER—We have taken Yorktown without fighting. The papers, of course, give you the main features of the event. Sunday morning it was our turn to go on picket; but before we got to our station, scouts came galloping in, announcing that not a rebel was in sight!

We struck camp immediately, and marched over into the enemy's works opposite our post; and camping overnight, we proceeded to Yorktown on the right, and camped again yesterday noon.

At six o'clock, last evening, we received marching orders; and after standing and *paddling* in the mud till three o'clock in the morning, and advancing only *about a mile*, we were ordered to return to camp and "make ourselves comfortable" till morning.

The army is in fine spirits. I never saw the men so enthusiastic. Every one seems to think *now* that we shall soon put an end to the war and be sent home.

The earthworks are tremendous—fort after fort, of the strongest kind, and mounted with an abundance of heavy artillery; but ours is so superior, *in range*, that they could not withstand it. The guns which they make at Richmond are very poor affairs. Five of them lay in fragments, burst by the overcharges in attempting to *reach* our batteries. The scoundrels buried bomb-shells and torpedoes in every road and all parts of the fortifications, so that when we first entered numbers were killed by their explosion.

I had a very narrow escape. I went up to one of the guns that had burst, to examine it. A few minutes after, a soldier, on the same errand trod on a torpedo, and the shell exploded, throwing him ten feet in the air, and burning him as black as a negro.

We are to embark on board transports for some unknown destination, probably West Point, and are now resting in line near the wharf. .... The army is in splendid condition. Every thing is on the move. McClellan is in high favor. It is "Onward to Richmond" now. I found the inclosed circular in the fort we have been besieging the past three weeks. Preserve it.

RICHARD DERBY.

LETTER LIV.

Addressed to a young lady who had put her name in a pair of socks, sent to the soldiers from the Aid Society, long after the person to whom written had "passed away."

NEWPORT BARRACKS.

You will, in all probability, wonder who this writer is, and how your name was found out by him; but, when you remember you sewed a piece of paper in a pair of stockings, sent by the Sanitary Commission, you will then know how I came to address you. This morning the paper was discovered, and, feeling very grateful for them, I was happy to know where to send an expression of thanks. You, perhaps, did not think they would fall into the possession of a Vermonter, but they have; and I assure you, they are valued as highly as they would have been, had they been received by one from my own State, and my opinion of the Sanitary Commission *is better than ever*. I think the ladies of the North have done nobly for the boys who have gone to fight for the dear old flag; and the prospect is, that this same flag will soon wave over every State in the Union. Perhaps you have a father or a brother in the army; if so, I know full well the fears you entertain daily of hearing distressing news. But I hope you will be sustained, and enabled to look on the *bright* side of things.

The above letter was answered by a member of the family, and the following lines sent to the soldier:

LETTER LV.

Ah, soldier! the offering of thanks fitly given
   May never be read by the friend
Who sent with good-will, in her dear handwriting,
   The name you so recently penned.

We think of her now, as you think of a comrade
   You know you will never more see
At "roll-call" or "drum-beat," when others assemble
   To answer the "shrill reveille."

You hear his name spoken, and then you remember
   How sad and forlorn was the day
You took a last look of all that was mortal,
   And silently bore him away.

In early spring-time, before the June roses
   Had yielded a breath of perfume,
Before her young heart with sorrow was blighted,
   We laid her to sleep in the tomb!

We may not tell now of the grief of the household
   When death his dread errand made known;
Or tell of the smitten—now ever lamenting—
   The loss of the dearly loved one.

But, stranger, we'll tell you, how at the leave-taking
   She smilingly bade us adieu,
As one who was going to far better mansions,
   As only the trusting can do.

She seemed as a seraph entranced with a vision
   Of pure unalloyed delight,
In haste to cross over the much-dreaded river,
   And join the pure angels in sight.

With songs on her lips, and leaning on Jesus,
   Rejoicing, we know she went where
The weary do rest, henceforth and forever:
   Oh, soldier! do strive to get there!

On the morning her pure spirit left its tenement, our village was clothed in gladness on the return of an officer left on the battle-field as dead, at the battle of Chancellorsville. Our flags had been at half-mast, and his friends had put on mourning, when, after two weeks or more, intelligence was received he had been paroled, and was doing well in hospital.

On his arrival home the bells were rung, and though the brave officer, instead of returning with the flush of health, was so pale and emaciated it made us sad to see him, nevertheless the band greeted him with "Home again," and the young lady referred to, on that morning rode out for the last time. Ere long she kissed the dear ones about her, sang verses of a hymn, folded her hands, and thus passed away.

LETTER LVI.

Battle of Seven Pines.

June 2d, 1862.

Dear Father—We have had a hard fight, and I am safe! and take the first opportunity to let you know it. Stevens, Anderson Loweree, and myself are all safe. Mr. Gore is wounded, but not dangerously. Lieutenant Fox is all safe. The enemy drove us from our position, and our wounded lay on the field till we drove them back. The fight commenced on Saturday, M., and to-day (Monday) the enemy has retreated, and we hold our old camp-ground again. We lost every thing we had. Casey's whole division lost all their tents, knapsacks, blankets, and provisions.

We were not supported as we should have been. We had to retreat, but fought as we did so. We fell back to our rifle-pits, and there stopped them. It is a wonder that any of the Ninety-second are left, as we were led up within twenty rods of the enemy, they being in the woods and we in the clearing. They poured in a perfect storm of bullets upon us, but we stood till ordered to retreat, and then left.

Our new colonel, L. C. Hunt, was wounded, and our regiment of 243, who entered the battle, lost in killed and wounded 74 men. Our artillery opened on the rebs first with grape and shell, and then with canister, turning it in by the peck at a time! and, from the closeness of the enemy, they mowed them down in windrows, actually piling them up in heaps. Our loss is great, but theirs must be greater. Our division (Casey's) is badly cut up, and we are ordered back over the Chickahominy. Casey's and Couch's divisions did the fighting till the reinforcements came up. All is quiet now. I will write more particularly respecting the battle soon.

John E. Whipple.

LETTER LVII.

Copperheads and copperheadism have no friends in the army. The soldiers know full well that their infernal treason is doing much to prolong the war. We feel indignant to think there are any citizens in the free and prosperous North, infamous enough to be working against a government that has protected them so faithfully, and secured to them more rights and greater privileges than any other nation under heaven. A child that, being cared for by a faithful mother, and drawing nourishment from her breast, plunges the dagger to her heart and spills her life-blood, is guilty of no more madness than such. We feel indignant, as we are marching through long cold nights and drenching storms, to think of this! The history of our country will be glorious, when it is written. But there is one thing that will be an eternal shame; it will rise like a cancer upon her glory: it is the copperhead spirit of a portion of the North. The names of its leaders will be coupled with those of Catiline and Arnold, and handed down into lasting infamy and disgrace.

REUBEN S. POTTER.

LETTER LVIII.

DEATH to the good is only a passage to a higher state of existence, while the soul will eternally progress in knowledge of truth; and when we have for ages sounded the ocean of truth, we shall but have only fathomed its surface. We can never reach the endless depths of its centre! When the mind of man dwells in darkness, he thinks there is no light; then a few rays enter, and he thinks he has seen and comprehended all. But, when he throws open the windows of his soul, and looks out with the spiritual eye of faith into the deep ocean of truth, he finds it as boundless and exhaustless as its Author. The whole universe is flooded with its glorious light. How sublime, how glorious the thought, that man is eternally to progress in wisdom, purity, and worth! If worthiness be our end and aim, how glorious that end!

REUBEN S. POTTER.

Reuben S. Potter was leading his men out of a thicket, in the "Battle of the Wilderness," when he received his mortal wound. After great suffering, which he endured with heroism and fortitude rarely equalled, he died in the hospital at Washington, D. C., June 13th, 1864.

W. C. Kenyon, of Alfred University, at which institution Reuben S. Potter was graduated the year previous to his entering the army, thus writes: "Brother Potter made a profession of religion publicly in the Baptist church, at the age of fifteen years. Meek, quiet, firm, he possessed talents that inspired hopes of great usefulness in his Master's service. With him every responsibility in life was measured by his religious obligations. He was always at the front of duty, and ready, as a willing and cheerful laborer, in every good work. He went to the field under a religious sense of duty. As a student, he had always been most faithful and scholarly; and the studious habits of his life he kept up in the army, using every spare moment in intellectual and spiritual culture. To him, all of science and literature was full of the unfoldings of the Divine plan and government. He wrote much while in the army on a great variety of moral and religious subjects, and sent home to his aged father and his sisters several hundred pages. The Church have confidently expected that he would enter the ministry at no very distant day. Nor was there a young man in all my acquaintance whose Christian graces and talents seemed so eminently to fit him for great usefulness. He has fallen, like tens of thousands of others, a martyr to the institution of slavery."

Reuben S. Potter was born at Hartsville, Steuben county, New York, 1837.

LETTER LIX.

HARRISON'S LANDING,
James River, Va., July 4th, 1862.

I RECEIVED your letter while out on picket duty, and since then, I can assure you, there has been little time for writing.

We continued on active duty until Saturday night, when we deserted our camp and commenced the retreat for the James river. General Sumner's corps being the reserve, it became our duty to act as rear-guard. At Savage's Station we had something of an engagement, though I don't know what the loss amounted to. After dark we continued our march, and by Monday afternoon nearly half our regiment had given out, exhausted by heat, fatigue, and want of sleep; and myself included among them. I was obliged to go to the baggage train and ride down here, and have not yet returned to duty. I am with

Major Phillbrick, two captains, and three other lieutenants, in a dwelling-house—all invalids.

Now that we are out of the *swamps* and have a chance to rest, I expect to return to the company very soon.

The "*retreat*" was a tremendous undertaking, and cost us a large number of lives and an immense amount of property. The fighting was continued for nearly a week.

I was under fire for three days, Friday, Saturday, and Sunday, but the Lord sees fit to preserve me still. The scenes along the line of retreat exceed any thing that can be imagined. If the authorities would permit them to be described, no pen could give an adequate idea of them.

When you see a ship-load of wounded soldiers landed at the Northern cities, you see comfort and perfect happiness compared with a field hospital, which *must* be deserted and left in the hands of the enemy!

The sick and wounded here are being cared for as fast as possible; but the rain of two days caused much additional suffering. There are plenty of gunboats lying here, which effectually prevent any attack on this point, and reinforcements are arriving.

Much obliged for the photographs. Don't think they flatter much.

An old darkey woman furnished us with an Independence dinner to-day: Bill of fare—stewed *hen*, hoe-cake, farina pudding, strawberry preserve; drinks — *muddy water*, doubtful tea, whiskey punch. Thanks to the Sanitary Commission for most of it, and a *dollar* to the old woman for the rest.

Your affectionate
Richard.

LETTER LX.

BATTLE OF GAINES' MILL.

HARRISON'S LANDING, Va., July 8th, 1862,
5th New York Duryea Zouaves.

I WROTE you a few days ago to let you know I was alive. In this I will try and state more fully our doings in the late retreat, or "*change of base,*" as it is called. A day or two before this movement we were in a constant state of uncertainty in reference to our future movements; orders were given and countermanded continually. On the 26th of June we all got ready to move at any moment. A tremendous firing was heard in the direction of Smith's division; all of General Porter's corps, including Duryea's Zouaves, were under arms all night. On the morning of the twenty-seventh we commenced falling back, and went over familiar ground. We did not understand what was the matter, but *supposed* the enemy were trying to get in our rear. After halting in several places, we were finally drawn up in line of battle, well to the front of the rest of our troops. We were here joined by a part of the provost guard, who were left behind to guard camp. They stated that the rebels had shelled our camp, and that they (the guard) had burnt up all the quartermaster's stores, ammunition, and officers' tents, and left in a hurry. The sick were obliged to turn out and hobble along as best they could. We now *began to feel as if we should have a fight.*

Colonel Warren, acting brigadier, selected his ground with great care, and we ranged the sights on our pieces to reach a wood in our front; we being in an open field just below the brow of a small hill, which saved us somewhat from the artillery fire of the rebels.

We soon spied a rebel battery getting into position. The shells now began to fly rather close, and we were ordered to lie down; and immediately two of our own batteries in the rear opened upon the rebels, which put us in a bad position, as we were between the fire of all three batteries. We lay here some time, once in a while firing a few shots towards the woods as feelers at the rebel sharpshooters, who were posted in trees on our right. We could not get out of the position, so we lay there an hour and a half, the rebels firing shell and grape and canister at us all the time! The solid shot ploughed up the ground all around, and the shells were bursting above us! I tell you, we made ourselves as "flat as pancakes." One of the men had a dog, who chased after the balls; he was wounded in the leg during the fight. Our red caps and pants were too good a mark for the sharpshooters, and the battery had got an exact range of us; so Colonel Warren conducted us through a little hollow to a road running at right angles to our former position, where we were somewhat protected by a brush fence on the top of a bank by the roadside. The boys were repeatedly admonished to keep their heads down below the bank; but some of them, not heeding the advice, were killed. It seems hard to see our own men killed by our own battery! One of our captains went up to Colonel Warren, a few yards off, and told him that the battery was "killing our own men." "Can't help it," says Colonel Warren; "they are Napoleon guns and American shot, and they must *work*."

I was peeping through the fence and saw a brigade of rebels marching by the flank and by fours, in the woods the other side of the field. I told Captain B. what I had seen, and *he* reported to Col. Warren. "Yes, Captain B., I am very much obliged to you for the information," said he, "but have I not eyes as well as you?" The captain "*sloped*," and at the instant the whole six guns poured their rounds into poor Johnny Reb trying a flank movement, and they were swept down in heaps, and those left of them were glad to get away where they came from.

Soon after, Col. Duryea said the rebels were coming out of the woods into the open field, just where we wanted them. We watched them through the fence. They were in splendid line of battle, and coming out at trail arms. They were after the two companies left out as a decoy, under Captain Partridge. After they were all well out in the middle of the field, Col. Hiram D. says, "Now, boys, your time has come, get up and do your duty."

We jumped up as one man, right in front of them. We gave them a volley, which laid many of them low: after a little more firing, we charged on them; they stood pretty obstinate, and some of them were even run through! The rest of them scattered to the woods; supports came up, and they had the woods: we being obliged to remain in the open field, suffered severely, falling in numbers all along the road, yet we obstinately held our own.

Our regiment had lost many men, and began to waver; Sergeant Varian seeing it (he carried the colors), walked, without flinching, right ahead of the regiment about thirty paces! Col. Duryea called to him to return, but he did not heed it. As soon as we saw that brave action, with one accord we gave a great shout, charged through the woods, completely scattering the rebels, and driving them in every direction. Some of them had thrown away their arms and were trying to climb up a bank; but their supports were coming up, and we had been fighting for nearly three hours. We (Duryea's Zouaves) were the last to leave the field of Gaines' Mill, covering the retreat. We went through some awful moments in this last fight: we were obliged to form again near night, in order to cover the retreat. Some of our troops were running, others falling back. Soon there was nothing in front of us but Stonewall Jackson's hordes. We were on a little knoll; there were about 150 of us (Duryea's Zouaves) who stood it out; we were supporting a battery, all ready to skedaddle at a moment's notice. As far as we could see through the smoke the rebels covered the hard-fought field, on which Union and rebel soldiers alike lay *together* in their last sleep.

The battery was firing its rounds as if life depended on it—which, in fact, it did; the shell and bullets of the enemy were flying like a storm over us; I lost my knapsack: we every one of us expected to sacrifice our lives or be taken prisoners,—"a fate worse than death."

The rebels were now so close to us that they began singing out, "Don't fire upon your own men." Many of us stopped firing; the smoke was so thick that we could not make out the flag. At that moment Col. Warren came up, and says, "Blaze away, blaze away, boys! if they are our own men, they have no business there;" and we did *blaze* away, and just then the colors fell! A ball came along and took about two inches of my coat away on the shoulder; the next instant Tom Carney, who was my file-leader, fell, as we thought, mortally wounded. We reported him "*killed*" to his friends, but he turned up among the wounded prisoners in Richmond, and joined us again. Some months after he saved me. We now heard the shouts of men in the distance towards the rear, and we knew that reinforcements were coming, but they were too far off to relieve us. Col. Hiram sat upon his horse, cool but anxious; said he, "I wish to God that we were relieved!" and it was time we were. The artillery now fired their last round and galloped off. It was now dark, and we, worn and tired out, followed along in the rear of it, missing many a familiar face; the fighting for that day was over. We were in it altogether, *in range*, five hours.

When we came to a halt, we were counted by our adjutant, and numbered 146 men. We slept soundly that night on the ground. In the morning we were drawn up in line of battle for twenty-four hours, guarding two roads at their junction. Again we were on the march, and came to what is known as Malvern Hill. We were here on picket between the Hill and Turkey-bend creek. If the rebels could have got in here they would have cut off our army from its line of retreat.
A. DAVENPORT.

LETTER LXI.

MALVERN HILL.

The great battle of Malvern Hill was fought just to the right of us, and I can safely say that I have never yet heard any thing like the thunder of the artillery on that day—it was one long, incessant roll. When we left the place the regiments were leaving in a panic—wagons, sick and wounded, artillery—all in one jumble. "Colonel Hiram" (Duryea) would not take us into such a disorganized mass, and we waited for the road to clear. He said he would rather face the whole Southern Confederacy than take his regiment into that rabble, and he backed his word by marching us down the road towards the rebel position, and there we were obliged to stay until the road was clear enough to march on and keep our order. We experienced that day the hardest marching we have yet seen, in mud knee-deep, fording streams to our middle, raining in torrents, and no place to sit down, unless we could sit in *slush* a foot deep; and to add to our misfortunes there was a hard slippery bottom under the layer of slush, which made it as difficult to walk as if we were on ice, and we were continually falling down. Everybody and every thing was wet through, and all tired out and half dead with the continual fatigue we had gone through.

We are now resting in a very fair camp on the borders of a small creek. General McClellan is fortifying the position, and unless the enemy could succeed in blockading the James river, they would have a hard time in driving us out. We must be reinforced, as the rebels are two to one, having concentrated most of their troops about Richmond, and they fight with determination; but they suffered more than we did in the retreat. Marching down Broadway our regiment numbered from 800 to 1,000 men, and on "Federal Hill," in Baltimore, in our glory, we had over 1,000. We now scrape together for duty 350. Three of our officers are under arrest for neglect of duty during the battle of Gaines' Mill.

We are all troubled with that soldier's curse, diarrhea, but are in fair spirits, and getting tired of this sort of life. It is a horrible life to lead, worse than being in prison as far as comfort is concerned, and there are few here who would not be willing to have some wound to get out of it, if the conversation of the men be believed. I have talked with men who have been in every station of life; men who have been in the navy, and sailed around the world; those who have been in the English and other European armies, and they say, without exception, that this is the hardest scrape that they ever got into. I lost my knapsack at Gaines' Mill. I wish the reb joy who found it, and I hope he enjoyed reading your patriotic letters, of which I had about fifty. The enemy are now some distance from us, and the remnants of bands of music are playing, and the drum is now heard for the first time since the evacuation of Yorktown. It seems like commencing our siege all over again. General McClellan complimented our colonel personally, and said that men never fought better, and that we did a great share in the saving of the right wing of the army at Gaines' Mill. General McClellan's address was read off to us on parade Sunday evening. It is very eloquent and *about true*, but the details are not thought of in a move of this kind—the dead and dying, the wounded and sick, left behind on the road, or prisoners. No one can tell the individual suffering and misery that takes place in such times as we have just gone through.

Good-by, and God bless us all,

A. DAVENPORT.

LETTER LXII.

BULL RUN.

CAMP NEAR CHAIN BRIDGE, Va.,
5th Regiment, N. Y. Vols., Sept. 3d, 1862.

DEAR FATHER—I received, about an hour since, yours of 12th and 21st August, and some papers; also just before leaving Harrison's Landing, mother's and Carrie's of 10th instant, but have had, as you may surmise, no time or opportunity of answering them until now. We have not even had time to rest or prepare our food since leaving Harrison's Landing. Three days before leaving that place our knapsacks were sent away; since which time have had nothing but the clothes upon my back, overcoat, haversack, canteen, and accoutrements. I am now writing this with the stump of a pencil, the only one in our company, I believe; have no envelope, or any thing to seal this with, but will trust to luck to close this some way. We marched from the Landing to Newport News in about three days and a half. The first day's march was one of the most severe that we ever experienced, being about thirty-five miles. We halted about a mile beyond the Chickahominy river, near its mouth, and were all exhausted, and about used up, and had to limp the last few miles, our feet being all blistered, and our limbs stiff. At Newport News we rested a day or two, and were joined by a batch of recruits; took the steamer Cahawba, on which our brigade, consisting of our regiment and the Tenth New York, about 1300 men, were crowded together for about sixty hours. I slept in a chair on deck, and hardly left it all that time, for fear I should lose even that berth. We landed at Acquia creek, and after some delay were crowded on platform and baggage cars; the one on which I was had no railing, and we sat with our legs dangling over the sides, and the centre of the platform crowded with our men, as best they could pack themselves. We reached Falmouth station after about an hour and a half's ride, and took up our march again; our arms being loaded, and sleeping under arms most of the time, often hearing heavy firing in the distance. We guarded several fords on the Rappahannock as we went along. As we came near Catlett's station, we saw our wounded lying about a farm-house, and they were burying our dead of a fight the day before. Some rebels were lying by the side of the railroad track in their gore, dead. At that place two locomotives and trains were destroyed; also bridges, burned by the rebels. At Manassas the destruction of railroad property was complete, the remains of engines and their trains, stores, and clothing scattered in every direction. From here we marched about eight miles, and drew up in line of battle, fired some dozen or so shell, but received no return; they were fighting some two miles below us, and there had been fighting in another direction the day before. We laid on the road that night, and the next day were at the scene of the previous day's fight, which it seems is what we call Bull Run; they were then carrying off the dead and wounded: we could distinguish the red pants of the dead of the Brooklyn Fourteenth, lying on a hill to the front of us, which was the disputed ground of the day before, our forces being driven twice from it, and soon to contain the dead and wounded of our own ill-fated regiment, of the same uniform as our Brooklyn brothers. We took our position well to the front, on the borders of the Run, and batteries to the left and right, shelling from hills in the direction of the enemy; there was a hill that rose up directly in front of us. The rebels replied; his shot and shell came whizzing near us, sometimes compelling us to lie down. While this was going on, we gathered some dry brush, made our little fires, and boiled our coffee in our cups, which is our principal nourishment during our long marches. After lying here some time, we advanced in line of battle to the top of the hill, supporting a battery still keeping up the shelling: when I speak of we, I mean the Fifth and Tenth regiments, the regulars were further to the rear. We were in advance of the line of our army, and on the extreme left: finally we again advanced to a hill on our left, and a little in advance of our former position, our battery shelling away in an open space, in which the country could be seen for miles in that direction, our regiment drawn up facing the woods, our left resting on them, the wood running all along our front, and again at right angels to our rear on the left; the Run was at the foot of the hill, and directly in our rear, and only a foot or so deep at this place. Six companies of the Tenth were in the woods in front of our right wing, the remaining four companies being out as skirmishers. The rebels had hardly replied to our shelling for some time, and it struck me that mischief was brewing: two rifle-balls came near us, one of which was picked up by our orderly sergeant; it looked mysterious, as not a reb was to be seen. It was not long before a company of the skirmishers came in on our left, all much excited, huddled together in a heap: they were much scared, and looked as if they had seen a ghost; they said the rebels were coming on, and were right on top of us, on our left flank. Before any orders could be given to change position, the balls began to fly like hail from the woods; it seemed as if the rebels had come out of the ground; it was a continual hiss, snap, whizz, slug. Pat Brady, who used to live opposite us in Lexington Avenue, in the wooden cottage, was the first one hit, he stood a few files from me. He fell without saying a word, struck in the body; he was dragged a few paces to the rear, to be out of our way, by the lieutenant, when he undid his body-belt himself: he died there without a complaint.

On account of part of the Tenth being drawn up in front of our right wing, only the companies on our left could fire. We commenced, but the rebel fire was now murderous, our men falling on all sides, like grass before the scythe; the Tenth had already broke and were flying to the rear. We had not fired more than two or three rounds, before the rebels were on us in front and flank, their object being to surround us and take us prisoners; the order had been given to retreat, by Col. Warren, and save ourselves, every man for himself, but we did not hear it; the recruits began to give way, and then what was left of the regiment broke and ran for their lives;—the rebels after us, yelling like fiends; they were Mississippi and Texan riflemen, and were six to one of us; they came charging on, yelling for "Jeff. Davis, and the Southern Confederacy!" They were mostly in their shirt sleeves, and looked savage enough. There was no hope, but in flight, of saving a man; all the time they were pouring in their deadly shots at short range; when we first broke they were not more than fifteen or twenty feet from us. The battery we were supporting got off safe, leaving Capt. Smead, its commander, dead on the field. He was one of our best artillery officers, and a graduate of West Point. Col. Warren and Capt. Winslow, acting in command of regiment, being mounted, got off safe, but it is a miracle that they escaped.

While running down the hill towards the Run, I saw my comrades dropping on all sides, canteens struck and flying to pieces, haversacks cut off, rifles knocked to pieces; it was a perfect hail of bullets. I was expecting to get mustered out every second; but on, on I went, the balls hissing by my head. I felt one strike me on the hip, just grazing me, and only cutting a hole through my pants. I crossed the Run in the wake of Col. Warren, he being about one hundred yards ahead of me, with his red cap in his hand, and his horse running at the top of his speed! I turned around to look behind once, and only once; that convinced me that it was no time to tarry. I saw two or three rebel officers on horseback, their swords drawn and waiving their men on; it occurred to me to turn and fire on them, but I as quickly decided that it was folly, as I could not stop long enough to take any kind of aim, and I would become a mark for a score of rifles, so I kept on. The rebels came on and swept every thing before them, completely turning the left wing of the army. There was no support whatever behind us, and somebody was evidently to blame; it looked to me as if it was left so on purpose to defeat Pope,—the old corps commanders of the army of the Potomac, being jealous of him, and not willing to co-operate with him. When we rallied, there were about forty of our regiment, and were joined by lost ones of different regiments. We were glad to see our colors safe, and the remnant of our once proud regiment rallying around them. The wounded were coming hobbling along in droves, covered with blood; some being assisted by comrades, some carried in blankets, with a man at each corner, all talking at once, excited. The poor wounded, joggled about from one side to another; some of them yelling with pain: but such is war. Men and artillery flying, the horses galloping like mad, the drivers bewildered; officers with drawn swords and revolvers, shouting, cursing, threatening, no one to obey; bullets flying, shells bursting, the rattle of musketry and roar of artillery, every thing enveloped in smoke; aids and orderlies riding back and forth as if mad; here and there a general with anxious look, giving hurried orders to aids, and, all together, the din and confusion like pandemonium, such as we might picture to ourselves hell in the day of Judgment,—such is what we call a rout. All this commotion as sudden as a storm at sea after a calm. There we stood excitedly looking on all this scene, in an agony of suspense as to the fate of our army, and what the effect on our cause. There our little band stood, with but one will to obey orders, *but minutes were ages.* Lieut. Colonel Marshall of the Tenth, was exhorting and encouraging his handful of men with tears in his eyes, "Be brave and resolute men," said he, "come what will; and for God's sake, do not let me be ashamed of you!" But in a few moments we saw Gen. McDowell ride along the front, amid the storm of bullets, and soon a long line of men were seen through the smoke following in the same direction: the men went along at a double-quick and with a cheer; at the end of the line, I saw one of our red boys, going along with them, although he had no business there. I never heard who it was, and he probably left his body there. It was a whole division of troops sent to the rescue; our fate and perhaps that of the Union depended on their success, in staying the onward rush of the enemy. Gen. McDowell's voice rang out clear and loud above the din—"*Let there be no faltering in this line!*" Immediately after a fearful rolling crash, as the whole division poured in their volley, succeeded by a fierce yell, told us that our boys had commenced the work of death, and were making a charge; at the same time some of our batteries on a hill opened with grape and canister on the rebel hordes. But darkness was fast spreading her mantle over the scene, and the army was saved. We immediately, under cover of night, commenced our retreat.

From the time the first shot was fired at our regiment to our getting off the field, it was not over fifteen minutes; yet in that time we lost eight out of eleven line-officers, killed and wounded,—they being all that we had left with us; among whom were Capt. Hagar, Capt. Lewis, acting major; Adjt. Sovereign, killed. *We* went in with about five hundred and eighty men, and now draw rations for two hundred and fifty men. Most of the recruits that had just joined us were either killed or wounded, having had no instruction, and not knowing by experience how to take common precautions. We have a lot more on the way to join us: little do they know what their trials and troubles are to be. Our company, G, being on the left, next to the last company, lost heavily: out of fifty-eight men, we have twenty-four left, non-commissioned officers and privates. We only had one commissioned officer to command us, Second Lieut. Martin, as brave a man as I want to see; *he fairly cried* when we broke. I went off the field about the same time he did. How I escaped I don't know, but I thank God for it! There are now only eight or ten of two-year men left in our company, who were at Fort Schuyler when the regiment was first organized; the rest have been killed or wounded, sick in hospital, deserted, discharged, &c. We had then one hundred and one men in our company, and I can hardly expect to survive another such engagement, if we should be unfortunate enough to get into another. I fear it will wipe us out as a thing of the past, eight more long, weary months of marching and misery!

Oh! this is a dreadful war, and it is my conviction, one of extermination on the part of the rebels; they fight with determination, and all the prisoners we take seem to be confident of success in the end; they still persist that the South *will never give in;* some of the Texans drawled out in a conversation, "We will foute you until we are all dead, Yanks, and I reckon then the women will foute you after that" (they say *foute* for *fight*). After the fight, we fell back to Centreville, which is strongly fortified, and by night we retreated to Fairfax, and from thence here, where we have just gone into camp, but how long to rest we don't know. The army of the Potomac is *most used* up, and requires rest.

We met Gen. McClellan on the road last night, who was on his way from Washington to meet the army. If any of his enemies and defamers amongst the "stay at homes" had been there, they would have held their heads in shame, at his reception; he has no enemies in the army, and the men would all die under him, if necessary. If he had been in command, there would have been no Bull Run No. 2! We were so glad to see him, that we cheered him until we were hoarse. He asked us how many men we had left, and seemed sorry at the reply; *we* were always favorites of his, and he always showed us off before visitors to the army. All the stories of the numbers in the rebel army are no exaggerations, but stern realities, and a million of men in Virginia alone, at this time, are none too many to conquer the State; our people at home are too apt to underrate them, but they will find out yet by hard experience that they must exert all their power and hang together, or they will never conquer the South; I can foresee it. In relation to a position that you spoke about, I will simply state, that I can do my duty as a private as well, and with as much service to our cause, as I could if I was an officer; and when I look and think on the moaning wounded, and the stark dead, the thought comes to me, what are all worldly glories? Here lies an officer with his gaudy trimmings; a few moments before he was haughty and proud of the very traps that drew on him the deadly aim of the sharp-shooter! He is like the butterfly, who, with gaudy wings, attracts the eye of the school-boy to whom he falls a prey; he lies in the dust, with the more humble, though not less honorable private. Death makes no distinction, they are *both* now before their Maker!

I could not help noticing the country in our immediate vicinity, and that which we have recently passed through: the former, although mostly deserted, shows some signs of cultivation, not having been troubled by desolating armies for some months; the latter, all laid waste. It is devastation in every sense of the word, and must be seen to be realized. I hope to God that Government and the North will be able to put the rebellion down; but our Army of the Potomac, in its present state, dread the idea of being obliged to go over the same ground again with doubtful success. In fact, we sometimes fear that the South, like our Revolutionary sires, are determined not to be conquered; but if so, it is God's will, but we should never submit until all means are exhausted. Now I must close this somewhat lengthy letter; but I hope that you will have the patience to read it through, trusting that if the Johnny Rebs follow up their intentions of taking Washington, that they will go back with a flea in their ear. Remember me to all.

Your affectionate son,
A. DAVENPORT,
Co. G, 5th Reg. N. Y. Vols., Duryea Zouaves.

P. S.—I forgot to mention that we lost both of our color-bearers, and four color-corporals killed, and two wounded. One ran away. Sergeant Alison, who carried the United States flag, was shot through the arm; he gave the colors up to a corporal, and went about twenty steps to the rear, but came back again, appearing as if he was ashamed. Shortly after, he was shot through the heart. Sergeant Chambers ran up and rolled his body off of the colors, and bore them off the field. Sergeant Spellman, who formerly tented with me, and carried the State colors, was shot through his neck, so his food came out that way; his arm was taken off at the socket, and he was shot through the side in several places. Medical Director Howard tried hard to save his life, but he died trying to hum a hymn.

A. D.

LETTER LXIII.

*On transport Mississippi, off Acquia Creek,
Potomac River, Aug. 27th, 1862.*

We "broke camp" at Newport News Sunday morning, and marched down to the landing. Went on board, Monday, steamer Mississippi.

Arrived here this morning. The order has just been issued, 3 p. m., to disembark. There are three regiments on board (about twenty-three hundred men), and ours being the last, we may not get off till morning.

We shall probably go direct to Fredericksburg, as there is no railroad communication to that point. Our voyage has been of great benefit to us, giving us good rest at night, and *mattrassed* berths, and pretty good fare at table. I expect we have got to go into rough living again, but it won't be as bad as what we have seen. The hottest part of the season is passed, and Northern Virginia is not as unhealthy as the Peninsula. Everybody is glad to get out of that *swampy desert*. We have plenty of rumors of the war, and most of them of a *disagreeable* character. I hope we shall get something *authentic*, even if it should be against us.

Alexandria, Va., Thursday morning.

P. S.—The first boat-load sent ashore at Acquia creek returned with orders to proceed to Alexandria; and here *we are*, lying in the stream opposite the city. We shall probably land during the day.

Richard Derby,
Lieutenant.

LETTER LXIV.

The "Box of Delicacies."

Frederick City, Md., Sept. 13, 1862.

We have just marched through the city, and are *bivouacking* in the clover-fields near by. There has been a running fight by our advance of cavalry and "flying artillery" all **day**, but several miles in advance of us. We saw the smoke of the cannonading on the mountains, across the valley, as we came down into Frederick, but it has gone over to the west side now. What the rebels mean is a mystery; and, of course, our movements depend upon theirs, and I cannot tell where we shall go next.

The "*box*" has come to hand at last! The lemons were so decayed that you could scarcely tell what they were. The can of raspberry smelt like a bottle of ammonia, and had leaked out a little. It was good luck that the cover did not drop off and spoil every thing. The little crackers were all musty, but the cake was still nice, and the sugar, but probably the tea is infected. You cannot send tea with other articles, unless put in *air-tight* packages. That which you sent before was *clove tea* when I got it. The raisins are nice and very palatable. I have not tried the "corn-starch," but the jelly was nearly eaten at the first opening. The *ginger wine* was *terrible* stuff—regular *Thompsonian* medicine! I had a man attacked with colic just as I opened it, and I administered a dose of it with beneficial effect.

I had got tired of cocoa. It is too heavy for hot weather; but now the mornings are getting cool, I can make good use of two boxes.

One box had some bologna sausages soaked in *Balm of*

Gilead, which was in a thin bottle next to them. They were not improved! ....

It requires constant care and attention in the enforcement of *judicious* rules to make well-bred children.... The *specimen* I send, which looks like coral, *is* a piece of coral; but how it came on Malvern Hill *I* don't know. Some parts of the Peninsula show numerous signs of having been at some former period covered with salt water. Whether that was there imbedded in earth, or carted there in sea-weed or guano, some geologist must determine. I saw several other similar pieces.

I haven't time to speak of the prospects of the war and the country; but I could not give you any thing very encouraging, if I had. The Northern people *labor under* a *vital* mistake as to the management of the war, and are *thoroughly* deceived as to the state of affairs. The views and comments in European papers are much more correct than those of ours. Your affectionate son,

RICHARD DERBY.

"This letter was," writes a near relative, "*received* on the 17th of Sept., 1862, on the morning of the battle of *Antietam*. The following letter was *written* on the same morning, before the fatal battle, and received three days after the dear one had fallen!"

LETTER LXV.

BOONESVILLE, Sept. 17th, 1862.

WE marched from Frederick, and are now encamped near Boonesboro, between that and the Potomac.

There has been some fighting, but we were not engaged. It looks now as though there would be a battle before Stonewall Jackson can get across the river on his retreat.

This is a beautiful country, and we have fared quite comfortably. . . . We hear very bad news from Harper's Ferry, but get no reliable particulars; yet prospects are bright with us for giving the rebs a good whipping at this point.

RICHARD DERBY.

Captain Richard Derby fell mortally wounded at Antietam. He was last seen cheering on his men in the most heroic manner. "I had found him," writes one who knew and loved him well, "such a genial companion, with so much to love and respect, that I could not quite reconcile myself to the thought 'that we were parted for this life;' and yet I almost longed to be with him, that I might leave such a fair name and glorious record. This line is constantly in my mind, and will always associate itself with his memory—

'That life is long that answers life's great ends.'

"The life of him we mourn was as pure and unsullied, from his birth to his death, as mortal man's could be. No pages to erase, his career was onward and upward till it is perfected in eternal day! Then I'll murmur not, but still must weep.

'The patriot's fire in my heart still burns,
Though I'm asking, Where is he?'

"Captain Derby combined courage and patriotism, with the polish of a gentleman, and the most prepossessing manners and form. He was beautiful, gentle, and sweet-tempered. Peace to the memory of a brave, manly, noble-hearted young man! And peace to the bleeding hearts of those who mourn!"

LETTER LXVI.

ANTIETAM, September 18th, 1862.

I HAVE lived through my first battle, and I am well. But when I think of the brave boys who lost their lives yesterday in defence of their country, I feel sad to think that Jeff. Davis did not die in their stead.

The men in my regiment stood their ground bravely; and fortunately for them, they escaped pretty well. When I was a boy I never thought I should be called upon to fight for my country.

But I am no better to die for liberty than any one else. If I lose my life, I shall be missed by but few; but if the Union be lost, it will be missed by many.

GEORGE I. FENNO,
107th N. Y. V.

LETTER LXVII.

JOHN MORGAN, THE GUERRILLA.

WE left Bowling Green, and came by forced marches to this place (Nashville, Tenn.) to save it, when it was as safe as could be.

The "Butternuts" are out here, though some twenty miles off, and we can gain no information as to what they intend doing. Whether they are menacing Nashville or not is a question of doubt. John Morgan is very lively, attacking our trains and "foraging" near our lines.

By the way, on our march here, our brigade, and further, our regiment, had a fight with Morgan and his band. Eighteen miles from here, towards Bowling Green, is a chain of high hills, around which the road winds into a deep ravine. The descent of the road down the hill to the ravine is a mile in length; when we were nearly at the bottom, Morgan's men, from the surrounding hill-tops, opened upon us with their musketry. We returned the fire, and charged upon them, when they "skedaddled" (*Prentissism*), with a loss of nine killed, and two left severely wounded on the field. We lost none, either killed or wounded. So much for our acquaintance with John Morgan, the Marion of the C. S. A.

W. H. TIMBERLAKE.

LETTER LXVIII.

CITY POINT, September, 1863.

TRULY I will not forget your kindness to me and others: my tongue and pen cannot speak the praises due, not simply for the many delicacies and comforts, but for sympathy and never-tiring patience. I was, I must confess, surprised to see so much sympathy for the suffering Confederates, and I thank God it was my lot to cast off on that beautiful little island (David's Island), which will remain as bright in my memory as it will on the pages of the history of this war. Write, write!

JAMES LOUIS.

(Testimony of an enemy!)

LETTER LXIX.

THE FREEDMEN OF NEWBERN.

I AM afraid you have given me an impossible task, when you say, "Tell me of the freedmen." It needs a far better pen-painter than I to do them justice. I have seen them in almost every condition, and can refute the oft-repeated opinion, that they would not try to help themselves were their freedom given them. A harder working, more frugal class of people or race of beings I never saw. Many of them have laid up considerable sums of money earned by hard work; some on the plantations, and others on Government work. They are the most jovial and happy things in the world; nothing puts them out of humor, and I am glad to say that of all persons congregated together in a place of this kind, the negroes give the least trouble.

From one year's experience in the provost-guard of Newbern, I can speak from facts. The free-schools established for them in 1862 were a decided success, and have added greatly to the improvement of their condition. It used to be a treat to go into one of their evening schools and watch their eagerness to learn, with even the most *primitive* of our *primers*; when one of them was able, after a style, to read, their delight was unbounded.

Poor people! the fever which raged so fearfully here in the summer carried off hundreds of them. They seem to droop very quickly; even in ordinary illness, such as we Northerners would hardly mind, they will seem to suffer greatly. I think that their religion is the most interesting thing connected with them. The *most* devoted follower of Christ among white men is fully equalled by any one of this race. Such perfect reverence for, and belief in Christ, I never saw. Their form of worship is *Methodist*; and I can only say that if the "chivalry" had the *fear of the Lord* that the poor uneducated negro has, this rebellion never would have taken place!

Capt. T. R. Heenan,
56th Massachusetts Volunteers.

December 5th, 1864.

LETTER LXX.

VICKSBURG, Miss., Sept. 23, 1864.

I WRITE to offer a notice of one of our noblest young men for the record. Early in the war, *Dougal McCall* felt it his duty to enter the service, for the noblest of governments was imperilled. He was accomplished and thoroughly educated. When he entered the service he was offered two commissions, but went as a private, saying, "If it were for position or emolument he was striving, his place was in civic contest." Though severely wounded in both arms, he has remained in the hope of doing something. He writes to his sister: "Dear sister, you know not how my trials in the army have intensified my love for those I left at home; but at the same time, each succeeding day expands my appreciation of the *free* institutions which a consistent patriotism must secure for after generations. In our march to the rear of Vicksburg from Milliken's Bend, I was four days with only one *hard tack* (a square of hard bread). I have had my feet so sore at night that I could not rest after walking for twelve hours; for they pained so that it was necessary to change position continually for an hour, until the outraged nerves would allow me to rest. But what has been borne can be again, and I thank God I have thus **far** been able to serve my country unfalteringly. As to bravery in the army, it is useless to make mention of any isolated instance, for I see none but brave men. *Every man* is willing to suffer or risk all, now that we have a prospect of success."

I **have** seen Dougal McCall go for shrieking wounded men on the field when no other man would venture; for there was not a prospect of living one minute, so rapidly flew the enemy's bullets. It was in a charge on the rebel works outside of Vicksburg. As soon as he brought one soldier to a place of safety, he went for another. He has remained as temperate and genteelly-behaved in the army as at home, where he was of model behavior. Mr. McCall is now an officer at Goodrich's Landing, La. He is now to be discharged on account of physical disability, and will soon return, to commence anew his civic labors.

Very respectfully,
A. M. LEWIS.

LETTER LXXI.

My dear Friend—I, a soldier of the Army of the Tennessee, send you greeting! I know not by what fortuitous circumstances the various parcels of "great price" came to us here in Vicksburg, instead of reaching our brave fellows in and around Chattanooga. 'Tis said truly, "Man *proposes* but God *disposes*," so I hope you will not be disappointed in receiving a letter from this place, instead of from the veterans of the "Army of the Cumberland," for whom the gifts were intended.

We, the soldiers of Minnesota, send greeting and thanks to the daughters of Maine, hoping God will keep them ever 'neath His all-protecting care, and reward them according to their works of love and mercy to the men now battling for the most glorious cause for which a soldier ever laid down life! Is it possible for us to fail? No! not while such love and devotion as is shown by the women of this nation makes itself so thoroughly felt among us, nerving us for the strife, and pointing us to the God of justice and battles as our chief Commander in the cause of humanity.

Our battery has participated in all of the great movements of Major-General Grant's army of the Tennessee.

Shiloh, or Pittsburg Landing, was our first battle. We helped to invest Corinth, entered after Beauregard ran away, rested there all summer, marched to the assistance of Rosecrans at Iuka in September, 1862; but owing to General Price's (of *running celebrity*) not waiting, we failed to arrive in time to help our "Rosey" to punish or capture the arch-traitor. Our battery was then, and is now, under the command of a gallant son of your own loved State of *Maine*. There are many *Maine men* in our company. Need I tell you they are brave? To resume: After the battle of Corinth we joined in the pursuit of Van Dorn and Co., and after rest and reorganization entered on the campaign that finally ended in the capture of Vicksburg. Thanking you in behalf of the patriotic armies struggling against the wrongs of the past, present, and future, never fearing failure while so sustained by such as you, and leaving the issue in God's hands, I am **your** sincere friend,

WILLIAM G. CHRISTIE,
McArthur's Div., 1st Minn. Battery.

To Miss Sarah Southworth.

LETTER LXXII.

BATTLE OF PERRYSVILLE.

HEADQUARTERS 81ST INDIANA VOLS.
(Bivouac at Crab Orchard, Ky.)
October 17th, 1862.

WHERE think you I was when your letter was handed me? It was on the battle-field, the morning succeeding the fight at Perrysville. The dead were piled around me in every direction—the wounded not yet taken from the field, groaning piteously in their agony. It was on such a spot, with all the horrors of war spread out before me, that your letter was given me by the chaplain.

I have witnessed an engagement between two mighty armies, and God spare me another such sight!

Not but that I am as anxious as any one *can* be, to see this rebellion put down by the strong arm of the Government, and intend to aid in bringing about this grand result by every means in my power. A large army like ours looks grandly magnificent in "battle array;" yet, to look over the same battle-field after the battle, and see many of those same men, *now* in all the pride of manhood, *then* mangled, torn and bleeding, with the wails of the wounded, the agonizing cry for their friends—to their Maker—their lamentations over the destitute condition in which their families will be placed, is horrifying—terrible to witness and know that *human* aid is unavailing!

I have read glowing accounts of such scenes, but imagination cannot depict or pen portray a *truthful* picture! It is *beyond* expression.

I will tell, as well as I can, the plan of the engagement; or how the different army corps constituting Buell's army were placed.

The army is divided into four corps, commanded respectively by Thomas, McCook, Crittenden, and Gilbert,—Crittenden on the right, McCook on the left, Gilbert and Thomas in the centre.

When we left Louisville, McCook marched through Shelbyville, thirty miles from Louisville; from thence to Taylorsville; thence to Bloomfield, where he united with Thomas, who came by another route.

Gilbert (in whose corps is the 81st Ind.) came by way of Bardstown; thence to Springfield; thence to Perrysville.

Crittenden came by way of Shepherdsville to Lebanon; thence to the battle-field.

By reference to a diagram I have made, you can see

how we marched from Louisville, driving the enemy, for they were threatening battle, in every direction, from Shepherdsville to Shelbyville. We drove them before us in our march, they not having time to concentrate with Kirby Smith until they reached Perrysville, where a junction was effected on the night previous to the battle.

The enemy's idea was to crush McCook and Thomas before Gilbert's and Crittenden's forces could arrive,—the road by which they were to come being very rocky and narrow, with large hills on each side for five miles, before the battle-field could be reached. But General Buell expected something of this, and marched Gilbert's forces up, the night before; so they were all ready to form the line of battle in the morning.

Bragg also, very artfully, marched his men up the creek bottom thereby concealing them effectually from the sight of our army, a mile distant. He at the same time made demonstrations against Crittenden with a small force, as though he were designing an attack there instead of where he did.

I was at the right, in Gilbert's line, next to Perrysville—the second brigade from the place. We drove the enemy from the town, entered it; thereby flanking the enemy and making him run, before Crittenden could wheel his about and surround him. The battle raged the fiercest from $12\frac{1}{2}$ P. M. to night; and had there been two hours more of daylight we would have captured Bragg's whole army.

As it was, it was the bloodiest battle of the war for the length of time in which it was fought. Our loss is at least 3,000 killed and wounded — the enemy's, 5,000. We have been chasing the enemy, skirmishing at every step. To-day we had a heavy skirmish at Lancaster, the county seat of Garrett county. Crittenden's forces had a little battle here at Crab Orchard. The enemy are probably retreating towards Cumberland Gap: at any rate *retreating*, and very fast, for we take a large number of prisoners every day.

Adjutant W. H. Timberlake.

LETTER LXXIII.

I WISH you could have read some of the letters found on the battle-field of Perrysville. It would have amused you beyond expression—so ardent, so impassioned, commencing, "Mi tru luv," &c. The ladies were so gallant, so affectionate, that some even wished to don "male attire" and go into the army, not to fight for Secessia, but separation was too terrible to endure. I do not believe it possible for a Northern lady to write such foolish silly letters.

LETTER LXXIV.

JUST ENLISTED.

NEW ORLEANS, Dec. 25th, 1862.

I TRUST that I have entered into the struggle actuated only by a love of country. As we passed, to-day, on our arrival, Forts Philip and Jackson, and saw for the first time ground that has witnessed gallant action, fierce resistance, and bloodshed, I have felt what it is to be in arms as the avenger of national honor, and, so far as my humble aid shall go, the protector of whatever our arms have gained, and to restore all we may have lost. If I succeed in doing aught of this, and live to return, I will willingly accept the thanks of the whole world's posterity.

I think I am not vain in saying this, for will they not be justly due? If the success of secession be a return to barbarism, will not its destruction in the land of civil and religious liberty call for the thanks of mankind? And should I fall, and fail to do all that *man* can, I am prepared, I think, to resign life for the privilege of *being one* to make this struggle for justice and the rights of humanity. God grant success to our arms, and nerve each man a hero in the coming strife!"

Lieutenant 156th N. Y. Vols.

LETTER LXXV.

Shiloh.

A wounded soldier on a battle-field says: "I could not help singing, 'When I can read my title clear.' And," said he, "There was a Christian brother in the brush near me; I could not see him, but I could *hear* him. He took up the strain, and beyond him another and another caught it up, all over the terrible battle-field of Shiloh! That night the echo was resounding, and we made the field of battle ring with hymns of praise to God!"

LETTER LXXVI.

Battle of Frederick City.

Camp Falmouth, Dec. 17th, 1862.

It has been an awful time with us for the last week. On the 10th, it was rumored through the camp that the army was to make a grand advance against the enemy, and in the evening it was a certainty.

Accordingly, at half-past two, on the morning of the 11th December, we were aroused by the sound of the bugle ringing out the *reveille* in the clear cold air. We turned out and immediately commenced our slight preparations for the march. We formed in line, and took the road, already blocked up as far as the eye could reach with moving troops. The sound of a heavy gun in the distance told us that the great ball had opened. From that time the roar of artillery was incessant. After marching about three miles, our division was turned into a wood to await further orders. We were finally marched from the wood to a spot just behind some earthworks on high ground, near the banks of the Rappahannock, from which we could distinctly see the ill-fated city of Fredericksburg, about two miles to the left of us, on the other side of the river, and our batteries playing on to the opposite bank.

Our forces were all day trying to lay the pontoon bridge across the river, but were prevented by the enemy's sharpshooters, who were posted in the houses along the shore of the city. This obliged us to turn our guns upon the town and shell the place. Soon the city was on fire in several places and continued to burn all night; it was a splendid sight after dark to see the flames burst forth. We could plainly see the enemy's works on the heights above the town, but they scarcely deigned to reply to our fire; it looked to me ominous. I thought they intended to wait until we crossed into the city, and then pay us off.

On the 13th our troops have all crossed, with the exception of one division, which is held as a reserve, generally composed of "regulars,"—our regiment is considered the same in point of steadiness and discipline. We had, however, besides in our brigade the 140th and 146th New York Volunteers, new men, never having smelt gunpowder before; but they were composed of a hardy set of men from the northern and western part of our State. Soon we were ordered to fall in, and marched towards the river. As we approached the bridge, there were signs of what was going on; pale-looking men limping along to the rear, and here and there a surgeon and his assistant with implements for use, with the wounded and dead lying about them; terrified looking soldiers skulking behind trees, where they thought themselves safe from flying shell.

We crossed the bridge and hurried through a business street, where whole blocks of houses were destroyed by fire, and desolation and destruction was everywhere visible. We turned into a side street, where the houses were all large—the residences of the wealthy inhabitants. The din of battle was terrifying, and from what we could find out the result was *uncertain*. We came to the end of the street which turned off into the country. It was now dark, and the "regulars" went into it "hot and heavy." We could have *been in* instead of them; but they were marching ahead of us, and there was not a moment to spare, and so they were filed off into the fight on a double-quick.

We were turned into a garden. The soil had recently been dug up, was wet and muddy; we were tired out, but there we had to stay, being the next in turn for the trying ordeal. We pulled down a fence, on which we could keep part of our bodies from the mud. The bullets whizzed over our heads from the firing just in front of us. Some of the boys were wounded. I curled up in a heap to keep myself warm, and to keep on the board,—my share consisting of a space two and a half feet long, and one and a half broad. I could not sleep; and few there were who closed their eyes that night. As I lay I thought of the morrow,—how many of us would live to come out—of home, and of eternity. But worse than all were the cries of the wounded lying between the lines without any one to help them; I could *distinctly* hear them cry for "water," and sometimes a chorus of wails and shrieks sent up on the midnight air, telling of human agony beyond the power of endurance! Thus the night wore through, and at daylight we were ordered to fall in. We had no sooner got up than the enemy opened on the "regulars" in front of us from their rifle-pits. The bullets flew around us thick, and began to thin our ranks. Our long line of fire told us where they were, for it was yet quite dark.

We were now hurried off, and went up the same street we came down, about a square, and closed up *en masse* to cover a body of men from observation, and into a garden with a dwelling in front of us, which somewhat screened us. We had not been here long before some of our men strayed off, and into the adjacent houses, and soon, jars of pickles, preserves, sugar, and all sorts of good things made their appearance; also handsome books, pocket-books of private papers, letters, silk dresses, and every imaginable article of use or luxury, were brought out, and wantonly destroyed by the thoughtless ones. It was ludicrous to see the boys come along with large doll-babies and children's toys: some of them with wigs on and white beavers, and women's bonnets and shawls on—but it made one sad to think how comfortable and happy the homes must have been in times of peace, now turned into desolation! It is surely no wonder that it is difficult to conquer such people, when they leave every thing, the houses and homes they were born and brought up in, and, perhaps, their parents before them, rather than surrender them willingly to us. In the afternoon we were marched down the street further, and turned into the yard in the rear of a large brick residence, one of a row, with piazzas, gas-fixtures, and water-pipes, which the rebels had shut off. The kitchen, a small brick house, was connected with the main building by a covered piazza. Back of it again were rows of neat huts for the colored servants: every thing was "in style." A bell hung out at the back of the house to waken the "people" in the morning.

We built a fire in the great stove, and there was the busiest crowd of cooks that ever were seen before! Plenty of flour was to be had in the house (all of them were well stored with provisions), and every man had a soup tureen, or some piece of crockery-ware, mixing flour and water to make slap-jacks.

The house was superbly furnished with every article that wealth could purchase or luxury suggest, and we were in need of nothing that could aid our culinary arrangements. We found splendid hams, preserved trout, farina, &c., and we lived high. The officers had feather-beds at night brought out in the yard to sleep on. We stayed there two days and a night, still under suspense, yet covered by the houses. The regulars could not get off the position assigned them the first night; they had to lay close to the ground, not daring to lift their heads, completely at the mercy of the rebels, who, in their covered rifle-pits, picked them off whenever they moved. They had no water, and suffered terribly. At night, when they crept away, they left ninty-seven of their number lying dead. This was the place we escaped from by a mere chance: our loss there would have been severe, as our red pants and caps make a splendid mark, as the result of the battles we have been in too well show, and the rebels are "down" on Zouaves, and ourselves particularly.

On the third day it began to look serious, as the rebels were advancing their rifle-pits nearer the city every night, and we were hemmed within its limits: the rebel balls were continually flying up the streets of the city: there was no position for our artillery, and, in "the front," death stared us in the face, and the wide river (Rappahannock) flowed in our rear, between us and safety. If the enemy, from the high bare hills commanding the city, which were crowned by their batteries, should shell the place, in which was massed nearly our entire army, a panic would probably have been created, and the army lost.

In addition to their batteries, they (the rebels) had a stone wall, two or three lines of rifle-pits, and a marsh, all of which we would have to overcome by assault if we gained the victory. General Franklin gained a mile on the left, but was then checked, and could go no further. General Burnside, it was rumored, wanted to storm the position, but was overruled by the other officers in a consultation. He would have lost half of the army! No less than seventeen charges had been made to no purpose: our dead strewed the field. It was sure death to face the batteries, and the wounded were left to die a lingering death between the lines; the rebels shooting any one who ventured to bring them off.

At this time every one's heart was down in their boots. Officers and men felt alike: the only alternative was a retreat across the river, or to meet sure death in the front. The suspense was worse than death itself, for it was apparent to the most simple that General Burnside had been drawn into a trap; we all knew and felt it. That which had been looked at by our people as so much gasconade in the Richmond papers, was being fulfilled to the letter.

On the third night, we fell in very mysteriously, and

were marched towards the front, down a street leading by the outskirts of the city. After some delay, we were finally marched into a large graveyard, with orders to keep very quiet. Here we laid down for two hours: every thing looked very mysterious; I thought that we were going to look for the bones of Washington! It was an aristocratic-looking place. We were then marched into another graveyard nearer *the front*. Everybody looked at each other and thought that our colonel's brain had been turned; finally, we were marched directly to the front, where we found some regulars digging rifle-pits for us. We were within three hundred yards of the enemy's pits; two of our companies, who went further out on picket, could hear the rebels talking. We fell back into the pits just finished. A battery for a few guns was thrown up in our rear. Towards morning we were told to put on knapsacks. The battery quickly moves off with muffled wheels, and it now flashed upon me that the army *was retreating across the river*, and we were the reserve to cover the retreat, and would be the last to cross over. It now commenced to rain in torrents, and filled the pits. We stood in mud and water up to our knees; the water ran down our backs and chilled us through: it was getting light, and before long our pits must be discovered, and bring upon us the rebels' guns and sharp-shooters. Officers and men would have given all they possessed to be out of that place. In the horrible moments of suspense, how I inwardly prayed for God to lengthen the morning and keep daylight from us! We could *now see* the rebel works loom up in the distance, and part of us were ordered to crawl away to the cover of a large storehouse, about two squares off, in the outskirts of the city: here we were soon joined by all the regiment, with the exception of a few men left behind to fire a shot occasionally from the pits, as if they were occupied.

It was now light, and they were popping away at our pits and at us, who were drawn up in a line across the street. We were getting very anxious for General Warren to appear (he had charge of the regiment covering the retreat), to give the signal for moving off.

We saw rebel officers on horseback going from fort to fort, and knots of men making observations, as if puzzled and not knowing the exact state of affairs. The suspense was now terrible: the officers looked at each other, and would have gladly marched us off themselves, but still General Warren sat on his horse, immovable, about two blocks up the street, and no signal given. At length, down came his aid for the second time, with the welcome order, "Right about face, and march *to the river*." Never was order obeyed with more alacrity! Though there was yet danger, the spell was broken; we were moving, and would soon know our fate, and were ready to meet it to the death. The rebels, on the discovery of the evacuation of the pits, would be down on us like a pack of bloodhounds, and we should be obliged to fight our way down through the city, and across the river, and most of us probably sacrificed. We were marching along briskly, when we met Major Cutting, aid to Gen. Sykes, who had been sent to see why we did not appear at the pontoon bridge.

A little further on we came across a brigade of regulars, who had been safe across the river, but were ordered back again, it being feared that we were in trouble. As soon as we got over a little hill in the street, out of sight of the rebels, the order was given "Double-quick," and we soon reached the pontoons, the brigade of regulars on our heels. As we went up the bank, on the opposite side of the river, we looked back, the rebel batteries had just opened on our rifle-pits, but we had fooled *Johnny Reb* that time!

We shook hands all around, and bivouacked for the night, thankful for safety; *and now here we are*, on the same ground we started from seven days ago, having accomplished *nothing*, our confidence gone, *fifteen thousand men less* at least! Is it not enough to make us sick of the war, to see how we are experimented with to satisfy popular feeling? I wonder who will be the next man to try experiments with us? By the time they have killed off a lot more of us, they may find a man that can face Lee with success. I still hope on, but I do not much think that I shall live to see you all again; I have had many narrow escapes, and I begin to feel worn out for want of a change of food. I eat very little, and what keeps me alive must be the coffee. I must now bid you all good-by, and may Providence favor our cause, and give to us the victory.

Your affectionate son,
A. DAVENPORT,
Duryea's Zouaves.

PART THIRD.

1863.

"The Lord to me a shepherd is,
   Want, therefore, shall not I
He in the folds of tender grass
   Doth cause me down to lie.
Goodness and mercy surely shall
   All my days follow me,
And in the Lord's house I shall dwell
   So long as days shall be."

LETTER LXXVII.

BATTLE OF MURFREESBORO.

CAMP AT MURFREESBORO, January 7th, 1863.

THE 42d was in the thickest of the fight throughout the day. We were on picket the night before the battle (Tuesday), and but few of us got any sleep, and we had nothing to eat.

At daylight the batteries opened, and the fight commenced. We were drawn in line across a cornfield. The forces in advance of us were driven in by the enemy, when Colonel Roberts ordered us to charge across the field and drive them back. We charged on the double-quick, Colonel Roberts at the lead—bullets, grape, canister, whizzing round our heads like hailstones.

We drove the rebels back nearly half a mile, and gained

an advantageous position, and would have held it, had not Johnson's division, which was on our right, given way, letting the rebels outflank us. This forced us to retreat, which was done in good order.

We took up a position in a cedar swamp at the left of the cornfield. Most of Sheridan's division were in this swamp. While here, the rebels outflanked and surrounded us, pouring it into us from every side. Our batteries returned the fire, making one continual roar, and mowing them down like grass before the scythe; but they immediately close up their ranks, never seeming to mind the shots.

It was after two o'clock in the afternoon. The right fell back and lay down behind the railroad. Here the solid shot and shell fell among us all the time.

We were now ordered to relieve the 2d Missouri, who were fighting hard up above us. We went up to relieve them; but *many* of the men *refused to fall back*, as their ammunition was *not quite* exhausted, though many had fired their last cartridge. *We* fired a few rounds, when the enemy retreated, and General Rosecrans ordered us to the rear to get rest. We fell back in a piece of timber and camped for the night. Thus ended Wednesday's fight, so far as *we* were concerned (the 42d), and a *hard fight* it was. I do not know the exact number our division lost in killed and wounded, but have heard it stated at 1795 —nearly one-half of the whole.

Well, I have to close if I expect to sleep any before morning, and be able to march. I could write dozens of pages; the half has not been told. You never *can* know or realize the horrors of a battle-field! I shall remember the sights and scenes of the past week till the day I die.

Affectionately your son,
Charlie Goodrich.

LETTER LXXVIII.

BATTLE OF STONE RIVER.

MURFREESBORO, Tenn., January 12th, 1863.

WE had a desperate battle here. For four days the fortunes of war seemed to be against us, but Providence at last turned the scales in our favor. I can yet seem to hear the din of the conflict—the whiz of the bullet, the scream of the shell, and the roar of the artillery! It is yet with me like one who has been on the sea; he becomes so accustomed to the roll and pitch of the ship, that it seems when on shore that the very earth is upheaving beneath his tread.

Our regiment was in the commencement of the bloody battle of Wednesday (December 31st), when our right was turned. General Jefferson C. Davis commands the division, and we stood the full shock of their concentrated charge.

General Johnson, who commanded a division adjoining us, suffered himself to be surprised and routed, thereby very nearly losing us the battle and causing the army to be annihilated. It seemed as if all were lost on that Wednesday. The enemy having massed their forces, or nearly all their whole force, against our right wing, commanded by McCook, swept over it like an avalanche! There was no resisting it. Our brigade gained more honor than any other on the right; but *we* had to fall back, leaving killed and wounded in their hands. Every thing went against us that day, and nearly every one prayed for night to come, that we might *retreat*. But Rosecrans knows no such word.

Thursday.—No advantage on either side, but the carnage terrible! Friday.—The battle commenced at two o'clock, and I venture to say more lives were lost in two hours there, than in the same time during the war. The enemy attacked our left wing, which resisted stubbornly, but, like ourselves, had to fall back from loss of numbers, but not until they had made sad havoc among the enemy.

As they fell back, General Negley threw his division forward, while our artillery was concentrated against their ranks. Then the rebels lost; they were literally mowed down! They had such an immense force, however, that Negley could not drive them. His men and the rebels were very much disorganized in the hand to hand conflict, when orders were brought to our general (Davis) to "forward with his division, and make a charge!"

Away we went, "double-quick," or rather, "on the run;" forded a stream over knee-deep three times; charged up the hill, where the rebels were, with a yell, and the rebs, panic-stricken, threw away their arms and fled. Such a sight as we saw! The ground was covered with the dead and dying.

The rebels admitted their loss in that one charge to be 800! This was the decisive blow of the battle. That night they commenced their retreat. But, in the four days' fight, with two days of heavy rain, cold, without blankets, no fires, and scarcely any sleep, our forces were entirely too exhausted to pursue.

How near we came to being defeated, only those who saw can realize.

ADJT. W. H. TIMBERLAKE,
81st Regt. Ind. Vols.

LETTER LXXIX.

REFERRING TO DISCOURAGEMENTS AND DEFEATS.

CAMP KEARNEY, near New Orleans, Feb. 5th, 1863.

I AM as sanguine of success in the future as ever I was. I care not whether Congressmen fight at Washington, or whether cabinets are dissolved, or Governor Seymour refuse the aid of the great State of New York, or if defeat should follow defeat to Northern arms, for I believe there is a God greater than all, who is interested in the strife. "Except the grain of wheat fall into the ground and die, it remaineth alone," was taught centuries ago, and its truth is just as applicable to-day. As with inanimate nature, so it is with individuals. Great men have been known in the world as such, not until they had died. Succeeding generations have exalted the memory of those whom their predecessors have imprisoned and debased. Our Washington was once not spared from slander and calumny, but where can be found a wretch so low as to speak his name but with reverence?

Nations, like individuals, are mortal—they sin, and like man, suffer the penalty, death. Greece and Rome lived, flourished, and died,—transgressing some law which God established as a rule of action, a proviso of existence. From the dead grain, though they fell, flourished a luxurious growth; and to-day, the world over, all that is beautiful in art, refined in taste, and elegant in design, is due to a former age of Grecian prosperity; while all that is sound in law is, wherever justice is dispensed, the fruit which has sprung from that dead but once mighty Roman empire.

We have not lived our allotted period, but some institutions have, no doubt. A fruit so luxuriant as general emancipation can only be the result of death. And what is war? Death, suffering, and despair; seed dropped into the ground to die, and germinate a glorious harvest! Man, short-sighted, asks little. The omniscient and omnipresent God plans, and demands more than man can at first comprehend, till it bursts upon him as a startling reality.

It was thus in our revolutionary struggle. Men at first were not prepared to ask for independence, but were willing to remain colonies, provided grievances were redressed, and a representation accepted: but God was not satisfied; a new form of Government had been decreed for this continent, in the councils of heaven. So, too, when our present war broke out, most seemed willing to yield to the demands of an antagonistical system, provided the two sections could again be united under one constitution: and I sincerely believe, drawing my conclusions from the progress of events, that this is God's campaign against the system of slavery on the American continent.

What fear then if God marshals our hosts? Defeat and the carnage of battle is the falling seed—prosperity, peace, reinvigorated nationality, and a higher civilization will be the fruit!

Lieut. ———,
156th N. Y. Vols.

Lines by the same writer.

February 23d, 1863.

There's naught to fear in sternest action
From bomb, or shell, or fuse, or paixhan:
But danger lurks where Northern faction
   In criminal sloth the end delays.
How base to falter in the struggle!
How sordid now to count the trouble!
God and our conscience pays us double,
   To know that unborn men shall praise!

Then come, oh struggle! fierce, and streaming
With hero's blood and death-fires gleaming:
If with the gift we are redeeming
All that is worth a thought on earth!

LETTER LXXX.

A BRAVE man has fallen, and in the remembrances of his comrades his worth is engraven; his little acts of kindness so natural, that at the time they were little thought of, now rush upon us with the force of our regrets, and although his name perhaps will never appear upon the great page of history along with names famous and infamous, yet often around many a fireside shall hereafter be related Edward Haggerty's deeds, worthy of all praise. *Requiescat in pace!*

LETTER LXXXI.
BEFORE THE FALL OF VICKSBURG.

I DRAW the conclusion that the next month or two will chronicle important events in the history of this rebellion. Perhaps hope, long deferred, has made many a heart sick; but mine will ever trust in the invincibility of the *American Union*, till the universal light of civilization goes out in an unending night of anarchy and death!

LETTER LXXXII.

Written by a member of the 124th Regt. N. Y. Vols., before the battle of Chancellorsville, to his wife.

CAMP NEAR FALMOUTH.

DEAR WIFE—I am in the regiment again, and I feel

better here than in the hospital. I shall *do all I can*, and go as far as I can, and then they can do what they please with me. I shall say nothing more about being lame or sick, but *stand up to the mark* as long as possible.

My dear, every thing shall work together for good to those that love God, and I do feel that I love him with all my heart. What would I do if I had no hope in Christ. I should almost be tempted to run away; but I will, with the help of God, do my duty as far as I know how. Pray for me, my dear, that I may be spared to you and our little ones; but if God otherwise determines, let us be sure to meet in heaven—we can if we will,—God is true.

We still have good meetings every night, and many are being brought to Christ. Write soon; good-by.

Lines written by his Wife.

[Sent to him and returned unopened; he was killed at Chancellorsville.]

Stand up, stand up for Jesus!
  Stand in His strength alone!
The arm of flesh will fail you,
  Ye dare not trust your own:
Put on the gospel armor,
  And watching unto prayer,
When duty calls or danger,
  Be never wanting there.

Stand up! stand up for Jesus,
  The strife will not be long,
This day the noise of battle,
  The next, the victor's song!
To him that overcometh
  A crown of life shall be;
He with the King of glory,
  Shall reign eternally.

LETTER LXXXIII.

Fort Federal Hill, Baltimore,
March 8th, 1863.

My dear Home—I hardly do work enough to pay for one meal a day, but eat three excellent ones. Each man is allowed a common-sized baker's loaf every noon; and it is splendid, too. Little children are in here every day for our leavings, and dozens of them go out with all they can carry. Bread we cannot sell, but all the rest of the rations we get the money for. The Government allows more than any one can eat; consequently each company has a surplus of coffee, beans, hominy, and rice; sugar (a pound a week to a man) is used up; coffee brings twenty-five cents a pound, and we sell from fifteen to twenty pounds a week. Some months we have saved twenty dollars; this is used for oil lamps, seasoning for soup, and many other things which we need.

LETTER LXXXIV.

Fort McHenry, April 10th, 1863.

Dear Home—History makes this fort famous. There is a shell here which the British threw in, in the war of 1812. . . . Some secesh wounded prisoners came in also, and some were unable to stand. One was so weak and lame that I had to carry him almost bodily. I won't abuse a man after he is down, and I treated those sick rebels kindly, hoping they will help some unfortunate Union man; but I am afraid they don't often do it. . . . If you have got an impression that our hospitals are hard places, I must correct it, for it surely is untrue. I have been in the large hospital at Stuart's Mansion, and at Patterson's Park, and

I have been in our own many times, and I must say that I want to go there if I am sick. Our sick boys testify to the nourishing food they get there. I had a horrible opinion of the hospitals, but it has changed wonderfully. About six hundred rebel prisoners have come in, all dressed in that dirty brown, and looking squalid enough.

LETTER LXXXV.

Fort McHenry, April 27th, 1863.

Dear Parents—In Baltimore there is almost as much Union sentiment as in Northern cities, and where you do find a secessionist they are so from principle; not like our Northern copperheads, Northern men with Southern principles. The policemen are strong Union, nabbing every person who ever hurrahs for Jeff. Davis. A secesh woman turns her nose on one side and gets as far away as possible when she meets a soldier. There are Union reliefs, Union reading-rooms, and Union assemblies, and scores of hospitals; in fact, this is the soldier's retreat. The sick, the lame, halt, and blind here meet; and many are the friendly acts done them.

May 13th.—Three hundred rebel prisoners came in to-day, and I had a good deal of talk with them, and found some fine fellows, though on the wrong side. They were captured out West, and by Michigan boys, and paid all Michigan boys the compliment of treating prisoners well, and said it was a general remark in their army.

May 25th, 1864.—We had a veritable hang here Monday morning of one of the worst guerillas that ever breathed, Leopold. General Wallace did not intend to have him reprieved; so, as soon as his sentence was approved, late on

Saturday night, General Wallace sent word to General Morris to hang him at sunrise on Monday morning.

LETTER LXXXVI.

FORT McHENRY, June 7th.

COL. PORTER was killed last Friday. Sergeant Hibbard carried the colors splendidly through all the battles, one nearly every day, till that fatal Friday when so many of our boys went down. He did not come into camp till Saturday night, and then came with both hands shot off at the wrist and wounded in the body. He laid on the flag all day, and crawled in, dragging it with him. The boys cheered him gloriously: that was a proud day for Hibbard. Company C lost twenty or thirty men that day. I ought to have been there; but it is not my fault, nor can I get there. General Morris told me I was to obey orders and ask no questions.

LETTER LXXXVII.

FORT McHENRY, Aug. 3d, 1864.

DEAR HOME—Grant has been unsuccessful in an assault, and some half-and-half patriots are feeling woe-begone, as if all efforts must succeed, or the whole cause fall at once. I hate this weak patriotism, which won't stand a failure.

LETTER LXXXVIII.

September 29th, 1864.

I AM in hopes to date from Richmond soon, with the stars and stripes floating proudly over the vile city. The capture of Richmond and Lincoln's re-election will end this war. You have no idea how hopeful the soldiers are. No croaking from them. None but non-combatants whine and find fault with the administration.

LETTER LXXXIX.

IN CAMP EASTVILLE, Northampton, Sept. 2d, 1863.

MY DEAR HOME—A lighthouse has been destroyed on Cape Charles, and the secessionists are taxed $8000 to pay all expenses; and if they don't pay, take them to Baltimore. Captain Hoyt gave me papers yesterday, and told me to take a guard, and go to work. I took two armed men, and went out about three miles after W. J. Nottingham, who was taxed about $5. I couldn't find him at home, but read the papers to his family, requesting him to appear in three days, or be arrested for disobedience of orders: his wife was scared half out of her wits to see a real live Yankee right in her own house, and she promised all sorts of things. I went a little way, and met Wm. J—— in a cart, drawn by a mule, with a darkie driver. I halted him, and highway robber style, demanded his money or his body. He willingly gave me the money. I signed a receipt, and bid him an affectionate adieu. The next man was Wm. P. Nottingham. I found him, and he counted out $41. He thought it was hard, when he handed me a $50 Baltimore bill; but as his dinner was ready, he thought it harder when I told him I could take nothing but greenbacks. The poor man was under the painful necessity of marching with us back to Eastville, to borrow the money. I then found Robinson Nottingham, about two miles from camp, who paid $10, after protesting against its injustice—all the comfort I could give them was they must not be secesh.

LETTER XC.

FORT FEDERAL HILL, Sept. 9th, 1863.

MY DEAR PARENTS—We left Eastville Sunday evening at five o'clock, getting to the wharf some time after dark, when captain gave me the order to pack up. Our company was full of negroes, who had been to church, opposite the camp, and I told them, if they wanted to go with us, to run around Eastville, and fall in below the village; and such a skedaddling as that started! A few decided to stay and go with us; but after we passed the village, over the fields they came in all directions. When we went aboard the boat, it was so dark the captain could not see them, so there was no trouble in hiding them in the hold: we did not start till the next noon, and a number of teams came there hitched, and the owners went aboard after their slaves. Mysteriously and unluckily for secesh, their horses got unhitched, and run off, although the few boys on shore threw stones at them to stop them. I followed the men to the boat to get up a little mob law, in case they got any of the darkies. But Major Hagner was enough for them, having practised law thirty-five years in New York city. He told them he was no slave-hunter, and they must do their own business in that line. In a few minutes the word blanket was called, and a stir among the boys was visible. Secesh began to look anxious and wild, smelling a rat. The major and other officers quietly moved to the cabin, and secesh hurried up their writing (having the sheriff with them to make out the papers), and started for the shore, about sixty rods; as soon as they touched land, one of our big corporals took hold of Mr. Sheriff, and cried, Rally! A dozen boys had hold of him before he knew it, and over he went into a blanket, held by as many men as could get hold of it, and one, two, three, and up he went into the air sprawling in all shapes. Three times up, and the yell Union, and he was free. Next came Mr. Jarvis, a perfect specimen of a fine Virginia gentleman, too fine to look at a laboring man, unless he was a black one. He had no idea of a vile Yankee throwing him fifteen feet in the air; but a few strong men soon laid him in the blanket, and up he went in all shapes, dropping his watch, and probably injuring it. Think of a F. F. V. being tossed fifteen feet in the air, three times, by Union soldiers—Northern mudsills. They got no slaves then, although there were lots of them about the field, afraid to come aboard on account of their presence near there. Off we started with fifteen free men and women (two women), and after a pleasant ride to Baltimore, took them to the headquarters of the colored regiment, and had all who were accepted, sworn into the United States service. I don't want any man to tell me how well off and contented the slave is. I know something of slavery, and can tell you a few things which I have no time to write.

Your affectionate son,
SERGT. EDMUND EVARTS,
8th N. Y. Artillery.

LETTER XCI.

The Battle at Newbern.

Newbern was taken by our troops on the 14th of March, 1862, and it was proposed to celebrate the anniversary of that day by the soldiers with great rejoicing, and all preparations were made accordingly. But it always takes two to make a bargain. The rebels proposed to retake Newbern as their part of the celebration. What they did on the other side of the river I do not know, only that they did not take the city. The fighting was several miles back from the river, and we did not hear much of it. But I do know what happened on our side, as you are aware we are on the east bank of the Neuse, just opposite Newbern.

About daybreak of the 14th, we were roused from our sleep by the roar of musketry on our picket-line, and soon the men were seen falling back on the Fort in quick time, but in good order, firing as they came; and then the rumbling of artillery wagons broke on the ear, when we knew full well that the "Philistines were upon us." In the dim gray light of the morning the enemy came down the road, filed off right and left in the field, and planted their batteries.

We had no guns, nothing but our rifles, and it would not pay to shoot with them; and so coolly they took their position, about a hundred rods from our fort! We watched them till they were all ready, and with the first flash from their guns, we dodged down behind our breastworks,—not a second too soon, for the first shell came directly over our company, and striking a post, burst into a thousand pieces, throwing sand and splinters all over us. No one was hurt, which was a great wonder. Cooper, Cunningham, and myself were standing close to the post, but it did not disturb us in the least. Then another gun opened upon us, and another, so we had grand music for a while. But all of a sudden the firing ceased, and a flag of truce came down: the colonel went out to meet it, and was told that Newbern was to be taken that day, and that we had better surrender, as we could not hold out against their force. Thirty minutes were given us to consider on it. Look at our position—not a single piece of artillery in our fort, every gunboat gone but one, and that aground near Newbern. No hopes of reinforcements in less than two hours, and we only three hundred men: while the rebels, with Pettigrew's brigade of 3,000 men and eighteen pieces of artillery, were ready to attack. The enemy before, the river behind us, there was no retreating, no falling back! The Ninety-second was fairly covered. Our fort is built of logs and sand, with a deep ditch around it; we tore up the bridge over the ditch—barricaded the gateway,—and presently when the flag of truce came for an answer, Col. Anderson replied, "he could not see the point." In hot haste the officer rode back to his men, and their bugles sounded the attack!

The Ninety-second sank behind their breastworks, every man grasping his gun in grim silence, when twelve guns opened on the doomed fort. Oh, such a shower of shot and shell you never imagined, and it was kept up for two and a half hours without intermission! We fired not a gun, nor had a man killed, and only three wounded very slightly. By this time some gunboats got here, and as soon as they commenced shelling in earnest, the rebels left us. I cannot tell why they did not charge on the fort with their infantry; they had ten men to our one, and could have walked right in, in spite of us, but their loss would have been great, for the Ninety-second had nothing to choose but victory or death, there was no such thing as running away.

*   *   *   *   *   *

The river is about one mile wide, the rebel batteries were eighty or one hundred rods off. The fort is quite small, about twenty-five rods long by sixteen wide; our tents were inside of it, near the banks: we kept close under the breastworks, but the tents being further back, were exposed to all the fury of the storm. The officers had procured boards and built houses, and in some instances they had torn down small houses, brought them to camp, and put them up again, so that we had quite a little village of houses and tents, interspersed with many small oak-trees and some stately pines, but you may well imagine it is in a sad plight now,—every house and tent riddled with shot and shell; two large tents were knocked down, and taking fire, were burnt up with all their contents.

Ever and anon a shell would explode in a tent or house, tearing every thing to pieces. The colonel's house had one hundred and fourteen balls through it, large and small. Whole charges of grape crashed through the trees, bringing down their limbs as the frost does the leaves of autumn. A tall pine-tree was cut down by a solid shot, and fell with a tremendous crash upon our tents: two horses in the stable were killed, and the doctor's saddle-bags smashed up.

A solid shot struck the chimney of my tent and knocked it endways; a charge of grape entered our tent, tore my knapsack, cut our blankets badly, taking them partly out of the tent. Our shirts and drawers hanging on a line in the tent, were wonderfully cut up. We found grape-shot in our bed, and pieces of shell were scattered all around; our tent seemed admirably adapted for the sanguinary business, by the sky-lights and side-lights it contained. Some had their knapsacks burnt up; others were struck by shell and completely emptied of their contents. In fact, it was almost laughable to see how things were smashed up,—dishes, cups, doctor's stores, sutlers' supplies, all gone to ruin. When a heavy shot struck the works, the bank being very thick and solid they would actually shake. The fun of the thing was, when a large shell would strike the embankment and burst, the sand would fly over us by the bushel, and we would shake it off and wait for the next one. After all, there was not much fun about it; for we did not know but that the next shot would shiver a post and kill some of us with the splinters. Then, again, we expected a charge by the infantry; if they had come we could not have lain behind our works, but should have stood up to meet them, and then something would have happened, "I reckon." "But what is good to give is good to take," and when the old gunboat Hunchback began to plant her heavy shells up among their batteries, we were well pleased. Then other boats commenced shelling, their shells passing over our camp; and what with friends and foes, we had shelling enough to satisfy the most inveterate lover of artillery music.

After a while the enemy withdrew, and at this time the 85th New York arrived on our side to help us, and the danger had passed.

At dark the rebs made good their retreat, having, as we afterwards learned, lost several men killed and wounded. They killed three of their own men by the bursting of one of their pieces; and one of our shells killed three, and wounded fourteen more. Sergeant Scott, of Hermon, is among the prisoners. None of the DeKalb boys hurt.

The firing of the rebels was splendid; one could but

admire it. If they took a notion to cut down a tree, down it came, and their shells burst just where they wanted them to. It would have done you good to see them. Nevertheless, I was perfectly willing they should stop; in fact, if I could have had my way, I should have stopped it before it began. For this lying on the ground two hours with shells bursting four feet above your head and grape and canister howling around, by way of accompaniment, does not suit me exactly. I reckon they will not come again soon, for we have our gunboats on hand now, and we have two guns mounted on our fort. The rebels dread our gunboats more than any thing else.

To-day it is warm and pleasant. The doctor has finished his garden in front of the fort; has sowed his onions and lettuce, and other garden seed. I really hope they will not be disturbed.

I have been on picket and must clean my gun, and therefore shall not write much more at present. With a thankful heart I recognize the hand of God in preserving my life through another battle, and render unto Him thanksgiving and praise. Ever trusting in Him, I remain yours,

JOHN WHIPPLE.

LETTER XCII.

THE MORNING REVEILLE.

LAKE PROVIDENCE, 1863.

FIRST we have the drums and fife, ten each to a regiment, at one hour before daylight; and as the regiments do not all commence at the same time, we hear plenty of music early. This is to call the soldiers out in line-of-battle to answer the roll-calls; then they turn in again. The bugles sound at half-past eight in the evening to retire, put out lights, and turn in until morning, when all the music is repeated. It sounds finely at night. At daybreak we have "sick-call" repeated through all the regiments. Two or three drummers and fifers stand in front of the "music tent," which is in the centre rear, and play an odd piece for three or four minutes; and it seems to say, "Come out, ye sick." This time *we* have to be on hand. The orderlies bring in the sick-list in each company, and such as are able come out. I take the book, call the names, and examine the men; feel of their pulse, look at their tongues, hear their story, ask questions, make a prescription, and mark their names *excused*, if really sick; if not, *duty* opposite; and those who need medicine step to my assistant or druggist, get the medicine, and leave. I do not get *fooled* very often. You must know if some can get excused, it saves going out on "picket duty" and standing guard nights. I feel sorry for the poor fellows sometimes. When it rains, and I find they are not well enough to bear fatigue and exposure, I favor them all I can; but not one overworks himself. The "sick-call" examinations last half an hour. If any are too sick to come up with the orderly, I go and see them at their quarters after breakfast. Next we go to breakfast; and then there is the beating of the orderlies' call; then another for the pickets, and so on until nine or ten o'clock: but, except the "sick-call," the medical department give little or no attention to the others. There is the officers' call to dinner, supper, etc., all in music. Once a week there is a general inspection of arms. Our regimental commander, Major Peets, tries to enforce discipline. He had, last week, four men tied by their hands up to a limb of a tree in camp, all day, for stealing. Our regiment has eight new drums; they are about fifty yards from my tent, in the rear of the regiment; and I can tell you I often wish I could put cotton in my ears, especially when they begin to roll out the noise at daybreak—about *twenty* bands of music, fifes and drums. The little fellow in our regiment that beats the bass-drum thumps away as if he expected the others would drown him down, and he is determined to be heard.

You would laugh to see the excitement when the mail arrives. It goes to the division headquarters, and is assorted for different regiments; then it is sent round to the adjutant of each regiment. The way we know of its arrival is, a man with a drum steps out before the adjutant's tent and gives the call for the orderlies. This call is a short prelude or roll and four separate taps of the drum; and moderately the orderly of each company goes to the door and receives the mail for his company: he takes it to the tent of his company and calls out, "Boys, come out for your mail," and then comes a rush!

H. H. PENNIMAN,
Logan's Div., 17th Army Corps.

LETTER XCIII.

CAMP NEAR FALMOUTH, Va., March 11th, 1863.

DEAR FRIEND—If you will permit me so to address you. There is in our company a sergeant by the name of Levi Rosa, whom I count among the men who serve faithfully and deserve well of their country. When, after enlisting, he passed the doctor, and told him, "Now, there are six brothers of us in the army, and we are *all* abolitionists,"—a solution of the question of how they all came to be there. One of those brothers has since died from the effects of wounds received at Bull Run. Another was killed in Missouri; he came from Kansas, and was orderly sergeant, but might have carried a commission had he been willing to disguise his abolitionism.

Sergeant Rosa received news from home not long since that his wife, who had recently lost two brothers in the army, was sick, and that her infant had died. He applied for and received a furlough to go home. When he reached Kingston he learned that his remaining child, a fine intelligent boy three years old, had been taken suddenly sick, and he too was dead.

You may think that he would have been justified in stretching his furlough for a few days; I certainly should not have blamed him: but promptly on time Sergeant Levi was at his post, ready to do his duty. In the hardest marches, in the worst of weather, I have never heard Sergeant Rosa complain or grumble. Now, he has a brother in the hospital at Point Lookout: I wish that you could see him. I am not acquainted with him, but he must be a man, or he would not be Sergeant Levi's brother. We can afford to lose our noblest men when it will tell, but not when it will not avail any thing. From your friend,

E. W. KETCHAM,
120th New York Volunteers.

LETTER XCIV.

ALGIERS, La., April 3d, 1863.

IT is with feelings of deep regret that I hear of the death of Captain Frank Leeds, of Stamford, for, though a stranger to me, there has been in his conduct that to honor and admire, though he had been an enemy. One generous soul gives all—gives life for the maintenance of his country's honor; another mortal, with equal capabilities for good, stays at home to plot the destruction of a government, whose continuance in its integrity alone procures him the security and blessing he enjoys while working his nefarious schemes. What a contrast!

A fit cognomen has the copperhead received! All my antipathies for the Angus tribe are revived by the mention of this class of men. I remember, in reading the Æneid, Virgil, describing the different kinds of crime punished in the infernal regions, depicts as one of the greatest magnitude, that of him who sold his country's honor for gold. Well says the poet, further, "*Auri sacra fames quid cogis non mortalia pectora.*" Oh, cursed thirst of gold! what will you not compel the heart of man to do?

But what do these vile creatures sell their country's honor for? I cannot imagine, unless it is their nature not to appreciate the blessings they have ever enjoyed under the best of governments, or because their hearts are naturally disposed for evil deeds.

How much better is the end of the honest and brave! They go down lamented to peaceful graves, and the love of their grateful countrymen will shield their honored names from the attacks of calumny.

LETTER XCV.

A WESTERN SOLDIER TO A NEW-ENGLAND WOMAN.

MY KIND FRIEND—I address you thus, because I believe you to be my *friend*. I am a little acquainted with you from having had the pleasure of reading two letters to other soldiers. In usual circumstances, I should not dare to write to a stranger lady from the "land of steady habits," but I know you love our country, and the principles for which I fight. I am a soldier in the service of the Government. I know what it is to live on short rations, to march through heat and rain, to hear the hum of bullets, the whistle of grape and canister, and the horrid shriek of shells from rebel works. I have been in a great defeat, and I know what victory means. You will, no doubt, remember about "Haines' Bluff," and the miserable retreat afterwards. Oh, those were sad days—there was no visible silver lining to the cloud. And there came such terrible news from every quarter; almost every general in the field had been defeated.

But the victory at Arkansas Post gave the disheartened ones here fresh courage; and in all that wretched retreat I was not discouraged; my faith and hope were strong. I believed in God, and in the justice of our cause; and have never doubted the final issue of the contest. Letters from home, full of love, hope, encouragement, confidence, and good advice do much, very much, towards keeping up the spirits of men in the army.

If such letters were oftener received, I am sure there would be fewer mothers to weep when they think of their wandering boys. The women of this country have done nobly for the material comfort of their soldiers, but I think they might be a little more prodigal of kind words. Oh, you don't know what letters are to soldiers! I have seen men who never flinched in battle, or faltered when one comrade after another fell by their side, weep like children because the mail brought them no messages from home. I am sure if those who love them could see their disappointment they would write very often, and tell them every little thing about home and friends. And we like, too, to hear from those whom we have never seen,—the good, true women of our land, whom we respect and honor, and for whose welfare we fight, and are ready to lay down our arms. Many a hearty "God bless the women" is heard from soldier-boys in hospitals, camps, and battle-fields. I hear that the President's wife gives a great deal of time to the soldiers in the hospitals in Washington; but Mary Lincoln is not the only woman who has now an opportunity to write her name where it will be cherished forever. Whoever, with kind true words, helps to lighten the soldier's burden, and give him hope, will be remembered with thankfulness even amidst the songs that go up from the hearts of the redeemed in heaven. It is worth something to live in these times, when the nation is marching on to a glorious destiny: we should rejoice that we are permitted to take part in the great struggle of right against wrong.

I am talking to a genuine Yankee woman, but do you know, may I tell you, how the rebels *hate* Yankees? They think they like us, Western men, pretty well, and they don't like to fight us; but when they speak of the "Puritanic Yankees," they can hardly find words to express their hatred and contempt.

I fear the picture you draw of New England would not be recognized, with their idea of the "fabled country away down east."

Their genuine Yankee never goes on foot, but always drives in a little *red* wagon, a lean ill-fed horse, loaded with basswood bacon, and white-oak cheese, and wooden nutmegs, all for the Southern market. It is really amusing to see how they *can* curl their lips at the name of *Yankee*. Foreigners are also the especial object of hatred.

A rebel staff-officer referred me to the foreigners in our army "as the off-scouring of the old world!" I laughed at him, pointing to some of the *same* sort by whose side he had been fighting. Evidently that staff-officer was one of the boasted "chivalry," but with all his contempt for Yankees, he lacked in himself the first qualities of a gentleman. I think there is, after all, a lingering love of the old flag *down* deep in the hearts of many whom we call *rebels;* indeed I could not call them *rebels*, when I saw the workings of their faces as they gathered round our fires on the boat coming up the river, and eagerly listened to the stirring notes of our national songs. I remember one spoke out, after listening to the "Battle-cry of Freedom" and "Star-spangled Banner:" "Yes, the old flag should still wave, if I had *my* say-so about it."

There will be victory by and by for the *right;* I am confident of it, and peace on better principles than our land has ever known. I believe that this war has done me good. I feel that I live for a nobler purpose than I ever did before; that I reach out after a higher, holier life in *every thing* in my great love to my country.

If you *can* write to me and will do so, I should like much to receive a letter; if not, *please write to some other soldier.* May heaven bless and keep you, is the prayer of your soldier friend.

LETTER XCVI.

On the Battlefield, rear of Vicksburg, May 21, 1863.

I have so *much* to write, I hardly know where to commence. On Tuesday, the 19th, we were drawn up in line of battle, and within eighty or one hundred rods of the rebs' pickets. Company B, of our regiment, was sent out as skirmishers. They attacked the rebels and drove them in; we followed, after the order was given to the Seventeenth Army Corps to advance, to attack them in their rifle-pits. But the attack was made about fifteen minutes sooner than ordered; and the Fourteenth also advanced on our right, but they were too fast. Then Col. Humphry ordered forward the Ninety-fifth, and we went with a will! But to our surprise the rebs were not where we expected, but some one hundred rods or more from us, and we were obliged to go down a hill and up another; and by that time the rebs had the timber all cut down, and every thing in the way, so it was almost impossible for a man to go down such a place. But the Ninety-fifth *did go down* and up the hill, the rebs sending their deadly fire on us from their rifle-pits and from their forts. John Benedict was killed, and has not yet been found. J. Wilcox, R. O. Gunn, D. B. Cornell, D. S. Gookins, J. Seberth, P. Byron, were all wounded. Benjamin Easton, too, one of the flag-bearers, was wounded in the hip, but we are in hopes all will get along safely.

We stood our ground till daylight, and were then ordered to fall back. *We* have the praise from all the generals, and from Col. Tom; *he is the man:* we want no other. Time will not let me speak of the bravery of officers and men, but the Ninety-fifth have gained themselves a name. Brig. General Ransom told us we did well. It is a perfect roar of cannon around us all the time.

By the way, we came very near being in a fight last Saturday; one hour more, and we would have had a hand in it: and there we got our first sight of dead and wounded, a sight the like of which I never want to see again; and that night we laid our weary limbs down on the battle-ground, amid dead and dying!

The next morning we marched nine miles on the double-quick, and our forces ahead were fighting on the Black river, at the bridge. We got there about noon, and laid our wearied bodies down for awhile, but we soon had to go and build a bridge that we could cross. The next morning, at nine, we crossed the bridge and marched about eighteen miles, and then encamped in the canebrakes, about half a mile from the rebels' pickets. I can hear their bullets whizzing over my head, as I am writing. I had to go last night, with about fifty, over the battle-ground to find the dead and wounded. We got all we could find. It was about 12 o'clock when we got through; the enemy firing at us, but they did not hit one of us!

We are gaining on the rebels every day, and Vicksburg has got to come as sure as there is such a place, and the boats on the river shell it every night. I must close.

Robert Horan,
95th Ill. Vols.

LETTER XCVII.

Fort Anderson,
Newbern, N. C., May 31, 1863.

It is the Sabbath-day. I tried hard to go to church, but could not, for all our boats were gone but the one belonging to the garrison; that ran on a snag and sprung a-leak as it was returning from town this morning, with a load of soft bread. So my attempts were useless. My pass ran till 9 p. m., and I could have heard two sermons if I had gone. So much for going to church in the army. When we do go, we must have our boots polished, brass bright, clothes brushed, dress-coat on, and side-arms, or we are not permitted to leave camp. Take it with the thermometer up to (as high as you please), and with heavy coats buttoned up to the chin, with belts on, it is not very comfortable, to say the least of it. It is very hot here indeed to-day; and as we have not had rain for some time, it is quite dry. If it was not for the breeze blowing from the river, we should find it almost impossible to live these days. I suppose you consider it rather warm up home, but if we were to go there we should undoubtedly find it cooler than this climate. The men stand the heat much better than they did last year, as they have become acclimated, and then they do not have to endure such hardships as they suffered in Virginia.

One year ago yesterday our pickets were within four and a half miles of Richmond, were driven in by the enemy, and twice the 92d was drawn up in line of battle for a fight. But yesterday every thing was as peaceable and quiet in the regiment as in a country town. Last night we slept in high tents with elevated bunks, board floors, good beds, with cooling breezes from off the river. But a year ago, last night, encamped on a muddy plain, so level that the water would neither run off or stand still, we of Casey's division were exposed to a tremendous rain-storm of several hours' duration, accompanied with the most terrific thunder and lightning. Our shelter-tents, open at both ends, were four feet high and no floors but our blankets, in which we were wrapped, on the ground. In the morning we found ourselves in the same predicament that you would, to roll yourself in a blanket, and lie down in the middle of a well-travelled road, when the frost is coming out in the spring.

One year ago to-day, even at the very moment of my penning these lines, I was on the battle-field at Fair Oaks, where shot and shell, grape and canister, were whistling in the air around my head. All around on my right hand

and on my left, men were falling like grass before the mower's scythe. Oh, the scenes of horror witnessed after the battle's close! Think you I will ever forget them? But to-day is as peaceful and calm as one could wish. Looking riverward I behold the wharf, the gateway, and the guard-house quietly reposing in the bright sunbeams. Hens are quietly walking around, croaking and cackling; flies all humming and buzzing around as they were wont to of a sunny afternoon at home. Amid such scenes as these, one almost forgets the days of conflict and suffering he has passed through; but we cannot, if we would, forget the gallant men who gave their lives that day for their country, and who now sleep in nameless graves far from their homes and friends! One of my company in particular I remember well that day—John Oliver, of Governeur, N. Y. He was only 15 years of age. Boy that he was, he flinched not under that murderous fire, till a ball pierced his heart. Then, true to the last, as he was falling he partly turned to Lieut. Fox, and said, "Lieutenant, I am killed!" He fell at my feet, and I think was dead as soon as he reached the ground. The son of a poor widow; yet none died a nobler death than he. There are others too, that I remember seeing for the last time that day; and if you see Albert Stevens, ask him if he remembers the dinner that five of us partook of together that day, just before the battle, and if he remembers that those five never met again! But all this is the soldier's lot. Without changes of some kind the world would grow monotonous; and as we have experienced a change from very hard to quite easy times, we should not complain: not only should we not complain, but we should be very thankful that Providence has so ordered that we are still alive and permitted to enjoy many of earth's comforts. As for myself, when I review the past, I am filled with the deepest gratitude to the Giver of all good for His mercies unto me; and, with the utmost confidence in His care, am willing to stand or fall, as seemeth good in His sight. Trusting that He will still continue to preserve us from all harm, I am, as ever,

Your son and brother,
JOHN WHIPPLE.

LETTER XCVIII.

FORT ANDERSON, N. C., April, 1863.

DEAR SISTER—Your letter and mother's of April 12th and 19th, with three packages of papers, arrived yesterday; and I improve this opportunity to thank you for your kind remembrance of me. I really had to smile when I read of the strange story that came to your ears in regard to my coming home. I regretted that you should have been caused unnecessary sorrow. Verily the fools are not all dead yet, or such a report would never have been started. I was glad to hear that you were well, and had got safely moved into your new home; but it would certainly seem very strange to me to go back and find you there, where I used to spend so many hours in other company. Life, however, is full of changes, and this is only one of them. Just at present there seems to be no changes here, for every thing is as still and calm as if there was no war. Our troops have driven the enemy from Washington, and in doing so they have secured the whole country around us from the depredations of guerrillas. They make no more nightly excursions to our pickets' lines, and for several days not a gun has been fired in earnest. There is some talk that the "old brigade" is going to Plymouth, and that we shall have to leave our fort to go with it, but nothing certain, however. Plymouth is on the Sound, one hundred miles from here. I had rather stay where I am, for I can get to church occasionally, and our mail is quite regular. We have more privileges here than we could get at Plymouth.

The city of Newbern is a very pleasant place to dwell in. It was founded many years ago, and its first settlers, as a matter of course in this hot climate, went in for shade, so that wherever there was a chance for a tree to grow it was improved. Years have rolled away since these trees were planted; and those who put them there have gone to their final home. But though they rest from their labors, "their works do follow them;" for the trees have grown old and gray, spreading their branches far and wide, and in some instances completely shadowing the streets. There is one street that it is almost impossible for the sun to shine on; for near half a mile it is like walking in a bower. You would admire it if you were here; for I rather imagine it would surprise you to see the leafy verdure of the trees, and to find the dooryards full of flowers and roses in full bloom. Yesterday I went to church. Do you wish to know how we go to church here? I will tell you. After morning inspection, which takes till noon, I write a pass and go to the first sergeant to see if I can go to church. "Yes." Then I get the company commander to sign it; then, going to the adjutant, I assume the position of a soldier, touch my hat respectfully, and ask, "Will I be allowed to attend church to-day?" "Yes." Then he signs my pass, which now reads as follows, omitting date and locality:

"Sergt. Whipple, of Co. I, has leave of absence from camp until 4 o'clock P. M., and pass to Newbern.
A. B., Commanding Co."
D. C., Adjutant 92d N. Y.

What if I should not return at precisely 4 P. M.? The provost-guard of Newbern would pick me up, and place me in "durance vile" until the next morning, and then send me to camp, and unless I had a good excuse for my absence, I might hear, at the next dress parade, something like the following: "Sergt. E. Whipple, of Co. I, for unsoldier-like conduct on the 26th of April, 1863, is hereby reduced to the ranks By order of," &c., &c. So you see that it is no easy thing to get to church in the army, and if you have any duty to do on the Sabbath, then, of course, you cannot go, no how. But I went to church, and to a negro church at that: about 150 members were present, all dressed decently, and some fashionably. Our officers and soldiers occupied the galleries; the congregation, the space below. Several of the ladies sported hoops and crinoline that would have done credit to whiter skins than theirs. This excited the wrath of the woolly-headed sexton, who declared that "de sisters as wore dem big frocks mussent crowd into dem seats any more:" whereat one colored lady indignantly declared "she didn't have on a big frock." "Oh, no, sister," said the sexton, "I didn't mean you, kase I knows you is allays trim." The question of "big frocks" being settled, an unusual amount of singing took place, after which came a stirring exhortation to repent of their sins, come forward, and be prayed for. "It will do no good for me to pray for you," quoth the preacher, "unless you pray for yourselves. You must come and kneel down here, and repent of your sins yourself; for God has declared dat every tub must stand on its own bottom." This appeal seemed to have the desired effect, for in a few moments several of the "tubs" were standing as requested, and were floundering around after the most approved style, crying and grieving as if their hearts would break. Some commenced a see-saw motion, sideways, others rolled their heads back and forth, or stamped with their feet. Two of the sisters, on their knees, threw their arms wildly in the air, and struck each other's shoulders many a hearty blow; while an old lady hard by seemed rocking another to sleep in her arms. But the oddest motion of all was that of a wench, who, placing both hands on the bench before her, in a stooping posture, spent her time in jumping from one foot to the other, a sort of hop-a-te-hop motion, more easily imagined than described, and very laughable withal. You will bear in mind that all this time they kept singing with all "their might and main." Every motion kept time with the music, changing whenever the time changed. Up in the galleries, soldiers snickered and laughed; corporals with two stripes slyly nudged sergeants with three, as much as to say "here is fun;" lieutenants with no bars winked and blinked at lieutenants with one bar; captains of the army looked downed and sneered; captains of the navy looked up and smiled, and everybody seemed well pleased, and voted it a fine thing, *this same negro meeting.* But all this made no difference with the worshippers, who seemed totally oblivious of our presence, and only intent upon their great work of saving souls. I noticed that when they prayed, every one of their number, men, women, and children, knelt, and when they sung, all joined in it. There was an earnestness of purpose apparent in their countenances, as well as their words, which kept me quite sober in spite of my great propensity for laughing. I wished to stay until the meeting closed, but fearing I might miss the boat, I left the church, and was soon gliding over the placid waters of the Neuse to my home in camp. We will now suppose supper eaten, dress-parade finished, bedtime come, and you bade good-night.

Truly yours, &c.,
JOHN.

LETTER XCIX.

CHARGE OF THE "NINETY-FIFTH ILL." ON THE FORTIFICATIONS OF VICKSBURG.

May 22d, 1863.

ONCE more, my dear mother, I have passed through one of those times and places which try men's souls.

Yesterday we made a charge, and were repulsed with heavy loss. Our brigade made a charge in front. We suffered more than any other; but the loss was fearful to us all, especially our regiment. The major was wounded, two captains killed, one mortally wounded, five lieutenants wounded; in all, eighteen killed, seventy-three wounded, and seven missing.

We had to advance over a hill; on the opposite side were posted the rebels, in great strength of position and numbers.

The colonel led the regiment (though badly wounded in the first fight) over the hill, and was seen to fall. The balls were flying as though all the rebels this side Hades were pouring their murderous fire upon us. We all saw our colonel fall, and supposed him dead: it cast a heavy gloom over our spirits, and checked our ardor.

You can better imagine than I can describe our joy, when, after dark, we saw him coming over the hill to us! Nothing but the providence of God could save men from death in such a position as was his! The regiment cried for joy at seeing him with us once more; it was as unexpected as though he had risen from the grave.

Our company lost one killed and ten wounded, and how I escaped is a wonder to me. Men were falling on every side, and the carnage was becoming too terrible for mortal to withstand, when we were ordered to "fall back," which we did in good order.

The groans of the dying, the shrieks of the wounded, and the almost unearthly screaming of shells and cannon-balls, mingled with the rattle of musketry, made up a scene that men see but a few times in a lifetime, and the fewer the better. The awful grandeur of some ancient Roman amphitheatre can bear no comparison with the sublimity of that charge.

The officers were brave and daring to a fault; our general, Ransom, is bolder than a lion. Captain Cornwall fell while cheering on and trying to rally his men; but all was of no avail. The rebel fire was too destructive for any troops to stand. We fell back, but this temporary check will not avail them any thing. We are just as sure to take Vicksburg, with all her traitorous inmates, as the sun is to make its daily revolutions on its axis. Give us a little time. I know you will wait.

Sergt. T. A. Rollins,
95th Ill. Vols.

LETTER C.

Fort Anderson, Md., April 14th, 1863.

Slowly the rain is falling, yet not steadily, and the wind blows by in fitful gusts. The night is very dark, and again I am alone. My partner is on picket duty, and I, seated in my camp, am writing to the "old folks at home." My candle is supported in a quart cup by the last week's "Herald" pressed tightly around it. I have no news of consequence to write, for all is quiet. The "expedition" I referred to in my last returned without accomplishing any thing, and to-day another has gone out to act in concert with one from another quarter, for the relief of Washington. Meanwhile the 92d "pursues the even tenor of its way," for with *us* "spades are trumps." We do nothing but *dig*, except guard duty, and we are not desirous of change; for as long as we stay here we can have things comfortable, and live about as easy as at home, excepting picket duty in wet weather.

In your last letter you advise me to come home. I should like very much to act upon your suggestion, but just at the present time I do not think it possible to do so. As for "playing off," as we call it, to get a discharge, I beg leave to assure you the time for that *will never come!* For if I could deceive man, I could not deceive my own conscience. I am coming home as honorable as I left it, or not at all. It is not the whole of life to live in this state of being, for when this world's night shall have passed away with all its darkness, its troubled dreams, its baseless visions, and we wake in the light of an eternal day, may we be spared the thought that *our* part in life's great struggle was not well played; therefore let us not be weary in well-doing. To you at the North, it doubtless seems the very height of trouble to be separated from your relations, children, and friends, knowing they are exposed to dangers and perils at all times; and yet *you* know but little of the miseries of war, compared with those who live in its very midst. If you could once see the country after an army has passed through it, you would be much more thankful than you are that you live in a land of peace. Only a few days since, our troops burned a widow's house and all the out-buildings, simply because she was *suspected* to be a spy! At times the rebel army marching through a neighborhood will take whatever they like; then *our* army follows, and take the rest. What would you think to see men come into your farmyard and catch your hens, milk your cows, shoot your pigs, and then make a fire of your garden fence to cook them; and not having the fear of the owner in their minds, upset beehives and carry off the honey?

A few days since, I was on an outpost, near the house of a citizen within our lines, who had just got a pass of the colonel, giving him permission to move his family and effects outside; in case of an attack, his house would probably be destroyed. The woman told me, with tears in her eyes, that she had lived there thirty years, with her husband, and that she herself was born and brought up there. They had determined to stick by, at all hazards; but our troops having planted a battery a few rods from the house the night before, to sweep the road in front of it, in case of an attack, their courage failed them, and they concluded to leave; and so the cart was brought up, and with many a tear and sigh, was loaded for the journey! It was the Sabbath morning, and as quiet, calm, and beautiful a day as ever dawned on the earth. We were far from the bustle and noise of the camp, and naught broke the peaceful stillness of the scene; the bees were humming in the bright sun, the leaves of the apple-tree were starting into life, the blossoms of the peach shook in the breeze, and the garden vegetables were flourishing luxuriantly; and yet, it must be *all* given up, the dear old moss-grown homestead, the valued possessions, and all the associations of a lifetime must be relinquished! Can you blame the woman for her tears, secesh though she was? I really pitied her; for, in all probability, when they return again to their old home, it will long have been laid in ashes! No neighbors were gathered there to bid them farewell, or assist them in their labors; for no one could come without a pass: only one old lady, who had been to town, stopped there awhile. The old man wished to give her some articles he could not take away, but was afraid to do so without orders, and the old lady was equally perplexed, for although she wanted the articles in question, she had no "creatur" to carry them, and she was too old to "tote 'em" herself, and "reckoned" if she got outside the lines, she "couldn't" get in again without a new pass.

Having charge of the post, and feeling sorry for the old woman, I told her to go for a cart and I would let her in when she came back: so off she started, and went *three miles;* getting a boy and a "creatur," she returned rejoicing. I told the old man he might give her whatever property he saw fit, and I would pass her out; for which he thanked me very much, and proceeded to put a "right smart load" on the cart, till the old lady "reckoned" she had got on all the "creatur" could "tote;" and he reckoning in the same manner, concluded she *had* got load enough, and then with protestations of love and friendship, and with hopes of better days to come, the old neighbors, with trembling voices, and tears coursing down their cheeks, bade each other good-by! When the cart and its big bundles, and the boy with the broad-brimmed hat, and the old lady with her flaxen hair and long-caped bonnet, and the sorrel "creatur" with its long switched-tail and flowing mane, were lost to sight among the solemn old pines, I sat me down in the pleasant sunshine, and throwing my gun across my lap, mused long on these trying vicissitudes, and the glory of war.

But I have preached enough, and, fearing lest my audience become weary, will even close, wishing you all success, with love to each and all.

JOHN WHIPPLE.

LETTER CI.

VICKSBURG, June 6th, 1863.

DEAR LITTLE WIFE—We still lie here waiting for the fall of Vicksburg, and expect it will be ours in from ten days to two weeks from this. Grant's fine army needs a few weeks of rest very much. Marching and countermarching, fighting, watching, and digging, with hot weather, dry and excessively dusty roads and fields, miserable camping-places on the ground, and great scarcity of water—and what we dig for is unhealthy, with very great excess of noxious chemical compounds—short diet, sleepless nights, dirty clothes, absence of tents, distance of wagons, and much confusion among these countless hills, all have aided in rendering the troops debilitated, and most decidedly uncomfortable. Still, there is less sickness than might be anticipated; but there must be a change soon, or we shall suffer much, as all these are gradually rendering the soldiers weak. Tuckered out will express the state of thousands of officers and men. We will get a long rest when we get this place, and there is great need. I did not stay at the hospital of our division, as another wanted it, and I was sent back to our regiment. As our surgeon, Doctor L. D. Kellogg, has just returned to our regiment, our medical staff is now full. Kellogg, Tompkins, and Penniman, is the full list. But we will not stay so long, probably. We all sleep in one little tent, eight feet square, and are fortunate in having this, as all tents were ordered to be left at Grand Gulf, even such as had not been left by previous orders at the Bend, sixty miles above. We lay under the side of a sharp hill, and our floor of clay is levelled by digging into the bank; and all sleeping-places are behind these ridges, to be out of range of shot and shell from the rebels, who often kill and wound men beyond us, even a mile out, if they can see them. They use splendid rifles, and best of English ammunition, and fire with incredible accuracy. I have had three bullets scatter the dust near me, in quick succession, while walking over a part of one of our roads exposed to view of these rebels. But I shall not go there again, so do not be alarmed, for I could tell you worse stories than this if I wished to alarm you.

The weather is oppressively hot, but I stand it tolerably well; and have only lost some thirty-five pounds since I left you, mostly within the last six weeks. I am, indeed, quite well, and eat our plain fare, and sleep well, and take things as cool as I can. I have plenty of clothing, and need nothing. Do not suppose I am suffering or sick. God be thanked for all his mercies. Our regiment go on duty every fourth day—that is, at 3 o'clock in the morning. We creep up to the front, and into the rifle-pits of the sharp-shooters, and relieve the regiment who have been there for twenty-four hours; and do not leave until just before daylight next morning. I and Tompkins stay at the foot of the hill (a mile from here), about twenty rods behind the troops, and, with our little equipment, wait any casualty that may call for our services. We take out rations and two blankets, and pass our time there; sleep on the ground, and fix up brush and wild cane to keep off the sun. The ground here is full of all sorts of insects; and at night, the bugs are plenty, and fireflies so numerous, that it is constant flash, flash, all around.

Heavy cannon boom over us all day, and occasionally in the night; and our men, in their pits, are shooting all day at any thing like a man's head they can see, or the place from which a little smoke issues from some rebel gun, distance about one thousand feet, over a deep and wide hollow. I will tell you all about these things, when kind Providence brings me to you again. I hope we will be paid some money—and all of us need it—when Vicksburg is taken.

War is a dreadful evil, and the army is a school of bad morals; about nine-tenths of the troops entering the army irreligious, become worse and worse. A great crowd of men, without the restraints of society, and no influence from woman, become very vulgar in language, coarse in their jokes, impious, and almost blasphemous in their profanity. I have never mingled, you know, with the lower dregs of society, and, every day, the associations are painful. It is dreadful and disgusting. Profanity is universal—often, and generally common oaths—sometimes dreadfully severe and heaven-daring in its tone. Such use of the name of the great and ever blessed God, and of the precious Saviour, causes me to feel shocked through and through. I am not squeamish, you know, and not very sensitive, and yet it is awful to hear the cold-blooded insults to God, and the contempt heaped upon the blessed Saviour of the world; and, with few exceptions, rare indeed, among some of superior education and high moral tone, cursing and swearing is common, and very frequent, especially upon the most trifling occasions, and even without any occasion.

This state of impiety will submit to no check nor admonition. The chaplains are of little account, and generally keep regimental post-offices; attend to such light duties, and, so far as I learn, are discouraged in endeavoring to reform abuses. Our regiment has had no chaplain for nearly a year. From all I can learn, his acquaintance had but little or no confidence in his piety. He had no influence; and, indeed, it is in some regiments like going among swine with pearls, and showing the brutes clean garments, to reform their habits. An occasional quiet remark, a question whose name the swearer used, and strict example in all I say and do, is about all I can do. It is dreadful to see how much worse a mess or squad will become after one of their number is killed. We had a fine young man killed out of our hospital mess, as I wrote you, and since that the balance, some nine or ten, are more profane, more trifling, more reckless, more every thing that indicates a worse condition of heart, than before. To pass away time, to play cards, to drink, to eat, to run round, to do any thing that will hinder the serious thoughts of eternity, this is all; and of the two persons in our regiment, reputed to be religious, one is not agreeable, and the other I tried in vain to draw into some very general religious talk, the other day, while we were both at leisure up the front: it was no use. Action, not thought; a man had better form his character and principles before he gets into the army. Drinking is abundant in the army, though this is a luxury denied at these situations except to officers. By liquor time is killed, spirits supported, care dismissed, and thought drowned. Indeed, I had no idea how dreadful are morals in the army. I will explain these matters to you. Every other man will get drunk if he can, and every officer is frequently drunk. General John A. L—— is stupidly drunk, report says, every night; and officers follow suit, generally. Sabbaths come and go unheeded, no difference; same cannonading, same duties, and all. It is a fact, that the blessed Sabbath has passed more than once, and I did not know it. Marching for weeks, fatigued, no books, no almanacs, no papers, baggage all behind, and up and at it again, hasty meals, and nothing to remind us, and not one in a dozen knows the day of the week with certainty. All this is dreadful; but true camp-life is rough and dreadful.

Your affectionate husband,
H. H. PENNIMAN.

LETTER CII.

VICKSBURG, 1863.

I AM now with my regiment, and have had an awful time. After heavy cannonading, Grant's army undertook to carry the forts in front of this place on the land-side. Got repulsed at every point, with piles of dead and wounded, many regiments losing 150 men. It was an awful day. Our hospitals are filled; surgeons are tolerably plenty. Our heavy cannon are throwing shells over our heads; but as we lay in a ravine, we are just now safe.

Vicksburg is one continued pile of hills, and on every hill a fort. It is very dry and dusty. Captain Cornell and two other captains in the "Ninety-fifth" were killed. Col. Humphrey, not killed, laid in a trench concealed till night, was wounded in the leg. It was useless to attempt to storm such forts. It is likely that cannonading and siege-ing at leisure will be the end of this affair. Both parties are skilful, and have plenty of powder and shot.

Our little regiment have fired away over 100,000 rifle cartridges since coming here. The most beautiful sight to us is the bombs at night. They are a great way off, about four miles, as it is three miles to the river, and our mortar-boats are at the other side. Two or three are climbing up at once high in the sky, describing, of course, a great circle towards us, and descend down into the town with an explosion like the heaviest cannon—indeed there is no noise round the place so awful and so loud. When they explode just above the houses, the scene is grand indeed, though they do the most damage when exploding in the streets or in houses. They have a fuse that shines all the way up and down, and it looks like a falling star, but much slower. The bomb weighs 245 pounds, has a shell or body three inches thick, and powder enough for a dozen big guns, and it is of the size of a common water-bucket. This mass of iron descends in its great arch from a height of from 1500 to 2000 feet, and when it strikes the earth explodes, opening a hole like a great cellar; or, if it bursts in the air, it throws its great pieces of all shapes, and some of them weighing twenty-five pounds, with a force that kills or crushes what of men and things are in the way. More than a keg of powder is used to load the mortar. No one can stand near at the discharge. A long string pulls the lock, and one can see the flash ten or fifteen seconds before the sound reaches one. And then, if one lived in the city, what an awful suspense as to *where* it will fall. The people are said to live in caves they have made in side-hills, and hide away.

The shell that is now fired from field-pieces, instead of the old-fashioned ball, is a long cylinder, like a good-sized long melon with the end cut square off; the point is towards the enemy, and at its end is a long percussion cap, as large as a small egg: when this hits any obstacle it explodes, the fragments being driven with great fury and destruction all around. These pieces will kill a man quick, though more often they make a great hole. I have dressed many a dreadful shell-wound.

The accuracy of their fire is wonderful indeed. They throw (the batteries) a shell a half a mile, and hit a man's head if he keep it up a minute too long above the top of the trench. We are *behind* Vicksburg, which has its front on the river. Our circle round, resting on the river from right to left, inclosing the town, is some ten miles in extent. They have a perfect circle of forts, one acre in extent each, all round on the highest and best-situated points; besides, they have connection from one to another by means of covered ways—i. e., by deep tracks, cut down so that men cannot be seen in their passages. They are covered or hidden from us only by being down below our shot: a man *mounted* may be seen moving about these passages, but troops can go six abreast, their heads below, all out of sight. So they can reinforce any fort that needs help; and when we tried to storm the forts, we could not make out more than two hundred or three hundred inside by the officers' glasses, but more than ten times the number were ready to receive us and drive us back from a position where one man is equal to one half-dozen, all hid but his head behind breastworks. Two of our regiments, 8th Ohio and 45th Illinois, moved one night close up to the forts, so close that the rebel cannon could not hurt them; and if any of their men reached over with their small guns, our men stood ready to shoot, with guns all cocked, at any moment. After staying there two days they were withdrawn, as they could not go over or up the works; besides they were in our way, as the batteries endangered them in bursting shell thrown at the fort.

The regiments all have their place or chance every

fourth day or night. The batteries thunder away all day, and sometimes all night, so as to hinder the rebels from coming out in force and escaping, which they have attempted two or three times; for we not only want their place, but their army. You may be assured there is sharp practice used on both sides.

H. H. PENNIMAN, M. D.,
17th Regt. Illinois Volunteers.

LETTER CIII.

VICKSBURG, June 23d, 1863.

WE have now another army, or rather a part of Grant's forces have come down from above. We have ample means, not only to take Vicksburg, but are not afraid of an extra hundred thousand rebels, as our reinforcements are said to be 40,000 strong. How we will come out is not known, but we are sure that we will be victorious; indeed, a fight is going on at Black river, a day's march in the rear. It is just a month last Friday (May 19th) since we began the siege, but we will blow up one of their forts to-night, it is probable, as we have mined it. Our parties are now digging 60 feet under it. We think the town will be ours by the 4th of July.

H. H. PENNIMAN, M. D.

LETTER CIV

VICKSBURG, Sunday.

IT is fine to hear the boys who lay in the trenches shout and yell at every extra good shot, as when timbers fly or an extra lot of dirt goes up in the air! So you see that I have had an unquiet Sabbath—very different from what you have in your peaceful town, away from war and noise of armies. It is a pity that men will be so wicked as to begin so dreadful a war.

H. H. PENNIMAN, M. D.

LETTER CV.

HOSPITAL, FREDERICKSBURG.

I ARRIVED at this place after lying in a field-hospital for two weeks. At one time our chaplain gave me up, and thanks be to God I felt ready to go or stay.

I would not give up the hope I have for the whole world. I found my Saviour to be a great comfort to me in my hours of pain. I have the Bible you gave me, through all my troubles. The ball passed under it. This is written by a friend. Write to

Your soldier-friend,
HUTCHISSON.

LETTER CVI.

[Written after the writer had volunteered in the storming party to scale the breastworks, had not the enemy surrendered, as was not anticipated.]

CAMP OF THE FORLORN HOPE,
before PORT HUDSON, July 3d, 1863.

I AM for the second time a volunteer—one of the "Forlorn Hope." Yet I think our party ought not to have this dismal name, we being, as General Banks has told us in an address, *the hope* of the country, and I am sure *that* is not forlorn; thinkest thou so? You must not think I have been rash in thus volunteering in the storming party, or that I was actuated by ambition for military glory, or anxious for promotion. I have acted only from principles of duty.

I have not before been among such a spirited body of men, so confident, so brave; one cannot be among them without feeling strong in the cause of right and justice, and hopeful for the result. Oh, the glorious thought that we are to be foremost in the struggle for victory, and that the hopes of our country come crowding after us!

LETTER CVII.

In Vicksburg (*not in rear of!*),
July 5th, 1863.

Dear Mother—The great work has at last been accomplished—the fight is fought, and the victory won! The great rebel stronghold has at last fallen, and let us thank God fervently. Your son has had the unspeakable pleasure of planting with his own hands the "Stars and Stripes" of America upon the strongest fortress of his country's foes! 'Tis a deed that must live with me and help me. 'Twere useless to add, I'm more than proud of it. Thanks be to God first, who has ruled our affairs to the dismay of our enemies! Thanks next to the patriotism, valor, ability, and energy of Major-General U. S. Grant! Thanks to the soldiers, who have nobly and patriotically performed so many deeds of valor, endured so many hardships, and bravely won so many victories! Thanks, also, to the hearty sympathy of the friends at home! The cause is worthy of their most cordial co-operation and earnest support.

Our only regret and sorrow is over the death of our comrades in arms. But they have not died in vain; their deeds will live in history, and their virtues be remembered until the day-star of Time shall have launched into an endless eternity!

Yesterday was a glorious Fourth. It was one that will live. Hereafter the day on which our fathers declared their independence, and threw off the oppressive yoke of England, will be doubly dear to the American heart. The enemy feel as much chagrined as we do joyful, over the fact of the city being surrendered on the 4th of July. Our brigade was one of the three that went into the city to take possession—a mark of honor in appreciation of our meritorious conduct in the siege of the last 46 days. Such marks of honor are highly valued by the soldiers.

I never was so happy in my life over any particular event; I was calmly happy. My feelings could well correspond to the description given by the newly converted sinner of his new-found happiness. Oh, how I longed to fly to the loyal North and communicate the glorious news! This is the severest blow the rebels have received since the commencement of this unholy rebellion. Thank God for it!

The rebels themselves I think do not feel very bad about it. They are the best-looking set of prisoners I have ever seen. They were "starved out;" that is the way we *took 'em*.

The munitions of war found in the city are unbounded. To-day we move camp into the city. A large force under General Sherman had gone to the rear last night to whip General Johnston: they'll do it too, or Mr. Johnston will skedaddle lively; which I think he will do. I am almost glad the rebs are making a raid in the Eastern States. It will waken them up, which they need very much. I hope the rebs will get all they want, and more too.

S. A. ROLLINS,
95th Illinois.

LETTER CIX.

The writer of the following letter, now a prisoner at Cahawba, Ala., was taken prisoner in the act of carrying his friend, S. A. Rollins, mortally wounded at Guntown, Miss., from the field. With rare self-devotion he remained with the heroic Rollins while he lingered; administering every alleviation in his power to his bodily sufferings, with the tenderest sympathy and affection. James G. Goodman passed from the dying bed of his friend to a rebel prison, with all its horrors.

Resting after the Battle.

NATCHEZ, Miss., 1863.

ONE year has passed swiftly by since Uncle Sam *adopted* me, and it has not been one of play, you may rest assured. From the time when the "iron-horse" bore us gently away from "Camp Fuller," of pleasant memory, to this moment in which I write, it has been crowded with events which tell us that we have not left *our all* for naught; and that the results in which we have borne a humble part, will live when we, as the "95th," shall be no more. And although we are but a remnant of that band of a year ago, while we sorrow for those that sleep their last sleep, we may glory in the laurels we have acquired.

As I review the road over which we have come, dotted by obstacles which we have surmounted with an undaunted front, though fatigued and careworn, and when at last Vicksburg loomed before our view, we have shown that we could brave the pointed steel and dare the iron storm of bullets.

Vicksburg has fallen, and with its fall the war in the Southwest resolves itself into a guerrilla horde, which, I trust, will soon be exterminated. We are resting now. Natchez, the "beautiful city," as it is called, holds us for the time being. Here we recuperate, in a clime that our fears have told us would be destructive to our lives; but experience has taught us to banish such idle fancies, and to enjoy what Nature has given us with a lavish hand. Fruit, and flowers, and shade combined, make our stay delightful; and here we find a place where war has not pressed its iron heel! No desolation, or fire, or sword, has here made havoc: all is quiet, peaceful, and (I was about to say) happy. But there is an under-current that, like the consuming fires of Etna, cankers the heart, and tell us, as though in words outspoken, that the poison of Rebeldom is here; and that, were the moment propitious, it would burst forth, destroying alike our happiness and theirs. But if it is but *seeming*, it bears to *us* the charm of novelty, and we see the citizen in dress and form much resembling our Northern friends at home; and, cheating thus our eyes, if not our intellect, we are reminded of that *home* where there are hearts and hopes that are with us.

James G. Goodman,
Co. B, 95th Illinois Volunteers.

LETTER CIX.

I think it was about a year ago, no particular army held Winchester, and it was subject to frequent visits by raiding parties from both sides, that Mr. Dooley ventured home, not thinking there was much danger from the rebels, and one night he rashly exposed himself to the eyes of the rebel citizens by going to church. As he was on his knees praying to his God, he was startled by the appearance of some half-dozen rebel soldiers, who commanded him to surrender. He refused at first, and showed signs of resistance, when one black-hearted traitor presented a revolver to his face and snapped a cap, but the revolver did not go off; enraged at this, he beat him shamefully over the head, and he was led bleeding from the church, amid the screams of the women and children. Some actually rejoiced at the act, and cries of "Good, they have got him now: I hope they will kill him," were heard in different parts of the house, from the mouths of persons who but a few moments before were bowed before the great God of mercy and pity: he was then robbed of money and watch, and taken to Richmond. Some people who saw him up the valley, say that "our misguided brethren" stripped him of his clothing, and gave him some old rags in exchange, and actually took the boots off his feet, and made him walk barefooted. He was taken to Richmond and confined in Castle Thunder, where he died, which appears to be very mysterious. I do not think he died a natural death; he was either shot or hung. The rebel citizens of Winchester say that he died, but will not tell the manner of his death. Mrs. Dooley felt her loss very severely (for Mr. D. was a good man, if there is any): she was left entirely destitute, with quite a family to provide for. Little Albert is dead; his remains now rest amid the bullet-marked tombstones in the cemetery.

Yours, respectfully,
Charles E. Hoover.

LETTER CX.

Dear Friend—I received your kind letter this evening, and it was like water to the thirsty soul.

Is not the President's message glorious? It must be now the "kingdom's comin' in the year of jubilo."

These little souls here are all absorbed in *rank*. You

can't think how I long to be powerful, so as to snub persons whose souls are made of such mean ingredients. I long to have a high position to see them *crawl*. Dr. —— I think has no respect for woman, religion, or God, which I believe are in close affinity; for as old Sojourner Truth, the Lybian Sibyl, said, "Was not Christ born of a woman?" One reason I hate slavery so, I imbibed it from my mother.

Perhaps you will think my letter rather stinging, but the day of wishy-washiness has passed; we have been a generation of mealy-mouthed beings, but that time has gone by. We must learn to dare to tell the truth, at least to our friends. I can't lick the hand that smites me, though I might turn the other cheek for a rebuff: the former is an action fit for a toady, the last for a Christian. The weather is exceedingly cold, Good-by,

LETTER CXI.

THE last number had a hit at the administration I did not like. Alas! our poor bleeding country receives more wounds from her internal and secret enemies than open and avowed secesh. Had all the North been a unit, this horrible rebellion would long since have been crushed out. But how is it?—the most of the democrats of the North would rather see the country ruined than their party broken up. The administration is crippled—they give aid and comfort for the Union! The Union they are fighting for, and not the negroes! It is the South, and a great many of the dough-faced North who are fighting for the negroes, or rather to perpetuate slavery; while the administration is stirring with the struggles of death to save, if possible, our poor country from utter ruin and desolation.

But, Mrs. ——, my faith is getting weak, I fear we are gone; the internal enemies are too many and great. Many of our own generals are no more than traitors; the soldiers are becoming discouraged, and we will be compelled, after a while, to yield or to compromise in some dishonorable way, I fear.

Yours, truly,
LLOYD KNIGHT.

LETTER CXII.

CAMP PARAPET.

I AM drilling every day more or less, and learning fast. I am in Company D, and it has the name of being the best-drilled company in the regiment.

We had a sad lesson showed us on the 25th of November; one of the Twelfth colored privates shot one of the sergeants with a pistol, and killed him dead on the spot: so he was tried and court-martialled, and sentenced to be shot to death by musketry.

On the day of his execution, the regiment was drawn up in line of battle, and about twelve o'clock he was led by an escort of four men carrying his coffin just ahead of him, and the twelve men that were detailed to shoot him. Poor fellow, he did not know that he had to be shot until three hours before he was tied to the stake of execution. He was from Philadelphia: he ran away from home, and left his mother, and the first word he said when the chaplain told his sentence, "Lord have mercy upon my poor mother." The last words he said were, "Tell my comrades to take warning from me." He was blindfolded, and in an instant afterwards he was pierced with bullets, and died without a struggle. It was a hard sight for me.

Tell the boys they need not wish to be a soldier, but stay where they have plenty to eat, with good beds to sleep on.

Yours with respect,

CORNELIUS W. HARRIS.
20th U. S. Colored Infantry.

LETTER CXIII.

DEAR FRIEND—I have related the destruction of your property in New York by the great Democratic copperhead mob: this, I told them, was the gratitude you received from the people of the great copperhead city. The answer they made when I asked them, "What ought to be done with such men?" was, as honest men would say, "Hang every one of them."

It has altered the political opinion of a great many in this hospital, so that we have a majority of sixty for Abraham Lincoln for president. Some of the traitors try to vindicate their right to murder negro orphan children, and burning their homes. I told them that I could produce a negro man that could defend himself against the best of them; but the cowardly traitors would not dare to meet a man single-handed, even if he does differ from them in color. They tell me I want to put a negro on equality with them. I told them, "No, I did not; that I should be very sorry to do so; but I considered negroes loyal men, and it should always be a part of my duty to elevate a Union man above a traitor. I should be very sorry to put him on a level with them."

Yours truly,

FRANK NICHOLS.

LETTER CXIV.

Dear Friend—We received your letter last night, and it gave us a great deal of pleasure to hear that Jeff. Davis's Democrats left your brother's roof standing to shelter you. I see the Democratic judges find rich Democrats to swear to the honesty of their thieving brother Democrats, who were engaged in plundering the houses of American citizens because they were loyal to their country. Judge —— was drummed out of the army, because he was a next-door neighbor to a traitor; it is a contagious disease, and he inhaled a large lot of it.

Frank Nichols.

LETTER CXV.

Sunday I took a walk through the contraband camp. I conversed with several of them, and they appear happy and contented, with good clothes, and plenty to eat. I visited also the colored regiment's camp. It was the first I ever saw. I was struck with amazement at the good order that prevailed, and the regularity with which every thing was laid out. The camp itself was a model for any veteran regiment.

The majority of them live in tents, erected on log foundations; but there are a great many of them who have built log huts, "old Virginia style;" in those they live with their families, for a great many have released their families from slavery, and they now refuse to leave them.

What astonished me most was the interest they took in trying themselves to learn to read and write. In one corner you would see a grown-up man trying to teach a drummer-boy to write; in another you would see a man about thirty, trying to learn his letters without a teacher. I think there should be a regimental school for each regiment; and I don't see why their officers don't take more pride in learning them. For my part, I should delight in learning them all I know myself. I learned two men to read and write when I was in my company, and took a pleasure in it; and I am sure they would be more apt to make better scholars than a white soldier, who has other things to engross his mind. I have a notion to apply for a commission in a colored regiment; and I believe I would be more competent than some officers whom I have seen.

The officer of the guard told me that, when they lay at Portsmouth, a colored soldier absented himself without leave, not being aware then of military discipline. He just came back the other day. He said a white soldier told him that he would be shot, if he went back; so he stayed away six weeks, and then made his way back to camp, saying that, "if he was to be shot, it would not be by a rebel 'scription." They are splendid marksmen, and invariably hit the target eight times out of twelve. What has become of Saunders, the colored man, that I freed from his shackles? Thank heaven, I can boast of freeing one slave during this war. Respectfully yours,

GEORGE O'MEALLY.

LETTER CXVI.

Bush River, July 5th, 1863.

I MENTIONED in my last the object of our mission in this secluded vale. There are ten high privates, two corporals, and a sergeant, quartered on the boat named the John

Tracy. We sleep on the deck and floor of the forward cabin, wrapped in our blankets, using our knapsacks for pillows, with boots and arms by our side ready for any emergency. We have one six-pound piece with which we bring to all vessels passing up or down the river. I think that if a good-sized oyster shell should float by on a misty twilight, we should be called to arms, and give it a shot, so vigilant is our look-out and martial our spirit.

Two poor mortals are kept stationed, day and night, one over the ammunition in front of the boat, the other on deck, who are returned every two hours.

The captain of the steamboat, his two mates, with the two engineers, take their meals in their shirt-sleeves first, having a tablecloth and china; while we, poor miserable soldiers, after, with our tin plates and cups. Our rations consist of hard bread, pork, rice, coffee, and brown sugar. We go on shore to buy milk, butter, chickens, and blackberries, so that we do quite well, although the cooking is none of the cleanest or best.

Yesterday I was on shore, with two others, when the colonel of the "troops on shore" told us to chase a suspicious vessel going down the river. We rowed to our boat, loaded our guns, weighed anchor, and off in pursuit. Various were the surmises as to the cargo of the vessel. All were full of the value of the prize. She had been twice hailed, but still kept on. Some of the more sanguine suggested a load of arms, others ammunition; but all most desired a load of soldiers to be found snugly stowed in the hold. In the mean time we gradually approached our formidable adversary with shotted guns and suppressed whispers, and exclamations denoting a more ferocious than pious spirit, as should be at such an anxious moment. Our small boat is lowered, five adventurous spirits, with loaded guns and fixed bayonets, leap in. I, being one of the artillery squad, am reluctantly detained; and now, with anxious hearts, perspiring brows, as we stand surrounding our beloved piece, exposed to the burning rays of a tropical sun, we watch the boat approach the prize. They fire a shot across her bows, but amid a death-like silence she keeps on; another gun, and then they leap on board and take possession. The hatches are down, and they are in ignorance of what smoldering volcano may be beneath; the helm is turned, and they proceed back to the bridge with visions of glory and prize-money floating in their minds. On casting anchor, an additional party of men were sent from both the shore and from our boat, to remove the hatches and guard the cargo, whatever it might be. I was one of those selected to go. We removed the hatches with due caution, the men standing with loaded arms around. The hold was dark; I jumped in; we returned with one small boy, who says " he is diff."

This morning, three of us went on shore with the avowed intention of getting some water, &c.; but the country looked too enticing to be resisted, so leaving one to guard the boat, we made a forced march of three miles, stopped, rested, and chatted with some country beauties, and returned to our envious comrades, from whom we received a rebuke for our rashness in venturing so far from our *base* in a hostile country without support, which we bore with becoming meekness.

I hope that you will not think that we are having a splendid time, or that we are not in the midst of imminent danger; but the party, I must acknowledge, do take some pleasure in recounting their deeds of valor, and by dint of mutual praise, and dwelling upon the dangers and hardships of a veteran's life, fondly imagine themselves equal to the mythological heroes of ancient times!

I have heard nothing from you since my advent on the scene of active life.

Yours truly,

H. P. M., N. Y. 7th Regt.

P. S. (privately.)—*I think we are safe!*

LETTER CXVII.

CAMP ABOVE VICKSBURG.

WE steamed down from Memphis a week ago. It took us from Monday noon until Friday, laying by at night—by tying up to the trees on the bank—down the Mississippi river. Our division (McArthur's) filled some fifteen steamers; when all in line the sight was beautiful, stretching away five miles!

Our men by thousands are digging the canal that was begun last year across "the bend." The greater part of the fleet remain quietly with the noses of the boats in the bank, and planks out for passage; they all keep up some steam. The expense to Government is great—some 150 dollars per day for transports, besides coal. We have plenty of food. Coffee is used by everybody three times a day, as hot and strong as they please. Plenty of sugar is furnished, and it is freely used; no milk is to be had. Bread is hard, baked in crackers six inches square and one half inch thick; it comes in boxes of 50 lbs. each. Butter has to be bought, also smoked beef and soft bread, the last in the towns; we have not bought any since leaving Memphis. We at the hospital mess are allowed to draw for white sugar and tea and some extra luxuries. Beans are allowed the army freely. There is no scarcity and no self-denial in any food we are allowed to use; so you see Uncle Sam intends to take care of his boys.

H. H. PENNIMAN, M. D.,
17th Ill. Vols.

LETTER CXVIII.

SNUFF EATERS.

CAMP NEAR NEWBERN, Feb. 11th, 1863.

As my motto is "business before pleasure," I will say, first, that I. received a letter from his wife, but C. C. did not, and he begins to think the Cooper family are all dead or married, or some other awful thing has happened to them.

We are still at work at our fort. When all is finished we shall be happy to see our Secesh friends, and would most assuredly give them a warm reception. The weather is now warm, but a few days ago we had a snow-storm, and we had no fire in many of our tents, and were put to our wits' end to keep warm through the night, and fain would have done it by lying spoon-fashion; but in spite of ourselves we kept just cool enough to prevent much sleeping. My sweet potatoes froze; meat shared the same fate, as likewise the water in our canteens.

The next night we dug holes in our tents, and filling them with coals, slept as warm as biscuits in an oven.

Do tell them to write, for C. is too good a soldier to be forgotten by any body. You in your pleasant homes, surrounded by the comforts of life, enjoying the society of friends and relatives, have but a faint idea of the joy a soldier experiences on receiving letters from the loved ones at home. Even if he knows they are all well, he is not satisfied unless he hears directly from their own hand.

Now that the weather has moderated, the dogs lie around the farmhouses basking in the sun, the flies are buzzing, the robins are singing, and after a brisk walk of a mile, one will get under a shade-tree for comfort. And now, all through the pleasant moonlight nights, the frogs croak and whistle the same old monotonous songs their brethren have so often chanted in my ear on the banks of the old Oswegatchie. But the banks of the Neuse differ greatly from those of the Oswegatchie. On the Neuse you find our ox-teams, the animal being hitched as a horse is hitched to a buggy, and is driven by a stick or by reins attached to his horns.

Here, moreover, are *snuff-eating women*, who take a small stick and pound or chew the end till it gets broomed, then wetting it in their mouth, put it into a box of snuff, and fall to eating and sucking it again and again, passing the snuff-box around like the old ladies of the North, only twice as often. While engaged in this delightful occupation the stick is seen protruding from their mouths three to five inches, causing the ladies to assume a very grotesque and highly interesting appearance, strikingly reminding me of the first lessons given to calves in the art of drinking by inserting a finger in their mouths. I should hardly have believed this if I had not seen it with my own eyes, and known by actual inspection that it was real snuff. It is just as common to see a young lady with her snuff-stick in her mouth here as it is to see one with knitting-work up in Yankeeland. In addition to those things on the banks of the Neuse, are sweet potatoes, which are selling at eighty cents per bushel. Such potatoes I never saw before. They are good boiled, roasted, or fried, and to-day I bought a sweet-potato pie; it is very skilfully made from the raw material by the good housewives of Craven County, wherein we now do sojourn. Your humble servant pronounces the potato almost equal to the pumpkin pie, resembling it in color and taste. Over across the Neuse, in the goodly town of Newbern, where "officers love to congregate," oysters most do flourish and rejoice in her marketplace; and many a broad grin of satisfaction illumines the countenance of the oyster-loving soldier as he pays his "quarter" for a fresh quart, or buys a whole bushel of them in the shell for fifty cents. But "there is a cobweb in every corner;" for although potatoes and oysters are plenty and cheap, every thing else is very dear. Poor envelopes sell at twenty cents a bunch, white chalk at twenty cents per pound, eggs twenty-five cents per dozen—and that in this warm country, where hens lay all the year round if they would. No butter or cheese is made here to sell, and but very few of the farmers make enough for their own use. Here are found large tracts of pine, from which our lean, lank, sallow, butternut-dressed Southern brethren obtain their pitch, tar, and turpentine. They first box the trees as some people do the sugar-maple, by cutting a hole in the side that will hold about one quart. Then they proceed to scratch the tree above the box, and the pitch runs down and fills it in about three weeks. As they box seven or eight thousand trees in one lot, they manage to get a large quantity of pitch, which they sell at from five to eight dollars per barrel, according to the demand in market. After running about four months it stops, and what dries and hardens on the trees is scraped off and sold with the rest. Each year they scratch a little higher up the trees; many are cut as high as forty feet or more, and have been tapped at least twenty years. As you may suppose, we of the Ninety-second have plenty of gum to chew, and all the fat pine we want for firewood. Thus you see how pine-sugar (as we call it) is manufactured in this portion of Uncle Sam's vineyard.

But I must tell you of another thing very common on the banks of the Neuse, which you do not enjoy at home, *i. e.*, "picket firing."

Last week, Captain Whitford's guerrillas came down, and getting in the rear of our outpost, fired on our boys, wounding four of them slightly. The pickets, being taken by surprise by being attacked in the rear instead of front, had time to fire but one volley into the rebels before they were in the woods out of sight. To-day, our quartermaster and their officer, riding beyond the lines, came unexpectedly upon a body of guerrillas, but by dint of good riding managed to run away unhurt. When they reached the reserve, the old pickets were turned out to deploy as skirmishers through the woods in pursuit. But the rebels had too much the start, and we only got one shot at them, capturing one haversack and canteen. Court Cooper was out, and managed to get one shot at them, and brought in a "johnny-cake" from a secesh haversack. He is going to send a piece home, so look out for rebel rations.

You must know that any alarm on the outpost is the signal for every man in the regiment to fall in. It would do you good to see the Ninety-second on such occasions. When the firing commenced to-day, I was out with a fatigue party cutting brush, and when the long-roll sounded, such a getting over brush and briers you never did see, for we had to go to camp on the double-quick. As it is natural for me, when any thing ridiculous occurs, I had to indulge in a hearty laugh, and more than usual at this time, to see the way they tumbled over the brush in their great haste to get their guns. I had ten men in my squad, and verily I thought some of them would break their necks before reaching camp. We knew perfectly well that there would be no great fighting, but we knew just as well that the long-roll means every man at his post, and orders must be obeyed. I must not write much longer, for a certain gun hanging in the tent needs cleaning, and who will do it if I do not? So, leaving picket-firing, pine-sugar, sweet potatoes, and snuff-eating girls to take care of themselves, I will bring my letter to a close by sending you all the love that such a letter is supposed capable of containing. I remain, as in duty bound, your obedient servant,

JOHN WHIPPLE.

LETTER CXIX.

FORTRESS MONROE, 1863.

WE can do nothing but fight for the country's cause; and that we will do until every man of us perish by the rebel bullet. In spite of all the prejudice that we have had shown towards us, we will stand by the old flag forever. If it should happen to prove of no benefit to us as a people, it will do good to the rising generation. So we will proudly fight the battles of our common country.

CHARLES A. HAITSTOCK,
Serg. 22d U. S. Col. Regt.

LETTER CXX.

HEADQUARTERS 119th N. Y. Volunteers,
BROOKS STATION, May 19th, 1863.

MY DEAR FRIEND— .... The 119th has again been subjected to the fiery ordeal of battle. Its men are now well-tried veterans, worthy the proud republic they represent, and the holy cause they defend: to lead such soldiers in the glorious struggle now waging, is an honor that even a Garabaldi might justly envy. If Romans could beautifully chant "It is sweet and becoming to die for one's country," when battling for conquest, in what glorious strains can we Americans indulge who fight for a government representing liberty, justice, truth!

This war was forced upon, it came through no fault of the patriotic North. It was begotten by the existence of anti-republican elements, whose growth depended not upon moral suasion, but upon the exercise of power; losing that power, it lost its capacity of resistance, and was imperilled. You know what I mean, the Slave Power, to which the whole patronage of the Government had been subordinate. Commercial interests, manufacturing interests, all, save the agriculture and literature of the country,—which, too, were unhappily part corrupted,—were dragooned in its service. Presses had been subsidized—senators stricken down with bludgeons—votaries of freedom martyred—freedom of speech and freedom of the press denied—religion corrupted—the virgin soil of our territories soaked with innocent blood—and tales of woe enacted, sad enough to draw pity from the very stones,—all for the benefit of that pernicious power, that it might be enlarged, popularized, and nationalized. But in vain. Though Truth slumbered, it was not *dead:* the earnest appeals of her vigilant sentinels reached and stirred the popular heart. Freedom asserted herself—struggled for supremacy, and triumphed. The Slave Power lost its props, foresaw its doom, and to save itself attempted the murder of the Republic. Thus came the war: hence Slavery *vs.* Freedom is its logical issue.

Therefore, whine not, though it has cost and will cost untold expenditures of blood and treasure. It is Heaven's opportunity to strike down despotism on this continent, and to make this government what it purports to be—a land of the *free*. We are not ripe for victory *yet*. It takes a four-years course of study to graduate in our universities, and the American people have far more to learn than is taught in our colleges. However, I do not complain.

"The mills of the gods grind slowly
But they grind exceeding fine!"

We are progressive. After a while we will learn the path to victory, recognize the difference between parricides and "erring brethren," conclude that Jefferson was not joking when he said that all men were free,—do justice to the slave, and *conquer* an honorable lasting *peace*. This consummation may require one, two, three, or even four years; be that as it may, time, reckoned by years, is nothing in a conflict whose result will affect human destiny to latest generations. There is just one little thing that we soldiers want, and shall have, whether it takes one or twenty years; and that is, complete victory. The cheaper we can buy it, of course, the better we will like it. To this fact the nation's foes, North and South, can accommodate themselves, steer clear and keep out of the way.

This Chancellorsville affair, through with a few days ago, may give you some little trouble up in the North, but let me tell you that we can readily digest a hundred such disasters. We are neither sick, disgusted, nor disheartened. Let perils multiply—we will nerve ourselves to a still loftier courage; in a just cause like ours, we must prevail. Short-sighted statesmanship, jealousies of rulers, and incompetency of generals, may protract our struggle; but they cannot, even when reinforced by the cowardly sneaks in the *North*—

who cry ruin and defeat, curse our noble President, magnify the reverses, and belittle the triumphs of our heroic soldiers—thwart the grand decree of Providence, that this Republic shall *survive*.

After all, this Chancellorsville affair was not so bad. The first day of the battle, by virtue of Stonewall Jackson's brilliantly executed flank movement—which resulted in an impetuous assault upon our rear and right wing, taking us by surprise, and driving a portion of our troops in confusion—was a sad disaster; and as for the 119th, they mourn the untimely death of their brave, chivalric colonel, accomplished in art, literature, and science, amiable and high-toned, who loved his adopted land as well as Leonidas loved Sparta. He was the idol of us all. Let the nation mourn when such heroes fall as he fell, in the far front, with the words, "You are doing excellently, boys; this is glorious: stand firm," echoing from his dying lips.

But as for the other days of the battle, the advantages were with us. We inflicted a far greater loss than we received, and never was disappointment more bitter than when we found that we were retiring.

Some attribute it to the sudden rise of the Rappahannock, which threatened to sweep away our pontoon bridges: some to Halleck's interference. Some to one thing and some to another. One thing I want you to understand— we were not whipped. We were not demoralized, and to day we are ready to push forward for another fight. We lost in killed and wounded about fifty per cent. of the men we took into action. Sad, very sad; but what would life be worth in a disintegrated, ruined country, torn by faction, and bleeding with oppression? All it becomes us is, to relieve their necessities—make the maimed and disabled soldiers children of the Republic, and, by the exercise of Christian charities, protect those made widows and orphans from crime and pauperism.

We shall move again on Richmond in a few days, unless perchance Lee, by an attempt at Northern invasion, necessitates our sojourn in the loyal States, which I most fervently hope he will. Unhappily, the foe, insolent enough to tread his foot over Mason and Dixon's line, if luckily he should return, it would be with ranks torn, shattered, and demoralized. I have no further time to write of war, as to that, &c. Faithfully yours, &c.,

BENJ. A. WILLIS,

H. T. S., Esq.   Major 119th N. Y. Vols.

LETTER CXXI.

THE FIRST COLORED REGIMENT.

STEAMER DE MOLAY, June 1st, 1863.
Off Cape Hatteras.

THE more I think of the passage of the Fifty-fourth through Boston, the more wonderful it seems to me. Just remember our own doubts and fears, and other people's sneering and pitying remarks, when we began last winter, and then look at the perfect triumph of last Thursday.

We have gone quietly along forming the regiment, and at last left Boston amidst a greater enthusiasm than has been seen since the first three-months troops left for the war. Every one I saw, from the governor's staff down, had nothing but words of praise for us.

Truly I ought to be thankful; and if the raising of colored troops prove such a benefit to the country, and to the blacks, as many people think it will, I shall thank God a thousand times that I was led to take my share in it.

ROBERT GOULD SHAW.

LETTER CXXII.

St. Simon's Island, June 9th, 1863.

We arrived at the southern point of this island at six this morning. I went ashore to report to Colonel Montgomery, and was ordered to proceed with my regiment to a place called Pike's Bluff, on the inner coast of the island, and encamp. We came up here in another steamer, the Sentinel, as the De Molay is too large for the inner waters, and took possession of a plantation formerly owned by Mr. Gould.

We have a very nice camping-ground for the regiment, and I have my quarters in "the house," very pleasantly situated, and surrounded by fine large trees. The island is beautiful, as far as I have seen it. You would be enchanted with the scenery here; the foliage is wonderfully thick, and the trees covered with hanging moss, making beautiful avenues wherever there is a road or path; it is more like the tropics than any thing I have seen. Mr. Butler King's plantation, where I first went ashore, must have been a beautiful place, and well kept. It is entirely neglected now, of course; and as the growth is very rapid two years' neglect almost covers all traces of former care.

June 12th.—If I could have gone on describing to you the beauties of this region, who knows but I might have made a fine addition to the literature of our age? But since I wrote the above, I have been looking at something very different.

On Wednesday, a steamboat appeared off our wharf, and Colonel Montgomery hailed me from the deck with, "How soon can you get ready to start on an expedition?" I said, "In half an hour," and it was not long before we were on board, with eight companies, leaving two for camp-guard.

We steamed down by his camp, where two other steamers, with five companies from his regiment, with two sections of Rhode Island artillery, joined us. A little below there we ran aground and had to wait until midnight for flood-tide, when we got away once more.

At 8 A. M. we were at the mouth of the Altamaha river, and immediately made for Darien. We wound in and out through the creeks, twisting and turning continually, often heading in directly the opposite direction from that which we intended to go, and often running aground, thereby losing much time. Besides our three vessels, we were followed by the gunboat Paul Jones.

On the way up, Montgomery threw several shells among the plantations, in what seemed to me a very brutal way, for he didn't know how many women and children there might be.

About noon, we came in sight of Darien, a beautiful little town. Our artillery peppered it a little, as we came up, and then our three boats made fast to the wharves, and we landed the troops. The town was deserted, with the exception of two white women and two negroes.

Montgomery ordered all the furniture and movable property to be taken on board the boats. This occupied some time; and, after the town was pretty thoroughly disembowelled, he said to me, "I shall burn this town." He speaks always in a very low tone, and has quite a sweet smile when addressing you. I told him "I did not want the responsibility of it;" and he was only too happy to take it all on his own shoulders. So the pretty little place was burnt to the ground, and not a shed remained standing—Montgomery firing the last buildings with his own hand. One of my companies assisted in it, because he ordered them out, and I had to obey. You must bear in mind, that not a shot had been fired at us from this place, and that there were evidently very few men left in it. All the inhabitants (principally women and children), had fled on our approach, and were, no doubt, watching the scene from a distance. Some of our grape-shot tore the skirt of one of the women whom I saw. Montgomery told her that her house and property should be spared; but it went down with the rest.

The reasons he gave me for destroying Darien were, that the Southerners must be made to feel that this was a real war, and that they were to be swept away by the hand of God, like the Jews of old. In theory, it may seem all right to some, but when it comes to being made the instrument of the Lord's vengeance, I myself don't like it. Then he says "We are outlawed, and, therefore, not bound by the rules of regular warfare." But that makes it none the less revolting to wreak our vengeance on the innocent and defenceless.

By the time we had finished this dirty piece of business, it was too dark to go far down the narrow river, where our boat sometimes touched both sides at once: so we lay at anchor until daylight, occasionally dropping a shell at a stray house. The Paul Jones fired a few guns as well as we.

I reached camp at about 2 p. m., to-day, after as abominable a job as I ever had a share in.

Remember not to breathe a word of what I have written about this raid, for I have not yet made up my mind what I ought to do. Besides my own distaste for this barbarous sort of warfare, I am not sure that it will not harm very much the reputation of black troops and of those connected with them. For myself, I have gone through the war so far without dishonor, and I do not like to degenerate into a plunderer and robber,—and the same applies to every officer in my regiment. There was not a deed performed from beginning to end, which required any pluck or courage; if we had fought for possession of the place, and it had been found necessary to hold or destroy it, or if the inhabitants had done any thing which deserved such punishment, or if it were a place of refuge for the enemy, there might have been some reason for Montgomery's acting as he did; but, as the case stands, I can't see any justification. If it were the order of our government to overrun the South with fire and sword, I might look at it in a different light, for then we should be carrying out what had been decided upon as a necessary policy. As the case stands, we are no better than "Semmes," who attacks and destroys defenceless vessels, and haven't even the poor excuse of gaining any thing by it; for the property is of no use to us, excepting that we can now sit on chairs instead of camp-stools.

But all I complain of is wanton destruction. After going through the hard campaigning and hard fighting in Virginia, this makes me very much ashamed of myself. Montgomery, from what I have seen of him, is a conscientious man, and really believes what he says, "that he is doing his duty to the best of his knowledge and ability." There are two courses only for me to pursue: to obey orders and say nothing, or to refuse to go on any more such expeditions, and be put under arrest, probably court-martialed, which is a serious thing.

June 13th.—To-day I rode over to Pierce Butler's plantation. It is an immense place, and parts of it very beautiful. The house is small, and badly built, like almost all

I have seen here. There are about ten of his slaves left there, all of them sixty or seventy years old. He sold about three hundred slaves about three years ago.

I talked with some whose children and grandchildren were sold then, and though they said that was a " weeping day," they maintained that "Massa Butler was a good massa, and they would give any thing to see him again." When I told them I had known Miss Fanny, they looked very much pleased, and one, named John, wanted me to tell her I had seen him. They said all the house-servants had been taken inland by the overseer at the beginning of the war; and they asked if we couldn't get their children back to the island again. These were all born and bred on the place, and even selling away their families could not entirely efface their love for their master.

The island is traversed from end to end by what they call a shell-road, which is hard and flat, excellent for driving. On each side, there are either very large and overhanging trees, with thick underbrush, or open country, covered with sago-palm, the sharp-pointed leaves making the country impassable. Occasionally we met with a few fields of very poor grass. Where there is no swamp, the road is very sandy.

There are a good many of these oyster-shell roads—for in many places there are great beds of them, deposited nobody knows when, I suppose. The walls of many of the buildings are built of cement, mixed with oyster-shells, which make them very durable.

I forgot to tell you, that the negroes at Mr. Butler's remembered Mrs. Kemble very well, and said she was a very fine lady. They hadn't seen her since the young ladies were very small, they said. My visit there was very interesting and touching.

A deserted homestead is always a sad sight, but here in the South we must look a little deeper than the surface, and then we see that every such overgrown plantation and empty house is a harbinger of freedom to the slaves; and every lover of his country, even if he have no feeling for the slaves themselves, must rejoice.

Next to Mr. Butler's is the house of Mr. James E. Couper. It must have been a lovely spot; the garden is well laid out, and the perfume of the flowers is delicious. The house is the finest on the island. The men from our gunboats have been there, and all the floors are strewed with books and magazines of every kind. There is no furniture in any of these houses.

Colonel Montgomery's original plan, on this last expedition, was to land about fifteen miles above Darien, and march down on two different roads to the town, taking all the negroes to be found, and burning every planter's house on the passage. I should have commanded our detachment in that case. The above are the orders he gave me.

ROBERT GOULD SHAW.

LETTER CXXIII.

ST. HELENA'S ISLAND, S. C., July 3d, 1863.

You will have been some time without letters from me, when you receive this, as the Arago was not allowed to take a mail last week, I understand, because of the late movement on Charleston. Last evening I went over to tea at a plantation four or five miles from here, where some of the teachers, four ladies, and the same number of gentlemen, live.

After tea, we went to what the negroes call a "praise-meeting," which was very interesting. The praying was done by an old blind fellow, who made believe all the time that he was reading out of a book. He was also the leader in the singing, and seemed to throw his whole soul into it. After the meeting, there was a "shout," which is a most extraordinary performance. They all walk and shuffle round in a ring, singing and chanting, while three or four stand in a corner and clap their hands to mark the time. At certain parts of the chorus, they all give a duck, the effect of which is very peculiar. This shuffling is what they call "shouting." They sometimes keep it up all night, and only church-members are allowed to join in it.

Their singing, when there are a great many voices, is fine, but otherwise I don't like it at all. The women's voices are so shrill, that I can't listen to them with comfort.

July 4th.—To-day there has been a great meeting for the colored people, at the Baptist church, six or seven miles from camp. I rode down there, and heard a speech from a colored preacher, from Baltimore, named Lynch. He was very eloquent.

Can you imagine any thing more wonderful than a colored abolitionist-meeting, on a South Carolina plantation? Here were collected all the freed slaves on this island, listening to the most ultra abolition speeches that could be made, while two years ago their masters were still here, the lords of the soil and of them. Now, they all own something themselves, go to school and to church, and work for wages! It is the most extraordinary change. Such things oblige a man to believe that God is not very far off.

A little black boy read the Declaration of Independence, and then they all sang some of their hymns. The effect was grand. I would have given any thing to have had you there; I thought of you all the time.

The day was beautiful, and the crowd was collected in the church-yard, under some magnificent old oaks, covered with the long, hanging gray moss which grows on the trees here. The gay dresses and turbans of the women made the sight very brilliant. Miss Forten promised to write me out the words of some of the hymns they sang, which I will send to you.

July 6th.—Yesterday I went to church at the same place, where the meeting was held on the 4th.

The preaching was very bad, being full of "hell and damnation," but administered in such a dull way, that sleep soon overcame most of the congregation, and we counted fifty darkies fast in the "arms of Murphy."

After the sermon, the preacher said, "Those who wish to be married can come forward." Some one then punched a stout young fellow in white gloves, near me; and as soon as he could be roused and made to understand that the hour was come, he walked up to the altar. A young woman, still stouter and broader-shouldered than the bridegroom, advanced from the women's side of the church, accompanied by a friend, and they both stood by his side, so that it looked as if he were being married to both of them. However, they got through it all right, as he evidently knew which was which, and they both said "Yes, sir," to all the preacher asked them; they were both coal-black. I couldn't find out if the bride had been sleeping during the sermon, as well as the groom.

At the church they sang our hymns, and made a sad mess of them, but they do justice to their own at their "praise-meetings."

9 P. M.—We have just had Miss Forten and two other ladies to tea, and entertained them afterwards with some singing from the men. It made us all think of those last evenings at Readville, which were so pleasant.

If there were any certainty of our being permanently here, you and Annie could come down and spend a month without the least difficulty. You would enjoy it immensely; there is enough here to interest you for months.

As you may suppose, I was bitterly disappointed at being left behind; but nothing has been done at Charleston yet, and we may have a chance.

To-day I went on board the monitor Montauk and the rebel ram Fingal. The latter is very strong and very powerfully armed; but the work is rough, and looks as if they wanted money and workmen to finish it properly.

We don't know with any certainty what is going on in the North, but can't believe Lee will get far into Pennsylvania. No matter if the rebels get to New York, I shall never lose my faith in our ultimate success. We are not yet ready for peace, and want a good deal of purging still.

I wrote to General Strong this afternoon, and expressed my wish to be in his brigade. Though I like Montgomery, I want to get my men alongside of white troops, and into a good fight, if there is to be one. The General sent me word, before he went away, that he was very much disappointed at being ordered to leave us; so I thought it well to put it into his head to try to get us back.

Working independently, the colored troops come only under the eyes of their own officers; and to have their worth properly acknowledged, they should be with other troops in action. It is an incentive to them, too, to do their best. There is some rumor to-night of our being ordered to James Island, and put under General Terry's command. I should be satisfied with that.

ROBERT GOULD SHAW.

Colonel Robert Gould Shaw fell mortally wounded in the assault on Fort Wagner, under command of General Gilmore, in Charleston harbor, July 18th, 1863.

Young, noble, heroic—an only son—but a few weeks married to the object of tenderest affection—forming the ornament and charm, by great social amenity and personal attractiveness, of a large and tenderly attached family circle—Colonel Shaw freely laid all, even life, on the altar of freedom and country.

Appointed, at his own request, by Governor Andrews, to the command of the first colored regiment (the 54th Mass.), which he formed and drilled to admirable discipline, the enthusiasm which greeted its appearance on the march of debarkation, with its gallant young leader at the head, unprecedented in Boston, will not soon be forgotten by those who witnessed the impressive scene.

Colonel Shaw entered the war as lieutenant in the famous Second Massachusetts, known as the "Fighting Second," having previously been a member of our Seventh regiment, which has furnished so many able officers for the army. He served in the Virginia campaign under General Banks, and fought at the battle of Cedar mountain, where he was struck by a spent ball, though not injured. His regiment on that occasion highly distinguished itself by bravery and forethought, and Colonel Shaw there won the rank of captain. At Antietam he became major of the regiment.

Thus has fallen, East, West, North, the very flower of society! men counting not their lives dear given in defence of and for the preservation of their noble inheritance—exhibiting a courage which in the teeth of peril knew no fear—a heroism which braved suffering, endured hardship—enrolling their names among Liberty's martyrs; a radiance of glory surrounds and hallows each—a glory that transfigures the pale forms of the battle-field, enfolding them with the mantle of immortality! to be held evermore with tender yet proud sorrow, in grateful, loving remembrance by their countrymen—dwelling now, we joyfully trust, in the "noontide of glory!"

> "Where should a warrior rest
> But with his braves?
> Hiding his loyal breast
> Among their graves.

  Laying his noble head
   Low, where theirs lie,—
 Where Southern waters chafe,
   Southern winds sigh.

"What though each dusky face
   Marks them to be
From that poor down-trodden race
   Over the sea!
There, where *his* grave is dug,
   Let *them* be laid :
They follow his death-charge,
   This brave, dark brigade!

"The rebels have made him
   A grave in the sand,
And there they have laid him
   With rough careless hand.
A hundred dark soldiers
   Are thrown by his side—
A hundred who gladly
   For liberty died!

"'*Bury him so,*'
   Said the traitors with glee,
'We'll let the world know
   How to make the slave free!'
Then dashing the sand in,
   They cover from sight
The hundred dark faces—
   The *one face so white.*

"Where should a leader sleep
   But with his men ?
Followers in such wild sweep
   Close round again !
Not now for fierce assault ;
   Not for the fight,
Silent martyrs, for *brotherhood,*
   Freedom, and *right.*"

LETTER CXXIV.

BATTLE OF GETTYSBURG.

July 25th, 1863.

We arrived near Gettysburg, Pennsylvania, on the eve of July 1st. The First and Eleventh corps had been whipped, and General Reynolds killed.

The morning of the 2d dawned gloomily for the last time on so many brave spirits.

There was skirmishing at different points along the line. About seven o'clock, our regiment was sent with one hundred sharp-shooters into the woods, on a reconnoissance, to see whether the enemy were there in force. We drove in their skirmishers, and then came upon them with a heavy force. We engaged them, and in ten minutes we had forty-five men out of one hundred and ninety shot down.

We were then ordered out, as the rebels were getting around us on both flanks: they pushed us so hard we could not bring off many of our wounded.

We soon after took up a position in a peach orchard, in front of our artillery, alongside of the Second New Hampshire. Soon after, a severe cannonading commenced, and was kept up for some time, when heavy masses of infantry came upon us. Twice we repulsed them. They would lie down in the grass and wait for reinforcements: at last they came close upon us. A great part of our men were shot down, and nearly all our artillery-horses killed. We gave and received two volleys, being only about four rods apart, when, most of our men having fallen, we were ordered back. We were pressed hard for about one hundred rods, and shelled much further: only about forty of our regiment (Third Maine regiment) got off, and in my company (Company F), only the captain, one sergeant, and myself got off! And we got bullet-holes through our clothes. I got two. Many of the boys, who had been in all the battles, and never got hit, there fell. The best men of the glorious "old Third"—heroes of many a battle—were there laid low.

3d July.—We were supporting the second line. The cannonading was fearful, the severest of the war, if not of *any* war—two hundred pieces on each side. When Longstreet made his last desperate charge, we were taken up to the support of the first line. Our position was good: the enemy had to come over a wide, level field, and our artillery made sad havoc among them. They charged up to the very mouth of our guns. Our infantry (Third Maine) met them, and the ground was piled with the dead. *They were driven back*, and nearly 2000 of them laid down their arms, and many colors were taken. Then the prow of the invasion was broken, and the tide rolled back. The homes of the North rendered secure, Freedom breathed *easier*.

I looked over the field, and covered many of the dead and wounded with blankets.

On the morning of the 4th we took the front, and I was upon the skirmish-line watching the enemy's sharp-shooters, and exchanging shots with them. We were in the grass, and they several times climbed trees to see us, but we could *take them out* the first fire. That night, the cries of the wounded, during the storm which raged, was *unpleasant in the extreme*. I gave many of the rebel wounded water, and covered them up, for which they were grateful, and would urge me to take money. Our boys would mingle with them with the *best of feelings*—brave men after a desperate struggle respect each other.

5th.—At daybreak on the 5th I ventured a little beyond my post to a wounded man, and not being fired upon, we *all* went forward, and soon learned the enemy had left. Ten feet from where I had been stationed lay Colonel Allen, dead (colonel of the 25th Virginia). I cut some buttons from his vest. He was richly dressed, and bore the impress of one of the F. F. Vs. I could look upon this sad remnant of humanity without regret, deeming it a fitting end for the *authors* of this rebellion.

Gettysburg is the bloodiest field of the war. Of the one hundred thousand invaders, one-third never recrossed the Potomac.

Each side fought with unsurpassed bravery and tenacity; but the oft-sneered-at and much-abused veterans of the Potomac Army, in fair and open field, defeated the entire host of the chivalry, led by the greatest general of modern times. And they did this unaided, not one of the much talked of *militia* being there. All were chagrined at the escape of Lee; all were anxious to make an attack, preferring to fight him here to Virginia, and we wanted to get that great humbug, the militia, in.

The military power of the rebellion was broken at Gettysburg, Vicksburg, and Port Hudson, and I am now hopeful of a successful termination of the conflict, and may sweet Peace delay not her coming.

On the 5th, when some of ours (Third regiment, Maine) were out burying their dead, a *citizen* told them, "They could afford to be shot once in a while, as they got their *pay* for it." I believe I should have broken the old ruffian's head with my rifle!

I hope this war will give the death-blow to slavery, and that I may live to see the end of the war; then I can return and meet the copperheads of our town with gratification—I had almost said, with defiance.

This is the great object of my life—to aid in crushing

this monstrous rebellion. I believe it matters little *when* a man dies, but *how* and *where*, that is all-important; and in no way can a man die so gloriously as when he dies for his country and race. One who has lived to serve his country two years in this war has done more than he that has spent a lifetime in self-aggrandizement. I have full confidence that the all-wise Dispenser of human events will not let this country, the beacon-light of the struggling millions, go down in darkness and despair. Such a disaster would cause a yell of triumph to be sent up from every despot who tyrannizes over his fellow men.

CHARLES N. MAXWELL,
3d Maine Regiment.

LETTER CXXV.

VICKSBURG, Miss., July 20th, 1863.

DEAR PARENTS—Now that Vicksburg is ours, and the din of battle has ceased, I will try to collect my thoughts to give you a short account of our part in the late Vicksburg campaign.

I need not give you a general account of the battles in which we have been engaged, as you have doubtless read all about them in the papers; yet a somewhat particular account of what I have seen, and the part taken by our regiment and brigade, may not be entirely uninteresting. By referring to my pocket diary, I see that we crossed the Mississippi River, at Bruinsburg Landing, on the 30th of April. In the evening, our regiment was addressed by Hon. E. B. Washburne and Gov. Yates, who flattered us not a little, and among other things, told us to sustain our past good reputation in the battle on the coming morrow. The next morning, we started early for the battle-field, and, after marching ten miles under a burning sun, encountered the enemy in force at Thompson's Hills, near Port Gibson. We immediately formed in line of battle, and sent forward skirmishers. After engaging the enemy for some time in front, to drive him from the cane-brakes and rifle-pits, we made a rapid movement to the left, and charged his right flank on double-quick, shouting as we went, which put the rebels utterly to route, and decided the fate of the day. It was a pleasing and exciting sight to us to see the terrific "secesh" leave their well-chosen position, and run for dear life before the charging columns of our enthusiastic brigade. After the charge, Generals Grant, McPherson, and Logan came riding by our regiment, with Governor Yates and Mr. Washburne, the latter of whom cried out, "I told you, boys, what you would do to-day, and you have done it." We pursued the retreating enemy about two miles, and bivouacked, using captured blankets in lieu of those we threw off on coming into the fight.

The next morning we marched into Port Gibson, singing "We'll rally round the flag, boys," &c. The fair maidens of the city looked quite sober as we passed, yet a few of the little rebels deigned to smile at the Yankee invaders, as they passed quietly through the streets.

Finding that the enemy had burnt the bridge over Bayou Pierre to prevent pursuit, we made a detour to the right; and after marching nine miles through woods and over fields, and crossing fords, we came again into the main road, and took up our line of march for Big Bayou Pierre, where we arrived at eleven o'clock at night, completely worn out with hard marching through the dust and hot sun.

On the third of May we crossed the bayou on a suspension bridge. On ascending the hill after crossing, the enemy gave us a morning salute by firing two shells at us, which exploded directly overhead, as we were marching up a narrow ravine. We again formed in line of battle, expecting the enemy would dispute our progress. We advanced in line of battle about a mile through almost impenetrable cane-brakes and brier patches, over deep gulleys and up steep hills. Our company was detached as skirmishers, and deployed in front of the regiment, and engaged the skirmishers of the enemy for some time, driving them from the woods, and putting them to flight. We then marched by a circuitous route to Black River, where we arrived about twelve o'clock at night, completely exhausted. Here we remained three days to give the men rest, which was much needed, as we had been on forced marches for several days on short rations, and many were shoeless and very footsore. My own poor feet were very badly galled, besides having four large blisters on the soles. On the 7th of May we removed to Rocky Springs, and halted another day. On the 9th, we drew about half rations, and marched through dust and a hot sun to Pine Hills, and bivouacked. The next day we marched on towards Jackson, passing through Utica, and camping at Utica Cross-roads. On the 11th I was detailed to take charge of teams and guard, going back to Rocky Springs after provisions and regimental property. General Logan would only send old worthless "confiscated teams," as he expected we would be captured by guerrillas, who were constantly hovering in our rear. I went back in the night over the roughest and darkest road I ever travelled.

The next morning we loaded up the teams, and started back to overtake the army, and made twenty miles before we halted for the night; we saw no guerrillas. On the 13th we came up with our troops, and found that they had been engaged in the battle of Raymond, an account of which you have doubtless seen in the papers; also the part taken by Logan's division, to which I have the honor to belong.

The right started soon after we came up, and marched to Clinton and bivouacked in mud and rain. May 14th we drew very short rations, and Gen. Logan said, "it was Jackson or starvation for us that night." The rain poured down in torrents, yet we moved forward at a brisk pace, expecting the enemy would give us a hard battle before giving up the capital of Jeff. Davis's native State. We advanced to within about two miles of the city, and formed in line of battle, as a reserve to Quimby's division, which was then fighting the enemy just ahead. After a short and desperate resistance, the rebels fell back before the successive charges of Quimby's gallant men. We then made a detour to the left to cut off the enemy's retreat towards Vicksburg, but he did not come that way, but fled across Pearl River, burning the bridge to prevent pursuit.

That night we bivouacked in mud and rain, and foraged enough to eat from the terrified citizens. I went into the city and saw the State-house and other public buildings. May 15th our army "changed front," and marched back through Clinton towards Vicksburg, and bivouacked near Bear Creek. The next day we marched four miles, and encountered the enemy in force at Champion Hills. Our regiment ran about a mile, under a burning sun, to get into position, and threw out skirmishers to protect the right flank of the army. We immediately advanced with the division to the support of Gen. Hovey, who was being very hard pressed by the overwhelming force of the enemy. We quickly got into the thickest of the fight, and opened fire. The battle soon raged with terrific fury. As reinforcements came up on both sides, the rapid volleys of musketry soon blended into one continual roar, only interrupted by the bursting of shells, and the constant discharges of artillery from both armies. The enemy had concentrated his forces on our right, and was making desperate efforts to drive us back; but Logan's division was not to be moved. The rebels moved up under the brow of a hill, evidently intending to make a desperate effort to take one of our batteries. I could not help but admire the fine style they moved up, and the splendid colors they carried. There was a short pause, and then came the order to charge. The brigade immediately moved forward, under a deadly shower of grape and musketry, and opened a terrific fire upon the stubborn foe. At first, he stood his ground manfully, but finally wavered and broke. Our brigade here captured about a thousand prisoners, and several pieces of artillery. It was a horrid sight to see the battle-field after the fight was over, covered with the dead and wounded of both armies. How little the folks at home, seated by their comfortable hearthstones, realize of the heart-sickening horrors of this unnatural war!

We pursued the enemy about two miles and bivouacked, almost worn out by the heat and fatigues of the day.

The next day we marched to Big Black river, and halted a short time to rest. On the morning of the 18th we crossed the river on a floating bridge (which the pioneer corps had thrown across during the night), and marched on towards Vicksburg, until 12 o'clock at night. The next day we started early, without rations, and soon came up to where the balls were whistling, and formed in line of battle for the final struggle of the Vicksburg campaign.

Here we had crackers dealt out to us, and cooked something to eat while the other divisions were getting into position. We then threw out skirmishers and advanced under fire of musketry and artillery, and after some sharp skirmishing drove the enemy within his breastworks. Sharp-shooters were sent forward, who crept up within a short distance of the enemy's works, and picked off his cannoniers whenever they attempted to load a piece. Our artillery was rapidly getting into position, and kept up a sharp fire wherever the enemy showed himself. One who has never seen them can form no idea of the strength of the enemy's works. Besides having the strongest natural position I have ever seen, he had been constructing breastworks for nearly a year, outside of which was an almost impenetrable abatis. The fight was constantly kept up by our sharp-shooters and artillery, until, on the 22d of May, early in the morning, word was sent round that we would charge the breastworks at 10 o'clock, A. M. You may imagine each man's feelings, about that time. We all felt that we could take the works; yet we knew that "many brave boys would fall" before we could drive the enemy from his fortifications, but almost all felt that it would be some one else besides himself who would fall.

The order of attack being arranged, we moved by the right flank of a road towards the enemy's works, exposed to his grape and musketry, most of which we avoided by walking as low as possible. We approached as near as practicable, and formed in line, and sent forward skirmishers to feel the enemy. Our company was detailed for this duty, and we advanced over a ridge, exposed to the enemy's fire, on quadruple quick, and got up behind logs and brush on the next ridge. After firing away all our cartridges we returned to the regiment, which was

soon ordered "forward" to the works. Just before we started, our brigade adjutant said to our regiment, "Now, boys, you must do your duty, just as you always"—just then a ball struck him in the thigh, and cut short his speech. Our major then said, "Let every man stand to his post. Forward, Forty-fifth."

The regiment started forward, as usual, with a yell, under the hottest fire I ever had been under before (and I was at Shiloh). The air seemed filled with bullets, which whistled with spiteful fury, like the winds around our Northern homes, in winter. The "hail of death" fell so fast that only a part of two companies, besides ours, ventured to run the fiery gauntlet. Our beloved major fell, mortally wounded, while gallantly leading the charge. After we had got under shelter of the enemy's breastworks, our men in the rear kept the rebels from shooting over at us; and we were so protected that we could keep them from firing much at the rest of our men, who came up a few at a time. We planted our flag, with that of the 20th Illinois, on the outer slope of the enemy's main fort, and remained there to defend them fourteen long hours. We were so near the rebels that we could pelt them with clods of dirt, on the other side of the works. They threw over an empty whiskey bottle, to show us what they had to drink; and we threw back crackers, to let them know what we had to eat.

The next day we were ordered to fall back, which we did one at a time, without loss. After that the fight settled down to a regular siege. Our sharp-shooters and artillery kept up a brisk fire to protect our men while working in the approaches. Sometimes all our artillery opened fire at once. You may imagine, but I cannot describe the scene, when one hundred and eighty pieces of cannon are firing together. In the night, the scene is terribly grand. The balls crossing and recrossing each other in their fiery circles, as they go shrieking through the air, seem like so many fiery serpents; and then the bombardment from the gun and mortar boats, together with the bursting of shells and deafening roar of cannon, make it a scene of imposing grandeur. By tireless vigilance and unceasing labor and fighting, we had run a sap up to the enemy's main fort, and had dug a mine under it, in which was deposited eighteen hundred pounds of powder.

At 4 o'clock P. M. on the 25th of June every thing was ready for the grand explosion. Our division was ordered out in line of battle, with our regiment in the advance in the saps, within a few yards of the fort. It was soon announced that the fuse had been lit, and we all stood in breathless suspense awaiting the explosion, which we expected would throw us all to the ground. It soon came, with a dull, thundering sound, that fairly made the earth tremble, and sent a large body of earth and several rebels heavenward.

Both sides immediately opened all the artillery and musketry they could bring to bear upon the contested point. Then, amid clouds of smoke and showers of dirt, and falling timbers, and more terrible fire of musketry, our regiment rushed to the breach, and planted its colors over the breastworks. Our lieutenant-colonel and major both fell at the head of their men, where brave men always fall; and our colonel and adjutant were both severely wounded. The explosion had forced out the earth so as to form a sort of breastwork, over which both parties fought with a desperation amounting almost to madness. The rebels had planted a cannon within 20 feet of us that poured a deadly fire into our ranks; and both sides threw hand-grenades, which made murderous havoc all around.

Of all the fights I have ever been in, this was the most desperate. The dead and wounded lying all around, and the men covered with blood and blackened with powder, fighting like madmen amid the smoke of battle, and bursting of shells, and roar of artillery and musketry, made it a scene to be remembered a man's lifetime.

After we had fought until our guns were so hot and foul that we could not use them, we were relieved by the 20th Illinois. We again returned soon after, and took our turn with the other regiments of our brigade. After we had held this "slaughter-pen" for 36 hours, and lost 300 men in killed and wounded from the brigade, we were ordered to fall back a few yards out of reach of the enemy's infernal hand-grenades. We only failed in our attempt to take the place by storm because it was not possible for mortal men to do it.

On the 4th of July, the enemy, unable longer to oppose our irresistible progress, surrendered this "American Sebastopol" to the unconquerable army of General Grant, after a siege of 48 days. Early in the morning of that memorable day we received orders to get ready to go in and take possession of Vicksburg. You may guess this was the most welcome order we ever obeyed. Our bullet-torn flag was sent for and placed on the courthouse; and our regiment had the honor of taking the lead of the army on its triumphant entry, as it had before taken the lead in storming the breastworks.

This was the most glorious Fourth of July we ever spent, and the proudest day of our lives; yet we could not help but drop a tear of sorrow for the many brave comrades we left sleeping on the battle-field, beneath the little mounds that mark their honored graves.

On arriving at the courthouse, our regiment, or rather the fragment of a regiment that is now left of us, was detailed as provost guard, on which duty we expect to remain for some time.

Notwithstanding the exposure and hardships of the campaign, I have enjoyed the best of health, and by the protecting care of a kind Providence have thus far been impervious to rebel steel and bullets,—I trust for some good purpose. With love to all the family,

I remain your affectionate son,

STEPHEN A. ROLLINS.

LETTER CXXVI.

[Written by Major-general Mitchel—the man of science, humble Christian, and patriot soldier-martyr.]

HEADQUARTERS THIRD DIVISION,
BOWLING GREEN, February, 18, 1862.

MY DEAR BARTLETT—I have to thank you for your letter, and the paper containing results of firing with the Parrot gun. It is not quite what I hoped, but exactly what I expected. I desired to learn whether, at the distance of 900 yards, as many shots had ever been thrown into a target of eight by twelve feet; this kind of record I presume has not been made.

The telegram will have announced to you the abandonment and capture of Bowling Green. On the 8th instant, I received a dispatch from Gen. Buell, asking me to come to Louisville on Friday, for consultation. On Tuesday, it was decided that my division should pass Green River. On

Monday morning, the entire column was in motion at seven A. M. On Monday evening, we were encamped near Roulete's Station, two miles south of Mumfordsville. From valuable information received on Tuesday, I became satisfied that the enemy had been enabled to weaken his force in Bowling Green, and I urged on Gen. Buell the propriety of attempting its capture by a sudden dash, while thus weakened. On Wednesday evening I received my orders to move, and with great caution feel the enemy,—the general doubting whether his force at this point had been much reduced. At six A. M. Thursday, the signal-gun fired, which ordered the advance guard to move. I am proud of this march, for it was executed beautifully. The 4th O. V. C., Col. Kennett, led the column, followed by —— brigade, the 19th and 24th Illinois, the 18th Ohio, and the 37th Indiana: the baggage train in the rear. At seven o'clock precisely, the entire train of the advanced guard had passed the bridge at Rouletes, and the head of the column was fairly under way. I looked with pride, I confess it, on this admirable movement. No confusion, no stragglers, no evidence of undisciplined troops, but thorough soldiers, with high spirits, and a martial look, passed in review before me, as I stood on horseback on the hill, near the bridge, which commanded the entire camp and the whole situation.

The main body, under the command of General D., followed with a precision and promptitude equal to that of the advanced guard.

Bartlett, it was a grand spectacle to see these 12,000 men, now thoroughly organized, moving quietly to their positions, without the slightest confusion, and to feel that all this was the work of a single determined will, steadily but firmly put forth.

My advanced guard encamped twenty-one miles from Green river, and the main body at Bell's Town, about a mile and a half in the rear.

The enemy had obstructed the road by felling trees from either side, with their bushy tops overlapping in the centre. Two companies of engineers and mechanics constituted my pioneer force, and they swept the trees from the way, with a rapidity incredible. Really we met no *obstruction*, as the most dense brush-heap in the road was swept away in fifteen minutes. During the night of the 14th, I made my headquarters at the house of a Mr. Cowts. About ten o'clock, my pickets brought the gentleman into his own house, a prisoner. He had left Bowling Green at five P. M. the same day, and brought valuable information of the burning of the railroad bridge at the time when he left town. He informed me that the turnpike bridge would be burned before daylight, and that although Hardee and Hindman did not know I was on the march south of Green River, they feared it, and hence the desperate measures to protect their greatly reduced force still in the town. I would have moved on at once and attempted a surprise, but for the fact of a heavy snow and rain storm, which lasted nearly all night. At daylight the column was in motion, and the march on Bowling Green will never be forgotten by those who participated in it. The cavalry threw forward scouts, with orders to move down and capture all beyond the enemy's pickets, and to cut off all communication with the town. The troops advanced in splendid order, at a quick-step, along the frozen and snow-covered turnpike. As I formed the line, each regiment sent up thundering cheers, and then shouts for "old Stars" and the "onward to Bowling Green," resounded along the entire column, for more than two miles. Some miles from town, I had no reliable information of the burning of the bridge. Here I found a good Union man; and mounting his son, a boy of thirteen, on a mule, I gave him a pass, and told him to *kill his mule*, and I would give him a five-dollar bill in case he brought me news that the bridge was standing.

I now ordered Loomis's battery of Parrot guns to the head of the infantry, leaving behind the caissons and battery wagons; and now commenced the chase in real earnest. The cavalry came forward at a round trot, followed by myself, and staff, and escort. Then came the artillery, thundering over the frozen turnpike, and pressing hard on their rear, the infantry almost at double-quick.

I received news four miles from town of the running down and capture of some of the Texas rangers who were on outpost duty, and soon after met my mule courier, who announced the firing of the bridge; and now it was a regular work to secure the heavy timbers.

October 11th.—My artillery was in position on a hill commanding the town, and spread out before me lay the Gibraltar of Kentucky.

The railroad depot was crowded, and two locomotives with steam on were working up a train. I determined at least to break up that movement, and when the first percussion shell went whizzing on its signal duty, to announce our arrival, and fell with loud explosion just beyond the engine, I felt that my work for the present was done. I walked into a building near by, which the enemy had just evacuated, sat down, and wrote a dispatch to General Buell. A flag was tied to the railing of the railroad bridge, and at one P. M. the firing ceased. The enemy, who had no suspicion even of our active approach, were taken completely by surprise, and our bombshells gave them the first intelligence of our arrival. They fled with the greatest precipitation. Hindman's brigade scattered in all directions, leaving their guns and baggage, which fell into our hands to a great extent.

I now determined, if possible, to pass the river. The enemy had failed to destroy our flatboat, which we found three miles below town; and during the night the advanced guard crossed the river with incredible labor, passing the cavalry horses down a rocky, precipitous river-bank by a ladder or steps of wood laid in the rocks, on which bags of bran were laid from the mill to prevent slipping. At daylight we entered a desolate and deserted town. The depot was fired by our shells, and lay in ruins. One locomotive had been hulled by a percussion shell, and stood on the track; some platform-cars and one horse-car stood near it. A six-pounder on the track was smashed in a platform-car, and was near the depot. A large amount of stores and great heaps of corn were on fire. Our troops soon occupied the town. Pickets and outposts were posted, and a patrol under a provost-marshal ordered. Colonel —— was left in command, and I crossed the river to prepare means to pass the division, with its train, over. Our boats are ready, our roads are finished, and as I write the artillery is moving on the turnpike to the lower ferry. It has been an herculean labor to build a boat and construct roads in mud, and slush, and rain. But it is done, and this morning at daylight we advance on Nashville.

Ever truly your friend,

O. M. MITCHEL.

LETTER CXXVII.

BALTIMORE, Md., Club-house, July, 1863.

You will, doubtless, be surprised when you see the stamp upon this paper. This morning our company was ordered to "pack up," and get ourselves in marching order. We were marched into the city to take possession of the Maryland Club-house, which has been seized by the order of General Schenck. So here we are, having full possession of a most splendid house, furnished luxuriously, and situated in the most fashionable part of the town. Our sentries at the front-door sit in splendidly carved chairs, and the rest of us pass in and out at our pleasure. We are having a most enjoyable time, though I think it will be short lived, as we expect to return in a few days.

They have got up a story here, within a few hours, that the expelled members are going to try to retake their club-house, so we have to keep a strong guard. In looking over the visitor's book, I see numerous names, even as late as the beginning of the week, with C. S. A. and C. S. N. opposite, written in full; also the name of the one who introduced them to the club.

I am writing on a large library table, around which we are gathered, some ten or twelve fellows, while the rest are playing billiards in a room adjoining, which contains three fine tables—so you see we have some relaxation to "temper the stern realities of war."

ROLAND GREENE MITCHELL,
7th Regiment, N. Y. V.

LETTER CXXVIII.

NEWBERN, N. C., July 25th, 1863.

WE have just returned from another march of six days' duration. We started from camp on July 18th, at three o'clock in the morning, and were in the saddle from that time until we got back to camp again. The sixth day out we arrived at Rocky Mount, on the Wilmington and Weldon railroad. As we charged into the town, there was a train of cars just ready to start, which was captured. Several rebel soldiers started to run for the swamp. I pursued and captured three, and brought them in. Myself and H. H. Hall, of Co. E, were sent on picket, and were not withdrawn. The column had marched about three hours before we knew they had gone: we were fourteen miles behind, in the enemy's country. We expected to join the army at Tarboro. Judge of our surprise when we found it deserted by the Union troops. Nevertheless, we advanced at a good round pace. When we were about half way through the town, four rebel soldiers placed themselves across the street, at about one hundred yards distance, and coolly drew up their pieces, and fired at us as though they were firing at a target. The first one fired point blank at me, and came very near knocking me from my horse. I loosed my carbine, but it missed fire. Then, drawing my revolver, I gave my horse the spur, and was alongside of them in an instant. I should have killed the one that fired at me had they not surrendered. They dropped their guns without orders, and I could not have the heart to shoot them. Hall snapped his pistol at them, but it missed fire. We got things arranged quickly, and started our prisoners on. We found Sparta also deserted by our troops. We had ridden about fifty miles that day, and were tired and hungry, but there was no alternative but to push on, and overtake the column, if possible. At length, too much fatigued to go further, we bivouacked in a door-yard, and fed our horses on whatever we could find. I told the boys to lie down—there were three of us—and I would stand the "first watch" of the prisoners. I laid down on my saddle, and tried to think of home and friends, in order to keep awake, but it was of no use: if I'd had Jeff. Davis to watch, I couldn't have kept awake. I slept till three o'clock in the morning. I then hurried forward as fast as I could, and just before daylight I heard talking in front of us. I thought it a relief picket, and told the boys that we might be fired upon, as it was dark.

In a few minutes a musket-shot was fired—then a dozen—then a whole volley. Some one shouted, "Don't fire, for God's sake, it is your own men!" All was still. I gave the order, "Forward." They heard it; turned a battery on us, and rained a perfect shower of canister, and short-range shell, which flew around our ears like hail. The prisoners were badly frightened. We fell back. At daylight we discovered that we had narrowly escaped capture, as we had got into a rebel encampment. The column, we found, had deviated from the main road. We took their track with two prisoners (two having escaped when we retreated), and joined the column in about half an hour, turning over my prisoners to the provost, and reporting to my company.

C. F. WAKEMAN,
Corporal, Co. E, 3d N. Y. Cavalry.

LETTER CXXIX.

November 29th, 1855.

I suppose that there are in the hospital one thousand rebels, sick; and to think how they are treated, to what our poor men are at Richmond! Oh, for another Luther, Knox, or Wesley, that he might arise in the strength of the Almighty, and stir the heart of the whole North to arise as one man, and go forth to deliver our poor fellows from those vile dens of filth and starvation! But it would not be right to treat their men as they treat ours. That is not the law of Christ. We must return good for evil; but, then, I don't believe in returning too much of it to traitors.

I am told that some of those beautiful white-bonneted sisters are better to the Johnny Rebs, than to Union sick. There are a great many visitors here, to see their rebel friends, and bring them nice things.

Yours, truly,

LLOYD KNIGHT.

LETTER CXXX.

THE SABINE EXPEDITION.

MY DEAR COUSIN—In compliance with your request, I will give you a description of the "Sabine Expedition." A year has passed since it became a matter of history, and I fear the lapse of time has abated whatever interest may have attached to it, when its events were fresh. Nevertheless, it forms part of the record of the rebellion, and therefore deserves to be remembered. It was the first invasion of the State of Texas. The object was to gain a foothold in the State, by which future military operations might be conducted. Besides, no part of Texas was under control of our armies, and danger was apprehended from separate negotiation between the people and the French in Mexico. Hence it was deemed necessary to plant the national flag on Texan soil.

Accordingly, on Thursday, Sept. 5th, 1863, a division of the 19th Army Corps, commanded by Brigadier-General Weitzel, embarked in transports, and assembled in Atchafalaya Bay. Another division, commanded by Brigadier-General Emory, embarked on the following day at New Orleans. The proper amount of artillery, quartermaster and commissary stores, and a small detachment of loyal Texan cavalry, were also placed on transports.

The expedition was organized by Major-General Banks. It was commanded by Major-General Franklin. The headquarters of General Franklin were established on board of the steamboat Suffolk—a small North River craft, not intended for service at sea, or in the rough waters of the Gulf of Mexico. Her history was not such as to inspire confidence in her passengers. She was formerly called the Niagara, and was wrecked when General Banks took his expedition to New Orleans. After her performance on that occasion, a change of name, and a new coat of paint, did not add any thing to her seaworthiness. Our only hope of reaching *terra firma* again rested in fair weather.

General Weitzel, with his division, started from his rendezvous in Atchafalaya Bay one day in advance of the main body of the fleet. The destination of the expedition was a profound secret, known only to the general officers. The orders divulging it were issued to the commanding officer of each vessel at the mouth of the Mississippi River.

These directed the command to proceed to Sabine Pass, on the coast of Texas.

Sabine Pass is the narrow entrance to Sabine Lake, which is the outlet of the Sabine River. It was protected by an extensive earthwork, mounting seven heavy guns. At the foot of the Pass it is three quarters of a mile in width; and there are two channels, one on either side, separated by oyster-banks. These channels were imperfectly known to us. The water is about five feet in depth.

Our fleet consisted of about fifteen transports, and four small wooden gunboats, viz., the Clifton, Sachem, Arizona, and Granite State. Captain Crocker, of the Clifton, commanded the naval operations.

It was arranged, as part of the plan, that these four gunboats and Weitzel's division, having started one day in advance, should enter Sabine Pass during the night, guided through the channel over the bar by signal-lights displayed by two other gunboats stationed there on blockade duty, and effect a landing at daybreak in the morning. By some mistake, these lights were not displayed, nor were there any gunboats stationed there. Consequently our gunboats and transports missed their way, passed the appointed place without knowing it, and did not find Sabine until Monday evening, several hours after our arrival.

When we arrived, none of our advance vessels being in sight, we supposed General Weitzel had entered the harbor and effected a landing. We therefore pushed boldly in across the bar, and approached the fort. Before we got under its guns, however, the absence of any signals from the shore aroused a suspicion that something had gone amiss, and our people were not there. We put back again, and recrossed the bar. This was a perplexing situation, and continued for five or six hours. What had become of

Weitzel's division and the gunboats? We lay out of the range of the fort during the afternoon, anxiously revolving this question in our minds. Finally, the missing vessels made their appearance, and the mystery was explained. This mistake prevented our taking the enemy by surprise, as we expected to do, in the gray of the morning. We had been in full view of them during Monday afternoon and night, and they had ample time to make preparations to resist us. At a council of war, held in the evening, it was determined to open the fight at daybreak the next morning, Tuesday. The plan was as follows: Three of the gunboats—the Clifton, Sachem, and Arizona—were to advance against the fort, and, under full head of steam, rush by it, discharging broadsides of grape and canister, so as to drive the rebel gunners from their guns, in the same manner as Admiral Farragut ran by forts Jackson and St. Philip in the Mississippi River, during the attack on New Orleans. At the same time a body of troops was to be landed under the protection of the gunboat Granite State and create a diversion in favor of the navy, by assaulting the fort in the rear. We entered the Pass according to the programme; but one of the gunboats and some of the transports ran aground in the shoal water, and we were detained several hours. At three o'clock in the afternoon we were all afloat again, and moved forward. At ten minutes past three, the first gun was fired by the Clifton, in the advance, followed by the Sachem and Arizona, the Granite State keeping somewhat behind to cover the landing of the troops. No reply was made by the rebels. Our heavy shells fall inside of the fort, and throw great volumes of dirt into the air. Yet not a rebel is to be seen. The guns are distinctly to be seen, but where is the garrison? Is the fort deserted, and no resistance intended? The

Clifton is now within five hundred yards of the fort, and in the opposite channel and directly abreast of it is the Sachem. The Arizona is some distance behind the Sachem. The Clifton is pouring in shells from the thirty-pounder Parrot in her bow, while the others are rapidly delivering broadsides. All is still silent in the fort, and no human being can be seen. The discipline of the rebel garrison is perfect, or curiosity would overcome it, and heads would appear over the ramparts. We were beginning to believe that our advance would not be resisted, and an easy victory awaited us, when suddenly the rebel gunners leap into their places, and their heavy guns belch forth their hostile thunder.

The battle has fully opened on both sides, and the excitement of the spectators on board of the transports is intense. Unfortunately, the Clifton has run aground, and we can distinctly see that, although her engine is still working, she does not move forward. The Arizona, too, seems to be hard aground, for she makes no progress whatever. The Sachem still steadily advances, and the rebels turn their attention wholly to her. Their shots penetrate both her sides and ricochet over the water beyond. The sixth shot burst her steam-pipe. A dense volume of steam enveloped her; her engine ceased working, and she lay helpless in the stream. A few more shells were fired by her, and then all was quiet on board.

The enemy next trained their guns on the Clifton, which was still unable to move. She could reply with her bow gun only. In a short time a similar cloud of steam rose from her decks, and the engine stopped. Her steam-pipe had been cut, and she too was disabled, and at the mercy of the rebels.

The Granite State, for some reason never fully explained, did not take the position assigned to her, and afforded no protection to the transports which contained the body of infantry to be landed. General Weitzel consequently found it impossible to land at the designated point. The rest of the coast was swampy and impracticable, and nothing could be done until the Granite State took her appointed position. She failed to do this; and therefore, through the fault of a part of the navy, no diversion was made in favor of the other part. Her commanding officer was afterwards court-martialed for disobedience of orders and bad conduct; with what result, I have not heard. It was evident that we had been whipped; and, accordingly, General Franklin sent me in a small boat to direct the captain of the Granite State to rescue the Sachem, by towing her away. Before this could be done, however, the Sachem and Clifton had surrendered, and the Arizona had retreated. Signal was then made to the entire fleet to withdraw across the bar, and one after another the vessels started in retreat. The gunboats shamelessly led the way, instead of moving in the rear for the protection of the unarmed transports, and the Granite State was among the first to gain the waters of the Gulf. Here the troubles of our military family on board the Suffolk began. As soon as the retreat commenced, two rebel steamers made their appearance, and steered directly for us. They were known to be gunboats protected by cotton bales. The Suffolk was bringing up the rear, and soon ran hard aground. This was somewhat of a predicament. The rebel cotton-clads drew nearer and nearer; there was nothing between us and them to check their advance, and we were perfectly defenceless, not having a gun on board. One of the transports, seeing our situation, threw a hawser to us and attempted to draw us off; but our progress was at the rate of a mile an hour, and gave us no hope, for the bar was two miles distant. Another transport, loaded with cannon, prepared one of them for action, and lay alongside of us. The prospect of such an unequal contest was rather exciting, and the result could hardly be doubtful. It seemed that we were doomed to become an easy prey. Fortunately, just at this time, the Arizona also ran aground not far from us. This frightened the rebel boats, and after considerable manœuvring, and keeping us in suspense for some time, they returned to the fort, and towed away the captured Clifton and Sachem. During the evening we succeeded in getting off, and once more reached the deep water outside.

Our loss in the action was two gunboats, small but well armed, and about three hundred prisoners. We had failed to effect a landing, and it was found necessary to return to New Orleans. Even if it had been possible to renew the attack after the exhibition of cowardice by the two remaining gunboats, the delay attending further experiments would have been out of the question. The troops and animals were beginning to suffer from want of water, and a supply could not be had except by returning to the Mississippi.

It was now ten o'clock P. M., very dark, and the sea rough. The Suffolk, while running about among the different vessels lying at anchor, delivering orders to them, collided with the Continental, a large screw steamship. I will not attempt to describe the scene that followed. The two vessels swung around, and lay alongside of each other. Each wave dashed them together, and the crashing of the sides of the untrustworthy Suffolk induced the belief that she would be knocked to pieces. On examination of the pilot-house, engine-room, &c., it was discovered that the captain and crew had deserted their posts, and leaped on board of the Continental. Nothing remained for us but to follow their example. Although the leap was extremely dangerous, all escaped, excepting, I believe, one or two soldiers, who were drowned. On the Continental were fifteen hundred panic-stricken soldiers, who could not be made to believe they were not sinking, and the darkness and the roar of the sea increased their terror.

As soon as order was restored, General Franklin sent an officer in a small boat to examine the Suffolk. He reported that she was not materially injured; the damage was in her false bottom, and above the water-line. The captain and crew were forthwith ordered back to their posts, and we likewise returned to the ill-starred craft.

The following morning we started for the Mississippi River. The passage lasted two days, and was highly exciting. The weather was very rough at times, and we had lost confidence, not only in the Suffolk, but also in her officers. Occasionally the water in the hold would gain on the pumps, and things looked rather blue for us. At one time it was thought that the ship was about to break into two parts, and we anxiously watched the movements of the beam, which indicated the working of the gap. By shifting the coal and horses in the hold, and extra labor at the pumps, we guarded against this catastrophe. Several of the transports had lost their smoke-stacks, and one of them had cast overboard two hundred and fifty mules. The poor animals had been in the water several hours when we passed, and were still floundering about. One by one they uttered their final scream, and went down! It was one of the most mournful sights I ever witnessed. It was a great relief from continuous excitement when, during that night, we descried Southwest Pass lighthouse, at the mouth of the Mississippi.

Thus ended the Sabine expedition, the first invasion of Texas. Its failure was owing to several causes. The rebel fort was stronger and more heavily armed than was supposed, and more than a match for the insufficient naval force sent against it. Our imperfect knowledge of the channel was also a source of great weakness. Perhaps there might have been a different result if the blockading gunboats had displayed the concerted signal-lights. We might then have taken the enemy by surprise, and gained a foothold without a contest. No blame whatever can attach to the officers who were responsible for the execution of the plans. Every possible precaution was taken to insure success, and we must regard our defeat as one of the unlucky chances of war. Whether an invasion of Texas was wise,—it being entirely cut off from the rest of the rebel Confederacy by that impassable barrier, the Mississippi river, and utterly unable to render assistance to the rebel cause,—I will not pretend to discuss.

Immediately after the failure of the naval attack, an overland campaign was inaugurated, with the same object in view. Before it had penetrated far into the interior it was discovered to be impracticable. A third campaign was directed against Texas last spring. This produced a concentration of the rebel forces of the Trans-Mississippi department, and ended in the Red River disaster. I cannot but think it would be prudent to let Texas alone until the rebellion is quelled elsewhere, and then turn our attention to it; if, indeed, it would be necessary to do so.

Affectionately,

GEORGE M. FRANKLIN,
Captain and Aide-de-camp.

LETTER CXXXI.

Vicksburg, Miss., Nov. 18th, 1863.

How this war has developed the noble and self-sacrificing traits of character in the people of the North! Many a man has shown himself a hero who would otherwise have lived and died in comparative obscurity. How much of heroic fortitude, high-toned patriotism, and self-denying devotion to the cause of truth and right, has been manifested by the American women since the commencement of the struggle! In my opinion, such women as Mrs. Swissholme and Mrs. Livermore should occupy a place in history equal to that of the greatest and best men the country has ever produced. Who shall say that the age that produced Florence Nightingale and Grace Darling has forever passed away? How different has been the conduct of the Northern ladies from a class of beings known by the very significant soubriquet of "copperheads." Instead of trying to encourage and cheer us amid our trials and perils, they have sought by every means in their power to injure us, by throwing obstacles in our paths, basely misrepresenting us at home, and depriving us of a voice in State affairs; seeking to render all our efforts of no avail, by giving all their sympathies, and rendering all the assistance in their power, to the rebellion we are trying to crush, thus making themselves far more despicable than their rebel brethren of the South. Their shameless acts and treasonable language have made them the equals in guilt of their prototypes, Judas Iscariot and Benedict Arnold. "May a traitor's doom be theirs," is the prayer of every true patriot; and by no man is the prayer uttered with more unction and sincerity than by the soldier.

Harry Washburn,
1st —— Battery.

LETTER CXXXII.

Vicksburg, Miss., Nov. 18th, 1863.

In the name and on the part of the "Vicksburg Literary Association," I heartily thank you and your colaborers in this graceful and charitable work, and assure you that we appreciate your kindness none the less that we are strangers, since it proves plainly that the great heart of the gallant North is throbbing with a glow of patriotism that puts those to shame who dare assert that "the people are tired of the war." We are tired of it, but not as they mean the word; and we will not be tired of it so long as a single rebel raises an arm against our country and our flag. Sooner than lay down my arms till rebellion is extinct, I would dig my grave in these trenches of Vicksburg, that we worked so hard to win. Tell your copperhead acquaintances they are insuring to themselves a fearful retribution, "when this cruel war is over," by their opposition to a just and generous government; and tell them one says so who knows the temper of the soldiers with regard to them and their designs.

You ask if I ever feel discouraged. Seriously, I do not. We have had backsets in the conduct of the war, for which *somebody* is to blame; but I do not lay the blame of any particular accident on any one, conceiving that the nation needed chastisement for national sins. And looking up to the brave old banner of our loves and hopes, and beyond it to Him who established us a nation, and who so long hath blessed us with more prosperity than any other people ever enjoyed, not excepting even His own chosen Israel, I recognize the fact that He is a God of justice, and that He will speed the right. The thought of the blessings and prayers coming to us from Northern homes cheers us through the long tedium of camp life, and nerves our weakened arms in the hour of battle. Yes, even when our lot comes to fall, such soft memories, pointing as they do to the land where there are neither strifes nor contentions, nor battlings, cheer the dying soldier, almost as if the soft hands of loved ones were wiping the death-damps from his brow.

WILL McLAIN,
Of Richmond, Va., 82d Regt. Ohio Vols.

LETTER CXXXIII.

You ask, "what do I think of the aspect of the military horizon?" This you asked last July, soon after this city (Vicksburg) fell into our hands. We were then full of hope and encouragement, having recently obtained many decisive victories. Now comes another impending crisis, and I hope, within thirty days, we shall hear of more and greater victories. We are now rejoicing over political victories at the ballot-box, and the horizon is evidently clear: soon the morning of peace will dawn; the Union *will* be re-established; the nation will be purified; the oppressed will all be free, and God will accomplish his vast designs, and make this now distracted people one of the greatest and most prosperous nations in the world. Already the freedmen here are enjoying their liberty in a greater degree than one could have supposed. Prejudice against color is fast going away, and the negroes, anxious to learn to read and write, provide for themselves, and show themselves men, will soon prove to the white race that they are not such an inferior race as they have been represented to be.

J. G. NIND,
127th Ills. Vols.

LETTER CXXXIV.

Vicksburg, Miss., Nov. 18th, 1863.

You ask me to "tell some of my own deeds of martial prowess." Now, my dear friend, that is a sensitive question. Suppose I have never performed any? I am the color-sergeant of the Ninety-fifth Ill. Vols. You have read all about the forty-seven days' siege of Vicksburg—*I was there.* And during the bloody battles that preceded the fall of that rebel stronghold—*I was there.* Our regiment lost one hundred and seventy-eight men during those terrible conflicts; but, God be thanked, the victory was ours. And on that memorable 4th of July, 1863, never to be forgotten, I had the joyful pleasure and honor of planting, with my own hands, the "stars and stripes" of my country's flag on the strongest fortress of my country's foes!

S. A. Rollins,
95th Ill. Vols.

LETTER CXXXV.

Vicksburg, Nov. 19th, 1863.

Have you concluded that the Western boys are not *grateful* for the kind remembrance of them by those who guard the hearth-stones of our own North (*one North*, from Cape Cod to San Francisco), or that they have not learned to read? Or do you wonder if the Christian Commission have carelessly failed to make good their engagements with the people?

In any of these possible surmises you are wrong; to show which is my present duty and pleasure.

Perhaps you are wondering who of the "Fourteenth Wisconsin" has the audacity—but wait just an instant.

There was *a little bag :* and now you know the whole matter in substance. I will tell you a few of the particulars.

We have a literary society here, albeit no man is certain of being left here one day after another, and it is on this wise. The good "Commission" have occupied the basement of one of the churches here, with a reading-room, where also are daily prayer-meetings, occasional lectures, singing schools, &c., and on Tuesday evening our society, mentioned.

On Tuesday last, the editor of our magazine *pulled* on a very mysterious expression of countenance, and announced a "telegram received from Maine," at the office of the magazine, and to be made known to the members of the society in the course of the evening. The event of the matter was the distribution of a *sack* full of *bags* to the boys, who hastened to their quarters in more than *usual glee*, each to light his candle and explore.

Of course I did my own share in the exploring line, with no needless delay. I am thankful for the kind thoughtfulness shown to a *stranger*, known only as one fighting for a cause dear to both.

The bag of *comforts* will be permanently assigned a post of honor and usefulness in my knapsack.

The ginger, pepper, and other items of like rank, though rather scarce in the army, all have useful qualities which are well remembered. The sugar, after undergoing a critical inspection by the captain, has been pronounced genuine Muscovado; the tea, by the same authority, is real black tea—the furthest possible remove from the "marsh hay" article usually dealt to soldiers. On properly august occasions, possibly not till our next weary march, I propose to submit the article to a final and decisive test.

Pins and needles, linen thread and yarn, were cordially

welcomed. A number of *complaining toes* will be presently *comforted*. To be sure, I had some thread, brought from home; but you know how thread will snarl when a man takes hold of it,—and I had carried this so long, it was in a terrible state of confusion. But I am glad you did not rob yourself of a thimble; for though I count myself pretty good at plain-sewing, I never could learn to use a thimble. And passing by many other things, I come to the letter, whose hopeful words of trust will be often called to mind in the future. It was written in Maine, but patriots know no sections. Maine is a part of my country, as Wisconsin is of yours. Virginian soldiers fought side by side with us from Illinois and Wisconsin, here at Vicksburg, and many of our best regiments are in the "Army of the Potomac." Let us be glad over the successes all along our far-extended battle-line, in the last few months. But we need not a whit less to look earnestly to Providence for direction that the coming peace may be more than a truce, to break out again in discord, after a little season, as it *certainly* will, if we do not do more wisely than our fathers did when they compacted the old Union.

HASSELTINE DUNTEN,
Co. 14th Wisconsin Volunteers.

LETTER CXXXVI.

THE SPY.

BRANDY STATION, Dec. 13th, 1863.

MY DEAR LITTLE COUSINS—Each a note in your own handwriting! What could I prize more highly than those two original mementoes of friendship? In them was contained much in little. Did you know that there are few persons in this beautiful world of ours who can speak volumes in a very few words. You have really done it. These missives of love shall ever be kept by me, for the purpose of remembering those "little people," who thought of a certain one; a soldier in a far distant country, who is struggling for his and their country's existence. Now, some "folks" are ignorant and simple enough to think and say that children are of no consequence; but what would society or the community at large be without them? Worse than a desert drear. Why, to have those little innocent, cheerful, and always playful people excluded, would be worse than death! We would all plead that time should end with the setting sun; for they, and they only, make the world what it is—happy or unhappy. So, my dear little cousins, bear in mind that your two little missives will be always carried next the spot that clarifies my blood,

"When the smoke of the roaring cannon surrounds me,
And the lightning of battle gleams brightly about me!"

What have I in my possession to send you, to show that I am of that class that can appreciate favors? A medal? Yes—a medal; and one which I purchased for the express purpose of wearing into battle, so that, providing I had been unfortunate and met the fate of many of my comrades, I could easily have been recognized by it. But, thanks to *One*, who is Ruler over all, it never had the opportunity of proving its usefulness. My name, place of residence, regiment and company, all the battles I was ever engaged in, up to Chancellorsville, is inscribed upon it; besides, there is attached to it the photograph of our old division commander, General Kearney, who had the misfortune to run against an obstacle in the dark, in the shape of a rebel minié ball, which caused instant death.

Above the photograph is a red square badge, representing the 1st division, 3d corps, Army of the Potomac.

There is a story connected with the medal, which is very interesting. Please listen a little while longer, and you shall hear it. The man of whom I purchased it had a roving commission as sutler, in the Army of the Potomac. He was known by every officer and soldier as a sutler, poet, musician, singer, ventriloquist, magician! He was also known as a professed Christian, a chaplain, an agent for the American Tract Society, and soldier's friend! He was a smart, shrewd hypocritical character—one that would take the advantage of a person the first opportunity. It appeared to me that *money* was all he cared about while he lived. Money, money, money; he would do any thing for money.

The last time I saw him was on our way back from the Pennsylvania campaign. He had been caught, tried, condemned as a spy, and sentenced to be hung on an appletree, southeast of Frederic City, Md. I saw him three days after, or rather his body, still hanging from the tree! He was to hang there five days and five nights. He made a full confession of his guilt after *the rope had been placed* about his neck! He confessed that he had been a rebel spy ever since the war broke out, and had been the cause of thousands of our troops being killed, wounded, and captured. The soles of his boots were *one and a half inch thick!*—it was the place where he deposited all of his important documents. I could tell you much more about his life since I became acquainted with him. In truth, the history of his career in the army would be worth reading. Twenty sheets of foolscap paper closely written over would not contain it! Suffice it to say, that it took *him* forty-seven long years to find out that the penalty of sin is death.

Now, little cousins, please accept this medal as a sort of romantic present from me. Now please don't stop writing, for your letters are better than the best.

LIEUT. HARVEY M. MUNSELL.
Penn. Vet. Vols.

LETTER CXXXVII.

"COMFORT BAGS."

VICKSBURG, 1863.

AFTER the closing exercises of the "Vicksburg Union Literary Association," the members remained; for we have always a large *audience,* and their names being called, each receives a bag out of *the bag.*

I need not say that the contents were all very acceptable, for *needles* are never *needless* to soldiers; while handkerchiefs, in the army, are like *hens' teeth,* or "angels' visits," *very* "few, and far between;" and the *condiments,* inclosed in the bags, prove a very acceptable subsequent to the "Attic salt" with which our meetings are *spiced!*

And if colds are not *kept down* from the ginger, etc., contained in my bag, I am very much mistaken. As for the thread and yarn, I must confess that soldiers have a very bad way of "darning" socks *verbally,* and throwing them away; also, that they generally subscribe to the maxim which declares "a hole more honorable than a *patch,*" since the first may be the result of *recent accident,* while a patch shows *premeditated poverty.* With all the incentives to a better condition that I now possess, however, I shall endeavor to improve my state.

W. M. McLAIN.

To Miss SARAH SOUTHWORTH,   32d Ohio Vols., Inf., 2d Brigade.
    Winthrop, Maine.

LETTER CXXXVIII.

Near Culpepper, December 31st, 1863.

Time passes very slowly here in camp. Nothing to excite or keep the mind enlivened. Far from home and friends, separated from all we hold dear on earth, what is it that binds us here? Why do we find so many *volunteering* to leave their homes, wives, children, parents, and sweethearts, to camp on the field of battle, to face the cannon's mouth, to undergo hunger, thirst, and every deprivation, and perhaps death in its worst form? Can any one imagine it is the *choice* of these men to live such a life? I answer, it is not in human nature: there must be something else to lead them on. Is it love of their country? I think it is. When true men see an armed force rising up to destroy that government under which they live, and for which their forefathers fought, they cannot stand still and see their country go to ruin without a struggle: none but cowards or traitors would do it. We have had a hard struggle, but the times are brightening. We look forward and dream of peace! May it come with all its blessings!

You ask "how cannonading sounds?" You must fancy you hear a hundred thunders at once, and as many hissing serpents flying through the air; then as many *little thunders* all around you, for the bursting of shells, to say nothing of the fire of the musketry and disaster surrounding you; and then you have but a *faint* idea of it!

George M. Doff,
1st Penn. Art., Battery B.

LETTER CXXXIX.

Germantown U. S. Hospital.

My dear Mother—Keep up your heart: if I am spared to come home, I will make you comfortable and happy in your old age. When my time is up, I will claim you, if I don't make up my mind to join the army again, if there is another *call for men:* but *don't be angry,* if I say I love my country's cause and the dear old flag, I may say, better. Do you blame me for doing so? Although I have a ball in my cheek, it will not stop me from *facing* the enemy. O dear Mother, if I *should* fall, you live in a noble country. It will not let you want, as you will be entitled to a pension. Dear Mother, I hope you will be praying for me, and I hope I will soon be able to rally round our dear old flag once again; and don't be afraid but we will shout the battle-cry of Freedom.

I must conclude, and remain your affectionate son, till death.

EDGAR WADHAMS,
Company A, 140th Regt.

LETTER CXL.

HEADQUARTERS, &c., KNOXVILLE, Oct. 2d, 1863.

DEAR MOTHER—I think I have told you of our campaign, up to the occupation of this place, which we reached September 3d; and after our three weeks' life on horseback, and in tents, dropped suddenly into semi-civilization. I say *semi,* for though our mansion is spacious, yet are the floors carpetless, and the beds sheetless. But we immediately got into our best clothes, and shook off riding-boots with delight; and though the pair I substituted have large holes in the toe, and are otherwise dilapidated, yet such slight matters are not thought of. But we did not enjoy our Capua very long, for, three days afterwards, Sunday, the General informed us we would start for Cumberland Gap, at daylight the next morning. And off we went about twenty-two miles very pleasantly, with no greater mishap than my horse casting a shoe, causing much temporary loss of temper, until the lucky discovery of a rustic blacksmith restored the shoe and my serenity.

Lunched in the front yard of a house, wherein abode the prettiest girl I've seen in Tennessee—a charming-featured, high-bred, intellectual-looking damsel of fifteen, who used horrible grammar, and who, doubtless, in a few years will follow her mother's example, and smoke a pipe. The mother, a good-looking woman of forty—born in Ohio, by the way—discoursed very sensibly and patriotically to us; notwithstanding she tilted her chair on two legs, and puffed at a pipe the while. Manufactured cloth has been beyond the means of these people, though the family were quite well-to-do; and she showed me a coat for her husband, the whole of which she had made in the house—making the cloth and lining, and dyeing the same with colors from bark of trees. Our houses, that night, were simply and scientifically constructed by placing a couple of rails against a high fence, and laying a tent-fly on them, with some hay on the bottoms of these tenements. They were quite comfortable, though somewhat airy about the head. But I use my Zouave overcoat, now-a-days, for a night-gown, and bid defiance to wandering orgies with aid of the hood.

Started soon after daylight next morning, stopping to rest at the house of a kindly old woman, who sat on the door-step, hugging her knees, and talked to us in a quaint, sensible manner, simply quoting much Scripture to prove the reward the rebels were laying up for themselves. She gave us a description of the way they had been harried by the rebs. Her two sons had gone to Kentucky, and enlisted in our army; and the third, a boy, had been, until within a few days, hiding in the woods and mountains, to avoid the rebel conscription. She hoped we would drive the rebels out, and make a "clean thing of it," but feared we would be unsuccessful; and summed up her perplexities with the odd expression, which has become quite a byword with us since: "It's who shall and who shan't, and weuns don't know what will become of none of us." That "weuns" means *we*. The country people in East Tennessee all say *weuns* and *youans*, for *we* and *you*. For instance, I heard one of them say to another: "Waal, if youans can stand it, weuns can." The old lady grieved much over her inability to get tobacco, thereby losing her accustomed pipe; but we made her heart glad by contributing from our stock. Among her peculiarities she had never seen a lucifer match.

Reached Tazewell, about 26 miles, at dusk, and went into camp. Were invited out to supper by some Union people, and had a jolly one, whereat I disposed of enough chicken and hot biscuit to cause Dr. Fowler grave fear for my safety, had he been present. Tazewell has been a very pretty place, mostly built of brick; was about equally divided between Union and Secesh. About a year ago most of the town was burned; by whom, seems rather doubtful, each side accusing the other. Whoever did it, the place presents a striking picture of the ravages of war, the whole of the main street being a mass of ruins. We left there very early Wednesday morning, and reached General ——'s headquarters, about three miles from the Gap, at breakfast time, and found he had demanded a surrender: Col. ——, who commanded the troops on the Kentucky side, had also. They declined. A flag of truce was then out, to which no answer had been returned: so, after waiting a while, the general sent me up with a letter, dated "Headquarters, Army of the Ohio," and signed by him, reiterating the demand for a surrender, stating that I was authorized to wait an hour at his picket for an answer,—rightly judging that Gen. Frazer would get the impression that the whole army of the Ohio was surrounding him, whereas, in reality, the general had only brought a brigade with him. Another officer went with me, a couple of orderlies ahead, bearing the white flag, and we galloped on at a great pace, haste being important. At our outer picket, found a rebel officer waiting an answer to a flag he had sent to Gen. S——. He desired to know if I brought him the answer. I told him nay, and rode on. Presently he came flying after us, told me he was authorized to receive any thing for Gen. Frazer, and would take any letter I brought. I told him I would, if he pleased, ride to their pickets, such being the regular course, which shut him up; but, as we rode on, getting nearer to the Gap, and no rebel pickets appearing, my friend seemed struck with an idea, and leaving us, rode in a hurry homewards. Supposing he had gone to draw his pickets further out, and animated by the laudable desire of seeing as much as possible, I posted after him, crossed the last ridge, and descended into a broad level space, just at the foot of the Gap, shut in by mountains, and looking very much like Franconia Notch. As we reached this plateau, a far away "halt" met our ears, and my *ci-devant* companion appeared in the distance with four others. He halted when near us, and I rode up and presented my letter.

He told me he would bring the answer out. Whereat, I again checkmated him by the information that I was ordered to wait an hour at his pickets: so we betook ourselves to the shade of a tree near by. He put his four dilapidated infantry men in guard over us, lest we should pocket some of his siege-guns, and departed up the mountain to General Frazer's headquarters. A delicious sulphur spring gurgled under the tree. We imbibed the waters thereof, and took a near view of the celebrated citadel of Cumberland Gap. The mountain rose a couple of hundred yards off, seamed in every direction with rifle-pits and batteries. Three casemated batteries were in sight, the embrasures masked with bushes to conceal either presence or absence of guns. The crest on the right was about 1300 feet above us, the one on the left 300 feet lower. The crests were lined with fortifications, and a casemate battery was visible at the head of the Gap.

I had some little talk with the pickets; but a sergeant kept close watch over them, to see they disclosed neither facts nor sympathy. And as the hour vanished and no officer reappeared, we mounted and departed for whence we came. I made my report to the general, and was talking with him over the plan of attack, a deserter having come in while we were out, and brought valuable information, when a flag of truce was reported at our pickets. I went out to receive it, and found my rebel friend of the morning, full of apologies for not having got back before the hour was up. He delivered me a letter, wherewith I posted back to the general, and found the rebels were beginning to draw in their horns, and offered to surrender on condition of being paroled. So another letter was prepared, setting forth the fact that he would be charmed to accede, but couldn't possibly; that an unconditional surrender was the only practicable arrangement; and in fact, that immediately on my return certain operations had been started which it would be impossible to stop. Just as the general signed his name to this, General ——, who had invited us to dine with him, announced dinner; whereat my mouth watered, twenty miles of riding having produced no small appetite. But watering was the only operation my mouth was destined to participate in; for the general coolly handed me the missive, saying he would like me to get up there as soon as possible, as I had to wait there an hour at their pickets. So I swallowed my disappointment, having nothing else to swallow, hoisted my white flag again, and pegged off to the Gap.

I got rather further in than before, and was brought up by a picket of four North Carolina soldiers, a venerable and rebellious sergeant and three homesick boys. I informed the sergeant that I had a communication for General Frazer from General Burnside, whereat he opened his mouth and said, "Wall," and kept it open. Thinking him a fit subject to "come the giraffe over," I continued: "Will you have the goodness to conduct me to General Frazer's headquarters?" "No," said he, "but I'll bring him down here." This was not exactly what I expected; but he "couldn't say no fairer nor that," as Mr. Peggotty phrased it, so I acquiesced, and dismounted to wait at the picket-station. One of the boys was dispatched to "bring General Frazer down." Presently, as I anticipated, the rebel officer of my morning's experience made his appearance, pouched my letter, and departed.

Major ——, the officer with me, a very talkative and facetious person, was soon on the most intimate terms with the picket, and they confided in him very freely, expressing great disgust with the war, and a determination to "bolt" whenever opportunity occurred, as many of their comrades had already done.

I found a soft stone for a pillow, and took a nap. About the end of the hour another long-haired rebel officer arrived, bringing the answer. Of course we had no conversation in regard to it; but from his exceedingly bilious and glum appearance, I inferred they had concluded to give up the ship. And it turned out so when the general opened the letter; whereupon, two of the staff were sent up to announce that the general would come up presently to receive the surrender. Then there was blacking of boots and dusting of coats, and furbishing up generally, that we might enter into our possessions in proper style.

About four o'clock we started up, with a regiment of cavalry behind us. As we approached the Gap, the general, fearing there might be some mistake, and some evil-minded artillerymen send us a present of grape, sent me ahead. I had to raise an impromptu flag—to wit, my handkerchief on my sword. Rode into the works, meeting many rebs lounging around, some sullen, many smiling, and some open in expressions of delight at the state of affairs. Went to Frazer's headquarters, and was introduced to a lot of rebel officers, with whom I was obliged to shake hands, to my intense disgust. Remained there till after dark, and then went back to camp.

October 5th.—Would like to describe the Gap, which we visited next day, but don't feel up to it, and it wearies me now to think of the interminable sandy ascents we toiled up that day; and before we reached the topmost crest there was a jolly view from there, some fifty miles into Tennessee. Dotting a few lakes and streams here and there, it would much resemble the outlook from the Rhigi; the smoky mountains of North Carolina forming the same background in this picture that the Bernese Alps do in that. So, perhaps, on the whole, it *paid*, though I didn't think so, as I painfully plunged and jerked downwards ankle deep in sand. A more desolate, dismal, and abominable place to be stationed at, I cannot conceive of. Here, not an atom of shade to be found; the burning sunshine fires it in summer, and the cold winds have it all their own way in winter. All paths lead either up or down; so locomotion is not an enticing pursuit, and the poor secesh have had nothing to do but sit still and look in each other's dirty faces. The only comfortable thing is plenty of good water from springs; one of which is so eccentric as to seek the light of day near the summit, upsetting the commonly received opinion in regard to the inability of water to run up hill. We corralled our rebel stock on the plain below, counted them, girdled them with bayonets, and early the next morning started them for Camp Chase, to await their time in the exchange mill. I imagine it will be some time before they are ground out. Two or three of the field-officers displayed their chivalry by deserting their commands immediately after the surrender, and, before we had taken possession, escaped into the woods. No doubt they will go home and boast of it as a good thing. Great is Southern chivalry, and such fellows are its prophets. General Frazer distinguished himself by getting rather intoxicated, and vaporing very valorously to some of our officers of what he would have done but for circumstances beyond his control. Possibly General Burnside was one of those circumstances. On Friday, about 2 P. M., we started on our return to Knoxville. Rode about eight miles, and went into camp soon after dark. Rose at three and a half the next morning, breakfasted on a cup of coffee and hard biscuit, and started on a ride to Knoxville. Bouted joyfully along for twenty miles or so, stopped and had the most starving of breakfasts at the house of the charming little Lucinda, of whom I spoke on the way up. Took a nap on the grass thereafter, and went the rest of the way to Knoxville with a rush, reaching here about five o'clock, Saturday afternoon, having made the fifty-eight miles in twenty-seven hours, bringing our headquarters train with us—the which is very fast marching. Took a bath and and dined; felt like giants refreshed with small-beer. Knoxville is beautifully situated, but rather dilapidated with two years of rebel rule. Very few shops open, and nothing to speak of in them. A number of nice people here, no doubt; but after my usual fashion, I am not going out at all. I was introduced to eight young ladies in about twenty minutes, the day the general made a speech; have not called since, and am constantly meeting them in the street, and not recognizing them till they bow—all of which is quite cheerful. A young and feeble mail came in to-day, bringing me one letter from Mr. ——, of Sept., nearly two weeks old: our advices are, you see, worse than Newbern. The mail goes in the early morning, and this budget must be closed. Good-by. Love to all.

Affectionately,

L.

LETTER CXLI.

ADVANCE UPON GOLDSBORO, N. C.

IN December, 1862, McClellan, prevented ostensibly by the difficulty he experienced in supplying his army with shoes, was delaying his pursuit of the enemy after the indecisive battle of Antietam. A move was ordered, on the part of our forces in North Carolina, upon the communications of the enemy in that State; and Major-General Foster advanced upon Goldsboro (the point where the Weldon and Wilmington railway crosses the Neuse river), at the head of a well-appointed force of fifteen thousand men, with a somewhat disproportionate train of light artillery.

My company of the 3d New York cavalry was in this army. The warm sun but bracing air of winter, at the South, made that successful expedition pleasant; and I well remember the light spirits with which our soldiers left Newbern and plunged into the labyrinth of swamps and savannahs which characterize the coast country. The cheerful bivouacs in the pitch-pine forest, lighted by unfailing fires, the merry *insouciance* of a soldier's life upon the march, the romance added by the dangers from our fleet-footed adversaries, to which our cavalry was particularly exposed, furnish memories agreeable to dwell upon.

Kinston, a town fortified by the enemy, was the first point where serious trouble was apprehended. Major-Gen. Evans (familiarly known to his own associates of the army as "Flank Evans," in allusion, I believe, to the length of his lower limbs), held a strong position on a causeway leading towards the town from the east. The principal, and, as the enemy judged, the sole practicable road, ran by this causeway. Another, scarce more than a pathway, called the Vine Swamp road, lay to our left. General Foster resolved to feint on the main road, and to turn the enemy's position by the left. As the head of our column reached the forks of the two roads, the chief of staff rode up to our major, and ordered him, in my hearing, to take his battalion and move up the right-hand road, and having attacked the enemy's pickets, to drive them well home; charge their first position, if he found it practicable; to act as though he had an army at his back, and on returning to light large fires, in order to deceive the enemy into the belief that an army was in bivouac in their front ready to assail their strong position in force on the morrow. Our kind, worthy major—a true volunteer—judged always that he could best secure the co-operation of his officers by imparting to them his plans; so we discussed the character of our undertaking as we rode along, and resolved that we would let the enemy know that it was *our regiment* with which they had to deal.

Fortune favored us wonderfully. The enemy's first picket-post was captured, horse and man; and it was thrown out to a distance of seven miles from the post of the grand guard, a practice common with them, as their horses are very fleet. A second post was taken in like manner, to our great exultation. Two miles further on, the relief guard was surprised at an angle of the road, pursued and overtaken by our videttes. Dismay was painted on the countenances of these last, and from this we rightly judged that the grand guard would be taken unawares, and that its fate was sealed. On we went, the slow march of the column adding to our impatience, till a negro informed us that the house occupied as the guard station lay at the distance of only one mile. "Trot—march!" commanded the major; "Gallop—march, draw pistols!" and the column was under full headway, thundering through the woods, and over the corduroy through the swamps. Not a word was spoken, for we knew not how soon the tables might be turned, and the biter become the bitten. Not much time to think, however; for in three minutes the clearing—with the plantation house in its midst, and the guard drawn up before it, a few figures galloping here and there—came in view. "Charge!" shouted the major. The yell of the cavalry mingled with the sharp spattering sound of the infantry volley, and we dashed in among them. No time to reload, and Colt's pistol at short range makes short work.

Apparently not two dozen loud reports of the pistols,

and thirteen of the enemy lay dying round the house; the rest of the guard of seventy, save the captain escaped on horseback, were prisoners in our hands. All would have been spared, had they surrendered promptly. One rebel dropped his musket, begged and received quarter, and when his pursuer had passed by, raised his piece and fired, missing his man. The cavalry-man turned his horse, deliberately rode up to him, and shot him through the head. The principle "porcere victis" can be carried too far. A few impudent shell were thrown from the mountain howitzer attached to the battalion, into Gen. Evans's face, as it were. The picket station was fired, and after retiring a couple of miles, we lighted fires over a wide space, and rested on our arms. Next day the heavy cannonading told of the battle of Kinston, in which Gen. Evans, having had his right turned by the carrying out of Gen. Foster's plan, lost seven hundred prisoners, and many in killed and wounded, before he could cross, with the remainder of his force, the bridge over the Neuse River, and thus leave the road to Goldsboro unobstructed for Gen. Foster's column to follow. We rested two days, living after the fashion since set by Gen. Sherman in Georgia.

A luckily situated grist-mill furnished us with bread, and the variety of food furnished by the neighboring plantations included every kind of butcher's meat and fowls: so great an improvement on the ordinary soldier's fare, that the men thought it hard that they should not be permitted to "campaign it" all the while. When we came by the Kinston battle-field, the traces of a severe conflict were everywhere manifest. I have nowhere seen the effects of cannon-shot upon the trees of the forest so curious.

Here, too, the sad sight of four officers of the Tenth Connecticut dead, all of whom I knew well, and with one of whom I had played billiards the night before we left Newbern, met my eye. Poor Lieut. Coffin, of the same regiment, shook me by the hand, and professed that he was bearing his injury (his thigh had been just amputated) grandly. He expired, however, in a few hours.

Here I learned of an amusing incident, illustrative of Southern insolence, which happened on the occasion of a flag of truce sent by Gen. Foster, after the battle. The flag was carried by the chief of staff, who held a commission as colonel of the First Loyal North Carolina regiment. Gen. Evans inquired his name and rank, and when he learned the title of his regiment, turned to his staff, and uttered a contemptuous *whistle*. The battle of the Monocacy ended the bad career of this general officer, I believe, a career actively begun at Ball's Bluff.

Pushing on past Kinston, our battalion overtook the army in the afternoon of the second day, drawn up in line of battle, near Goldsboro bridge. The enemy, who had already a considerable force there, had been driven from the ground which he occupied south of the bridge; the bridge itself had been fired by a forlorn hope, and our artillery was pouring into it a convergent fire, to assist in the fall of the timbers, and to prevent it from being extinguished.

The country, generally covered with a dense forest, is more open near Goldsboro, and a clearing, a mile or more in extent, afforded us good opportunity for our operations. A slight rising ground gave us a fine view of the position of the army which remained on the field, for the return line of march had already been taken up, and the scene was beautiful,—the long lines of our blue-coated soldiers, under the folds of the starry flag, contrasting with the shining of the brass Napoleons, and relieved by the more picturesque forms of the cavalry. Soon—enough was judged to have been done—the column began to defile slowly past us, and shortly only Lee's brigade remained, and they were withdrawn under cover, leaving a section of Morrison's battery of the 3d New York Artillery to protect the rear, which we were ordered to support. We took up our position on the left flank of the section, when, to make sure of the complete destruction of the bridge, which was hidden from view by a broad screen of trees along the river, the lieutenant-colonel of my regiment ordered me to take ten men, and go down to the bridge, and report upon its condition.

The railway ran southward across the open space, and I had to urge my horse with much difficulty up the steep sides of the embankment on which it was carried to the bridge. I rode down the track through the screen of woods, and found the bridge to have been completely destroyed; wheeled my horse, and was returning, peering cautiously through the thick undergrowth beneath me, when an individual, in "butternut," and having a musket in his hand, called to me, in uncomplimentary terms and with many expletives, to halt. I remember he used the word Yankee, so that I was at no loss to know whom he was addressing. This demand was instantly repeated by many other similarly attired and repulsive-looking fellows, who now swarmed out of the woods beyond the railway, to the number of a regiment or more.

My tactical words of command came not to my aid. I could only shout to my men to gallop and save themselves; a command they were not loth to obey, but found difficulty therein, on account of the exposed ties of the track, and the narrowness of the embankment, down which it was necessary to go to reach the cleared field again. Such a gauntlet I hope I may never be called upon to run again. It was, in imagination at least, like being blown from the mouth of a cannon, they were so near; and yet, through providential grace, this proved our salvation, for rifles over-carry at short range, and we were so high above them that we all escaped unharmed, though with bullet holes through the clothes of some of the men. I reported to the colonel that I had developed the enemy's position, and could be of use in directing the fire of the section, as I knew of my own personal knowledge where they were. Several shells were accordingly pitched into the right spot; but, as no more was seen or heard of our friends for some minutes, Captain Morrison pronounced it as his opinion that these fellows did not want a fight, and, limbering up, withdrew his pieces to the rear. Our cavalry gave three parting cheers, when suddenly the enemy responded, not with a cheer—that is unknown among them—but with many savage yet ludicrous yelps, and lo! two regiments in "echelon," and I must say, at a distance presenting a fine appearance under the "stars and bars," came over the embankment, and advanced towards us at a double-quick.

> "But on the British heart was lost,
> The terror of that clanging host."

Morrison brought up his six guns, unlimbered them and placed his pieces in battery, in two minutes, and just in time; for the first discharge of shell, which burst too far beyond, encouraged them greatly. I felt relieved when the captain, jumping off his horse and exclaiming, "This won't do!" substituted double charges of canister; the effect of the first of which was to open a lane through the first regiment of a company front, carrying with it the rebel banner.

Captain Belger, of the 1st Rhode Island, now brought

his battery of 24-pound howitzers into position, and the five of the twelve pieces soon *annihilated* the First Regiment (the South Carolina Legion of Pettigrew's brigade of six hundred men), and drove what was left of the other behind the embankment for shelter. Lieutenant Williams, of the 62d North Carolina, whom I afterwards took a prisoner, told me that he was present in this affair, and that the "Legion" lost five hundred and sixty men out of six hundred who went into action. The fact was, the regiment was in the very focus of the fire, and could neither advance nor retreat. They lay down, but this did not save them; for the canister could be *seen*, as it tore up little jets of dust, in skipping over the sandy soil, as thick as drops of rain, and tossing the bodies of the living and the dead, as it struck them lying on the ground. We did not charge, and our lieutenant-colonel was blamed for not ordering the movement; but we had the advantage of active firing, a rare scene in war, and one which so engrosses the memory of all who beheld it, that it can never be obliterated. The lesson was a salutary one, for it is somewhat remarkable that not one hostile shot was fired on the return march to Newbern, where we arrived in three days, and rested for a while from our labors.

ROWLAND MINTURN HALL,
(late) Capt. 3d N. Y. Cavalry Volunteers.

PART FOURTH.

THE BEGINNING OF THE END.

1864.

"When Freedom from her mountain height
  Unfurled her standard to the air,
She tore the azure robe of night,
  And set the stars of glory there!
Flag of the free heart's hope and home,
  By angel hands to valor given!
Thy stars have lit the welkin dome,
  And all thy hues were born in heaven.
Forever float that standard sheet!
  Where breathes the foe but falls before us,
With Freedom's soil beneath our feet,
  And Freedom's banner streaming o'er us?"

LETTER CXLII.

A Soldier's Prophecy.

The dawn of a conquered peace is breaking upon us. Ere another year rolls round, the plaudits of an admiring world will be sounding in our ears, and the nation everywhere rejoicing in praises and thanksgiving over the triumphs of self-government and civil liberty.

And then, who can depict the future glory of America? With an area of over 3,000,000 square miles, comprising almost every variety of soil and climate; possessing all the arts that bless and the sciences that elevate mankind; prosperity and Christianity in every home; the asylum of the oppressed of all nations; the "Land of the free and the home of the brave;" queen of this broad continent and arbitress in the councils of earth's emancipated peoples;—we shall then be the terror of tyrants and the friend of liberty, throughout the world; while each *sovereign* "can look on this picture" of happiness and honor, and say with proud satisfaction, "I, too, am an American citizen." This will be the soldier's reward; the highest, the noblest, the greatest, that ever repaid the true and the brave.

And then, wherever from the rock-bound coast of New England to California's golden shores is heard the busy hum of millions of spinning-wheels, the merry shout of the schoolboy, or shrill whistle of the steam-engine; wherever, from the St. Lawrence on the north to the silvery waves of the Gulf on the south, the iron horse with his thundering train crosses our broad prairies, or the noble steamer ploughs her way through America's mighty waters; wherever the free press, on its holy mission of knowledge and truth, blesses the land, or the winged lightning flashes the news with thought's velocity; wherever the husbandman gathers in his golden harvests for the feeding of the nations, or our merchant ships, whitening every sea, are protected by that proud banner of liberty; wherever and whenever liberty and freedom are proclaimed to man, and above all floats the untorn flag of my country, *we* can look around and say, "Behold the monuments of liberty, and the triumphs of the Union arms!"

SERGEANT S. A. ROLLINS,
95th Illinois Volunteers.

LETTER CXLIII.

Our regiment (59th Massachusetts) supported Martin's battery at the battle of Hanover Court-house, and tore up three miles of track on the Orange and Alexandria railroad. The second day of the "seven days" fight before Richmond I was wounded, at Gaines' Mill, quite severely, a minié ball whizzing through my left shoulder, and disabling me from holding my musket. I was taken prisoner, and marched into Richmond, June 29th, 1862. I was located in the cock-loft of the Libby Prison until July 19th, when I was paroled. At City Point my eyes were gratified at the sight of the star-spangled banner, after they had been *bleared* with looking on the dirty secession rag which floated from the top of the capitol at Richmond. I arrived at David's Island on Thursday, July 24th.

Ward B. Frothingham,
Lieut. 59th Mass. Vet. Vols.

LETTER CXLIV.

Vicksburg, Miss., January 2d, 1864.

Our division is now stationed at this place, but we soon expect to join the "grand army" that is now gathering as the thunder gathereth, under our loved and triumphant General Grant.

The great rebellion seems to be fast approaching a grave of infamy and dishonor, and the only wish of our army here is to be there to help in giving it the death-stroke.

Oh, how I long for that day to come when we shall stand forth once more a free and united nation. I am fully determined to do my own full share of this "awful work," until victory shall crown our arms. But my heart sickens at the thought of our once happy country, now wrenched by civil feuds, and weltering in the blood of brothers. But still I would not give up one single principle of our free institutions to stay this carnage of human life, but rather would carry on the war a hundred years than sacrifice principle for the sake of peace. I think, and hope, and pray that the day is not far distant when the nation will be everywhere rejoicing in thanksgiving and praise for the triumph of liberty, a reunited territory, and the more enduring bonds of national affection.

But the work is not yet done. Many a hard-fought battle must be added to the historic battle-grounds of the '61 war, ere the bloody strife shall cease.

I have yet eighteen months to serve, unless sooner shot.

S. A. ROLLINS,
95th Ill. Vols.

LETTER CXLV.

SANITARY FAIRS.

CAMP KEARNEY, near NEW ORLEANS,
Jan., 1864.

THEY will unite more closely in bonds of love our whole people, working together in the cause of humanity. .....I have been reading in the "Sanitary Com. Bulletin" for December a well-written and affecting article on the great Northwestern Fair. As I read that the rich and poor gave of their abundance and their scant means; that they came hundreds of miles under difficulties; that those who had no worldly goods gave labor, and that "one and all" gave sympathy—there ran through me a thrill of pride that I am of the same people, the great and true elements of whose character is being tested with the fire which either purifies or destroys. All contributions were of little value compared with the great unanimous expression of the people's faith in our armies, our leaders, our country, and in God!

The moral effect of such an exhibition will, I believe, be as valuable and thankfully received as their contributions will be grateful and pleasing to the soldier in the field

---

LETTER CXLVI.

VICKSBURG, Jan. 15th, 1864.

LET us thank our heavenly Father for the many efforts of loyal and patriotic hearts that remember the families of the defenders of our country. I frequently feel sorrowful that I was not able to leave you and the children better provided for. Had I not felt that I could lean upon an Almighty arm that can uphold and sustain you, I never should have enlisted in the service of my country. But, bless the Lord, he can provide a table in the desert for his children! Do I hear a voice saying, "He repents his bargain?" Let the echo come from my soul to those who say such a thing, Never, never! I regard my present calling as most noble and honorable. Our cause is God and Liberty!—more precious than rubies. Four millions of human beings are now to come forth redeemed from the tyrants' chains—from the clutch of this monster iniquity! Hereafter, under the ample folds of our starry banner, no human being is to be sold for shining gold. Liberty and freedom henceforth are to be our country's glory and password: a home and an asylum for the oppressed of all nations.

The church I attend shows the marks of the siege in

three places. It has a nice organ, which is played by a soldier; a choir of soldiers, with one or two lady singers. The chaplains preach alternately, and the audience is mostly composed of officers and privates. Most of the ladies are their wives and daughters, who come down to "Dixie" to spend the winter with their husbands and fathers. In fact, the worship of God is performed by the soldiers.

LETTER CXLVII.

The Green-house.

Vicksburg, Jan. 18th, 1864.

In days as "big with fate" as these that have fallen to our lot, the individual is very apt to lose his individuality, and all his labors go like drops to an ocean, to make the great whole, which is the grand result that people have time to look at. There were, no doubt, many acts of individual bravery at Mission Ridge or Lookout Mountain (I speak of them as representative battles, and refer through them to any and every field that we have won or lost during the war); but "the people" have only time to recognize the fact that a battle was lost or a victory was won, before the quickly passing phantasmagoria calls them to another, perhaps more exciting scene! But if any event can dwell long in a soldier's mind, it is the arrival of news from home, or any thing showing that we are not forgotten in the loyal States. If any persons desire their names to be long remembered, let them write letters to soldiers! They shall certainly gain the meed of long and loving remembrance.

Our regiment once left the paymaster's table to fall in line, when the long-roll was sounded and a skirmish was coming on; but they would leave the fight or mess-table to get the mail at any time!

Do you love flowers? Of course you do. Then I wish you had been with me this afternoon, although it might have made you very sad when you remembered that this was but one case of a hundred—yes, thousands. Perhaps you know that we are building a new set of works (technically, line of works) to protect this good city of Vicksburg from any future irruption of rebels. Well, I used to be something of an engineer (civil); and to-day, in laying out work for my "fatigue-party" to do, I had a new fortalice to lay out. It was plainly marked upon the plot, but I used every means in my power to misunderstand said plot; and why? Because, on going to the place where this little fort was laid down, I found the point of the Bluff to be occupied by a splendidly arranged *green-house*. I reset my instrument and took another view. It was still there! There was no going around it. I went to the civil engineer: told him the circumstances. "I know that," was the reply. Went then to Gen. Leggett, in charge of the post and garrison, and told him. "Go to the chief engineer," said he! No satisfaction there. So went back, and staked out the lines to be dug. Lady came out begging: went back crying. Could not help it. Tried to see it in the proper light, as a "military necessity," but could not. Tried to remember that the rebels brought on the war, and that the war brought on the destruction of property; but I, although *logically convinced*, was *morally doubtful*. Lady's beauty dazzled my eyes and clouded my memory of rebel misdeeds. *Still it had to be done*, so I compromised between my conscience and my duty. I suppose war is the only thing that could give rise to such a compromise as that! In any other line of life conscience and duty would be apt to point the same way. Still I *compromised*, and set the "fatigue" to carefully removing the flower-pots, and taking down the glass-work, and putting all in the lady's cellar: thereby incurring multitudinous expressions of gratitude from the beautiful lady, and, tell it not in Gath! invitations *to dine at her house* as long as we were at work in that neighborhood. But it is the *flowers* I was going to tell you about!

There are more varieties, and more beautiful of their kinds, than I ever saw before. Some of the very finest cactuses and other tropical plants, all in full bloom. Century plants; pitcher plants—those "springs of the desert;" night-blooming cereus,—every flower that is beautiful, that I ever heard of! I am very fearful that she cannot keep them until another house be prepared for them. Oh, horridum bellum!

And yet this is one of the least sad sights that war brings to our eyes and ears. The field where we are now encamped, is one on which a Tennessee conscript was executed for writing *treason* to his lady-love! Treason indeed! *Treason against traitors!* I was engaged some time ago on a court-martial, and found, among some rebel documents, the records and history of his case. It was really touching. The letter to his *engagée* (which was intercepted) was there. I have kept the papers, and have written a sort of story of the whole case, to commemorate his name. Poor fellow! He is only one of thousands of heroes who have gone down beneath the wave of this terrible tribulation of our country.

WILL. M. McLAIN,

32d Ohio Vols.

LETTER CXLVIII.

THE RAID.

Vicksburg, Feb. 2d, 1864.

Already the rattle of the army train is heard, and soon we will have to join in their wake. Every thing portable is in readiness to move at the shortest notice. The night is far advanced, yet I cannot retire to rest—the duties so soon to devolve upon me, drive away all thought of sleep. Perhaps you will be envious to know our destination. Anticipating this, I will give you the little knowledge I have acquired of the movement.

In the first place, we are to penetrate the country as far as Jackson, Miss. After taking that place, we will form a junction with a portion of Grant's immediate command, and destroy a portion of the railroad now in communication with Bragg's army. Farewell.

W. S. Hubbell.
32d Ohio Vet. Inf.

LETTER CXLIX.

Indeed, of all the white-robed martyrs which this war has sent, or shall send, from a glorious death on a field of glory to a glorious eternity in a land of *unpaling* brightness, there will be none to lift up *whiter* hands, nor to sing praises with a purer heart, than Stephen A. Rollins!

If pure patriotism be honorable; if self-immolation on the altar of principle avail any thing before the tribunal of Deity, then indeed he had something wherewith to console his last sad moments. I hope and trust there was

> "Nothing to stain, no lure to stay
> The soul, as up it springs;
> God's sunshine on its gladdened way,
> God's blessing on its wings."

Dear Rollins! None of all those he electrified with a sudden, sweeping eloquence, loved him better or appreciated him higher, or feel his loss deeper than I.

W. M. McLAIN.

LETTER CL.

THE EMANCIPATION PROCLAMATION.—A FALLEN HERO'S WORDS.

VICKSBURG, 1864.

THE great cause of the war has received its death-blow. Believing this, I cannot pronounce that decree of liberty any thing less than one of the grandest strokes of statesman-like policy ever achieved by a magistrate in power, when, by one dash as it were of his magic pen, the shackles of slavery, which had for ages ground them to the dust, fell from four millions of human beings, and they were ushered from the thraldom of servitude into God's sunlight of liberty!

Let no weak imbecile tell me, hereafter, that we cannot conquer this disloyal people; for our cause is just, and as such, must receive the aid of the Most High. Justice may sleep, but it never dies.

> "Truth crushed to earth shall rise again,
> The eternal years of God are hers!"

SERGT. S. A. ROLLINS.

To Miss SARAH SOUTHWORTH,
  Winthrop, Maine.

LETTER CLI.

The Prison at Elmira.—Lookout Mountain.

Elmira Barracks, N. Y., Jan. 1864.

My dear Sister—On the morning of December 17th, 1863, cold and stormy, at the hour of 4.30, the Buffalo Express left the Elmira station, bearing away among its living freight a party of fifteen men and two officers. Six of the men were guards, armed and equipped as the law directs; and the remaining nine were deserters, also equipped as the law directs, i. e., handcuffed and strung on a chain—said handcuffs or bracelets being far more useful than ornamental. Thus the whole party of nine were bound together by the very strongest of ties! Myself being one of the aforesaid guards, "know whereof I affirm," when saying we bowled merrily over the wide guage of the Erie road, for the first hundred miles on our outward trip to Chattanooga, Tenn. I saw nothing of interest till we arrived at Dunkirk, the western terminus of the road. At this place we took the lake-shore road for Cleveland, through a very pleasant and level country. We arrived at Cleveland, Ohio, at 8 o'clock, P. M. It was dark and stormy outside, the waves were dashing on the wharf, and the gaslights were vainly striving to mimic day where there was none! Here we took the Bellefontaine train for Indianapolis, Ind. All night long we rode. The morning dawned, and a broken rail delayed us; and it was high noon before we saw the spires of Indianapolis. Here we turned over our prisoners to the provost, till the arrival of the next train, and roamed about the city as best pleased us. Drawing three days' rations, we put our prisoners on the 8.50 P. M. train for Louisville, Ky.—not, however, till one of them had stolen an overcoat from one of the provost guards, wherewith to keep himself from freezing on the way. In nodding, sleeping, and grumbling, we passed the long hours of the night; and, just in the gray dawn of morning, we found ourselves on board a boat crossing the Ohio River. Our steamer rejoiced in the somewhat singular name of "John shall Cross." So far as I know, John* had no objections to crossing; and it was unnecessary to say he "shall cross," for he was perfectly willing to cross. Nevertheless, we did cross on the Shall Cross; and, with a keen and sharp-cutting wind blowing in our faces, we proceeded to the provost-marshal's, and turned over our gang till the next morning train.

At 7 A. M. of the 20th we took the train for Nashville, Tenn. We were now in a country that had been wrested from the rebels, and this road is under military control, having two conductors, one civil and one military, to collect fares and examine passes. Attached to our train is a guard-car containing 50 Enfield rifles, all ready for use, with plenty of ammunition; and in case of an attack by guerrillas, the passengers are expected to use them. Every bridge on the road is guarded, and all large ones are protected by stockades and rifle-pits.

For the first fifty miles the country is rough. A huge hill is seen here right ahead of us on the track! There is no getting around it, and we commenced going up at the grade of 120 feet to the mile, which is very steep, you will observe, for a railroad. We soon arrive at the top, and then find that this is only a small part of the whole ascent— that we must now jump from the top of this hill to that of

---

* The name of the writer.

the other ;—and away we go over a trestle-work bridge of dizzy elevation, and still on up the hill again, winding around ledges and angles, while far below us are seen the tops of the loftiest trees; till at last, as if in utter despair of ever scaling the top, the "iron horse" gives a fierce snort, and plunges madly into the bank, and away he goes through a tunnel in total darkness and a mile in length, and then down the plane on the other side much quicker than we ascended.

The bridges over these mountain ravines have been burned four or five times by Morgan, the guerrilla; and all the trains run by daylight for better security. Morgan always notifies the trains on the road after he has burned the bridges, which shows he is something of a man after all—nay, an honorable man; for if a train should go down through these trestle-works, not a soul would be left to tell the tale.

This day we passed Munfordsville, Bowling Green, and other places of note in Kentucky since the war commenced, the battle-fields and skirmishing grounds of contending armies. At dark we found ourselves at Nashville, the capital of Tennessee, and straightway proceeded to a large brick building, partly furnished. It was commenced by a man in the rebel army named Overton, termed by the Nashville people "Overton's Folly," but named by the soldiers, Zollicoffer House. It is an immense building, containing 360 rooms, not one of them furnished, and is used by Government for barracks, guardhouse, &c. Its owner being a rebel, it is of course confiscated property. Here we passed a cold December night, with no fire, the wind whistling through the open windows like fun! We were lodged in the third story, the rooms large and airy, and all but pleasant! There were guards at the doors and guards at the windows, guards from the cellar to the garret, and several stationed on the roof, and all for the better security of the property and persons of the guests! And yet all this was provided by the gentlemanly proprietor free of charge; however, with all these rare accommodations and advantages, I cannot conscientiously recommend the Zollicoffer House to the patronage of my travelling friends. Should you visit Nashville, do not, I pray you, stop at the Zollicoffer!

At 3 P. M. of the 21st we train for Stevenson, Ala., 123 miles, over the roughest road in the world. About noon we passed through the battle-field of Murfreesboro, Tenn., with its long lines of breastworks and rifle-pits, and its half acre of graves of gallant men, who met their death on the bloody field. It is now still and silent, and all overgrown with weeds, bushes, and grass, as if Nature were trying to hide from all eyes the evidences of "man's inhumanity to man."

Our train this day, not only carried a guard-car, but also a guard well armed and ready for action at any time, numbering some thirty or forty men, who guard the train, and see that nothing is stolen from the stations where the trains stop. The road is heavily guarded, and patrols pass over every mile of it once in two hours, day and night Any damage to this road endangers the whole army of the Cumberland, as all their supplies must pass over it, and though they run from five to seven trains a day, it is impossible to supply the army with all it needs. At 10 P. M. we arrived at Stevenson and changed cars for Bridgeport, ten miles, which distance we made in about one hour. We were travelling in an open car by moonlight; had to go back about a mile after some cars that broke off from our train, and came near being left altogether.

At Bridgeport we took the steamer Point Rock for Chattanooga, distant sixty-five miles. The road runs direct from Bridgeport to Chattanooga, but the rebs destroyed all the bridges between the two places, and until they are rebuilt, we must needs travel by water, using the Tennessee River for that purpose. We left the wharf at Bridgeport at 2 A. M. of the 22d, and at noon were at Kelly's Landing, about thirty miles from the starting point. Our boat run till it got out of wood, then stopped at a fence and took the rails for firewood, and so on from one fence to another. The shores are bold, and the water very deep, therefore we experienced no difficulty in running close up.

The river winds among hills and mountains, and the scenery is, in the highest degree, romantic and sublime. The day was beautiful, and we enjoyed it exceedingly. Shortly after leaving Kelly's, we passed the "pot" and "suck," places where the water runs rapidly, and so adverse to our course, in the latter place, that our boat went backwards, consequently a line was taken ashore to tow her safely through. We passed on, and just as the shades of night were gathering over us, we wound around the base of a huge hill, when lo! far ahead, standing alone in silent majesty, rearing its head far above all its fellows, was "Lookout Mountain!" Soon the moon arose, shining mildly athwart the landscape, adding new charms to the beautiful scene. For two hours or more we glided smoothly on the bosom of the placid Tennessee, under the shadow of the eternal hills, and at 9 P. M. the pontoon at Chattanooga opened to admit us to the wharf (which, by the way, was only the muddy shore); throwing out our plank, we landed, and forthwith went on our way rejoicing to the provost marshal's, where we turned over our prisoners for the last time. Having delivered them in safety at the place specified, and having fulfilled our orders to the letter, we sought quarters in a large brick house (once a fine dwelling, but now deserted by its owner), and going up stairs, started a roaring fire in the old fireplace, and boiling our coffee and broiling our bacon on a long stick, we ate our supper. Then reclining on our blankets, with feet to the fire, we were soon clasped in the arms of the drowsy god, and enjoying sweetly that repose of which we had been deprived for the past five nights.

In the morning, I took a walk over the town, which is almost destroyed by the ravages of war. I saw, among other things, thirty pieces of artillery captured from the rebels at the last battle of Chattanooga. One fine brass piece bore the name of "Lady Buckner," and another "Lady Breckinridge," both wives of Kentucky statesmen. But, alas, for all human calculations! the Yankees now hold both the guns, and the traitors they are named after are now powerless to do us harm, as the pieces are. Chattanooga was once a good-sized place, and considerable business has been done here in days of yore, but now her glory hath departed. The buildings are burnt; her pleasant groves laid low in the dust; her gardens, her orchards, and her fields, are turned into desert places; her sightly hill-tops are covered and disfigured with breastworks, rifle-pits, and forts; all, all the bitter reaping of the fruits of her own sowing.

About noon we left Chattanooga for the Twelfth army corps, then lying in the Lookout Valley, and where we expected to find the 60th regiment from St. Lawrence county, and also the 191st, to which our captain belonged. We had about seven miles to travel, over the roughest kind of a road, and partly over the point of the mountain, and thence down to the railroad track on the bank of the river. The road here winds under the base of the mountain, some forty or fifty feet above the river. The cliff rises up on the other side of the road from one to three hundred feet perpendicularly; nay more, it actually hangs over the road in places.

At this point the rebels used to amuse themselves by rolling huge rocks down on the track, which, it is needless to state, smashed rails and tracks all into a "cocked hat." Here we found a large cave, from which the rebels procured saltpetre for the manufacture of gunpowder. We went into it a long way, and having but one candle, could not prolong our stay beyond reasonable bounds. Towards night we separated, some going to one regiment and some to others. I made tracks for the 60th, and the first man I saw, with whom I was acquainted, was Frank Reed, who gave me a hearty welcome, and at once set before me a plentiful repast of pork, hard tack, and coffee, to which I did ample justice. After talking over old times, I stretched my weary limbs on a soldier's couch, and, side by side with Frank, soon passed into the land of dreams.

The camp of the 60th is situated high up on the mountain side. When, at sunset, as I stood gazing into the beautiful valley of the Wanhatchie, dotted with its white tents and newly-built cabins, I saw far below me, on the brow of another hill, a company of men gathered around an open grave to perform the last sad rites for a comrade who "had fought his last battle." At the foot of a tall pine-tree "they laid him to rest," and I almost expected to hear the solemn words floating up to me on the evening breeze, "Ashes unto ashes, dust unto dust;" but no sound broke on the calm stillness till the last tribute of honor, the parting salute, was fired over his grave. They heaped the cold earth on the rude coffin, and left him alone, the tall pine keeping lonely watch, and the evening wind sighing through its branches a mournful dirge over the dead patriot. Need I tell you my view of the valley was obscured by tears?

The 24th of December opened bright, and procuring a pass, signed by Colonel Goddard of the 60th, and countersigned by a brigadier, I started with one of our party for the top of Lookout. It was only about three miles to the foot of the mountain; we were soon there, and then commenced some going up hill, I reckon! This mountain, you will remember, was occupied by the rebels, and taken from them on the 25th of November last by General Hooker's troops, at the battle of Chattanooga. The mountain was taken by storm; our brave men charging boldly up its steep sides, exposed to a heavy fire from the rebel works, drove all before them, and planted our glorious old flag on its very summit. It is astonishing how men could ever get up that hill and fight as they went along. Going up with no gun or equipments, I had to rest a dozen times. It is necessary to pull one's self up by the bushes and twigs. We had to climb two long ladders to get to the summit. About half-way up is a level piece of ground—that is, when you get to it; then comes a long distance, steeper and harder to climb, and after that a high perpendicular rock. Over all these heights we toiled, till at last we found ourselves on the highest peak of Lookout Mountain.

It is possible there are words in the English language that may express the feelings of some, as they gaze from this point down on the world beneath; but I confess I am ignorant of them. I shall not attempt it, not being equal to the task. I can only state a few facts, from which you may draw on your imagination to produce the scene before me. Standing here, I saw directly beneath my feet the town of Chattanooga, which, although very hilly, appears from this point perfectly level. On the left I notice Wanhatchie Valley and the valley of Lookout. On the right, stretching back from the river for miles, is that long chain of hills called Missionary Ridge, while far back among the hills is the battle-field of Chattanooga. Every foot of this ground has been consecrated to freedom by the best blood of her valiant sons. Here it was shed freely by willing hearts, who counted it no loss to die for their imperilled country.

Away, far away in the distance, almost illimitable, I behold heights peeping over heights, and mountains piled on mountains; till the eye grows weary with gazing, and the soul that had gone forth seeking some resting-place, returned back to its frail ark, wondering at the impenetrable depths of space spread out before it. From this summit can be seen the mountain-tops of seven States.

> "Lives there a man with soul so dead,
> Who never to himself hath said,
> This is my own, my native land ?"

Standing here, I seemed to behold the gallant men of Hooker's division charging up these rocky steeps, with cheers of victory! I saw, "in the mind's eye," a long line of fire bursting from the rebel rifle-pits, stretching far away from this point to Missionary Ridge. As our men moved up to the attack, I beheld the crest of the Ridge enveloped in smoke and flame, as, from guns double-shotted with the death-dealing grape and canister, the enemy thundered death and destruction on our advancing columns, mowing them down like grass, yet not for a moment checking that torrent of freemen who, steadily pushing on, overcame all opposition, became masters of those very guns, and turned them with fearful effect on the fleeing masses of the enemy.

I heard, again, the cheers of victory, the shouts of the conquerors, and the groans of the wounded!

All this I heard and saw only in imagination, for the terrible reality had passed away; the only sound that now breaks upon the stillness is the wind whistling through the tree-tops; and in place of contending armies, is seen on that peaceful plain a moving panorama of soldiers, teams, and laborers, on the roads and fortifications. Cutting some canes from the hickory-trees growing on the mountain, and taking a few specimens of rock as memorials of our visit, I returned to camp, and "went in" for a ten-hours snooze.

The next morning was Christmas, and, demolishing an alarming amount of "pork and tack," we went down to division-headquarters, and passed the forenoon, and were treated with a sumptuous dinner of hard bread, coffee, and pork (Christmas dinner, you know): the best they had in the house. After dinner, we started to visit the cave under the mountain; and being well provided with candles, we went in as far as it was safe without a guide, procured some specimens of stone, and made tracks for the mouth.

The cave is seventeen miles long, and runs through the mountain; it has many branches, and it is not safe to venture far without a guide. Soldiers have been lately lost here, by venturing too far.

While passing through Wanhatchie Valley, we came to the place where the 137th N. Y. Regiment were surprised by the rebels, on a dark night of November last. They were just coming into the valley, when they found themselves surrounded by the enemy. Other regiments of ours were near, and the fight soon became general. After a desperate conflict of several hours, the rebels were repulsed at all points.

On this Christmas day I stood by the graves of the men who had fallen in the fray. The sun had sunk behind the hills, and the winds blew cold and cheerless over the plain, rustling the yellow and withered leaves of the beeches, and sweeping moaningly through the sombre hemlocks—sighing a dirge over these silent graves. A feeling of sadness crept over my soul as I thought that, on last Christmas, these men were in full enjoyment of life and hope; and that this night, far away in Northern homes, stricken hearts were weeping over their dear ones who went down to death on that bloody field, and are now sleeping in their lonely graves in the Wanhatchie Valley. Sadly thinking on these things, I turned my face campward, and left the consecrated graves, dropping a tear to the memory of the silent sleepers. "May they rest in peace."

On the 27th we left Stevenson, Alabama, for Nashville, over the most dangerous road in the country. Almost every day men are killed by trains running off the track; in many places we beheld cars and engines turned bottom upwards, and smashed to pieces off the embankments. As none but soldiers are killed in these somersets, it is not supposed that as much notice will be taken of it as though they had fallen in "battle's deadly breach."

Although jumping, jolting, jerking, and rumbling slowly along like an old lumber-wagon, we made the trip to Nashville in safety. We "reported" at Elmira, N. Y., at 4 o'clock, A. M., having travelled six hundred miles in twenty-four hours. We were absent fourteen days to an hour, were in eight different States, and travelled twenty-two hundred miles.

I have been obliged to condense into lines what might have well occupied pages. I have told you nothing of the people, their experience, and general appearance; nor of the desolation and misery everywhere visible in Tennessee,—of fields grown up to grass, and overrun with weeds,—the thousands of acres with no one to till or care for! Neither have I told you of the negroes, dressed in their very best, spending the Christmas holidays in "Old Kaintuck," every one of them supremely happy. I have written in a room full of men, talking around me and at me, till I do not know half the time what I have written. I have no doubt that you will have many a hearty laugh over my attempts at "murdering the king's English." Inclosed please find a ball of cotton, picked with mine own hand from a deserted field "'way down in Tennessee," as the song has it. Good-night.

JOHN E. WHIPPLE.

LETTER CLII.

ON BOARD STEAMER JOHN RAINE, for Red River.

WE are lying at the mouth of the Red River, but have not commenced to move—General A. J. Smith's command. How far we shall ascend it I do not know, nor the object of the expedition, which is secret; but that it may tell to shorten the breath of the dying rebellion I hope; and if our successes are in consonance with our hopes, the present summer will have struck the last and fatal blow that rings the knell of the slave power, and restores us once more to peace and prosperity.

JAMES C. GOODMAN,
95th Ill. Vols.

LETTER CLIII.

WASHINGTON "HOSPITAL HOME."

EVERY thing looks bright now. Victory has perched upon the banners of the "grand (now valiant) Army of the Potomac." And they have a leader who has led and will lead them on from victory to victory, until Lee and his followers are completely wiped out. Sherman, now in Georgia, is tapping at their vitals in the very heart of the Confederacy; and, better than all, "Old Abe" is renominated, and I feel confident will be re-elected! God bless him, and save our country!

THOMAS SULLY,
15th Illinois Infantry.

LETTER CLIV.

ALEXANDRIA, La., April, 1864.

FIGHTING in the immortal name of Liberty, we feel that not only the right of four millions of down-trodden human beings, but the great questions of the right and power of a free people for self-government, now rest upon the decision of our arms.

And there is no other country on the face of the earth where the poor man can rise to distinction by the power of merit alone. All the enthusiasm of the past, and aspirations for the future, the weal or woe of posterity, down to "millions yet unborn,"—all that we are, or ever hope to be, is involved in this life and death struggle!

And, if the flag of our country must go down, let us too fall beneath the shadow of that glorious and immortal emblem: wrap it around our fainting forms, and let its sacred folds remain for us a winding-sheet forever!

But our victories have given us great hopes of the future. We shall try to do our duty, and trust to God the issue.

OSGOOD J. NOYES,
8th Wisconsin Volunteers.

LETTER CLV.

You cannot imagine how it cheers me—a letter even from one I never saw. It seems almost to say, "Fight on, Mac! There is something left in the gallant North that is worth defending—*something* worth defending. There are true hearts beating there yet; and warm souls that remember you!" And it does make me bear hardships I once thought did not exist, with a light spirit.

W. M. McLAIN.

LETTER CLVI.

ON FURLOUGH.

ON the morning of the 4th of March, after spending one short night in our old camp at Vicksburg, we were ordered to turn over all the camp equipage, and prepare for a trip homeward. Oh, my joy can never be told with our simple language, when the old familiar command, "Pack up!" echoed through our little camp! Just at nightfall we floated gently down from the old wharf where I had spent many a night of toil. Somehow, I hated to leave the place; though, not far before lay the prospect of again beholding the home of my childhood with all its endearments and comforts. We reached Columbus. It was but eighteen miles to my home, so that the next morning's sunlight streamed again through that same space between the curtains of my little bedroom window and rested on my face, just as it did ere I had dreamed of war. It awakened me, although nature had not taken the usual amount of rest. I arose, to sit again by the old fireside, while my father read a chapter—one that I had before listened to, and fretted and wondered why it was so long! But I could listen now; each tone of that dear voice seemed to waken some happy dream of the past. It was then I missed my mother! A *brother*, too, was wanting. But, with a sense of his absence, came the hope of again meeting him in this world; for he, like myself, had been *ashamed* to stand an idle spectator and see the cherished institutions of our country strangling and drowning in the angry surges of rebellion! Poor boy! to-night he sleeps within the gloomy walls of a rebel prison. He is only sixty miles away, and yet I cannot go to his help. I must wait events requiring time for their consummation.

In regard to *copperheads*, I do not know *one* who claims a place in the first class of society. There are quite a number who have attained rank and influence; but I find that, prior to their espousal of this infamous cause, there was a depreciation of their political value, enough to insure defeat, should they aspire to any station of advancement, and that they have made a sacrifice of what honor yet remained, and become not only the fosterers of this trouble, but its leaders. Their ends are entirely selfish: they will hold to this treasonable policy until the ignorant people of our land abandon them. The wise were never so foolish as to listen with favor to them.

W. S. Hubbell,
32d Ohio Volunteers, Infantry.

LETTER CLVII.

The following letter was written by a young man of eighteen years of age.

He enlisted at the opening of the war, while only seventeen, from a conviction it was right he should do so. He had belonged to a military company, joining, as a boy, for the drill. The company being offered to the State, and he having had the advantages of it, insisted upon going.

Through home influence, and his own qualities being known, he was promoted higher than he would have asked, into another regiment. By a consolidation of two regiments, he was mustered out, but at this time the papers were made out for a better appointment for him. He did not wait, but went at once to another State, and enlisted as a private, sending his mother this letter as explanatory of his views.

"I shall enlist here, because I think there is more prospect of seeing active service, and because it is not pleasant to be in the ranks, where you have many friends to come and see you; for a private is looked down upon by the rules—and good rules, too—of military discipline.

"As a common soldier, I enlisted to fight against the rebels. I was made a lieutenant simply because I had influential friends, although there were hundreds of others who have proved themselves more worthy of promotion, but are still in the ranks. Into the ranks I shall go again. I can certainly do my part there as well as any one, and if I deserve promotion, I shall rise; and if I do nothing special to merit a commission, it is certainly better for me to remain in the ranks than to cheat some one out of that which is his just reward.

"Do not think that this is a hasty or rash decision; for I have thought it over, and looked at the question on all sides, and to me my duty is plain and clear.

"The lot of a common soldier, physically, is not worse

than that of an officer; and there are just about as many fine men in the ranks as there are among the list of fellows with 'gilt' on their shoulders."

He has since been promoted, and is now a staff-officer, and has shown himself so brave and noble, as to have made his family justly proud of him.

LETTER CLVIII.

The brother of the preceding, a young lieutenant, has sent me an incident for you.

He himself was taken prisoner, at the battle of the Wilderness, and sent to Lynchburg, where, with a "brother officer," he escaped by the aid of a negro escort.

They travelled on foot, more than two hundred miles, mostly at night, being kept from starving by the blacks, who always aided them with their own food. They forded rivers, and passed many perils, but seldom went into the houses of the whites. One of them had the accent of a Southerner, and he did the talking. While in one house, the owner remarked, "he was confident some Yankees were there on the previous day;" saying, "I cannot be deceived. I should know at a glance *you* fellows were *Southerners*." His wife then said, "You can always tell Yankees, they are so *polite*." Was not this an admission from the chivalry?

They at length reach Harper's Ferry, and the young man has been promoted to the staff, and is an honor to his widowed mother, and the name of his family.

The following is an instance of the love felt for "Phil" Sheridan, by all those who served under him in the Valley campaign.

The day before the battle of Fisher's Hill, a young fellow, named George Sheely, 122d New York, was wounded on the skirmish line, and brought back under a tree where Gen. R. had temporarily established his headquarters. The poor fellow was badly, and as he himself supposed, mortally wounded; but while waiting for a stretcher to be brought, he looked towards Gen. R., who was kindly administering to his wants, and asked, "How is Sheridan—is he safe?" and upon being answered in the affirmative, exclaimed, with a smile in spite of his pain, "Bully for him!"

LETTER CLIX.—(Extract.)

VICKSBURG, 1864.

IF the army could be made to feel that they are an isolated set of *hirelings*, uncared for at home, our cause would be lost; but with the sympathies and prayers of our friends and sisters at home we *will* succeed. I gave up high hopes and bright expectations—all, every thing, to fight for freedom and freemen's rights; am an "Abolitionist" in sentiment, and desirous of having that poor, ignorant, down-trodden race do nobly for themselves."

D. McCALL,
Lieut. 66th U. S. Infantry, colored.

From Kalamazoo, Mich.

LETTER CLX.—(Extract.)

YES, I do heartily wish I could repay the New England ladies for their nobleness in this war. I think they are jewels! I can exclaim, in the language of the glee, "New England, New England, I love thee for these!" One sentence in a letter lately received sinks deep into my heart:

"A soldier who knows why and for what end he is fighting, has a greater claim on me and on every one than we can cancel by any ordinary exertion." You may appreciate my gratitude to appreciative hearts, which are caskets of purity and loveliness; pure in their loveliness, and lovely in their purity.

Remember me as a willing soldier, who knows the trials of camp, field, and siege, but whose hopes are for a more noble, pure, and free government. Remember me as one who honors and will cherish as his true friends those whose labors are for the suffering, but not the "*poor* soldier."

LIEUT. D. McCALL,
66th U. S. Colored Infantry

LETTER CLXI.

SURRENDER OF VICKSBURG.

VICKSBURG, Miss., February 18th, 1864.

THE mere act of taking possession of the city, and the deafening, reiterated, thundering cheers of the soldiers, as on that memorable 4th of July we took possession of their works, and cheered around the stars and stripes, was but a side-play to the awful fights that preceded the surrender. The soldiers of the enemy in the city seemed almost as happy as ourselves. They were a starved, dirty, squalid set of rascals. They would come to our camps and beg rations from us, which we freely divided with them; and those who had been so recently opposing each other in deadly conflict, now met as friends and brothers!

What strange contrasts this world of ours presents! The citizens were silent and moody; but I thought I saw a pleasant twinkle in the eyes of many of them, occasioned, as I thought, by the prospect of a speedy change of quartermasters.

I find these Southern nabobs, yes, and nabobesses, who were going to die in the last ditch, are quite willing to swear any amount of oaths in order to taste the sweets of Uncle Sam's pantry. Oh, thou god of Southern chivalry! art thou dead, or art thou gone on a journey? Why are thy worshippers so delighted at the prospect of a change from thy "fat mule meat" to Uncle Samuel's Yankee flour and Western pork? Something must ail thee! I opine thou art sick!

Thus I have told you something of that glorious victory; and yet I have told nothing, for I have not spoken of its effects.

SERGEANT S. A. ROLLINS,
95th Illinois Volunteers.

"This young hero fell in defence of the old flag he loved so well, at Guntown, Miss., June 10th, 1864. He was true as steel, and brave as true; a soldier from a sense of duty, as we know from his own words."

LETTER CLXII.

VICKSBURG, Miss., February 9th, 1864.

I FEEL hopeful and confident of the future, and am of the opinion that the rebellion will be crushed this coming campaign. Yet no one can say *when;* but I think I can tell quite surely *how* it will end. I recognize the overruling providence of God in the affairs of nations, and therefore, in the darkest hours of our reverses, have never doubted the final result.

> "For Right is Right, since God is God,
> And Right the day must win;
> To doubt would be disloyalty,
> To falter would be sin."

Yes, this is truly a glorious age in which to live, if we act well our part. I think we will come out of this furnace of war purified of our prime national evil—slavery, and that it will be a glorious consummation.

S. A. ROLLINS,
Sergt. 95th Illinois Vols.

The noble young patriot lived not to *see* the "glorious consummation;" but if the spirits that inhabit the kingdom of the blessed take cognizance of the best of earth's victories, it would appear that it might enkindle a deeper glow of even celestial joy—the triumph of right over wrong—of justice over oppression—the triumph of heaven-born liberty!

LETTER CLXIII.

HUNTSVILLE, Ala., May 24th, 1864.

WOULD God I could see the olive branch of universal peace! However, He who tries the reins of the children of men, has the direction of this whole affair. If He grant victory to our arms, we may be assured our cause is just: if otherwise, if our foes prevail, we can but say, "It is the Lord; let Him do as seemeth to Him right!" But whether there be such a word as "fail," in a cause that to outward appearances seems so just, so upright, so sanctioned by every precedent of justice, by every maxim of law, I cannot tell, but I do not believe it!

One thing is certain, that when the issue was pressed upon us of slavery or freedom, setting aside even the pre-existing issue of Union and Secession—when, I say, the case was simmered down to this, *no true man*, whether from Virginia or Maine, could have done otherwise than I did, if he believed in the first, chief, corner-stone of our institutions, and the prime cause of our differing from all the other nations of the earth, which is found in the tenet that "all men are born free and equal!"....... We have received orders to issue five days' rations to-day to the division, and we will march to-morrow.

Forward! It is a gallant old shout; especially when the blue steel is glittering in the sunlight, and the bluecoats stand shoulder to shoulder, waiting for its sound to cast themselves forward. We had a commander once who pronounced it "Vorwarts;" and he never said it but we answered with a cheer, and sprang to obey him. He was our major, and was killed at Harper's Ferry. We go from here to Rome, Ga., where Sherman's headquarters are said to be. I may soon be,

"Where low sleep the brave,
No tombstone memorial to hallow his grave!"

WILL. M. McLAIN.

LETTER CLXIV.

CONTRABANDS.

After returning from Sherman's raid in Feb., 1864.

Do you suppose that it was without a thought of the hated race of "Abolitionists" that I, a slaveholder, when the war began, found and freed a negro one day during our "raid" through Miss.? He was handcuffed and tied to a tree on the bank of Chunkalo Creek, where his master had left him: when our cavalry came up he was trying to "run him off to Georgy."

I went with him a mile or so to find a key to unlock

his handcuffs, and brought them in as a relic for a very kind friend of mine, Mrs. Ex-governor Harvey, of Wisconsin, who is staying here devoting her time and money to alleviating the hardships of the soldiers. God bless her!

Next, I found myself put in charge of *seven thousand refugee negroes!* with two hundred and fifty teams, of every description under the sun, and found it devolve on me to get these "grown-up children" from their camps in the morning into column, on the road, and then in the evening to get them into camp again, for five long days: until at last I thought them safely within sight of the frowning battlements of Vicksburg, and turned them over to Colonel Thomas, chief of contrabands in these parts. I never worked so hard in all my life, as I did those five days, and never expect to again.

I don't say it was exactly a "labor of love;" but I found that I could understand and handle them better than more Northern-bred men; and so I conceived it my duty to tell the colonel so, and he immediately set me at it. I could fill sheets with an account of those five days, but am filling too many already, and must postpone rendering an account of my command until some other time.

But I have been "superseded:" indeed I was on the day I reached Vicksburg, by one of the best and noblest women I ever knew, Mrs. Ex-governor Harvey, of Wisconsin. She has spent time and fortune, freely, for the last two years or more, in behalf of soldiers; and incidentally of refugees, either black or white. She, with Colonels Thomas and Ridgely, took charge of the latter, and separated or rather scattered them over the plantations near Vicksburg. There they now are at work.

WILL. M. McLAIN,
82d Ohio Vol. Inf., of Richmond, Va.

LETTER CLXV.

After Returning from the Red River Expedition.

Memphis, Tenn., May 31, 1864.

Oh, how many events are now crowding with their momentous issues before the nation! Surely we are being tried in a furnace!

The news of Grant's great battles still come like "tidings of great joy;" but oh, how many homes are in mourning, how many families are in agony over a manly form crippled for life! And still the awful work goes on, every hour increasing in fury and savage determination. But I think God will bless his own cause.

I think General Grant and his brave men will bring the rebel capital to a loyal state of mind before he leaves the contest. But even if he fail this time, my principles would say, "Do not give up the struggle until treason is crushed on any consideration." May God defend the right!

"Truth crushed to earth shall rise again,
The eternal years of God are hers."

Sergeant S. A. Rollins,
95th Ill. Vols.

LETTER CLXVI.

Camp of 108th Vols.,
Fort Morton, Va., May, 1864.

Dear Friend—As I have a little time to spare after dress-parade, I will improve it by writing a few lines to you. It has been a beautiful May day, and we think the last one we shall see in this camp. This is Sabbath-day; our chapel is gone, so to-day meeting was held in the open air. The men were seated on the ground, and the chaplain used part of an old cheese-box for the pulpit, but for all that, I never heard a better discourse. You would say we could not get a better chaplain. We all think a great deal of him, even those who are not interested in religion. Manley has my best wishes and prayers for his temporal as well as spiritual welfare. How we are all scattered, and not likely to meet again in this world! There is not a day but I think of it; and may God help us so to live that we may all meet in that better world, and know each other there. What a blessed thought it is to a soldier that, after all the hard weary marches, all the trials and temptations, all the dangers of the battle-field, if we fight the good fight and keep the faith, our weary souls shall find rest from them in heaven: not by our own good works, but by the precious love and redemption of our blessed Saviour. God grant it may be so with us all. Excuse me if I let my feelings run away with me; but I do love to talk of the love of Jesus and how he has blessed me.

I see, by the "Washington Chronicle," that General Grant has won the sword which you spoke of, at the Metropolitan Fair; and am very glad he got it. I thought he would. McClellan has lost a good many of his friends during the past year. The most of the soldiers like General Grant and A. Lincoln, and hope he will be our next President. No news in camp at present. Did I tell you how the rebs are coming over to us? While I was on picket, one week ago last night, down by the Rapidan, a rebel sergeant and eight of his own company, and two from another—all belonging to the 50th Va. Regiment—came over. None of your old friends were among the number. If ever I see any of them, I will put them in mind of David's Island. But I will bring this to a close.

Truly yours,
C. HUTCHINSON.

LETTER CLXVII.

Kenesaw Mountain, Iowa Regt.

Dear ——— A man belonging to the 76th Ohio had served out his time, was discharged and ready to start for home, went out to the skirmish-line to see some of his friends before leaving, and was killed! I will tell you of another instance that I was eye-witness to, the other day. When the charge was made on the rebel works, quite a number of prisoners were taken. Some of the boys belonging to the 53d Ohio, had taken a squad of Johnny Rebs, and were guarding them out to the rear. Just as they were nearly out of danger, the rebels fired a volley at them, wounding one of their own men; and one of ours was struck in the side, the ball passing clean through his body. He ran up to our company, and fell down behind the works, saying that he was killed. Just, then, his brother came up; he, also, being one of the party that was guarding the prisoners. I will not attempt to describe what followed, but I am sure the scene will ever be impressed on my mind. Yours,

R. A. Talbot,
4th Iowa V. V. I.

LETTER CLXVIII.

A Rainy Day in Camp.

Huntsville, Ala., May, 1864.

It is pretty early—say 7 o'clock, A.M. We are about a mile from Huntsville, Ala. We have no tents; but I have an abundance of India-rubber blankets, or ponchos. With these I fix up my roving tent, wherever we are encamped. Last night I built my shelter here, because it threatened rain. This morning the rain began to come down. I am a firm believer in the promises of Holy Writ, or I should have expected a second flood. But although it rained and rained, and rained, still in my cabin I kept dry. I am tired of counting the drops of water as they fall on my roof, so I am resting while breakfast is getting ready.

Our "intelligent" is hard at work preparing our coffee, &c.; while the rain-drops are tumbling off his cuffs (or the place where cuffs ought to be), his elbows and coat-skirts are dipping into the coffee-pot and skillet, making a frizzling sound peculiarly agreeable to our ears. But I hardly think you would have much taste for the breakfast, if you could see (as I do) the preparations therefor. But we are on a campaign, and a great many discomforts attend a march that camp-life is free from; and I am so much better off than many poor fellows who are within sight of me, as I write, that I dare not complain. I have a shelter, and half a dozen boxes of "hard-tack" make an excellent bed; at all events, it keeps me out of the mud and wet grass,— although, in appearance, it makes me think of a small-sized ark, floating on the surface of the waters.

Will. M. McLain,
32d Ohio Volunteers.

LETTER CLXIX.

In the Trenches.

Petersburg, Va., June, 1864.

We are on duty every day and night, sometimes all night, for three or four nights at a time. We have only one allowance of eating; and, as a matter of course, where we draw four or five days' rations at a time, we are liable to be short the last day or two. Yet our Government is not to blame; there is plenty furnished for us, and somebody must put some in their pocket. But in spite of all the hardships we have endured, our army is in the best of spirits. Indeed, why should we not be in good spirits? We have beaten the enemy at every point. We have driven him from positions that were deemed impregnable, with comparatively little loss. They say, when the Diamond comes on a charge, they might just as well lie down, and not fire a shot, for there is no use in trying to stop them fellows. This is what their prisoners (the rebels) say. So much for the old Third Corps.

The question arises, to whom are we indebted for these great victories? To Grant?—to Mead?—to Hancock?—or to the men who fight under them? No! Then, to whom is it? To none other than the great Supreme Ruler of the universe,—to Him who made the world, and all that is therein. Then, to God let the nation give praise! Her foul sin is about to die; and now God in his goodness has seen that blood enough has been shed, and will soon cause this war to end, and peace will be seated here again, and the banner of freedom will float over city town and village once more. How many of us here in front will return to enjoy this anticipated blessing. Who can tell? God alone knows. In his hands I leave myself, and our cause, to do with us as to him seemeth good.

J. R. PILLINGS.

LETTER CLXX.

SPOTTSYLVANIA COURT-HOUSE.

WE are now on the road to Richmond! Left camp at Brandy Station, on 3d of May; and, since that time, have been constantly marching and fighting. Have been in seven engagements. Our first engagement was a few miles below Chancellorsville, on the 5th, and we have been under fire constantly since; am writing this letter, as we lay in the rifle-pits; and since I commenced, the rebels have made a dash at our lines, and we are expecting an engagement every minute. Our regiment, as well as the brigade, has lost heavily. I have had several pretty close calls, but to this time have remained unhurt. We have had to endure great hardships, and I have had hardly any rest in a week; but if we can use up Lee's army, I shall be content. Give my love to 'Ma, Annie, Emily, and Louis.

JAMES R. AYRES,
3d Michigan Regiment.

LETTER CLXXI.
"THE WOMEN OF THE NORTH."

THE women of the North are doing a glorious work for the sick and wounded soldiers! *God bless them!* When the women are so zealous in their loyalty, the Republic is safe. Hopeless would be a cause that they could not sanction and aid! How noble the position of the true woman! Our country will come forth from this terrible conflict redeemed, and will have blotted out from her fair escutcheon the foul stain of human bondage. The cost is fearful, but we will gain results commensurate with it.

BYRON B. WILSON,
Vermont Vols.

LETTER CLXXII.

EXPECT good news soon! The star of hope shines brighter and nearer: it no longer remains in the misty dimness, a great way off, but burns brighter and nearer as each day rolls by.

God, *our* God, does still make His great mercy manifest towards me, in sparing my unprofitable life and health, and I look forward to soon being able to rejoin my friends and church in civil life. Ah, that war and its horrors were laid aside, and our country again clothed with peace-vestments! But we must abide the time of our King and ruler; may that time be very soon, is the prayer of yours, &c.,

J. R. PILLINGS,
86th N. Y. S. Vet. Vols.

LETTER CLXXIII.

"Lieut. Charles De Mott, of the First New York Artillery, was killed June 3d, 1864, having served his country faithfully just two years and eight months. I send you a few lines of his, that though dead he may yet speak for the great cause for which he gave up a life. Young, strong, with aspirations high for the future—yet God saw fit to take him, and he now awaits our coming instead of our waiting for him. May our grace be sufficient for our day."

BRANDY STATION, 1864.

PREPARATIONS are rapidly going forward for the coming campaign. If our own northern people were all *truly loyal*, there would be nothing to fear; for then, if we *should* be defeated in the field, it would only fire the hearts of our brethren with *new zeal*. But if we are defeated, what will be the effect upon the coming political struggle? These are dangerous periods even in peace, but more so when distracted by war. I trust the "Ship of State" will safely outride the awful maelstrom through which she must pass during the next six months! We can afford to be defeated in the field far better, and with less calamity to our nation, than it would be to be defeated in electing our candidate for the presidency at this crisis. There should be no division in the ranks of the Union party; yet I am sorry to see dissension, and unmistakable evidence that all is not right. I forget you are not a politician. We, as soldiers, *feel* we have each a *personal* interest at stake; and indeed it is so.

CHARLES DE MOTT.

LETTER CLXXIV.

ON THE BATTLE-FIELD,
BATTLE OF THE WILDERNESS.

THIS is the seventh day of the most awful carnage the world has ever known. Our battery opened the fight. I have not yet been scratched! God has been good in his preserving care of your unworthy husband! I believe there will be no end until the rebellion is annihilated or we are. We are doing well, but our losses will be frightful.

CHARLES DE MOTT.

P. S. I came near losing my left hand.

LETTER CLXXV.

IN THE CAMP, ON THE FIELD.

How grateful I feel this morning, no tongue can tell. I cannot give you a detailed account of the great battle going on for the last eight days—the battles of the Wilderness.

Fighting is still going on at the front, and *we* are expecting every moment to go in again. We have been for eight days on the front line of battle: last night we were relieved; unharnessed our horses, and gave our men an opportunity to sleep. For *four* days we have been in position, and fought where we could not raise our heads above our works without being shot at. Many a rebel bullet has whistled past my head so near, I could almost feel the wind of it! I have no time to tell of narrow escapes; "suffice it to say," *you yet have a husband* and our little boy a father, with an unshattered mind and body.

I have received compliments from officers of high rank: I tell you this not to boast, for *I feel humble*, but that you may feel proud. We captured, yesterday, 7,000 prisoners and thirty pieces of artillery.

Thoughts of my family come to my mind while in the midst of battle, nerving me to nobly dare the dangers that surround me. I did not know how much I loved you; you must have then been praying for me. I felt the affections of my heart welling up as pure and warm as ever. Dangers are not yet past. Continue to plead with my Heavenly Father for my welfare. I have great hopes of returning safely to the bosom of my family; but if I never do, I know I shall not be forgotten away down in the vista of the future; when my body has mingled for years with the dust of the brave men who have fallen in battle, you will think of me.

News has just come in from the front; the enemy has fallen back. Now for Richmond!

Your affectionate husband,
CHARLES DE MOTT.

LETTER CLXXVI.

THE ROUTE OF THE THIRTEENTH ARMY CORPS AT PLEASANT HILL, IN THE RED RIVER EXPEDITION.

April, 1864.

WHEN we started from Alexandria, we found the Twenty-ninth Maine transferred from the Second to the First brigade, under General Dwight, a splendid officer, as he has lately proved himself. Tuesday was occupied in searching for a horse to which I was entitled, but could not get, on account of the scarcity of said article. Succeeded better in finding a very good colored boy for a hostler and waiter; of his good qualities I will hereafter discourse. Wednesday morning, at eight o'clock, we again took up the march, on the Texas road, from Natchitoches, halted, and camped at six o'clock P. M., by a small lagoon, having marched eighteen miles further to Pleasant Hill. On the way I bought, for a trifle, a young mustang pony, and having borrowed a saddle, got along very well. Arriving here at five, found that the cavalry corps, which was in advance, had encountered the enemy, and lost several in killed and wounded, and report of two hundred prisoners,—the Eighty-seventh Illinois mounted infantry being mostly engaged. The Thirteenth and Seventeenth corps encamped here, General Smith and his force being one day in the rear. Here our brigade was in a small ward-house, apparently new. Next morning we moved on towards the enemy— General Lee with cavalry, and the Thirteenth army corps in advance of us, skirmishing along the road: halted near a sawmill, and having got all prepared for rest, orders came to go on and support the advance. On we went six miles further. The first intimation of the enemy was, of course, the firing, which might be heard before we started. Having gone about five miles, on came a negro, bareheaded, and running as if for life. Soon came more, and then by hundreds, on foot and mounted; nor knew they scarcely why they ran, only that the rebels were coming. Then came cavalry, infantry, artillery, and wagons, crowding the road and each side, making advance almost an impossibility. In short, it was a perfect stampede of the

Thirteenth army corps. We had now gained the top of a small hill, and the smoke of battle now came rolling up from the valley, and the rattle of rebel musketry was fast advancing. General Dwight had then gone in the rear of the brigade to meet an envoy.

By some one's order the whole brigade tore down the fence on their right, and moved into the field. This, too, was full of forces. Our general (Dwight) brought order by forming his brigade in line across the crest of the elevation, behind a fence. The 29th had the key of the position. Every man held his post nobly, and the rebels had a warm reception. The Second and Third brigades formed on our right, and in reserve. The First had the brunt of the battle, and great honor is accorded to the men and to General Dwight, for saving the whole army from utter annihilation. The enemy made three desperate attempts to break our lines, but were as many times met with terrible volleys which turned them back. They had been rushing on, mad with success, and had no idea of meeting such opposition. Our men lay close to the ground, and reserved their fire till the enemy were in close range; so their unsuspecting ranks were terribly thinned. The fire continued till dusk, during, perhaps, two hours. The rebels then retired. Skirmishers were thrown out in front of each regiment, first four hundred, then six hundred yards—no firing allowed, if possible to avoid it.

The wounded were then brought in and cared for; all ambulances and wagons were then put *en route* for Red River. I have no authority for stating the loss. Two thousand prisoners are said to be in our hands. Captain Gordon had command of the pickets in front of company C, and he set a complete trap for the rebels. His line running across the main road, he secreted his men from this road, and just allowed the stragglers to pass right inside the lines, before they knew it.

At twelve o'clock these pickets were very quietly withdrawn, a few paces at a time, and the column moved towards Pleasant Hill in good order, and without a single halt, the distance being about fifteen miles. So still were all the movements of retiring, that the enemy never mistrusted it, and next morning began to shell the position they supposed us to occupy. Arriving at Pleasant Hill at half-past eight o'clock the next Saturday morning, we took precisely the same position we occupied Thursday night. Here we were met by General A. J. Smith with his forces, which took the front line. The enemy's cavalry soon came up, and by afternoon their infantry forces came also. Some skirmishing was kept up nearly all day, and occasional shot and shell were exchanged; but we rested very well, and partook of some hard bread, tea, and hot coffee. At five a fire of infantry and cavalry was briskly opened upon our centre, and in a moment the fight became general.

The attack was concerted and desperate, the enemy moving from one point to another very quickly; no doubt, they intended to make quick work of us, but happily they were disappointed. I think there was one time when all feared the result,—the left flank had been turned, and bullets came fast from the right flank. The 29th was not brought into close action this time, but was moved back and forth ready to support the weak parts of the line. Nearly all the enemy's large shot and shell went high over our heads. Here, again, darkness put an end to the conflict. Nearly every regiment had expended its twenty rounds, and some more of its ammunition. The rebels then retired a respectful distance from our pickets, leaving us in temporary possession of the field. The ambulances went out, in some cases, far beyond the pickets, and brought in the wounded. At one time the portico of our headquarters was filled with dead and wounded. The former were buried, each with its slab at the head of the grave, to mark its resting-place. The latter were soon removed to the hospitals, where their wounds were dressed; after which they were started off for Grand Ecore. I helped to put the last of these wounded into a wagon—he was a rebel, and severely wounded in the thigh. A consultation of commanders was now being held at Banks's headquarters. Meantime, we of the staff lay down in our old quarters for a little rest. It may be possible that I slept an hour, but not more than that. This, of course, was all the rest we had for two nights. At twelve o'clock I went out with Captain Matthews, to carry instructions to the several colonels of brigades to be ready to move at an instant's notice. After this, we walked out some distance towards the field, but did not think it prudent to venture far. A heavy dew, mingling with the thick volumes of smoke, veiled stars and earth from view, as with a dingy mantle; and all was silence, except now and then the voice of one wounded calling for help. The men, the moment the action ceased, lay down upon their arms, to rest and sleep, such was their exhaustion. They were able, thus, to get several hours' sleep.

At two o'clock the column moved on again for this place (Grand Ecore); all were sleepy and tired, and marched in silence. The train moved with little hindrance, and we halted frequently. If I dropped asleep on my horse once, I did a hundred times. I never was so completely in the power of drowsiness before; and, had my horse been willing to keep his place without my constant attention, I should have slept for hours in the saddle. Having marched eighteen miles, we halted for the night, in the old place of Wednesday night before, knowing well that no rebels would trouble us with pursuit. The train had gone on still further, and here we had no tents, but slept in front of the fire, the general having a tent of boughs. Next morning, at 8 o'clock, we resumed the retrograde, and arrived here safe, at 5 o'clock, P. M. Thus endeth my first lesson, and the first glorious defeat of our army on the Red River, Thursday, 14th April. Yesterday, while writing, the enemy were reported advancing. Men donned equipments and attached arms; and horses were saddled, as a precautionary measure. Still I kept on writing, not at all disturbed by such slight reports,—for now I am a veteran, have been under fire several times, know that I *did not* run, and estimate the future by the past. Many little incidents of the past few days I may, from time to time, add. The main story may not agree with newspaper reporters; therefore, such as conflicts with better authority, is hereby declared null and void. Of one thing you may rest assured, that I always contrived to keep my face towards the enemy, even when occasion required me to turn from them.

If I know myself, I knew no such thing as fear, and did not hesitate to go into the thickest of the fight. The balls flew pretty thick, but somehow not very near me; a charm seemed to preserve me; my time had not yet come. Of General Dwight's staff there were five, of whom not one was injured. Captain Matthews was touched on the arm by a spent ball, and his horse shot slightly in the flank. I was close by, and just in front of General Franklin when his horse was shot from under him. Neither were more than six paces in rear of the line of battle. General Franklin afterwards had another horse shot. The country through which we marched was barren of every thing, and, of course, the men have been on short rations for several days, but that is not to last any longer. The transports that had gone up to meet us at Shreveport with supplies are arriving here again. Four or five came down yesterday, and fifteen more are to come. Admiral Porter reported all within twenty miles, and accompanied by the gunboats. The rebs are on both sides of the river; the last of them some fifteen miles above here. He had an attack from fifteen hundred of them at one place, killed one hundred and fifty, among them, General Greene, so it is reported. General Mouton was killed in the first day's fight, which has been named the battle of the Sabine Crossroads.

The cause and consequence of this inglorious rout of the Thirteenth army corps will be explained, of course, by those who know. One thing sure, they were woefully deceived in regard to the enemy's forces, and very unsuspectingly trapped by the more sagacious rebels. Had the Nineteenth corps been fifteen minutes further behind, I believe no earthly power could have saved our whole Army of the Gulf from utter destruction. In this action the First brigade bore a noble part, and the general gained much glory, as well as the perfect confidence of every officer and man in his command. A gracious Providence has preserved me. I am forcibly reminded of a friend's benediction when I left the State, his prayer that God would cover my head in the day of battle. Has it not been fulfilled?

A little season of quiet has come once more in our busy campaign, and I find myself sitting down to write to you of the return trip of the grand army down Red River. All Northern papers seem extravagant in their expectations of Banks's Red River expedition. I am very sorry, but fear they are to be slightly disappointed. I wrote from Grand Ecore the news up to the 21st. Here, let me begin again. That day (Thursday) the regiment was detailed on picket, about one mile beyond the marks, which let me here describe. The line ran from a river to a lagoon, on the brow of an elevation, with a slight slope towards the enemy. In front of these all the trees were fallen from the wall towards the enemy, for about a quarter of a mile, and out among these fallen trees were small works thrown up, to hold a few men each. The wall itself was of large pine logs, two trees, about six feet apart and five feet high, and filled between with sand, making an impenetrable wall; on the inside tier was one more log, so placed as to leave about four inches space between it and the next lower, through which the infantry might discharge their pieces with comparative safety.

To return to the picket-post. I remember to have heard a whip-poor-will all night long, from a tree close by us. At half-past ten o'clock, I simply wrapped my rubber around me, and lying down at the foot of a tall pine-tree, dropped asleep. It was a brilliant night (full moon). When I awoke at twelve, it had rained a little. The village of Grand Ecore had burned to the ground, and the reserve had all fallen in, and lay on their arms, thinking an attack might be made by attraction of the light. Major Knowlton said he stood watch by me to wake me, but found no occasion.

The regiment moved Friday morning to join the column. The country, for some distance, was literally in flames. At one time, I counted fifteen burning houses or mills. This lighted our road most of the way. The value of the piles of cotton and corn in flames cannot be estimated, but the heaps were very large. Cavalry were in advance of us.

In the rear were the trains. Then the 13th and 16th Army Corps in the rear of them. Near five o'clock, when near Cloutierville, we halted a short time, and I went in pursuit of some cistern-water to drink. Forded the bayou Kain through three feet of water, and found my object; water clear and cool. Here, too, were some fine rose-bushes, and I confiscated several of course. We had all sorts of rumors of rebs in front and rear, and of trains surely lost, unless Grover arrived in season from Alexandria with his forces to meet us; but all this did not cause any one to fear, though, I must confess, I was ready to give the enemy the credit of being too sharp to let so good a chance pass without a trial, with the force they showed at Pleasant Hill. It seemed absurd that we should retire unmolested. As we neared Kain River crossing, the picket and skirmish firing became quite sharp and frequent. The cavalry were busy, and the artillery ordered forward. This began at half-past six o'clock. As the forces moved up towards the river, they were all drawn up in an open field, between which and the river was a belt of woods. This suspense of waiting and expecting was more than going into it pell-mell, as we did at Sabine Cross-roads. At half-past eight o'clock a rebel battery opened, off towards the right; and ours, which had been drawn into position, gave rapid and forcible replies. Our brigade was now ordered forward into the woods. I could just see the position of the rebel battery, which, however, was soon silenced. The brigade moved for some distance into the woods, when I, for one, expected to come upon the enemy's line of battle, at any moment, but they were not there. The 27th and 153d New York, being on the left, came to a deep swamp, and were obliged to halt, while the right went further forward. The shelling was kept up quite briskly till ten, and occasionally till twelve. It was rare fun to hear them sing: one cut a big limb from a tree, close to the right of the regiment; but we were at no time in range. Here we lay till half-past three P. M., then moved through this wood to an open field, at the side of the river. The mounted infantry had driven the rebs across the river, and from their position on the other side. At five, we moved over and enjoyed hot coffee and hard-tack. At half-past eight, crossed into Piney woods, about five miles, and halted at eleven near the old ground, vacated March 30th. Next morning, after counter-marching several times, we came to the Red River, and found the gunboats.

That day A. J. Smith had a sharp fight with the enemy, but repulsed him handsomely. It is very amusing to read the newspaper accounts of our expedition. Yesterday, I heard a description of the battles of the 8th and 9th from the New Orleans "Times;" one would hardly know it was not an extract from "Paradise Lost," or some other history, but for the names of generals and places. There was such a coloring of every fact, that nothing seemed like truth. I don't know but I shall yet have to write a history of the whole thing myself.

S. A. ROLLINS.

ALEXANDRIA, La., April 27th, 1864.

LETTER CLXXVII.

MILLIKEN'S BEND, April 19th, 1864.

ANOTHER twilight and moonlight has gone, and my letter is not finished. Last night I stopped writing to assist in putting up earthworks. We are only about 300 strong, and 1500 are reported as marching against us.

Possibly, ere this leaves my tent, we will have suffered the fate of the troops at Fort Pillow. It is currently reported that the fort was taken by the rebels, and the garrison massacred. If I must lose my life thus, I will not die begging; and if this report be true, I look for the time when they will be rewarded. There seems to be excitement in camp. The adjutant is giving orders as to the disposition of the forces. I have my letter nearly done, and am ready for battle. We are in much more danger than white troops, because few of us together.

Lieut. D. McCall,
66th U. S. Colored Regiment.

LETTER CLXXVIII.

Motto—"Remember Fort Pillow."

Vidalia, La., May 17th, 1864.

There has been a party of guerrillas prowling about here, stealing horses and mules from the leased plantations. A scouting party was sent out from here, in which was a company of colored cavalry, commanded by the colonel of a colored regiment. After marching some distance, they came upon the party of whom they were in pursuit. There were seventeen prisoners captured and shot by the colored soldiers. When the guerrillas were first seen, the colonel told them in a loud tone of voice to "Remember Fort Pillow." And they did: all honor to them for it.

If the Confederacy wish to fight us on these terms, we are glad to know it, and will try and do our part in the contest. I do not admire the mode of warfare, but know of no other way for us to end the war than to retaliate.

Lieut. Anson S. Hemingway.
70th U. S. Col. Regiment.

LETTER CLXXIX.

Halted on the Peninsula, near the Pamunkey River, May 29th, 1864.

Dear Friend—This is a splendid Sabbath morning. I will occupy my time in giving you a brief review of this campaign thus far. Perhaps you will say it is not right to write on such subjects on the Sabbath-day. Now, I ask which is the most right, to write a letter showing the mercy of God to me, or to idle away my time in useless regret?

May 3d.—On picket at Kelly's Ford, Rapidan River. Weather fine and warm. The country all around smiles as the green garment is being spread over vegetation. At eight p. m. we drew in our picket, went back to camp (seven miles), and drew six days' rations. At twelve the whole army took up its line of march for the Rapidan.

When we reached Fredericksburg plank-road, we threw up some logs for breastworks, firing in front. Moved by the right of companies, the front into column, and advanced through some underbrush. Soon the balls whistled over our heads, and we were about to engage the enemy. There was one brigade of ours then fighting them; and we had not yet come into line of battle, but were by the right of companies to the front, and so close together, that when the order was given we could not get into line. Then I saw at once if we were attacked we would break and run. Soon after, all was confusion. The brigade in front was overpowered, and ran through our imperfect line, which made our line worse than it was before, if such a thing were possible. Soon the rebels advanced; we fired about eight rounds; then the left centre gave way, and all ran for the breastworks; passed in our turn through the First division of the old Third corps, and got behind our own breastworks. Soon the rebels came out, and were handsomely driven back.

May 6th.—As soon as it was light, our columns advanced and drove the Johnnies before us as nicely as you ever saw any thing done. About 11 A. M. the rebels turned our left flank, and again we had to fall back to our breastworks. The rest of the day was very quiet until about 4 P. M., when the rebels closed *en masse*, charged on our works, and of all the sounds of musketry ever known in history, there never was or could be any thing produced to equal the firing that continued for about one hour; it was just like a million drums beating one continual roll. About 5 our works caught fire on our left, and we had to fall back to our second line; the rebs came up as far as we had left, and then ran back for dear life, and the victory was ours. Such was the two days' fight in the Wilderness, near Chancellorsville.

7th.—At 4 P. M., moved out by the right flank, crossed the plank-road, and went into works: soon, General Grant passed along the line: the enthusiasm was very great. A few moments later, General Mead went by, followed by a brigade of cavalry, then artillery, and as I laid me down the Sixth corps was passing.

8th.—Arose before the sun this morning; troops are still going by, and have been all night. At eight the last of the corps passed. At 9 A. M. we move off to the left. At four heavy skirmishing in front. A detail from our brigade went out to cut off some rebel cavalry, but found it supported by infantry, and returned unsuccessful.

9th.—Early in the morning we were taken to the left, past Todd's tavern; commenced building earthworks;

finally put into earthworks already built; picket kept up a steady fire, so that we got no rest.

10th.—The Sixth corps had hard fighting all day. At 5 P. M., our division made a charge on the enemy's stronghold, near Spottsylvania, but were unsuccessful, and ran back under a heavy fire of shot and shell. This is only an outline of ten days' fighting, working, and hardships never before known in this army.

June 1st.—Since I wrote the above, I have again been engaged with the enemy, and, through the mercy of God, am permitted to live, sound and well, to write a few more lines to you. Yesterday we had orders to move, and went out in front, charged on the enemy's pits, and took his first line of intrenchments. We were stationed on the extreme left of the line, and the rebels had a flanking fire on us, killing and wounding our men at their leisure, until we dug a flanking pit, when we very soon dried them up. While I was digging, two balls hit me, one went through my knapsack, and the other hit the strap across my shoulder, but neither hurt me or scared me, for my trust is in God, and whatever may be His will, will be accomplished. Remember me in your prayers.

Yours as ever,
J. R. PILINGS.

LETTER CLXXX.

ARMY OF THE POTOMAC.

BARTLETT's MILL, Va., June 10th.

AGAIN I seat myself to continue my sketch of this campaign. 11th May.—Moved to our position after the charge, and laid still behind breastworks all day. In the afternoon the Fifth corps came, and formed three lines of battle on the right of our brigade, as if to make a charge; but at four o'clock it began to rain, and at five they moved off by the right flank to their former position. At sundown we occupied a part of the Sixth corps' intrenchments, and drew three days' rations, and built breastworks all night.

May 12th.—Daylight: the whole field is covered with troops, closed *en masse;* there are two lines in advance of ours, which is the third line, and there is still another behind us, also a line of artillery as thick as it can be conveniently planted; surely this must mean something. Ah, we have not long to wait. There they go. It is a grand charge. The first line has advanced, the second followed; now it is our turn; steady boys, keep cool; forward now, remember who you are; double-quick, steady. Here we pass through the line which went in advance of us; the prisoners captured by the first line are being marched in by thousands. Now we are up to the breastworks (rebel), and the first attacking line. Now, excelsior; forward over the work; over we went; but by this time the rebels had awakened to their danger, and were well prepared to receive us with shot, shell, and canister, so we contented ourselves with bringing off one piece of artillery, and one rebel color. Thus was conducted one of the most brilliant, successful charges of this war. It was a complete surprise to them, and many were prisoners ere they had awoke from their sleep; many more would have been captured but for the second line cheering a little too soon; but, as it was, we took 6,000 prisoners, eighteen pieces of artillery, and thirty-two colors. All this was done before 8 A. M., and any of us had had a mouthful to eat. Now, as there was a lull, we put a few hard-tack out of the way.

Soon the rebels formed their troops again, and were determined to retake the works so lately taken from them. They charged time and again, but all in vain; our boys are not now to be intimidated by a few minié balls; they have the death of many brave comrades to avenge, and it seems as though, to a man, they are unmindful of personal danger.

About noon, the rebels showed a flag of truce in front of our right, and our officers ordered us to cease firing, which order, after some delay, was reluctantly obeyed. They came up, and some said they wanted to come and give themselves up; we told them to come on: a few started, and the rest fired into us; this was more than we bargained for, and we gave it to them back with interest; but, with the aid of the "white flag," they had managed to creep up to the other side of the works, and there we stood, their flag on one side and ours on the other, not more than ten feet apart, firing into one another as fast as we could. We kept up a steady fire all night, to prevent their getting over the works under cover of darkness. In the morning they were gone, but in a space of three rods they left over one hundred of their dead on the field. Such a sight I never saw.

May 14th.—Called up at three A. M., moved off to the right, and occupied the intrenchments we fought behind on the 12th. Rebel sharp-shooters busy all day, but do not accomplish much. At three P. M. moved still further to the right, and built strong breastworks. After work was done, I went out to review our position, and came back perfectly content to lay down and sleep, as safe as if I had been at home in my mother's arms.

May 15th.—Moved and connected with Burnside's forces on the left. Johnnies threw shell at us all day.

May 16th.—Moved further to the right into a dangerous

pit; twelve men hurt yesterday: but felt that God was near me to protect me from harm.

May 18th.—At early dawn we were again in motion, perfectly at a loss to account for some moves, but have confidence in our leaders, and take every thing as it comes; soon we filed right, and faced the enemy. Brisk fighting for about three hours. Twelve o'clock, midnight, took up our line of march towards the left.

May 19th.—Marched until eight A. M. this morning. At last, we have come out of the Wilderness into as pretty a country as I ever saw.

May 20th.—Started for Simea Station, as wagon-guard. Marched twenty-five miles through a beautiful country; vegetation seemed to be in a prosperous condition.

May 22d.—Moved into intrenchments by the right flank; cut a road for artillery through the woods.

May 23d.—At six P. M. were within half a mile of the North Anna River; we charged and took a redoubt and some rifle-pits; got possession of the bridge (Taylor's). My company were on picket at the bridge all night, with orders to hold it at all hazards. The rebels tried to burn it several times, but we sent too many minié balls at them, and they left with their object unaccomplished. We held the bridge until four P. M. the next day, and then all our corps were on the other side, and there was no more need of our staying, so we rejoined our command.

May 25th.—All quiet during the day; at seven P. M. we went out and built breastworks in front, and from that time till to-day, the 11th of June, we have been building works, having an occasional skirmish. Here we are, where McClellan was two years ago. I wonder if, on the 25th of this month, we will have another such move as he made: let us wait and see what the future brings forth.

The last month has been one of particular trials and hardships, such as even this army never before endured, and through the whole God has been ever near and precious to me, and I can unfeignedly thank Him for His great goodness to one so unworthy of even His notice. Last night we had a very nice prayer-meeting; eight of us went out in front and enjoyed a pleasant hour in sweet communion with God; how pleasant it is to one's soul, after a month of entire abstinence of gathering together, or even seeing one another (to speak a word), to meet and lift up our hearts as one to the Ruler of all events of life! Oh that I may ever feel my dependance upon Him, so that if I am spared to return home, I can tell the world of his exceeding great goodness; or if it is His will that I see home no more, that I may be so prepared as to go home to my Saviour in heaven above!

Your loving
J. R. PILLINGS.

LETTER CLXXXI.

The Prison Camp.

ELMIRA, N. Y., July, 1864.

My dear—"When, in the course of human events," it becomes necessary or desirable for one individual to endeavor to convey a correct and distinct conception of the impressions and surroundings of a certain locality to the mind of another individual at a distance, it is apparently evident that the former must call up the powers of description, while the latter must exercise the faculties of imagination. You will, therefore, give full play to the working of those combinations of phrenological developments which are said to produce this state of mind, and soaring aloft on the bright pinions of fancy, look down upon that portion of this mundane sphere, which the United States Government has been pleased to designate as the "Prison Camp of Elmira," while your humble servant attempts a description of the same.

We have in a square form about fifty acres of land, surrounded by a board fence, twelve feet high : said fence is made very tight, and whitewashed on the inside. Outside, at proper intervals, and within four feet of the top, are the sentry-boxes for the guards, thus enabling them to overlook the whole camp. Inside are thirty buildings, capable of quartering from one hundred and sixteen to one hunhundred and sixty men each. Besides these are mess-halls and tack-rooms, &c. We have barracks for about 4,000 men. The remainder are put in tents.

The officers on duty inside are quartered in tents, and we now mess in the old cook-rooms of the Sixteenth V. R. C., which were formerly inside with us. The regiment doing duty outside are, as a matter of course, "dwellers in tents." Those of us who were so lucky as to be put on duty inside, are the happiest men in the world; we live, eat, drink, and sleep among the "Johnnies;" have abundant opportunities for studying their characters, habits, dispositions, &c. We are not obliged, neither are we allowed, to go to the city every day, which proves very beneficial to our purses; neither are citizens allowed to come inside, so no one molests or makes us afraid; thieves do not break through and steal; the draft does not trouble us; the constable and sheriff cannot get at us; no collectors bother us about taxes, and we need take no thought for the morrow, for regularly our beloved commissary sendeth us our daily bread, and soft bread at that; we toil not, neither do we spin, and yet we lack not garments, for our quartermaster hath always goodly apparel for such as we.

Here, within these happy walls, docile insects most do congregate, and crawl at random over many a Johnnie's back, or pursue the even tenor of their way through many a bed and bunk. It is here we enjoy the most abundant facilities for giving away tobacco, paper, envelopes, postage-stamps, clothing, and whatever else we have to dispose of. I can assure you, that the Southern chivalry are too well bred and too polite to insult us by offering pay for these things. Ah, happy place, where we have most of the necessaries of life, besides some of the unnecessaries! But I fear I am digressing from the main subject, and will return to my starting point, if I had one.

The prisoners were sent here from Point Lookout, Md., which place has been used as a prison camp for a long time, but it is now broken up on account of its unhealthiness. They hail from nearly every state and regiment in the Confederacy. Some of them have been our prisoners one year, and some two years, but the majority of them were captured this summer by Grant's army in Virginia. Among the rest are several citizens of Petersburg, who turned out to defend their city against Spear's cavalry raid, and were taken prisoners; they had been in the trenches about an hour when captured; they hate the Yankees with a deadly hatred, being much more bitter against us than the soldiers. It was rather hard, to be sure, for when the bells sounded the alarm they ran out of their houses into the trenches, and being soon taken prisoners, had not time to say "boo" to their families before they were started off. Their families are now in Petersburg, exposed to our shells; under such circumstances, one can hardly blame them for being a little "edgeways."

Every man of them declares they want the war to close, and the sooner the better; yet they all say we can never conquer them, and some say that rather than yield their slaves and property, they would fight ten years longer.

From what I have seen of Southern men, there is a certain class, I believe, who would make their words good, but, unfortunately for them, there is a larger per cent. of their army who are not such property owners, and, as they have but little to lose, care but little to fight, and will take the first opportunity to get out of it.

Two hundred of them have already expressed themselves as willing to take the oath of allegiance, provided they shall not be made to serve in our army, as in case of recapture they would doubtless be shot. There is but one thing in which they all agree, and that is hatred of the negro. The greatest insult that can be offered them, is to place a negro guard over them; it galls them terribly. It is needless to remark that this hatred is reciprocated by the negro to the fullest extent.

At Point Lookout the guards were all negroes; and it is well known that they improved every opportunity to testify their peculiar regard for their former masters. They would shoot down a rebel on the slightest provocation, or infringement of orders. A prisoner said to me: "If we got only one foot over the line of our camp, we could not get back again too quick;" for the guard had rather shoot them than not.

For the first nights after their arrival here, the night-patrol was composed of negroes; and the universal exclamation was: "Let white men guard us, and we shall be satisfied. We do not want them d——d niggers over us;" and here, permit me to remark, although slightly foreign to the subject, that the most trustworthy and reliable guards we have at this place are negroes, and, next to them, the drafted men. So far as my observation and experience have gone, singular as it may appear, negroes or drafted men have been more reliable thus far as soldiers, at this rendezvous, than either volunteers or substitutes.

As a general thing, the prisoners are very destitute of clothing; many being barefoot, and destitute of pants and coats. Some of them had nothing but shirts and drawers on, when they came; and when they essayed to wash their linen, were obliged to adopt the costume of our first parents—a very close-fitting suit, most assuredly! As for blankets, they have not enough of them to render themselves uncomfortable by any means; and with most of them, going to bed is a very simple process indeed, as they are saved all the trouble of shaking up, smoothing down, and tucking-under of bedclothes. In fact, they have nothing to do but to select the softest board in their bunks, and stretch themselves out upon it. Whether they have the ability to determine the exact shade of difference between the softness of a pine or a hemlock board is, as yet, unknown to the writer.

Their rations are good, and amply abundant to sustain life,—no such miserable trash as is doled out to our men whom their government hold; but good bread, meat, bean-soup, &c. Every man of them has a plate, knife, fork, spoon, and cup; and eats at a clean table, in the large mess hall. The dishes, tables, and hall are kept clean by the company's waiters. They have two meals a-day; one at 7 A. M., the other at 3 P. M. Several of them are on daily duty, such as digging wells and ditches, carpenter-work, repairing and building a hospital. All men thus employed get five cents per day, and extra rations. Our Government allows the prisoners, I think, full soldiers' rations; but it is not all issued to them, a certain part is sold, and the proceeds go to form the "prison fund," out of which appropriations are made for the purchase of dishes, brooms, pails, kettles, and whatever else the prisoners need,—and, in fact, all expenses connected with the management of the camp.

It is not strange if one's teeth do sometimes shut a little closer together than they ought, and a dark scowl come over the face, indicating that wrong feelings are rising up in the heart, when observing how well these men are protected and fed; and our poor, unprotected fellows at Richmond and other places, in the usurper's dominions, are starving. But after all, these ignorant, semi-barbarous men, are not to blame; it is their aristocratic rulers, who, I am afraid, will not in this world receive all the punishment they deserve.

Many of the prisoners were found to be blind on their arrival at this place, and from this cause. Point Lookout is a point of white sand, extending out into Chesapeake Bay, with water on three sides; so that nothing can be seen but sky, water, and white sand. Looking on this sand has produced their blindness, which is similar to snow-blindness. Many of them had to be led by their comrades. In furnishing them with rations, the first night, I offered one his rations; and he would not take it. I then stuck them close up to his face: still he did not offer to take them; and I was about to send him away, when they informed me that he was blind. And sure enough, he could not go without being led. As there is plenty of grass and trees to look at in this place, I presume they will soon recover their lost sight.

Like all soldiers from the field, they do greatly and exceedingly abound in that species of vermin once a great plague to ancient Egypt; but as Egypt had seven plagues, you must exercise your own discrimination as to which of them I refer. Perhaps you may think I allude to the frogs, and then perhaps not; but, at any rate, whatever they are, the "Johnnies" can be seen at all hours of the day with their shirts or trousers in their hands, engaged in the delightful occupation of hunting and catching these friendly little fellows, which, I almost shudder to say, are instantly slaughtered on being taken alive. These little exercises (called "picket duties," on account of the picking done) are no new thing to the writer, for he has a distinct recollection of the time *he* was obliged to engage in business of the kind, and with the most gratifying results.

These "Johnnies" are possessed with the insatiable desire for writing to some one for assistance. It matters not whether they had any personal knowledge of one, or whether they have heard some one speak of him, it is all the same. If they ever knew a man down South that has or had relatives in the North, they are sure to remember it, and the said relatives are just as sure to receive an application for the relief of the prisoner, based on the grounds, "that about six years ago we used to be acquainted with your grandmother, or some of your first wife's relatives;" or, perhaps, some sixteenth cousin of yours kept store down in Mississippi, about twelve miles from where they used to live. Those who cannot possibly think of any one to write to, will ask us if we know some one that would be apt to help them; and if so, will please give them their name and address. We have had some very good jokes out of this, and we hope to have more: if some of the "Copperheads" in this vicinity do not get applications enough to suit them, it will not be our fault.

There can be no doubt that the religious element predominates (outwardly at least) to a far greater degree among the followers of Jeff. now in durance vile at this place, than among our soldiers; whether this is to be attributed to the chastening and subduing of their rebellious natures by long confinement and separation from their families and friends, or whether they are only "playing possum," and appearing to be good only for the sake of the loaves and fishes that might fall to the lot of the Christian prisoner, through some pious Yankee, moved to sympathy at their suffering, is not entirely clear to the writer: whether this spirit prevails extensively in the field, is equally a matter of doubt, although our "cook" (a Methodist by the way), a very quiet, still young man, a native of South Carolina, remarked to me, "It seems to me as if our men were a heap wickeder than theirs;" and I must frankly acknowledge that I have heard more swearing in a regiment of our men in one day, than I have heard among these two thousand rebs since their arrival here.

Two or three times a week they hold prayer-meetings, which are always largely attended, and seem to attract much interest. They usually are held after retreat (or roll-call) at sundown, but sometimes in the middle of the day, as they have nothing to busy themselves about. Some might imagine these meetings were held simply for the purpose of passing away time, while others would claim that these men were actuated by higher motives. To the latter view the writer is very strongly inclined, not believing they are all hypocrites.

A few evenings since, sitting in my tent door, I saw the blue smoke settling over the Chemung hills and valleys far away, hazy and dreamy, obscuring the roughness of the numerous peaks, and smoothing their slanting sides to graceful curves. The bayonet of the sentry men flashed in the rays of the setting sun, as they paced their measured rounds, and as the orb of day sank behind the distant hills, I saw the "Johnnies" assembling on the grass in front of their quarters, and suspecting the purpose of their gathering, resolved to attend and witness what they had to offer.

Procuring a bench, I proceeded straightway to take up my position in the outskirts of the congregation; all front seats were appropriated by the worshippers, which seats, by the way, were simply the verdant bosom of mother earth; opposite me, seated in high-backed board chairs, a captain and lieutenant, alike curious to know to whom and for whom a rebel would pray.

After singing a hymn in Southern style, very slow and drawlingly, they commenced praying. In all their prayers they expressed the utmost willingness to have the war closed, without giving the slightest intimation how it should be closed; Jeff. and his followers were not so much as noticed, and the Confederate cause was badly slighted, not a single blessing was invoked upon it! I half suspected that the presence of the aforesaid officers gave tone and bias to their petitions; as to that, you must be your own judge. Respecting Father Abraham, I doubt if so much as a thought of him entered their heads during the whole performance, unless it was when they prayed for their enemies; and yet I would not judge these men harshly: most devoutly they thanked God for all the blessings they were enjoying. Meekly they bowed to His will, without a murmur or complaint at their present lot. They believed that God, in his providence, had caused them to be brought here, and were willing to abide His guidance.

They commended to His merciful care their wives, children, and friends, and asked to be restored to them once more; but if that could not be permitted on earth, that they might eventually meet in heaven.

Their apparent confidence in God, their faith, their hope, all bespoke the true Christian. After the Doxology had been sung, I returned to my quarters, and asked myself: "Who art thou, man, that judgest thy brother?"

The moon was slowly climbing up the spangled heavens, shedding its silver light upon the earth. It shone equally upon the prisoner and his keeper; and I reflected: "Is not the infinite and abiding love of the Eternal also manifested unto all these men, as unto us? Hath not God made of one blood all nations to dwell upon the earth? and when we stand before him, will not these minor points of difference that now separate us, shrink and vanish away?" Thus meditating, I entered my room, remembering a prayer once offered: "Father, forgive them, they know not what they do;" and, likewise, the injunction: "If thine enemy hunger, feed him; if he thirst, give him drink."

When the drums had beaten "lights out," as in duty bound I locked my door, turned down the kerosene, crept under my blankets, and soon, under the soothing influences of Morpheus, I was sojourning in the land of dreams.

Yours, as ever,
JOHN WHIPPLE.

THE SNOW AT FREDERICKSBURG.

"FALL over those lonely hero-graves,
   O delicate drooping snow!
Like the blessing of God's unfaltering love
   On the warriors' heads below;
Like the tender sigh of a mother's soul,
   As she waiteth and watcheth for one
Who will never come back from the sunrise-land,
   When this terrible war is done.

"And here, where lieth the high of heart,
  Drift, white as the bridal-veil,
That will never be worn by the drooping girl
  Who sitteth afar so pale.

"Fall, in thy virgin tenderness,
  O delicate snow! and cover
The graves of our heroes sanctified—
  Husband, and son, and lover.
Drift tenderly over those yellow slopes,
  And mellow our deep distress;
And put us in mind of the shriven souls,
  And their mantles of righteousness."

LETTER CLXXXII.

Patriotism and Hard-tack.

January, 1864.

As far as my wound is concerned, I am entirely recovered, and eager to join the army once more, and lend a good right arm, to give my blood, and, if needs be, my life, to the service of my country.

A word about the hard bread used in the army. It goes by the name of "hard-tack," "eyelet-pie," and other euphonious names. It was also aged, if you could judge by the dates stamped upon each one. Some bore the date of 1810, and were supposed to be a lot left over from the war of 1812. They were pretty good. Some were dated 1796, and, to all appearance, were part of a lot baked for the revolutionary army; and were so hard, that they had to be brought in contact with a boot-heel to break them. Lastly, there came a load of hard-tack, marked B. C. This "knocked us." They looked as if they might have been baked before "the flood;" but they did not flood the Army of the Potomac a great while, as they were mouldy and decayed, and were speedily thrown away.

June.—I awoke, this morning, amid the sweet singing of innumerable birds, and the crashing of bullets among the trees over our heads. A curious mixture of my sweet, happy, dear country-life at home, and the miserable, hungry, dirty soldier's life in the army!

WARD B. FROTHINGHAM,
Lieut. 59th Regt. Mass. Vet. Vols.

LETTER CLXXXIII.

NEAR THE CHICKAHOMINY, Va.,
June, 1864.

How good it would seem to hear a sermon after so long a lapse of time, for it is impossible to hold a meeting such times as these; yet we can all hold a continual meeting within our own hearts, with the Spirit of God dwelling therein. Oh, what joy and consolation religion gives me now! In the heaviest of the fight I can always say, "Thy will, not mine, be done." We are on the Peninsula again, twelve or fourteen miles from Richmond, and I hope, ere long, to write to you from the rebel capital.

JOHN R. PILLINGS,
N. Y. Vols.

LETTER CLXXXIV.

Red River Expedition.

My health has not been good in this expedition. We have marched double distance on half-rations, besides fighting the enemy nearly every day; but the love of country, duty, and the outlay of our little family pluck, has kept me at my post of duty,—every hour and in every emergency,—and if I am not (as the song goes) a perfect used-up man now, I never was, nor ever expect to be.

We have had more hardships in this expedition than we have ever experienced before since we came into the service; but our regiment has been very fortunate. We have never sought, in a single instance, what is termed by the soldier a *soft place*. We have even courted dangers by volunteering, in one or two instances, to go in advance. Our loss in this expedition, in killed, wounded, and died, is about twenty. Company B, ever fortunate, and in two more hot skirmishes than the rest of the regiment, have not lost a single man!

But we have had a great many sick. We have marched on the retreat a distance of one hundred and twenty miles, fighting the enemy in many instances in the daytime, and marching most of the night! One day we forced the enemy, and four hours in the forenoon fought a right smart skirmish, and marched thirty miles, before we halted for the night! This was the first day we started from Natchitoches. You must remember that the part of the army from Vicksburg covered the retreat of Banks' army, with his paraphernalia.

We have been in five or six fights, and have faced the enemy almost every day, for the last month, in some shape or other; but, thank God, we are now out of the Department of the Gulf. We have been outgeneralled, but not a private has been whipped! I can say in all truthfulness that the "expedition" from Vicksburg have whipped the enemy every time we have faced them! We (the expedition from Vicksburg, I mean) have whipped them at Pleasantville, Caen River, and Bayou Glaye, and covered the retreat of Banks and his army all the way from Pleasant Hill to the Mississippi River. And in every instance, and in every place, we Western boys have acquitted ourselves with credit and success. But as I intend to write a long account of the whole expedition, from beginning to end, I will not write any more at this time.

S. A. ROLLINS,
95th Illinois Vols.

"But the poor boy," touchingly writes his mother on the same sheet, "fell a victim to the Guntown disaster in a few days, and never had the opportunity to write the 'long account.'"

So the "long account" was rendered above, and a *good account* had her noble "boy" to render!

LETTER CLXXXV.

AFTER THE RED RIVER EXPEDITION.

ALEXANDRIA, May, 1864.

I AM pleased to be able again to greet you, being well, and *far from disheartened.*

The first day of May, with its many pleasant reminiscences of roses, and hilarious innocence around village May-poles in merry England, and *once* in our dear peaceful land, has been with us, and is already numbered with the past. As night came, proclaiming at an end the bright May-day, so I felt that war has cast a sombre shadow over many a bright picture and joyous time-honored custom.

War is no patron of poetry and the roses. The feet of innocent childhood dance not to its measure. And no fair May-queen graces a festival of flowers.

God is uniformly good; as though it were his blessing, flowers *do* smile for us, in gardens, in the woods, and by the wayside, as sweetly as they did in Eden. But, we bearing with us the cares of war, the remembrance of recent battle and death, cannot turn aside to contemplate aught but the useful, the *practicable* — the most practicable method of disposing of an enemy, or burying our dead, and the most useful instrument or means for the greatest destruction of human life. It is this contrast with the condition of things in peace which makes war deformed, hideous, and revolting.

I am boarding, while here on detailed duty, with a lady, once the owner of a large plantation and many slaves. She has lost her husband and her property during the war, and has only a house remaining with garden attached, and she has a great variety of flowers. She is a consistent secessionist, if that is not a misnomer—a good Catholic—and I admire her for her Christian resignation under all her losses, and a true lady-like character.

On May-morning, when I went over to breakfast, she said to me very sadly, "Our lines have not fallen in pleasant places, surely; especially on this May-morning do I remark the great changes, *always* heretofore honored by us as a children's floral festival;" and as though she were unable to see one May-day pass by, that was not a link in the great chain of custom, she had placed upon a stand in the hall, a great white bowl of beautiful flowers. It was a sad, though appropriate offering to the day, to a custom displaced by war; an offering to the better, nobler, poetic feelings of our nature.

I am always interested with flowers, and ever sensible to their beauty, but I felt that *these* were eloquent. In their presence I could but forget war, ignore the *battle of yesterday* and its sad results, for the lilies spoke of purity and peace, and the roses of a love that shall make man forget war, and the little forget-me-not said plainly, "forget not that you knew me, growing in the green, peaceful valleys of your home." And I did not forget, but thanked God that he had given us grace still to retain, as a connecting link with home and peace, our love of flowers.

What contrasts are not suggested by the incidents and accidents of war! Shall we not mourn and long for the time, the "good time," when the "nations shall not learn war any more?"

LETTER CLXXXVI.

May, 1864.

WHILE at Baton Rouge, I made the acquaintance of Captain Lathrop, of the Thirty-eighth Massachusetts. I often met with him: he was one of the best of fellows, and a true friend: he was very fond of telling long stories, and many are the jokes we had about the captain's proclivity.

At Caen River he was wounded, and has since died. I am more than sorry. I wish to tell some one that I knew him, honorable, brave, good. I wish to put in writing the fact (which my conscience never reproves me for doing), that he fell while nobly rallying a party of soldiers: brave fellow! a hero to be envied: he has told his last story with his lips; but the record of his life, and the last act of his manhood, will be a story cherished as a sacred legacy in the home made lonely by his death, and in the memory of his friends who knew him as I did.

LETTER CLXXXVII.

FREDERICKSBURG, May 2d, 1864.

I ARRIVED at this place last evening, after lying in a field hospital for two weeks. As our army advanced, it left "a few of us" at the mercy of the rebel cavalry, who, however, did not trouble us much, as they had their hands full to take care of their own wounded. They pretended to parole us, but it did not amount to any thing, for we were brought away under a flag of truce before they took our names. I was wounded in the second day's fight; shot through the left lung; the ball entering under my left arm, and coming out at the back. I think I shall come out "all right" again, as I am now where I am getting nourishing diet, which I trust will give me more strength than I have just at present. At one time our chaplain gave me up, but thanks be to God, I felt ready to go or stay. I would not give up the hope I have for the whole world. I found my Saviour to be a great comfort to me in my hours of pain. I kept the Bible you gave me through all my troubles. The ball *passed under it.* This is written by a friend lying by my side, wounded slightly in the right hand.

I remain your friend,
CHESTER HUTCHINSON.

LETTER CLXXXVIII.

Army of the Potomac.

May 18th, 1864.

This is a very hard but very successful campaign. We have been under arms now fifteen days, and under the enemy's fire every day in succession. In this struggle our loss has been heavy; yet there must needs be blood spilled—blood is required for our sins! With the strong arm of God with us, a good and noble army, and confidence in our leader (General Grant), we are sure soon to see the wings of peace spread over our blessed country.

My dear friend, whatever may befall me, my trust is firm in the Lord; and when I have seen my comrades fall on every side, and heard the mournful cries of the wounded, and shot and shell were flying close around my head, my thoughts were, and ever are, with my God and those whom I love at home. Oh, what bliss to feel that you are ready to fly to the world above without a moment's notice! Now is the time that I find the value of secret prayer. Oh! the comfort I get from this source cannot be explained! Pray for me, for I am weak and sinful, and need the prayers of all Christ's beloved.

J. R. Pillings.

LETTER CLXXXIX.

Guntown Expedition.

Memphis, July 1, 1864.

I thought I would not be too hasty, but wait and tell what I knew of the facts of General Sturges' defeat and sad disaster, at Guntown, Miss., before writing; as I knew there would be plenty to bring up an evil report and say, "There were giants in the land:" but I believe that the only "giants" there was giant Rum, which got the better of the general, as was plainly shown in his suggestions to General Grierson, when Sturges told him that the best way would be to surrender to the rebels. The reply extorted from Grierson was: "General, I will never surrender my cavalry, and no man but a coward could ask it." My soul loathes the man! Oh, *Rum*, thou wretch! that such men should be led to slaughter as Colonels Humphrey, Bush, Rollins, and many others equally brave and patriotic, in the line and rank; as good men as ever shouldered a rifle in defence of their country. Oh, noble General Grierson! Thou livest yet, in the mercy and providence of God, to help repair the disaster. These traitors will pay for this, sooner or later, for our God will plead our cause.

May we not justly hope for a peace, in righteousness, when we are sufficiently humbled for our national transgressions?

LETTER CXC.

HEADQUARTERS IN THE TRENCHES.

In front of KENESAW-PIT, en route for ATLANTA, Ga.,
Almost dusk of June 28th, 1864.

FROM my heading you may see that we are arrived in the "front" again. We joined Sherman's army on the 8th inst., at Ackworth. He sent us to the extreme left of his line on the 9th, and we have been fighting ever since, with very few intervals of rest. As soon as we arrived here the colonel sent for me, and said he wanted me to come back to the regiment, to act as a kind of regimental engineer, or rather boss of fatigue parties; my duties being to superintend and direct all our breastwork digging and intrenching, and every thing of that sort, of which we have abundance to do just now. So I left the division supply-train for the time, and find my new sphere more active than agreeable; almost all our digging has to be done at night, to avoid the rebel sharp-shooters; and as the men work by reliefs, and I attend each relief and each working party, it keeps me from getting much sleep except in the daytime, when it is entirely too hot to sleep. Then, too, the moonlight nights of a week or two back, gave the rebels an excellent opportunity of supervising our work almost as closely as I did; and their supervision was not of as gentle a style as mine, since, where any thing in the shape of a trench went wrong (which means rebelward), they expressed their disapprobation loudly, and using harder metal than is put in *lead* pencils.

Musket firing at night, however, is not a scary thing when one gets used to it; and they have hitherto hurt but few out of our working parties. Thus the loss of sleep is the worst thing about the present position; but this is amply repaid to my mind by the excellent opportunities afforded me (being on our foremost line) of seeing every thing that is going on, and watching all their manœuvres, as well as frequently having an opportunity of trying my horse's speed rearward.

I may very appropriately date my letters from the trenches, since I have not been out of them (except to reconnoitre forward for new positions) since the middle of this month. I'm so used to ditches and ditching, to scarps and counterscarps, lunettes, salients, and re-entrant angles, bastions and lines of crests, that I expect when the war is over, I'll have to employ three hundred Irishmen (about the number of a night fatigue-party on our lines), and go about ditching farms by the wholesale! But I can hardly see the lines, and must postpone further scratching to-night, since to light a candle would be to draw on me a shower of rebel shell, as well as anathemas from the boys who are completing this work, which is a redoubt pierced for four guns, which we are throwing up in a thicket on the crest of a hill; and it being nearly done, we shall unmask by cutting away the timber as soon as it is dark, and then—woe to the rebellious rifle-pits in front of us to-morrow, at daybreak! We shall have a band of brass 12-pounders to pay reveille for the "Johnnies," and they'll like it less than "Federal Doodle Dandy!"

June 29, half-past five A. M.—We woke 'em up this morning, and as we are done for the forenoon, I will try to finish this letter. Would you like a description of our whereabouts here? If you can make out the diagram I will put in this, you may perhaps get an inkling of our situation.

Our signal-corps not only signal all around our own lines, but flag across from our extreme right to our left, behind the rebels; but there is a vast difference between sending an occasional signal across the space, and occupying with the stout forms and bright bayonets of the "Yanks." Still we are surely, although slowly, contracting our lines, and we shall inevitably make a corral of Kenesaw Mountain, unless the "Johnnies" right-about skedaddle, and that right early! Thus you have our "position," or as much as I comprehend, which is all you can ask of me. For further information, apply to W. T. Sherman, at Big Shanty Station, and you'll not find out any thing, for a more reticent individual don't live. I'll tell an anecdote or two now. *I guess* when Hooker's corps took the rebel works on Pine Mountain, on the 15th, one of his divisions charged six times upon a certain salient containing two 12-pounders, but were each time repulsed. A seventh time they flew at it, and this time reached the very deep fosse or ditch. Here they lay, and kept the rebels from showing over the top of the embankment. At last they set to digging with their bayonets, and one or two spades. They undermined the works right at the portholes, and dragging the guns out, climbed in and took the place, driving out with their bayonets or capturing the garrison.

One of the acting engineers of my corps yesterday took a prisoner handsomely: in his shirt sleeves, and with his pants so dirty with mud from the trenches that you couldn't really tell whether they were blue or "butternut," he found himself close to a rebel picket-post, and between it and a deep ravine; showing himself to the pickets suddenly, he cried out (in a stage whisper): "Boys, here's a Yank in the gulley! Come, shoot him!" Unsuspecting, Johnny rushed to have a shot at the "cursed Yank;" and getting down below the crest of the hill, out of sight of his comrades, was immediately "gobbled" by my friend, who whipped a pistol out of his shirt bosom, and told John to "keep silent, or die the death!" John saw that it was a Yankee trick, and oh! how cheap he looked!—cheaper than Confederate bonds, and meaner too!

The day we charged these works (Sunday week), the skirmish line of the 78th Ohio advanced on a thicket of underbrush in the woods and there halted, the captain on their right and on our left. Presently the rebs began throwing their bullets pretty thickly, and a voice called out from the thicket (so loud that several of our company heard it): "Cap! come in here, the rebels have range on you there!" He stepped in; and when he went out, it was towards the rebel lines, as a prisoner: the Johnnies beat him that time. One more, and I'm done. But you must excuse me a moment or two.

Breakfast (what an insult to the white rolls, coffee, &c., on my mother's breakfast-table just about this time this morning, to call that stuff on yonder piece of bark, breakfast!) is ready. Don't it seem to you a sad and low state of demoralization, when the whole man and manhood is concentrated in the query, what shall (or will) I have for dinner? And when echo only answers, it betokens something more unpleasant than even demoralization. Well, it has brought about such a pass with me. Now James Contraband, Esq., informs us that "there's nuffin mo' to eat: just some coff!" Can't you telegraph me a dinner? Oh! why did I leave the commissariat, where, if there was no fun, there was plenty of "grub?" But we'll let that pass, though this is a poor country for ravens, even if I had the claims of the prophet!

The incident I was going to relate happened to a friend of mine, by which he came near going home, i. e., to Richmond, or some other depository of prisoners. Two of them went out on a wooded hill, in front of our extreme left, to look for a new line on which to build a work. We had hardly reached the spot, when a rattling and tramping announced somebody's approach; so we sat still, on our horses, awaiting developments. They came, and soon, in the shape of a squad of rebel cavalry, who almost immediately saw us, and gave chase. My old horse could not make time enough; and their bullets whistled merrily around us, as we lay down on our horses' necks, and fairly sailed through the trees. I found their horses had the speed on me; and, watching my chance, I slid off the saddle into the bushes, and let the horse go on. He went; and, as I found out afterwards, a bullet just grazed his neck, which would have settled me, had I been in the saddle. I crawled into the brush, and lay close behind a log. The rebels flew after the other fellow and my horse, who accelerated his speed somewhat, I expect, having no load to carry, and passed by my hiding-place without discovering me. But I had to lie there a long, long time, before I considered it safe to go towards our works; and then, the pickets arrested me, and carried me to headquarters, as a suspicious person found lurking outside the lines. But I showed General Leggett what I wouldn't gratify the lieutenant of the picket enough to show him, my papers, and then told how I came to be dismounted; and was, of course, released. Lowes, my companion, and my old horse, had gotten safely into our lines; and one, at least, was wondering what had become of me. I don't go so far out now.

No, I cannot admit that "barbarism" is the exact word that applies to that state of society where slavery has existed. I am unwilling to acknowledge that I was, even accidentally, born in a barbarous state of society; or was principally raised, and have seen the American Congress sitting, and the United States President inaugurated in such a state; and, although I exclaim heartily, Thanks be to God who giveth us power to wipe out this stain upon us, and to do it with even-handed justice now, yet I cannot consent to have been a barbarian until now! " 'Nuff said." There's a job for us to do here,—breastworks to charge, a hill to climb, a river to span, a city to take! Then an enemy to defeat, a government to demolish, home-traitors to defeat, and a Government to establish. In all this I have some part to act. Well, God bless and keep you; and pray for me and all others who are working in the dismal trench, out in the midnight air.

WILL. M. McLAIN.

LETTER CXCI.

PETERSBURG, VA., July 25th, 1864.

WITH regard to re-enlisting, I do not regret the step I have taken; for rebellion exists in our land, and some people must be out in front, with their faces towards the rebellious part of the nation, in order ever to get rid of it. Why should not I be one of these? I see no reason in the world. If I fall, it is not as with thousands of others, who have wives and children to mourn them. No, I am young, single, and without engagements; so that my loss would not be felt as deeply as would others, in different circumstances.

It was looking at things in this light that I re-enlisted; and now I cheerfully submit to all things necessary to accomplish the restoration of an honorable Union; yea, if it is necessary, to the last drop of my blood. I have been in conflicts from which it would seem impossible for any one to escape unhurt; yet, here I am, safe and sound in limb and body. The mighty Ruler of the universe has been good and gracious to me, thus far; and I have no reason to doubt but that His goodness will carry me safely through the ensuing two years and six months. Then, should I survive the perils of war, will be the happiest and proudest days of my life,—to know that I have done all in *my* power to destroy the vile serpent that reared its head a little over three years ago. But if it should be my lot to fall, my friends will console themselves with the knowledge that I fell in a good cause, triumphing over death through the interceding power of a merciful Saviour. Believe me, as ever,

Your friend,
JOHN R. PILLINGS,
86th N. Y. Vet. Volunteers.

LETTER CXCII.

IN FRONT OF PETERSBURG.

THIS has been an excessively hot day; and even now, though the sun has gone down, the air is hot and sultry. What with the great heat and the scarcity of water, our army's sufferings are greatly increased; but there is no grumbling, or if there is, it is only in passing a joke. It is truly wonderful to see the spirit of unity that has all along prevailed in our army. No amount of duty, no sufferings will bring out a word of complaint, except where a subordinate officer imposes on the men.

JOHN R. PILLINGS.

LETTER CXCIII.

IN one month and four days we have driven the enemy from one stronghold to another; have fought him day after day and gained victory after victory. We have compelled him to abandon his fortifications at Mine Run, at Fredericksburg, at Spottsylvania, North and South Anna Rivers, and the Pamunkey, and now we have him a cowering foe within ten miles of Richmond! He has tried three times every day for the last four days to break our centre, and has each time been driven back with heavy loss, while our loss has been very small.

JOHN R. PILLINGS.

LETTER CXCIV.

PETERSBURG, Aug. 1st, 1864.

WE have been undermining a rebel fort. After placing seven tons of powder underneath it, all was ready on the morning of the 30th. It was to be blown up, and the line was to charge the works, and take them. With what anxiety we watched the fort! At last it went up! What a sight it was! At that moment our men rushed forward and took the ruins. Our colored troops were engaged: they were for the first time under fire. They moved forward under a heavy fire from the enemy's infantry and artillery, but they never faltered once: their colors no quicker fell than another took them up. They took one stand of rebel colors, and a large number of prisoners. We held the works for six hours, when our line was ordered to fall back to their former line of works. That ended that day's work. We expect to try them again in a few days, and then we hope to take the whole rebel army. We await the time to come with patience.

SERGT. JOHN W. STARKINS.

LETTER CXCV.

Four miles north of Atlanta,
July, 1864.

I GOT the little book, and I am very much obliged for it, for it is a very good book. I have lent it out in the company to almost all of the boys, and they are all pleased with it. Our army has got along finely. We have crossed Chattahoochie River, and are now within four miles of the city. The army is in good cheer, better than ever before. I am glad Frank looks so well, but I hope he will try it over again, for I think it every single man's place to keep at it until it is over. If my time were out I would re-enlist, for I feel the duty of serving my bleeding country more than ever I did. This war is coming to a close fast. Our army is doing some good every day. We have a noble commander over us. I hope cowards and copperheads will be made to go into the army, for they are a disgrace to the country they belong to. I love to get patriotic letters.

      I remain
        Your Soldier Friend.

LETTER CXCVI.

THE THIRTY-SECOND OHIO IN THE BATTLES OF JULY 22D AND 28TH NEAR ATLANTA, GA.

      Camp of the 17th Army Corps,
    Near Atlanta, Ga., August 8th, 1864.

You may be aware that on the 22d ult. our army of the Tennessee, to wit, the Fifteenth, Sixteenth, and Seventeenth corps, distinguished themselves, although, about 2 o'clock P. M. of that day, I feared very much that they would have been extinguished utterly before night. Truly, our corps was never in as tight a place before.

Our regiment was at the extreme left of our corps, and it was the intention for the Sixteenth to have joined us, and formed as flankers; but, instead of being in position at 9 A. M., as ordered, they were lounging along at one o'clock, and a great gap was left between their right and our left. The rebs found this out at about twelve, and attacked us simultaneously in line on our flank, and in column about the right of our corps, and the centre of the advancing Sixteenth corps too. The first balls that were fired came in lengthwise of our work, and it was scarcely any time before they came in *perfect sheets.* Our works were not complete, but they would have afforded considerable shelter had the attack been from the front.

But they came upon us in every direction, and from three points of the compass. Our first manœuvre was to face by the rear rank, and to form on the outside of our ditch, using it for defence. Here we repelled the first and second charge of the rebs, which came "slantways" from the northeast. But we were attacked then in our own rear, and again jumped our ditches to reform on the other, or proper side, and here again we repelled a charge; but they began to come too thick, and the section (two guns) of the Second Illinois artillery, which was on our left, ceased playing, so we were ordered to "change front," and form at right angles with our own works.

Our regiment, by this new disposition of the division, was thrown out of the works entirely, into the edge of a cornfield, while the Iowa brigade formed a continuation of the line inside our trenches. This we did under a hot fire from infantry, and from two or three pieces of artillery, which the rebels had just gotten into position on our left, or rather where the extension of our left would previously have been. When formed, we lay down, and it stood us in hand to lay close, for the unevenness of the ground was our only shelter. Without thinking of that, I had lain down (I was overseeing ditching when the attack first began, but with the chaplain I soon found a musket, and fell in with our company on the left); and now I found that we were on a little crown or hillock, and entirely unsheltered; but we were afraid to get back further where the ground was lower, on account of a lot of recruits who were in our company, and close by us, and whom I could occasionally see casting furtive glances to the rear. The chaplain and the sergeant-major were both alongside of me (the chaplain always assumes "the weapons of carnal warfare" when the regiment goes into action), and on my right were three others of my comrades. We lay there until the rebels got within about thirty yards of us, when they took possession of our old works, and then we had it *hot* and *heavy*. For nearly an hour we fought without change of position, until the word was brought that the Iowa brigade (inside the works) had fallen back from our alignment, and the rebels were now completely between us and the rest of our forces. I looked at St. Duncan, A. A. G. of brigade, and saw that he thought it a bad position of affairs; but he didn't despair, so I concluded I wouldn't. He ordered us to fall back to the woods in our rear, a company at a time; and they began at Co. "A," on the right. We kept up a steady fire from our flank to protect the manœuvre, and soon our turn came. I was starting, when one of my comrades on my right, who was shot through the chest, turned his face and said, "Oh, Will!" I thought he wanted water; I knew we couldn't carry him off, and stooped to give him my canteen; but he didn't want water, and caught me by the hand. He tried to say something, but could not; and while he held me, he gasped his last.

I rose up from my knees, and looked around. Company was out of sight in the timber, but rebs were in sight, and plenty of them. I saw it was too late to run; there was nothing larger than a cornstalk to hide behind, and I had to come the strategy. I lay down on my face, and lay stark and stiff, as if I were as dead as poor Mitchell, beside whom I lay. On came the rush. I expected every moment to feel a bayonet between my ribs, or a musket-butt on my head. But they passed, and I was safe! Still the balls were falling around me from our own men, and the battle raged fiercely on the top of the hill about a hundred yards off; but it was in the woods, and there was only one line of rebels, and I felt confident that our regiment was good for them, so I began looking for a hiding-place to bide my time. I had no desire to be captured, having tried that twice during my three years. But here came the rebels flying back, their line broken and mangled; while our boys raised a shout such as I never heard a regiment give before. Oh! I wanted to add to it to the top of my lungs, but I didn't dare: I had to play dead man again. I tell you it was a terrible moment. I wouldn't take a thousand dollars to pass another such. Still the good God was overseeing all, and he preserved me. Never did I utter a more fervent prayer of thanks than I did that night.

They passed, and I took a gun and drew my revolver, to be ready for any straggling or wounded Johnny that might be between me and the regiment, for I was determined to get to it or die; so off I started. But there were only dead and badly wounded along my route, and they let me alone, so I didn't bother them, and I regained the regiment; but we numbered one hundred and two less men than we had an hour previous, and Co. "B" was shorter by eleven files—twenty-two good men and true. I mentioned the men who were around me at first. Of the five, two were dead; Chaplain Bennet, Sergeant-Major Hyde, and my cousin, were all severely wounded;

and I, worthless and unworthy of such a favor, was unscathed.

Yet our regiment was separated from the rest of the Union troops, and we were a half mile out of the line of works; but we soon formed a line in the woods, and as a portion of the Third Division, our own glorious old Buckeye brigade (we were transferred early in July to the First brigade, Fourth Division), made a sortie out of the works, we, on the other side of the rebels they attacked, charged down the hill at a double-quick, and with a cheer, and taking the rebels by surprise, forced a number of them clear into our works, where the provost-guard soon took care of them, and they went to the rear. At last night came, and oh how glad we were! Towards the afternoon we moved to a bottom, where the rebels had charged our men three times, and where numbers of the graybacks paid the penalty of their treason. A little stream trickled through the bottom, and our boys hadn't had water since morning. It was muddy, and dead and wounded lay thick along inside it. But our boys were forced to drink it, or to parch; so they drank it, blood and all.

Close by was a wounded lieutenant, calling (he was crazy and dying) to his mother, to give him water. Poor traitor! Can't you pity him? His mother lives at Athens, in this State; and after he died, one of the boys took a photograph from his pocket, which is very probably hers.

..... The chaplain gives me the credit of killing a colonel or field-officer commanding a regiment; and I know that I did my best. I drew as level a bead on his belt, as he waved his sword and cheered his men forward, as ever I drew on a squirrel—and I know I can cut a pigeon's head off with the same gun, at the same distance he was; and I know, too, that when my smoke blew away, his saddle was empty! Sometimes I wonder if it is right for a man to single out his mark that way; but I couldn't help it. That colonel was doing more against us than any man I could see, and I felt that it would help us the most to drop him. Was I justified? .... Our army was broken up a great deal, many men losing their commands, and even brigade commanders losing their brigades in the turmoil; but not a man of ours did I see that wanted to do any thing but fight—*fight*—FIGHT, until the foe was driven back. In one place, when our regiment crossed the works among our old friends of the Ohio brigade, it got broken up and scattered. But two or three cries of, "Rally here, Company B!" "Here, you Thirty-two's!" soon brought most of them back. In one place, in the 16th Corps, a party of stragglers gathered in a rifle-pit for shelter. They were unsupported, having been thrown out as skirmishers, and were in front of the main lines. The rebels made a charge upon them; and as the Johnnies first came in sight, our boys raised a white rag on a bayonet, intending to surrender. The rebels took no notice of it, but continued firing, when the boys took down the white flag, and went to work and whipped the rebel line that charged them,—holding their ground until they were reinforced! Many such incidents I've heard of, some not so much to our boys' credit. In one portion of the line the rebels reached the works, and bayonets were freely used. Both our men and the Confederates lay dead from bayonet wounds there, the next day.

A flag came from General Hood the next day, to bury the dead; and there is no telling—it never will be known —how many were buried. Our loss, notwithstanding the disastrous nature of the attack upon us, and our bad success at first, was not heavy—not over three thousand three hundred, at the very outside; while our division passed under the flag over one thousand seven hundred rebels, dead. But the usually allowed proportion of five to one wounded to dead, will not hold good in this battle. Three to one will fully cover the wounded, I believe—for our firing was terribly deadly.

Well, on the 25th, we left that wing of the army, as it seemed to be Sherman's intention to run the Army of the Tennessee as far as he could; and we passed the rear of the rest of the army, and extended our right flank. On the morning of the 28th we were taking our position, when the rebs tried the same game of hitting us where they supposed our extreme flank was; but they missed it most egregiously. They could not find the flank; and if they had, it would have only made more widows and orphans in the Confederacy. For the right was a breastwork on a hill-side, with our 32d behind it; while in our rear was the artillery of all three corps, all massed and masked, and ready to hew down any force that came against it. Our orders were: "Right step." They were "not to leave the rifle-pits for ANY cause, while life lasts." Our regiment is to be armed with Spencer-rifles—"seven-shooters," "wind-up-on-Sunday-and-shoot-all-the-week-guns"—as a reward. And that reminds me, your gallant "one-armed man, with the empty sleeve," commands the Army of the Tennessee now, in place of McPherson, who was killed on the 22d. Howard took command of the Third Corps, on the night of the 27th; and he handled them right gallantly on the 28th. At the close of the action he came along the line; and when he reached us, he asked (he was in front of our company): "Boys, do you know what orders I sent you, this morning?" "Aye, sir." "Well, have you left the pit?" "Nary time!" "Well," said he, "if this is the way the Army of the Tennessee fights, I don't wonder McPherson called you heroes; and I am well satisfied with my command!" We gave him three cheers, and he bowed and retired, and the next day issued an order complimenting us, and promising us the "seven-shooters." On the 28th, the Forty-sixth Ohio, armed with "seven-shooters," were assailed by three attacking lines of rebels. They had only rail-piles to fight behind—no pits at all. But they planted their colors in the rail-piles, and told the rebs "if they wanted those colors, to come and take 'em!" It was the same corps that had attacked us on the 22d—Hardee's; and they thought the Yankees were cowed at last, and rushed forward with a cheer to take the works. They came within forty feet, when the Forty-sixth rose up and began "pumping death" at them, as one of the wounded called it. Before the seven loads were exhausted, the line was broken; and they reloaded for the second line, which staggered up, fearful, only to be beaten back again, and so for seven separate distinct charges. . . . .

I have heard of the death of a dear friend and comrade-in-arms, lately. Alas! alas! Yet such may be the fate of any of us, any moment, here. But I always feel

"Whether on the scaffold high,
Or in the battle's van,
The noblest place for man to die,
Is where he dies FOR MAN!"

Yes, I'll concede that slavery has done it. Ten thousand times ten thousand crimes are hers; and now we see the fearful reckoning that awaits her. But, alas that the just and the unjust should suffer together!

WILL. M. McLAIN,
Co. B, 32d Ohio Infantry.

LETTER CXCVII.

PREACHING AN ABOLITION SERMON.

DID you send me a little poem, with these words in it?

"In the beauty of the lilies Christ was born beyond the sea,
With a lustre on his forehead, that transfigures you and me:
Since He died to make men holy, let us die to make men free!"

That is all I remember of it; but so much has been running in my head, all the evening. It is very late. I have just returned from the ladies' "Soldiers' Aid Society," which met to-night, and I was chosen to tell a tale, or preach a sermon, or read a lecture to the ladies, while they sewed away on the different things they were making for "the boys." Somehow I couldn't think of any thing amusing, nor any thing exciting. That verse kept ringing in my ears all the time. So I told them about that band of Ethiops coming out of bondage, that I told you of once; and, indeed, I preached them a first-rate abolition sermon before I was done. . . . . The time is coming when, not only here, but from Maine to Georgia, from Atlantic to Pacific, all over our broad land, the people everywhere will believe that that "old man honorable" who wrote his name in letters an inch long on the Declaration of Independence, and said he did it so that George the Third might never be mistaken who it was; and that other old man who penned his name with a palsied hand, but a brave and determined heart; and all those other men, who threw into the balance "their lives, their fortunes, and their sacred honor;"—the time is coming—yea, is almost here—when the people everywhere shall know that they were in earnest. And they were right, when they declared that "all men were created free and equal!" God speed the day! I look for it more longingly than the watcher for the day-star.

The best argument I ever heard in favor of abolition I heard in the battle-shouts and battle-shots of 19 battle-days that I have passed in the last three years. And I can cry, with a whole soul and fervent heart, "Hurrah for Freedom!" God speed the day when

> "Hills fling that cry to hills around,
> And ocean-mart replies to mart;
> And streams whose springs are yet unfound
> Peal, far away, the startling sound
> Into the forest's heart!"

WILL. M. McLAIN,
Co. B, 32d Ohio.

On furlough after the long campaign "before Atlanta."

LETTER CXCVIII.
MAJOR-GENERAL FRANKLIN'S CAPTURE AND ESCAPE.

PORTLAND, MAINE, Aug. 26th, 1864.

MY DEAR COUSIN ANNE—In compliance with your request, I will give you a detailed statement of my capture by the rebels, and my escape from them in July last.

I left this place on July 4th, to make a visit to General Grant, at his headquarters at City Point, Va. I arrived there on the 7th, stayed with him until the 10th, in the mean time making a visit to General W. T. Smith before Petersburg, and left City Point on the 10th.

I arrived at Baltimore early in the morning on the 11th, and finding that there was no excitement in the city, and that the Philadelphia trains were to run as usual, no military pass being required, I started for Philadelphia in the first train, which left Baltimore at 8.30 A. M. I was suspicious of an attack upon the road that day, and took the earlier train, because I gained an hour at the dangerous end of the road by taking it.

I considered the Gunpowder Creek Bridge, about fifteen miles from Baltimore, as the dangerous point. It, however, was crossed in safety, and I imagined that the danger was over.

But I was mistaken; for at Magnolia Station, a mile further, the rebels made their appearance just as the train stopped! The train was at once captured, and guards were placed over every car, so that all chance of escape was cut off. The rebels were a portion of a rebel Maryland regiment, under the command of Major Gilmor, a Baltimore man, and they numbered about one hundred and twenty-five men.

There were about twenty Union officers on the train in uniform, who were soon marched out. I was in citizen's dress, and flattered myself that I would not be recognized. But there was a rebel officer on the train in citizen's dress, a spy, who pointed me out to the rebel captors as soon as the train arrived, and my car was particularly well guarded.

After about half an hour Major Gilmor came into the car, and asked an officer who was sitting in front of me whether his name was Major-General Franklin; when he replied in the negative, he searched his papers, and then returned them to him. He then asked me my name, and not wishing to have my papers searched, as one of them contained information that would have been exceedingly valuable to the rebel authorities, I at once replied, "I am the person that you are looking for." He then said, "My name is Major Gilmor, and you will have to go along with me." I replied that I was disabled by a wound, and could not walk or ride on horseback, and did not think my detention would be legitimate. He intimated that his opinion was different, and I left the car with him. He obtained my valise from the baggage-car, and I was placed in charge of two men. A buggy was procured from the station, and I was seated in it. In about half an hour the second Philadelphia train came up, and was captured just as the first had been. In the mean time a party had been sent out to Gen. George Cadwallader's place, a few miles distant, to steal horses. There were about one hundred and twenty-five horses on the place, but the General's manager knew what was going on at Magnolia; and I have learned since that they only succeeded in stealing twelve or thirteen horses, the manager having hidden the others.

Both trains were burned; and that which arrived last was backed on to the Gunpowder Bridge, which consequently was destroyed for a distance equal to the length of the train. Some of the baggage was rifled by the rebels, and some of the passengers were robbed by them. So far as I could observe, the robbery of individuals was not general, but the rifling of baggage was; for I saw scarcely a rebel, from Major Gilmor down, who did not have about him some article of private property, taken from the trunks of the passengers.

About one o'clock P. M. the cavalcade started from the station, in a southwesterly direction. I accompanied it in the buggy; another captured officer driving me and two others on horseback. The remainder, who were captured, were set free or paroled, and some escaped before we started.

We crossed the Gunpowder Creek five or six miles from the railroad, and had a good view of the burning bridge.

About ten o'clock P. M. we arrived at Towsontown, a village near the Northern Central Railroad, ten miles from

Baltimore. I believe we remained here for a short time, when a skirmish began between the rebels and a party of our cavalry, which had been sent out to intercept them. I do not know its result, for, as soon as it commenced, I was sent off in charge of Capt. Owens, and a party of six or eight men, which was increased by stragglers coming up to about twenty. We travelled in a southwesterly direction and at a fast trot for about two hours, and then for another hour at a walk. By this time we had crossed the Reisterstown turnpike, ten miles from Baltimore.

At this point we stopped on the road to feed and rest the horses. I was allowed to get out of the buggy, and some hay was brought for me to lie upon in a fence corner. A sentinel was placed over me, and Capt. Owens was sent off to a house near by to get something to eat for us all. As soon as he left, another sentinel came to keep the first one awake; but finding him quite wakeful, he "went to sleep" himself.

When Capt. Owens returned, the first sentinel soon went to sleep; and the captain, who *found* him wide awake when he arrived, went to sleep himself *almost immediately*.

During this time I had been wide awake, scarcely daring to hope for what had just occurred. But this was the *fifth* night that these marauders had had no sleep, and as they had drank a good deal of whiskey during the day, the fatigue had been too much for them.

I now saw that the opportunity for which I had been anxiously watching, ever since my capture, had arrived, and with an earnest prayer for strength, I resolved to attempt an escape.

I rose to a sitting posture, coughed, yawned, and finally got up, and hobbled to the buggy. Seeing that these movements attracted no attention, I *deliberately* walked through the line of sleeping troopers! A dark wood bordered the road where I had been lying, and further on a thick row of trees ran along the road for some distance. I attained the shelter of these trees, and kept along the road for about two hundred yards. Then I crossed the road and went through an open grass-field, in a northwesterly direction, for about three-fourths of a mile. Then I went through a thick wood, and upon emerging from this, found myself upon the brink of a broad, well-cultivated valley. As it would have been broad daylight before I could have crossed this valley, I determined to *hide myself* for the day, near where I then was. I therefore went through a wood which I knew no mounted man could pass through, and finding beyond it a small stream of water, and a clump of blackberry bushes and weeds, I crept into the clump, and burrowing a passage for myself, laid there securely all day; merely leaving my hiding-place to get water.

I had become so exhausted from want of food and the fatigue of my lame leg, I could go no further; and yet from about one o'clock, when I escaped, until broad daylight, about four o'clock, I learned afterwards that I had not gone more than two miles. Before I lay down for the day, I found three ripe blackberries, which I ate, and drank a little whiskey which remained in my pocket-flask.

In my weak state, annoyed by the sun and musquitoes, I passed an exceedingly uncomfortable day. I distinctly heard my rebel friends inquiring of the harvesters, in the fields near by, if they had seen me, and could hear their conversation at a picket-post on the turnpike. But I was not disturbed during the day. My imagination, however, got the better of my senses, and several times I thought I heard the tramp of large bodies of men and trains of artillery passing towards Baltimore.

The noises were caused by reaping-machines in the fields near me; but even after I became convinced of this fact, the hallucination would return.

About nine o'clock, in the evening, I started to cross the valley, keeping the course upon which I had travelled in the morning. The valley was about one mile broad, but I was *three* hours crossing it.

About the middle of the valley was a large cornfield, through which I was obliged to go. Here again my weak state forced itself upon my notice very unpleasantly. While waiting to gather strength to get over the fence, I imagined that the field was filled with men armed in antique style, with shields, lances, battle-axes, and coats of mail!

Knowing that it was an illusion, I crossed the fence, but the illusion was not dispelled until I placed my hands upon the cornstalks, which were the imaginary soldiers.

On the further side of the valley I passed through a garden, in which were some cabbages; I pulled up one of these, and was a good deal refreshed by eating its leaves. Then I reached a wood which bordered the valley, and finding in it a small stream of water, spent the remainder of the night there.

I had become so exhausted that I was determined to get something to eat on the next morning, either from friend or foe; so, at daylight, I went through the wood towards a small house. When I arrived near, I saw two men coming from its direction, with bundles of hay, and accosted them, telling them that I was a refugee, and asking for breakfast.

They told me that they were Union people, and sent me to the house, where I saw the proprietor of the place. I was treated in the kindest and most hospitable manner by him and his family. They gave me an excellent breakfast; and afterwards, the proprietor (whom I shall call Mr. B.), with a friend who was staying with him, went out to learn whether any rebels were in the vicinity.

I returned to the wood; and while I was there, eight rebels passed along the road near the house, within two hundred yards of where I was hidden! Shortly afterwards I returned to the house, and stayed there during the remainder of the day.

Mr. B. and his friend returned about twelve o'clock, and reported that the country was still infested with straggling parties of rebels. Mr. B. offered to take a note from me to the commanding general in Baltimore, and started off with it about one o'clock. In the note I informed the general of my escape, and asked him to send out to Mr. B.'s some cavalry as an escort, and a buggy for me, as I was unable to ride on horseback.

About 1 A. M., on Thursday, the cavalry and buggy arrived, and Mr. B. drove me into Baltimore, escorted by the cavalry. We arrived at Barnum's Hotel about four o'clock; and I was once more within our lines, in the hands of friends, thankful that I had this time escaped the horrors of a rebel prison!

I am glad to be able to state that my kind friend, Mr. B., has reason to believe, through the liberality of my friends, that he did the most profitable day's work of his life, when he devoted the 13th of July to my service.

Affectionately, your cousin,

W. B. FRANKLIN.

LETTER CXCIX.

ARMY OF THE CUMBERLAND, W. VA., Sept. 15th.

I HAVE been so busy making out the company pay-rolls, that I have not had time to write before. Well, are you aware that the time for election is drawing near, and the soldiers have received the news and the result of the Chicago Convention; and almost all with whom I have spoken on the subject, who *were* McClellan men before, are, since his acceptance of the peace platform, strong against him; for how can a soldier be a peace man when they are fighting to crush the rebellion by force of arms? Do you or any one suppose I would be willing to give up all we have gained in this great struggle for liberty, Union, and the *dear* old flag? What! now lay down our arms and offer terms with traitors in arms against the United States government! Oh! no, no, no. The spirits of our murdered comrades would stand constantly before us, calling on us to avenge their death.

There was one little fellow killed in the battle of Winchester, as brave a little soldier as ever fired carbine; for *his sake* I will never vote for such men as McClellan and Pendleton.

There is no soldier or citizen more anxious for peace than I am, yet I want peace on such terms as we may dictate. Let the citizens of the North come out and carry the election at home, and the soldiers will do their part to elect Abraham Lincoln, the faithful ruler of the people. I am certain that if he be re-elected, the war will soon be ended. I will stake my life on it.

Aunt Julia, if it will not be giving you too much trouble, I should like you to ascertain the price of a really handsome cavalry sword; some of the *boys* are going to present our captain with one, and of course it should be a good one, for he is a soldier and a gentleman. To be a *soldier* and a *gentleman* is the only distinction of which I should be proud; indeed such honors I hope to claim. Is it not a title of which an American should be proud? I will close this epistle, and subscribe myself, along with Robert—two of the best *Union men* between Richmond and Canada—

Your affectionate nephew,

EDWIN J. MARSH.

LETTER CC.

CAMPBELL HOSPITAL, WASHINGTON, D. C., 1864.

THE "God of battles" has kindly watched over me, and my life has been spared through nearly three years of active service, with its hardships, toils, and privations. Many of my brave and noble comrades have given their lives to aid in the maintenance of our laws. Out of the original 1200 members of my regiment, only about 300 now remain, and they have re-enlisted. You cannot imagine how much real good results to the disabled soldiers from your contributions at home. Every thing around us in the hospital reminds us of our friends at home, and how kindly they remember all the needs of their sick and wounded sons, brothers, and friends. We bless you all for your patriotic efforts in our behalf, and the strength and courage you impart to us by your aid and example. *You* are doing *just as much* for the "holy cause" as we, who have the glorious privilege of fighting in the field.

Our hospital will soon be filled to overflowing with our wounded brothers from the *front*, but they will be made quite comfortable by the thousand and one needed things sent from our "reserve corps" at home. Heaven bless the women of our dear, free North!

C. P. PARKER,
Com. Serg't 1st Michigan Cav.

LETTER CCI.

"Chicago Convention."

In the Field, Sept. 20, 1864.

I am happy to know that the wicked prosper not, and that the traitorous schemes of our political antagonists, the enemies of our country and our cause, are in a fair way to come to naught.

How sublimely ridiculous has been the performance of the whole farce—the terrific splutter and fizzle at Chicago—the high horse which they rode after "little Mac" was announced as the nominee of the party, and their subsequent great trepidation and disgust upon the receipt of the letter of acceptance of the little saint! I have always thought that the true and loyal men of the North would prove sufficient in the contests between parties, where the questions at issue are of so great and vital importance, involving, as they do, the principles upon which our government is based, and we exist as a free people, independent and united; besides the consideration of the great problem of humanity and morality which is now being solved, and which is to affect the whole human race, and influence the destiny of coming generations.

When I read the proceedings of the Chicago Convention, during its organization and continuance, crouching as I was behind a friendly heap of dirt, which only protected me from the balls of the sharp-shooters—amid the roar of cannon, the bursting of bombs, the screeching of shell, and hurtling balls and hissing of bullets—tons of iron and lead being pitched about in a most promiscuous and careless manner—my heart almost failed me. I was fain to give up in despair and disgust. Then, in a day or two we got more particular accounts—the speeches, platform, and nominations—and my blood boiled in my fierce wrath and impotent rage!

I have no doubt but I made some wicked and foolish remarks and resolves, but I finally cooled off a little, and took a more extensive and reasonable view of the matter. I thought of the character of the men engaged, compared them with many others enlisted in the good cause and true party; compared platforms, &c., and came to the conclusion that the thing wouldn't work. The people wouldn't swallow it, and although the party might cause us much trouble and sorrow, yet the mass of the people would, all in good time, show the true mettle, and come to time.

"Eternal vigilance is the price of liberty." We must use every means of an honorable character to controvert and overthrow the designs of our enemies. Grant and Sherman are great generals; Farragut is king of his craft or art—yet, would they make good presidents? It demands different qualities to constitute a soldier and a statesman and ruler of a nation; much besides scientific knowledge, or the great qualities even of patriotism, determination, and strong will.

Please excuse this hastily written letter; it is after tattoo, and I am sleepy.

    I remain your affectionate cousin,
        C. C. CONE,
         Lieut. 8th U. S. Cavalry

When the rebellion broke out, Lieut. Cone was a student at law in the office of Hon. Albert Cone, Wellsboro, Tioga county, Pa. He at once enlisted (June, 1861) as a private in the Sixth Regt. Pa. Reserve Corps, and fought in all the battles of the army of the Potomac, to February, 1863, when he was promoted, for bravery and good conduct, to a lieutenancy—raised his company, and went to *Florida;* fought at the battle of Oulousta, and was wounded, and sent to the hospital. On his recovery, his regiment was assigned to the army of the James, under Gen. Butler.

Lieut. Cone fell mortally wounded at the battle of *Chapin's Farm*, Oct., 1864. A young man more beloved by a large circle of friends and relatives, was not offered as a sacrifice to the demon of slavery.

LETTER CCII.

"The Hero of Chickamauga."

Our colonel is the same officer whom the newspapers praised so much at the battle of "Chickamauga." He being on Gen. Negley's staff, was cut off from his command, and nothing daunted, he reported to the first troops he met. Gen. Thomas happened to be with them. "Who are you?" asked Thomas. "I am Capt. Johnson, of Negley's staff."

At the same moment was seen in the distance a cloud of dust from approaching troops: if the enemy, the "Army of the Cumberland" was lost—if not, possibly saved.

Gen. Thomas wished to know which he had to expect; but the mission was perilous: "Who will go and bring me information who those troops are?" said he. "*I will,*" said Capt. Johnson, and away he rode.

Between him and the coming troops was a thick wood, filled with the rebel skirmishers. He bowed his head to his horse's neck, and rode the whole length of the line, amid the awful hail of bullets which were shot at him alone!

He reached the troops. They were General Gordon Granger's. Captain Johnson told him where to lead his army, and led the way, and the Army of the Cumberland was saved! He was called the "Hero of Chickamauga."

W. H. TIMBERLAKE,
13th Ind. Cavalry.

NASHVILLE, Tenn.

LETTER CCIII.

HART'S ISLAND, N. Y., 1864.

MADAM—I seat myself at this time, as an opportunity affords itself to me, to drop you a few lines in way of a communication, to inform you that I am well; and I hope when this comes to hand that it may find you all the same. My object in writing is to inform you that I have enlisted in the army of the United States for one year; but having faith and confidence in my Father above, I live in hopes to get back home once more, when I expect to find my work and old customers waiting for their old whitewasher and house-cleaner to resume his old station. As time is short and business so brisk, I will have to come to a close. I now remain yours most obediently,

ISAAC STOKELEY,
N.Y. Colored Regt.

LETTER CCIV.

"THE MINE."

BEFORE PETERSBURG, VA., Aug., 1864.

IN my last I wrote you of what I thought was the charge on Petersburg. Events have shown that I was right. With the first streak of daylight we blew up a rebel fort, and our columns advanced steadily to the fray, driving the "Johnnies" before them, until we had possession of two lines of the formidable works. We then advanced on to the third, when General Grant and others showed themselves on the field, and ordered the "right wing" to fall back in good order, keeping the "left" firm in its place. This order was not understood along the whole line; and when the men saw the whole right wing swing round, they took it as a sign of disaster, and fell back pell-mell! The "Johnnies" took advantage of this, came out, charged our men, and drove them back into our intrenchments.

Thus, by the misunderstanding of an order, one of the most brilliant affairs of the war was converted into a disaster for us. I feel proud of the honor of my own corps: had they been in the position that the others were, all rebeldom would never have driven them back. Why, do I hear you say? Because in a fight every man is his own officer, and each one has had so much experience in the business that we know just what is wanting. As soon as we get on the ground, our first object, after getting possession of a line of the enemy's works, is to get the lay of the ground in our heads; it is then easy for us to surmise our chances, and to learn whether any changing of front is necessary; and, if it is to be done, to do it quickly, without waiting for orders. When the gun is thrown down the shovel is taken up; and by the time our enemy is ready to attempt to drive us from the position we have gained, we are ready to receive them with military honors!

There is a report this morning that they are going to call for volunteers from our corps to charge these works again. If they should, or even call from the army at large, the name of John R. Pillings will be among the first to respond to the call.

Yours,
J. R. PILLINGS.

LETTER CCV.

Before Petersburg.

Our main line of battle runs along the edge of a piece of woods, and the picket lines are about 100 yards directly in front, and along the railroad bank of the Petersburg and Norfolk road. The pickets have little pigeon-holes dug in the sides of the railroad for their protection. These moonlight nights we have to wait till the golden orb goes down behind the tree-tops, and then proceed with noiseless tread, with canteens, cups, &c., muffled, so as to make no noise to give the "Johnnies" intimation of what we are up to. When once out there, there is no returning till darkness again befriends us.

At night picket duty is pleasant, as out there one can see the shells from both mortars and artillery that are constantly passing between our lines. There is scarcely 15 minutes during 24 hours but that shell are dropping in the fort on the enemy's right. Our artillery will tear the works to pieces in the daytime, and at night they (the rebels) will build it up again. But they are going up one of these days. I don't believe you will impart the secret to Jeff. if I tell you. We have now a shaft out under the work. Under the fort we have got a chamber capable of holding one ton of powder, and when the proper time comes the powder will be put in and a fuse laid. It seems horrible to contemplate, but it is one of war's stern necessities. You cannot realize the soldier's life, because you cannot believe that human nature can endure what soldiers do. You do not realize the horrors of war, because you do not believe that men can become so hardened as regards these dreadful scenes as are every-day business. To-day I command a company that formerly mustered 92 men, and of which the effective force is now 9 men. The regiment to-day numbers 92 men for duty, and is now commanded by the only remaining captain. We have five first and second lieutenants with the regiment. Many of our men are sick in hospital, but the number of killed and wounded is between 400 and 500.

That is a bloody but honorable record to show; for the 59th has given the State of Massachusetts no cause to be ashamed of it. Our colonel, Wm. F. Bartlett, has been recently made brigadier-general, and is the youngest officer that wears stars in our service. He most truly merits his position, for a braver man never wore the blue uniform.

God grant that day may soon come when the dark cloud that now overshadows our beloved country may be swept away!

I once had a company that I was proud of; but now, but a remnant of it is left. I will send you some relic or trophy from before Petersburg, the first opportunity. With best wishes of your friend,

JOHN H. COOK.

LETTER CCVI.

COMPROMISE.

MAINE and Mississippi!—the Northeast and the Southwest!—the Alpha and Omega!—the loyal and the traitorous!—yet both sister States of the once glorious family sister-stars of the once bright galaxy—now "severed, discordant, belligerent!" But yet, thought I, there is a chord thrilling which shall reconnect and rejoin these sundered people—shall reunite these parted friends, until they shall meet again like parted streams, and mingle as of old.

They of the South shall see what a generosity there is in these people of the North, whom they have so long called "mean and niggardly;" they shall see that it is no vain boast that the North makes—that her people sacrifice all that is needed on the altar of their country. You ask, "Am I in favor of compromise?" Well, I do not know that such a thing is *possible*. *Light* and *darkness* may compromise and give us *twilight*, but God and Satan, never! The man who pretends to compromise between *right* and *wrong* does no such thing, but is *all* wrong. It can be no otherwise. With our own gallant Grant, I am for "unconditional surrender," and that is *my* only compromise with traitors in arms.

I have worn out my health in the service until rejected by the surgeon. I, not yet twenty-four years of age when I offered to re-enlist as a veteran; never did a day's work in my life (manual labor, I mean), until I went into the service, and having (three years ago, come next 17th of April, when I first enlisted) as stout a constitution as forty-nine out of fifty;—I was rejected and laid on the shelf, like some unserviceable old wreck!

Well, it makes me a little mad; though it is not much matter. I *can, and will* re-enlist as soon as my present time expires, for I don't feel worn out yet—only I can't walk like I once could. But what I meant to say was, that sooner than see any other compromise than the above, I will wear out just as much more as I have within these three years, all to a month, and then *three more* on that! I am in for life, or until the close of the war! That's all.

WILL. M. McLAIN,
32d Ohio Vols.

LETTER CCVII.

[Written after returning from Sherman's raid to Meridian, Miss.]

DAVID'S ISLAND.

DEAR MADAM—I suppose you begin to think the little drummer-boy has forgotten you. I have been in hospital ever since. I was offered my discharge; but I preferred to go in the Invalid corps, and was transferred. I expect to go in a few days to Elmira, to guard rebel prisoners at that post. I found the people of Buffalo and Rochester just as good and attentive to the sick and wounded soldiers as at Willett's Point, yet my affections seem to centre more strongly there. I suppose it is because there I suffered most, and needed most the sympathy of friends. My wound is healed, but my arm is withered. I like the service, and only wish I might be of some use to my beloved country in this hour of national peril. I am determined to do all I can, and if I could only get back to my regiment I would be satisfied. But that cannot be! I feel as if I had discharged my duty, and that is all that is required of me. I should be glad to hear from you. Perhaps we may meet again. I remain

Your affectionate friend forever,

OSCAR BENNETT, Drummer boy,
14th Artillery, N. Y. Vols.

LETTER CCVIII.

"A VIEW FROM A SOLDIER'S WATCH-TOWER."

SYSTEM, for the first time since the war began, is apparent in all military operations; but there are many ways for disaster to raise his hydra head. It is a strange thing that the jealousy of the Old World powers must add its weight to our discomfiture! France, with her wily words of oil, studies the deepest diplomacy to devise our overthrow. England preys upon our commerce. "Right must and will prevail." Great are the encouragements to-day, that we knew not of one year ago. . . . For the first time in my recollection, a U. S. Senator gives as a reason *why* a measure should pass that body—"The President recommends it;" and it passed almost unanimously. It was Sumner's Liberia Gunboat bill. . . . The United States Army is commanded by General Grant. The commanders have learned that they must work in harmony with the general plan. General Thomas is very able, and will give Hood a plenty of work.

Lieut. Dougal McCall,
66th U. S. Col. Infantry.

LETTER CCIX.

A Happy New Year.

Newbern.

"A happy New Year!
  Oh, praise and tanks! De Lord he come
  To set the people free,
An massa tink it day ob doom,
  An we of jubilee.
De Lord dat heap de Red Sea waves,
  He jus as strong as den;
He say de word—we las night slaves,
  To-day, de Lord's free men!"

This will be, I think, a really *happy* new year. The great question will be finally settled between a *free* or despotic slave government before another year dawns upon us. What a superb affair was Sherman's march in Georgia, and how true has "Alexander Stephen's prophecy" turned out! "If they went out of the Union, they would 'sow with the wind and reap the whirlwind!' Their homes would be laid waste with fire and sword!"

The *invincible* chivalry thought they had only to say to the North, "Down, sir!" and we would cower like a whipped cur. The "greasy mechanics" and "mudsills" won't fight: "a Southerner can whip *five* Yankees!" What a grand mistake "somebody" made to be sure! Let the world produce a finer spectacle than the uprising of the North, or an army that more perfectly understands what they are fighting for, sustained in that work by the glorious result of the election, and I'll say no more. It cannot be done.

The flight of the slaves in Sherman's march brings to mind the flight of the Israelites out of Egypt. As the army advanced, there came in crowds from every direction slaves of all sexes and ages, going, they knew not where, but following the stars and stripes with the one thought of *freedom*, their blessed birthright, restored to them. Twenty thousand, old and young, took up the wearisome march at scarce a moment's notice, with heart and soul rejoicing. They were free. Twenty thousand people born again!

"Massa Sherman," says one old woman, "be bery fine man, but dis am de *Lord's work*." Verily more truth than poetry in that.

The great celebration of January 1st came off on Monday. Just imagine, if you can, a procession of some 5,000 or 6,000 men, women, and children, with flags and banners, and all in their brightest colors, marching about the city for hours, stopping at almost every street corner to shout and laugh. To a stranger it would seem as though they were all crazy; it may be so, but there was "method in their madness." The motto on one banner was this: "North Carolina colored volunteers, as good on the battle-field as on the cotton-field."

Late in the afternoon they came to a halt in the big square, and some hours were then devoted to speeches, General Palmer, Harland, and others addressing them; the bands at intervals playing national airs. My ears yet ring with their hearty cheers for "President Lincoln," and "de Yanks General," Butler. The scene will not readily be forgotten by those who witnessed it. Ah, it was a day we never dreamed of seeing two years ags! Thank God for it!

CAPTAIN S. R. KEENAN,
56th Mass.

To Miss Sarah Southworth,
   Winthrop, Maine.

LETTER CCX.

THE MINE.

BEFORE PETERSBURG, Aug.

I AM tired and sleepy with a hard day's work: it is so hot, can't go to sleep, and the flies have bothered me nearly to death—made me nervous and twitchy. My temper is getting horribly irascible under these afflictions, joined to chronic mental irritation, occasioned by the prevalence of knaves and fools. I probably shall not write long, but go and sit under the general's tent-fly, and gnash my teeth.

I suppose you would like to hear my account of the affair of the 30th, and my part therein; but I have not dared to write about it, fearing I should say things I ought not to. Matters are mixed enough without my getting into a scrape.

But here is a sketch. But, by the way, don't you admire my reticence in saying nothing of the Mine, though my mind has been full of it for so long? Tell Heinrich I have a pipe for him, made out of clay dug out of the face of the Mine, clear under the enemy's works.

I was up the Mine the day before it was charged. Conceive, my child, entering the earth by a hole about four feet square, and continuing up that hole, bent nearly double, for nearly six hundred feet; lighting your uncertain steps through deep and sticky mud, by a candle held in one hand.

Arrived there you sit down, panting and perspiring, and listen to our friends the enemy pegging around over your head, hammering at gun platforms, rolling barrels, &c., which noises come to you very distinctly, though dull and muffled. It is a very odd sensation. Perhaps the rest can best be described by mingling it with my personal experience.

Three of the staff were detailed to go with the First, Second, and Third Divisions. I was to go with the Second Division, under General Potter. I awoke at 2 o'clock, A. M., received instructions from General ——, and rode over about 3 o'clock. Went to the front with General ——, where we were told that the fuse at the Mine had been fired, and the explosion would take place at 3.41. It was still quite dark, and we stood on a hill-side, opposite the enemy's line,—fifteen thousand men lying on their arms just below us, ready for a rush at the enemy's position.

The appointed time came—no explosion. Ten minutes passed—twenty—we began to look blank at each other. I got on my horse and rushed over to see the general, who was further to the left; wondered with him what the row was, and rushed back. Officer came up, and reported failure in the fuse; had been relit, and would be off at 4.42.

By this time it was quite light, and not much chance of taking the fellows in their beds. Punctually, at 4.42, we felt a trembling of the earth, a dull heavy explosion; and I jumped out upon the parapet in time to see a huge fountain of rebel fort and smoke, rushing 150 feet into the air. One hundred and twenty guns opened with a terrific crash. Our columns charged,—the enemy's line was gained, and the ball opened. But now the bad effect of our six weeks' crouching behind breastworks was apparent. The enemy opened a hot fire, and there was some difficulty in getting the men beyond the shelter of the enemy's line, towards the crest we were to take. Started after fifteen minutes' delay; but the head of the column was shivered by the hot fire, and came back. Other troops were put in, but the line of works they had to cross was so crowded with men, that confusion resulted. But Potter's Division went in well, and nearly gained the crest, but were driven back by the concentrated artillery fire. The Third Division went in on the left, and captured another fort, part of their line, and some prisoners.

I began to get anxious, and went down myself. The process of getting from our front line to the crater of the Mine was not pleasant, the rebs keeping up a cross-fire on the space between. I climbed over our works, and ran like a trooper to the other line, some one hundred and fifty yards, and stopped behind a large chunk of earth on the outer slope of the crater to rest, surrounded by a mass of dead rebels, and some of our own wounded, one of whom kindly suggested to me that I was on the wrong side of the chunk; and a bullet nearly taking the top of my head off, proved he was right. So I proceeded inside the crater, where I found some of the brigade commanders. I brought orders to advance; and just as I got there, written orders from General —— came to his division; so Colonel —— and I went down the rebel pits to the right, dead and wounded rebels so thick you couldn't avoid stepping on them. Two or three hundred yards down the line we came to the end of our troops, and the beginning of the rebels, who were firing at each other round an angle in the works, and twenty feet apart, quite sociable and pleasant. I helped —— form his brigade, and we jumped upon the bomb-proof and tried a charge, but ran into so hot a fire that the men broke. Were just reforming them, also the brigade behind ours, when the colored troops came bulging down the pits, knocking our line all to pieces. The colonel who was leading them wanted instructions where to go, and I gave them, showing how we could take a crook in the enemy's line, and probably bag most of the rebs there. So we got the fellows out of the pits, and made a rush for this part of the line, and took it, with a battle-flag and a lot of prisoners. It was exceedingly hot for a few minutes; but I have wonderful fortune, and came out unhurt, though with my clothing spattered with the blood of fellows hit around me. The darkies, certainly, went in well. I then went back, and met the other brigade of negroes coming in tip-top style. I stood in the centre, cheering, waving sword, &c., as did the other officers there, and urging the darkies to go in well. The ridge of the crater where they had to cross was pretty well swept with bullets, and not a pleasant place to go over; and there they betrayed rather a tendency to crawl. So I stood near there, and distributed cheers, blessings, expletives, and whacks of my sabre with great liberality.

At last the most of them were through, and were being formed towards the enemy for a charge, and I sat down to rest, nearer dead than I care to be again. The sun was frightfully hot, no water to be had. I was without breakfast, and it is a mercy I didn't have another sunstroke. The crater was filled with the debris of regiments broken up going through, the sides black with men; the enemy were getting the range of it with shell and schrapnel, rendering it unpleasant. Spang! a shell would strike right in a swarm of men: two or three would turn over dead, and others limp away wounded. Slap! a lot of case-shot would strike the other side, while overhead the canister was almost like a horizontal hailstorm—musket-bullets were, of course, also prevalent.

I forgot to say that during this last charge through the crater I was powerfully reminded of the picture of the taking of the Malakoff, of which you have a print. There was the same rugged blown-up appearance, fragments of gabions, sand-bags, gun-carriages, dead men; great chunks of earth, with perhaps a man sticking out from beneath; and ghastly dead all around—color-bearers, waving their flags—officers their swords and hats, &c. Of course, there was not the hand to hand skirmishing there is in the picture I speak of, still the general features on a somewhat smaller scale were like it.

I then went down the line again to see the commanders of the negro brigade that was to charge, gave him final instructions, and then started back to communicate with the general. By this time the enemy had got perfect range of the space between the crater and our advanced line, and it was more unpleasant going back than it was coming out: the whole crest of the crater was swept with a storm of bullets. I don't think I ever disliked a trip quite so much;

so I rested for a few moments behind the edge, talking with the colonel of one of our black regiments, then started over the top and ran like a good one for our lines, about one hundred and fifty yards, but it seemed *about a mile and a quarter.* Took a flying leap over our breastwork—safe and surprised—worked my way up to the general and reported.

Just then the darkies charged—were repulsed, and came back confusedly; adding to the crowded crater and pits of the enemy a mass of panic-stricken negroes.

It was a great mistake putting in the colored division at that time, but the general had imperative orders from General Meade to do so.

Directly after this repulse of the darkies, the rebs came down on our position, but were very handsomely repulsed. Then came an order for us to withdraw from the enemy's line, and close the fight. And so we quietly backed out with much loss from a half-fought field, with three corps behind us who had not been engaged; only one brigade of any other corps than this was engaged—the 9th Corps.

STAFF-OFFICER.

LETTER CCXI.

It's not the perils of the battlefield the soldier fears. Oh, no! it is the terrible, the awful, the inhuman *prisons* of rebeldom—prisons upon whose infernal gates seem written, "All hope abandon, ye who enter here!" Talk of the barbarity of the middle ages, or any other infamous or inhuman episode that ever cursed this beautiful world; they sink into insignificance compared with the barbarity which Federal prisoners receive in the *bull-pens* of the professedly hospitable and amiable South!

J. E.

LETTER CCXII.

AN EXODUS IN THE NINETEETH CENTURY.

"John Brown's body lies a-mouldering in the grave,
But his soul goes marching on!"

In the month of February, 1864, General Sherman organized and led an expedition from the city of Vicksburg into the heart of the Confederacy, which is known in history as the Meridian Expedition. Its chief objects were the destruction of the Mississippi Central Railroad, from Jackson to Meridian, and the capture or dispersal of the forces and destruction of the stores and machine-shops at the latter place. These aims, undertaken with boldness of conception, were accomplished with vigor of execution, and with slight loss of life on either side. The columns composed of portions of the 16th and 17th Army Corps, commanded respectively by Hurlbut and the gallant, lamented McPherson, left Vicksburg on the 3d of February, and the advance of their return re-entered the city on the 3d of March. But it is not concerning the main objects nor attainments that we intend to speak. They are already history, and little could be said which would add to the praise which the originator and leader of the foray already receives from his grateful countrymen for this, as for many other deeds of patriotism and devotion.

As the returning columns approached Black River, the eastward outpost of the defences of Vicksburg, there was a strange sight that met the eye. Following the vanguard of two or three regiments was a strange and motley gathering. There, toiling slowly along the rough road, might be seen old-men with gray heads and stooping forms, hobbling along on canes or crutches towards their not distant graves; there were stout, stalwart men in the prime of life, with brawny muscles and limbs strong for labor; there were young men and youths and boys and babes; there were girls and young women and matrons, and old withered crones who looked as if they had numbered far more than threescore years and ten of trouble and of toil. There was to be seen in the throng every hue known to the tillers of the Southern soil, from the pale, chalky albino, with his pink eyes and fawn-colored hair, through all the shades of flesh-color, cream-color, olive, chocolate, umber, and brown, to the deepest and jettiest of blacks. Every mode of conveyance known in that section of the country was in requisition to move this mass of humanity. Wagons of every description were there, from the light spanker-wagon to the great lumbering "conestoga," built high up before and behind like a Chinese junk. There were wagons with two, four, six yoke of oxen, wagons with horses and wagons with mules. Some were drawn by a combination of the two latter classes of locomotives, and some by all three together. One cart to which were hitched a sluggish ox and a mettlesome, restive Spanish ass, reminded me forcibly of the *ox* and the *ass* who have been tugging for years at either end of the Union yoke. Many of these travellers rode in carriages that had brought a thousand or more dollars to Northern mechanics; some were in buggies, some in carts, many had hand-barrows, one or two had small carts drawn by dogs, while to many—very many, old and young—fate had allotted only the progressives which nature furnished. A sulky that might have figured on the Pharsalia or Métairie race-courses, would be followed by the heavy plantation wagon, made by the "hands" and ironed by the rude "blacksmith" of "Marster's place." There were horses of the purest blood known in America, side by side with others who could boast no ancestry except the pair that Noah carried into the Ark, and their age made them appear as closely related to those. But all these vehicles were heavily laden. Many of them had nothing but human freight. In one broad-tread wagon I counted over thirty little round woolly pates, besides a couple of women, who were up there to keep the young ones quiet. Another scene for the artist was a sulky drawn by a raw-boned horse, with corn-shuck collar and rope harness, in which sat, in native dignity, a matron holding two small children; while hanging on the back of the conveyance was the father's eldest hope, a bare-legged boy of eight or ten, the color of gall-dyed charcoal; and to cap the climax, *paterfamilias* bestrode the rosinante, his long legs protruding *two feet* through his coarse homespun pants, and dangling over the shafts. For humanity's sake I made him dismount and lead his "forlorn hope" of a horse. I have said that many vehicles were loaded entirely with human beings, but many others were laden with household goods;—mattresses of straw, shucks, cotton, or feathers, bedclothes of every dye, pattern, and thickness; chairs of antique or modern make; even looking-glasses and musical instruments. For these people had gathered up in the short time intervening between their determining to "go with the Unioners" and their actual starting on their weary pilgrimage, not only their own possessions but every thing that struck their fancy, which they could lay their hands on. There were shawls of crape and cashmere, which had once hung in graceful folds from the rounded shoulders of Mississippi's belles as they whiled away the summer evenings of long ago, on the cool verandahs, or whirled in the schottische and mazourka, to the music of the bands at Saratoga or Newport. There were robes of silk and brocade and satin that had flaunted themselves beneath the gaslights of Southern palaces in the gone-by years; yes, there were even jewels of value, whose sheen had intensified the light that fell upon the fair bosoms of their wearers ere they cast it back; and which had been buried at the approach of "the Yanks," yet not so well concealed but that they had been found by the hitherto trusted lady's-maid or gentleman's valet. And it was not uncommon to see a valuable brooch shining on the bosom of a very dirty shirt of homespun cotton, or a sparkling ring contrasting with the finger of a sable damsel. Table-linen of the finest damask, magnificent carpets, rich curtains, "young mistress's" guitar, or "marster's" silver-mounted flute, even silver spoons, forks, and goblets, were to be found in old hair trunks, or rough deal "chests," or little wallets of the pilgrims, all of which had been "captured" or "confiscated," I believe the technical term is—here in civilization we would say stolen. Verily had the bondmen despoiled the Egyptians, their taskmasters!

But among all their luggage, useful or otherwise, it is a noticeable fact that hardly any of them had bethought themselves to bring food, from the abundance they left behind. Cooking utensils they had in abundance,—pots, skillets, gridirons, kettles—even a cooking-stove adorned the stern of one of the boat-like wagons; but nothing was there to cook. From the overflowing corn-cribs and smoke-houses they left, scarce one had brought a ham, or a "side," or a squash, or a sweet potatoe, or a sack of meal. Unaccustomed to think or to provide for themselves during their whole past lives, now, when cast upon their own resources, and possessing finery and gewgaws enough if sold to sustain them for months, yet the first great necessity of their condition was forgotten. Moreover, the bare thought of freedom had so enraptured them, that in their dreams it had painted with rosy colors the unknown fate to which they were tending, and caused the land of the Yankees to seem a land flowing with milk and honey! What need, then, to provide themselves with the "cornpone" and the rusty bacon?—coarse and unwelcome food of their former slave-lives. Freedom! and I suppose the very sound awoke as wildly thrilling an echo in their bosoms as erst in the heart of a Moses, or a Brutus, or a Tell, or a Washington. Freedom! and were the everyday things of their hard, past life necessaries which should enter into that elysium? What wonder, then, that they failed to provide food, and thus, alas! that so many mourned for the flesh-pots left behind! Our troops had started with but twenty days' rations, and a portion of these had been spoilt by weather, so that they were in a bad condition themselves, and but little could be spared for the destitute pilgrims. They could offer occupation to some as cooks, and to *all* protection from recapture; but it was impossible to feed the vast army that followed them, from the scanty rations which the depleted commissariat issued. Furthermore, a sharp cold spell came on about four days' march from Black River, and the poorly clad pilgrims fared hardly, sleeping in the frosty air at night, and marching (many of them barefoot) over the frozen ground in the morning. It is no wonder then, that, hungry and cold, strong men should hang their heads with overpowering sorrow, and children should weep at the unaccustomed hardships. It is little wonder that one mother, with two children in her arms, herself almost starved, should have thrown the smallest into the swift-running Pearl River, as she crossed the pontoon; and, when accused of the crime, palliated it by saying, "It had better drown than starve.'

Is it much more wonder that another woman should wrap her babe in a large blanket, and cast it into a great burning heap of rails, as she was about to start forward on a cold frosty morning? These things happened. The fault was not with the people, it was in their education. Nor is it wonderful that, on arriving at Vicksburg, and "corraling" near the pest-hospital, they should have taken the infection so quickly and so generally into their emaciated systems, and died off so fast before they could be sent to the plantations destined for their reception. And here let the record pause a moment, while I pay a merited tribute to a lady whose mission on earth seems to be that ascribed to genius:

> "——— To uplift,
> Purify, and confirm, by its own gracious gift,
> The world, in spite of the world's dull endeavor
> To degrade and drag down, and oppose it forever;
> . . . . . . to watch and to wait,
> To renew, to redeem, and to regenerate!"

I allude to the widow of a late governor of Wisconsin, who lost his life in the same employ in which she is spending hers—attending to the wants and well-being of the soldier and the freedman. To her individual and untiring efforts it is to be attributed that more of these poor creatures did not perish by the small-pox; and to her does many a soldier revert as to an angel who, when he was "sick or in prison, visited him," and ministered to all his wants. Many a heart in the Mississippi Valley blesses her. To resume. "What does all this mean? Who are these people? whence come they, and whither going?" were questions asked more than once by the spectators who saw the passing of the long array. The latter question was answered, in a manner, by one of the youngest of the pilgrims. He was a little fellow, not over three feet high, and made much broader than due regard for symmetry and proportion would warrant in a sculptor. Slung by a piece of rope and a strap over his shoulders, knapsack-wise, was a huge roll of blankets and comforters, looking larger than himself; and with this load he was trudging along with a bright eye and a firm step, each moment lengthening the distance between himself and the associations of his childhood, even as he was putting upon himself the duties of a man. As I rode alongside of him, I asked him, "Where are you going to, youngster?" Looking up at me with a smile on his face, and a sparkle in his eyes, he replied, "I'm gui-in to glory, marster!" There was the secret, the main-spring of the movement. That was the day-dream of all of them. And were they wrong? True, the road was long and stony. True, famine and pestilence and death stood immediately before, and only a portion of that vast multitude could pass these by unscathed; but are we so short-sighted as to look no further than that? I do not strain my mental vision to be able to see away yonder, in the ages that are to come, ere the millennium dawns—in the distance, and dimly foreshadowed, but yet discernible without a prophetic eye—a nation free, vigorous, educated, virtuous, religious; their commerce whitening the oceans, and their industry gladdening the land; their matrons teaching the children at the knee, their men busied with the affairs of life, their soldiers going forth to battle, and their sages sitting in council; their vines and fig-trees shadowing the earth, and their fanes pointing up towards the heavens; and over the door of their great temple, and on the folds of their stripeless, starry flag, I see written, "These are they which came out of bondage, and out of great tribulation!"

Glory! Is not that glory enough, distant though it be? and is not that deathless glory shared by those by whose strong right arms this people is disenthralled? Yes, in very truth it is; and this makes us forget all the heavy anguish of the labor. O ye dusky sons of Ham, deep and long and sad hath been the curse upon you! deep and long and sad is the travail by which ye are made free! O Ethiopia! to-day fulfil the prophecy!—to-day "stretch forth thy hands to God," and thank Him that a nation has been found by whom ye are made free!

WILL. M. McLAIN.

URBANA, Ohio, Feb. 15th, 1865.

LETTER CCXIII.

BATTLE OF THE WILDERNESS.

November, '64.

DEAR FRIEND—During the summer I received one or two letters from you, which I was unable to answer, in the midst, as we were, of the constant changes of the campaign; I might have sent you a short note acknowledging the receipt of it, but I felt that that would not be satisfactory. So now that I am once more in the bosom of home and at rest, after the long months of marching and fighting, I can please myself, and I hope you, with a somewhat full narrative of events. The "Legion" joined the Army of the Potomac at Spottsylvania, 16th of May, and on the 17th distinguished itself in a charge, losing a couple of hundred in killed and wounded; Col. Murphy wounded (left arm); Flood wounded (in thigh and abdomen), since dead. Capt. Dwyer, Col. De Lacy, and Major Byrne (since recovered), reported for duty about August 1st, and at the battle of Reams' Station, on August 25th, was captured, and is now in "Libby Prison." I was with Gen. Tyler, at Bull Plain, acting as aid-de-camp. Gen. Tyler joined the army with a heavy artillery division, 10,000 strong. On the 18th and 19th had a fight, whipping Ewell's corps, and losing nearly 1,000 men. Ewell's corps attempted a raid in our rear. Next day or two after we commenced a forced march from Spottsylvania towards Richmond, outflanking Lee's army. The weather was hot, and we marched night and day, through a beautiful country,— as yet untouched by the ravages of war,—to the North Anna River, where the enemy contested our crossing and further advance. As we were in the Second corps, under Gen. Hancock, and had the advance, we did nearly all the hot work—charged the fort that connected Chesterfield Bridge, capturing its guns and prisoners, in as hot a little musketry fight as I have seen for the short space of time. The Legion were engaged on the other side of the river (about the 24th of May), losing quite heavily, from the 170th particularly (five officers). The 69th acted well upon the occasion. We were shelled very heavily here by the enemy on the day we withdrew to continue our flanking process. Kinney, a brave fellow in action, received a wound through the arm from a sharp-shooter; however, he continued to do duty. We marched from here to the Pamunkey, crossed in pontoons, halted a day on the other side for rest; when Tyler's heavy artillery division was broken up, and he was given command of the Legion again, together with the 8th New York heavy artillery,—a regiment from Central New York, composed of splendid material, Col. Porter commanding, numbering 1,500 men. This was then called the Fourth Brigade, Second Division, Second Army Corps; but a month or two after its number was changed to the

Second Brigade, and numbered about 300. Tyler was as much pleased to get with old friends as was I. Tommy (the mail carrier) acted as mounted orderly, and afterwards carried our brigade flag through many a fight right gallantly.

From the Pamunkey we marched to a creek called the Tolopotamy, some fifteen miles from Richmond: here we had some severe attacks from the enemy, all of which were repulsed. From the Tolopotamy we marched to Coal Harbor, reaching there June 2d, and proceeded to build breastworks in the face of the foe, who were heavily intrenched behind the outer defences of Richmond. At daybreak, on the 3d of June, was inaugurated the great battle of Coal Harbor. In our brigade Gen. Tyler was wounded, and has not been able to return to the field since. The gallant MacMahon was killed. Col. Porter was killed, bravely doing his duty. This man was a true patriot; one who, though worth millions of money, yet gave up every thing, even life itself, to do his share towards putting down the rebellion. Schuyler was wounded, and afterwards died in hospital; he too had a fearless spirit. Owen was wounded. Captains Butler and Nugent, of the 69th, were killed. Capt. Carolan and Winterbottom also wounded. Many other officers were killed or wounded, that I do not now recollect. Lamotte and I escaped, though I was mounted and on duty through the pandemonium made by shot and shell! I can only attribute our preservation to Providence. We lost about 1200 killed and wounded here, *one out of every three* of our brigade,—only think of it!—over which Gen. Gibbon assigned Col. Ramsay, of the 8th New Jersey. Our headquarters were always under fire, and the sharp-shooters' bullets were constantly whistling through the trees. At night the rebels frequently assaulted our lines, about 8 or 9 P. M., when the most infernal racket would be kept up for about an hour, shot, shell, and musketry intermingling promiscuously.

From Coal Harbor we made another shifting flank movement to the James River. This was a terrible forced march, lasting all one night, and next day, and half of the ensuing night, before we halted to eat or sleep. Here we were so close to the enemy that we had to send all canteens, &c., that would rattle when the men moved, to the rear; and at dark made the band play until the brigade had crept silently away to the rear, from under the very noses of the unsuspecting "Johnnies." It was a beautiful moonlight, and the long columns of dusky warriors with bayonets glistening in the mellow light, moving so silently, gave the whole thing a bewitching air of mystery. Our line of march led us to the Chickahominy, which we reached and crossed on pontoons—(River of Death!) And well named it is, for thousands of our poor fellows of the 69th christened its banks with their life's blood. It is a horribly muddy, swampy, sluggish stream.

The country between this and the James we found flourishing and full of growing crops. We crossed the James on the eve of the 4th of June in numerous steamers, with our band playing, smoking our pipes in the moonlight. It seemed a fairy scene!

The next morning about 9 we started for another long march to Petersburg. When we had marched all day up to 9 P. M. we halted within five miles of Petersburg, and met ambulances full of colored wounded soldiers. They had just had a fight, and captured the strongest line of defensive works in front of the city. If we had been told, tired and worn out as we were, that by keeping up our pluck, and marching on for a few miles further, the city lay at our mercy, we could have marched right in, but delayed until 5 P. M. the next day (the 16th); then made a grand charge, which, as the rebels had been heavily reinforced, they were enabled to check us in some parts, but couldn't in others, as they evacuated their second line of works next day.

On the 18th we were in another fight. Again on the 22d we got into it hot and heavy.

I forgot to say that Colonel Ramsay was wounded on the 16th, and that Colonel Blaisdell was assigned the command—as brave a man as ever lived; had been through all the Mexican war; his time had expired, but he would not leave the new recruits of his regiment behind, so re-enlisted.

On the 22d, the second and sixth corps, in extending our lines around Petersburg to the left (where that misfortune occurred in which we lost McKnight's battery and about 1200 prisoners), in making a movement a gap was made between the sixth corps and first division of ours: the rebs in one heavy column turned the flank of our corps, and in overwhelming numbers poured in a rear fire before we noticed them. Our brigade happened to be in reserve, and was immediately ordered to the front, to charge and retake the guns; but Gen. Pierce, who was in command of the movement, delayed the charge for some reason, when he was placed under arrest by Gen. Gibbon, and our Colonel (Blaisdell) ordered to make it. We aids flew around giving the necessary orders, and with a rush the brigade pushed ahead to retake the breastworks; but they were full of new reinforcements, and we were met by such a galling fire that we were obliged to halt, although some of our men got into the ditch. All through the night we worked like beavers, throwing up counter works within a few yards of the enemy, who kept up a continual fire on us, hitting some poor fellow every minute. Balls were cutting through the trees continually. I was up all night with our indefatigable colonel, running along our lines at times to see how the work was progressing; at others hunting up ammunition, tools, stretchers, to carry off the wounded, &c. I was worn out the next day. At daylight we worried and frightened the Johnnies to such an extent by our noisy working during the darkness, that they expected a charge, and evacuated. So we eventually gained the position captured the day before. This was our last battle for some time. We were often under fire though, both from artillery and the balls of the sharp-shooters. Our corps was held in reserve, or as a flying corps. We were all OK until the next "orderly" should ride up in haste with, "You will hold your commands in readiness to move at a moment's warning"—"Gentlemen, mount," from the brigade commanders; and then, under guidance of some staff-officer from headquarters, we'd move away, expecting every moment to be put in another fight.

Some of those hot, dry, dusty marches in the summer months were fearful. I have actually seen scores of poor sun-stricken soldiers by the wayside, many of them dying. They dreaded a hot march worse than a fight.

Our corps and Sheridan's cavalry were sent by night across the peninsula on which Bermuda Hundred is situated. Here we charged a rebel brigade, dashing in on them so impetuously that they, seeing our overwhelming numbers, precipitately fled. We captured two of their batteries, which proved on examination to have formerly belonged to the United States. In the night we made a forced march back to Petersburg.

I had the honor of taking dinner with General Foster, an old friend of Suffolk days, then a colonel.

We reached our lines about sunrise of the day on which the great mine was exploded. Soon a grand bombardment was opened all along our lines, and at four-and-a-half the mine blew up. Then that charge was made by the Ninth corps. . . . . Our corps, being fatigued by the fighting at Deep Bottom, was held in reserve. We still remained in close proximity to the enemy, skirmishing continually.

About August 20th, Gen. Grant had pushed the Fifth corps across the Weldon Railroad, and met with little or no opposition, thereby destroying one of Lee's chief lines of communication. Our brigade supported this corps whilst it fortified and destroyed several miles of the road.

On the evening of the 25th, the first and second line of our corps, numbering, with Spears' brigade of cavalry, 5,000 or 6,000 men, were sent down to Reams' Station on the railroad, to continue its destruction. Gen. Lee soon knew our numbers, isolation, &c.; and on the 25th sent down Hill's corps and Hampton's cavalry "to use us up." There was skirmishing and change of position going on all day, but it was not until 5 P. M. that the battle really commenced, the rebels outnumbering us five to one. It was a busy day for the "staff." We were flying about continually. I had just got in from the picket line, which I had been inspecting, and was thinking about eating (having fasted since morning) some dinner, which our boys had just brought in, when Colonel M—— posted me off again in our front to see about the skirmish line. I found it was weak, and the rebels pouring in; but although an occasional bolt was shot from a battery in our front, the fight had not yet opened in earnest. Our front was held, protected by a swamp and woods, so I did not anticipate much trouble there; but when I returned the second time, and reported progress, the enemy suddenly opened on us from two batteries planted about 500 yards from our right flank, in the edge of the woods. These batteries enfiladed us, and such another dose of shot and shell I have never experienced. We sent our horses in the rear in time to save them, and got close to the works. The missiles fell high and low around and amongst us. We lost many officers and men from this hot fire. I expected my time had come, but I was protected by a merciful Providence. After enduring this demoralizing attention awhile, we heard them coming on all sides—front, flank, and rear. Soon our men became unmanageable under the bewildering fire. The colonel ordered one or two regiments " to try and save the Rhode Island battery," which was abandoned by its gunners; but it was impossible. The horses were nearly all shot, and no road was open to drag the guns away by hand. All the brave boys could do was to load and fire as fast as possible, but it was no use against such odds. One shabby rebel, after I had been slightly wounded in the right arm by a piece of shell which disabled me, pointed his piece at me, and remarked, "Come in." I raised my cap in token of surrender. At the same time two officers rushed at me for my sword. I refused to give it to them, desiring to be permitted to do so to the commanding officer of their regiment. But they "couldn't see it," and one impatiently drew his rifle and threatened to run me through " if I did not give up immediately." We were all then hastened under guard to the rear, whilst shots from our own guns flew over our heads. On our way back we passed the two batteries which had paid us such particular attention, and one reb remarked, "Those are Pegram's guns—the best in the service." When we reached an open space, well to the rear, we were halted until about 8 or 9 P. M. After dark a thunderstorm came up and drenched us completely. We were given nothing to eat, were marched through the mud about five miles that night, and then permitted to sleep until morning on the wet ground—no blankets. It was rough, I tell you. Hungry, tired, and wet through, we started at daybreak, and marched all day long, taking a wide circuit to avoid the left of our army, and reached Petersburg about 5 P. M. We were quartered for the night on an island on the Appomattox River, given nothing to eat, and again we were allowed to sleep in a pouring rain, unsheltered, on the ground. About 11 A. M. on the 27th we were fed—hardtack and bacon.

We were taken about noon to Richmond by railroad, and marched in triumph through the city to the Libby Prison. We were searched, and ordered to give up our greenbacks for "safe-keeping;" then marched up-stairs to our "quarters," and once there, our monotonous life began. At daybreak half-a-dozen colored men (also captives) came up under guard and swept the room. We were given a dirty blanket and one tin plate. We ate, sat, and slept on the floor. About 9 A. M. we were fed with a piece of corn-bread and a slice of bacon or boiled beef; at 3.30 P. M. dinner—the same quantity of bread, and half a pot of black, buggy beans. We had a bath-tub and plenty of water—a great blessing. We could of course keep clean by washing, but we could not keep away vermin, which abounded. I got that army scourge, the diarrhea, badly, and had to go into hospital. Here we had straw beds, and plenty of (dirty) linen and blankets. I began to improve a little.

The flag-of-truce boat, the New York, came up with a load of prisoners, sick and wounded, and great was the speculation in hospital as to who would be sent away in exchange. A medical inspector came around one afternoon, and examined us all. My name was put down to go. Oh, what a happy night that was! The next day the rebel boat took us down the James, to Aiken's Landing, where we were transferred to the New York, and were once more under the Stars and Stripes. I never realized the beauty and value of our flag until then.

Down the James we sailed, passed City Point and Fortress Monroe, steamed up the Chesapeake to Annapolis, where we got 20 days' leave; then on home, where I have been spending the time " happy at home."

I hear the brigade did not number 200 men after the battle of Reams' Station!

Please answer soon. Your comrade in arms and ever true friend,

J. T. CONOLLY, A. D. C.

LETTER CCXIV.

" Lost Mountain."

CAMP MARIETTA, Ga.

SINCE leaving home and joining the *gallant Sherman* once more, we have been continually moving;—not over five miles in the last two weeks, but it has been almost as hard as steady marching. We are causing the enemy to abandon one position after another, only to take *a new one*. We have to-day been at work on a new point. "Lost Mountain" is almost surrounded by us, and yet they linger there. It stands alone, towering high above the surrounding country, and so steep as to render impracticable an advance. We are about ten miles from Atlanta, but many brave boys must fall before we reach there. I know of four being killed to-day in our brigade by stray shells. I have to jump occasionally, when a ball crashes through the timber above me. Somehow I *cannot become* careless of life. Now I am compelled to close, in order to take my scanty allowance of supper; yet I am content with it. Once, during our raid with Sherman in Mississippi, we lived three days on parched corn, and such articles as could be gathered to supply the place of bread. But we bore it like men, *without a murmur.*

W. S. HUBBELL,
32d Ohio Vols.

LETTER CCXV.

BEFORE PETERSBURG, 1864.

THESE men who take one another by the hand this minute, may the next send one another to the spirit-land. These who are now trading tobacco for coffee and sugar, may, ere another hour rolls round, be trading lead for lead. It seems as though men in the time of war lose their civilization. Oh, how fearful must be the punishment of those who were the cause of all this sacrifice of human life! How bitter must be the pangs of conscience of its leaders, as they feel the iron hand of the North taking its vice-like grip on the throat of this Rebellion! Would I change places with any of them? I believe they are fighting to establish a monarchy, as much as any thing else. This I get from reading their letters and hearing them talk: for "*Nobility*" is the burden of their sigh!

LETTER CCXVI.

CAMP PAROLE, ANNAPOLIS, NOV. 28, 1864.

"As one from cruel hands I come,
From hearts that know no pity, dark and vengeful,
That quaff the tears of wretches, bathe in blood,
And know no music but the groans of men!"

YES, I have just escaped from the horrible, terrible, the abominable, the indescribable Camp Sumter or Federal prison—alias Bull-pen—at Andersonville. How came I there? On the 19th of last June, a division of cavalry, under the command of a certain poor individual misnamed Gen. ——, started on a ten days' raid, for the purpose of destroying the Petersburg, Danville, and other branches of railroads that helped to feed the rebel army. We started—accomplished our object, but not without considerable hardship and fighting. Returning, we were met by the enemy at Stony Creek, and after a night of hard fighting, succeeded in routing them. They fell back, formed at Reams' Station, where they were reinforced by three brigades of infantry, among which was Mulligan's. Outnumbered, and without any kind of position, we were, after some hard fighting, compelled to retreat. And such a retreat! why, it would have made a mouth hermetically sealed with taciturnity burst out in most uproarious laughter. Why? Apart from the wonderfully confused and jostling position of our cavalry, each seemingly anxious only for his own safety, the general included, upwards of five hundred head of negroes of both sexes and all ages (picked up here and there, and brought along in compliance with their own wishes), fled helter-skelter at both flanks, howling and yelling with an almost insane fear, forming the most panic-stricken, obstreperous, and indeed comical crowd I ever witnessed. Indeed, the whole scene was truly ridiculous and laughable, and I could not help indulging in a most risible fit, despite the peril that environed me. My horse having been played out two days before this disaster, I was mounted on one of those gallant animals that, like a great many of their masters, have more strength than knowledge—a mule. He was completely used up, as indeed were all the animals; and after a terrible but vain dose of kicking, spurring, and licking, I succeeded in getting him along for some distance, when coming to a large ravine, he, with several of his cousins and brethren, rolled headlong in, nearly crushing to death themselves and their luckless masters! Rousing myself from this, I, with some fifty others, now started on foot (as did hundreds of others whose horses were fagged out), and just as we were about darting into a wild, woody recess, the better to aid our flight, a party of about two hundred rebels flanked us on the right, calling loudly on us to surrender. Some did; but others more anxious for their freedom, among whom I was, continued to flee: when some were stricken down dead, and one of those death-dealing blackguard bullets, fond of a fleshy residence and a bloody drink, took up its lodging in the calf of my right leg, and causing its unfortunate owner to whine and growl with an agony as keen as his late laughter was hilarious.

Enough—I was captured, and brought with hundreds of others to Petersburg prison that night. Next day, hungry and weary, painful and wretched, about eight hundred of us were started to Richmond—marched into the Hotel de Libby, where we were robbed of every thing we possessed. After starving and suffering here for about fifteen days (I was in a wretched ward that was honored by the name of hospital, where my wound, much to my astonishment, succeeded in getting better), we were started for

Danville prison. From thence we were removed to Andersonville, where, after eight days of the most cruel misery and starvation (seventy of us being crowded in every freight-car, and fasting most of the time during the journey), we arrived more like dead than living beings. We were then marched into the prison or stockade (a piece of most uneven ground of about thirty acres, bare as the palm of your hand, fenced round by a large, high, wooden wall, to the height of forty feet), where upwards of 35,000 human beings were huddled together in the most awful and fearful misery imaginable—misery and privation beyond all description and conception. Nor was this all, for the utmost heartlessness, the most cold-blooded inhumanity pervaded all ranks; the weak were robbed and kicked about by the strong; the sick could not get a drink of water from the convalescent or well; gangs of thieves and rowdies roamed and plundered with impunity; the dying, devoured by vermin of all kinds, could be seen in numbers everywhere. Death was too common a thing to notice; and villains there were, many who slept without fear or remorse, in wretched tents, beneath which lay the bodies of wretches they killed and plundered! Good God! there is no such thing as describing this horrible place, or the misery and villany that reigned there.

I should have remarked, that around and within ten feet of the stockade, at every side, ran a "dead line," and woe to the wretch who, not only ventured without, but even leaned upon this accursed mark. He was shot down like a dog. There was a wretched creek running through this bull-pen, a part of which was the filthiest and most disgusting sink ever seen; another part from which we drew water, came in contact with this dead-line. In order to get the water clearer, some would now and then lean their heads beyond the dead line, when they were instantly shot down by the fiendish sentries on the top of the stockade. Report had it, that those sentries received two months furlough for every Yank they killed, and one month for every one they wounded.

During my time in the stockade, I had no shelter from the sun by day, the dew by night, or the terrible rains that so often visit that State; but, indeed, I was not alone in this, for thousands of others were in the same sad predicament. The only shelter, if such it could be called, which many had, was either in the shape of holes dug in the ground and roofed over with mud and rags, and would-be tents, made out of old clothes, pieces of old blankets, and now and then some brush, the best of which was unable to keep out the rain. Men died at the rate of three hundred a week! The records show, that from the 18th of March to the 10th of November, 14,690 human beings died at that fearful place!

Our rations consisted of a piece of corn-bread, made out of the coarsest unsifted meal, and a few ounces of pork. Men who entered there stout and strong, in a short time staggered as they walked, and looked more like a ghost of mendicity and privation than aught else. Without, and to the south of the stockade, was a miserable institution called a hospital, composed of a few rows of condemned tents, to which none was admitted till just on the eve of death. Indeed, the majority died ere they arrived there. Wounded and sick men were thought nothing about. My wound having broke out anew, was frightful to look at, from want of care. I looked upon it for a long time as a lost limb. How I limped for water and other necessaries; how I spent the cold, cold nights with that dreadful limb, none save God and I can ever tell. At last, by much ado, I succeeded in getting into the hospital for the purpose of having it amputated, but, thanks to God, after burning it with nitric acid, nitrate of silver, and keeping turpentine and linseed meal to it for about six weeks, I succeeded, but not without infinite pain, in getting the gangrene out. This demon once ejected, I was soon fit to report for exchange. In a lucky, most lucky moment, I told the doctor that I was prepared to meet all difficulties, and deemed myself in every way fit to go. He consented, my name was taken down, and in a few days afterwards I was on my way, with eight hundred others, to Savannah, for the purpose of being paroled. O God! what joy I felt, all felt, as we saw once more the glorious stars and stripes! And as I stepped on board the "New York," receiving boat, I felt, as it were, that a new spirit had taken possession of me, that all my misery was over, and that a happy longevity was still in reserve for me. Be this as it may, I shall ever, whilst life is mine, celebrate here the glorious anniversary of the 20th of November, that set me free.

We are paroled for 90 days, and are now at this camp, where every thing is comfortable. I am in the convalescent section, and for once in eight months I have taken off my pants and enjoyed the downy raptures of a tick of straw and two new blankets. Besides, I now enjoy the luxury of a drawers and shirt, together with shoes and stockings, articles of which my flesh was entirely innocent since my capture.

I speak seriously, most seriously, that if ever there was a being chastened, humbled, and purified by the absolute experience of misery, I am that being. There was a time when I couldn't appreciate any thing, being tired and satiated with every thing; but now, oh, now! the smallest, the humblest of God's blessings, even to a piece of bread, has a rapture and charm for me never known before!

I am now able to walk, but not without limping, but thank Heaven, after passing through the most horrible ordeal of misery ever endured upon this earth, I stand to day the same being I was before, only wiser and better, though I may be perchance somewhat sadder.

JOHN ENGLAND,
Co. E, 2d N. Y. Cav.

LETTER CCXVII.

GENERAL MCPHERSON.

In the "Front," near ATLANTA, GA., 1864.

THROUGH an all-wise Providence I am yet spared, although my regiment has been continually in the front, and on the 22d inst. helped to fight the hardest battle of the campaign. Our corps (the 17th) contended with double its number, and handsomely repulsed charge after charge which they made on us. In this day's engagement we killed, wounded, and captured over 8,000 of the enemy, which was more men than we had in action. The forces engaged on our side, on the 22d, were a part of the 15th, 16th, and all of the 17th Army Corps. This was to the left of our line east of Atlanta.

On the same day (the 22d) we lost our noble, brave, gentlemanly department commander, Major-General J. B. McPherson. A more noble, kind, consistent general never was known. He for a long time commanded our 17th Corps, and we have had every opportunity to become acquainted with him, and at all times he took every care to preserve the lives and health of his men. In him the country has sustained an irreparable loss, and the soldiers of the 17th Corps the kindest friend.

On the night of the 26th, our corps and the 15th and 16th commenced a movement from the left to the right, where we arrived on the afternoon of the 27th, formed into line, advanced nearly a mile, bivouacked for the night, in the morning commenced our advance again, moved about 80 rods, when the 15th was heavily assaulted by the enemy, coming on with shouts and yells, determined to drive the 15th back, which they found to be a serious matter. They were handsomely repulsed with heavy loss, and so with seven successive charges which they made on it. Their loss was very severe, ours slight; so thickly was the ground covered with slain that one could have stepped from body to body over the ground without touching it! One who has never seen a battle-field can form no idea of its horrors. The groans and cries of the wounded and dying as they wailingly cry for help, is enough to call down tears from high heaven for the inconsistency of the human family. How many are being laid beneath grassy mounds, in the land of treason!

We are not yet in possession of Atlanta, though very sanguine of success. Our operations here are now in the form of a regular siege. We are gradually approaching the enemy, who most obstinately contest every inch of ground that we force them to abandon.

Our regiment is now within 300 yards of the enemy's main line of works, and their balls are continually whistling over and in our bivouacs, frequently wounding and sometimes killing our comrades. I know not how long it will be until we get possession of Atlanta, but I think there is a move on foot which will cause the "Johnnies" to resume a backward movement and give us possession of the city, from which I hope to date my next letter. If you could but see how thankful the sick and wounded soldier is when he receives the comforts and delicacies given him by the Sanitary Commission, you would never tire in your work of love and charity for us.

One of my brave comrades fallen! A true patriot; an ornament in any society which might be graced by his presence. Nobly has he fallen, as thousands of other brave men in defence of his country, which traitors North and South are endeavoring to destroy.

W. R. SNOOK,
68th Ohio Vols.

LETTER CCXVIII.

BEFORE PETERSBURG.

WE know that our services are appreciated by friends at home; and that the prayers of those for whom we are suffering hardships and dangers follow us in the camp and on the battle-field, encouraging us in the path of duty and right. This has been a long and cruel war; thousands of brave men have fallen in defence of that "starry banner" you love so dearly. How anxiously do we look for the dawning of that day when those "bands of white and rosy light" shall float from every town and bay and hill of our national Union! Then, and then only, will our task be finished.

When rebel shots were thundering against the walls of Sumter, and rebellion had just begun to show its serpent head, I was impatient to meet the traitor foe.

The pickets keep up a constant rattle of musketry, and about once a minute the "Petersburg Express" (a huge mortar) sends a shell into the fated city. There is not a minute, day or night, but what we hear the cannon's roar or the rifle's crack. But we don't mind it much. We have gotten used to it. It is our trade; 'tis music to us. We go to sleep to it, we wake to it; but I cannot say we like it. You have doubtless heard of Burnside's old Ninth Corps. We have followed him since his great expedition in '62, and he thinks a great deal of us, and we love him.

CHARLIE H. WHITE,
21st Mass. Vet. Vols.

LETTER CCXIX.

"THE VICKSBURG UNION LITERARY SOCIETY."—BROKEN TIES.

YES, we are all scattered now! Some are gone away forever—some are here, others there! Hardly two together anywhere! One night, about a year ago, the "Vicksburg Literary Society" held a "sociable," with a supper afterwards. It was nearly three o'clock in the morning when we were done; and Rollins and McCall and I concluded not to go back to camp, but stay all night in the church, where we held our meeting. But the boards were very hard, even for soldiers, so we took down the large "storm-flags" that we had used to ornament the room with, doubled them, and made a bed of them, and then we took others for a covering,

> "Laid peaceful down, as brothers tried,
> And slept until the morning beam
> Purpled the mountain and the stream."

I assisted last evening in arranging our Lyceum Hall for a public meeting, and carried my own flag in. It became untied, as I rode along, and I wrapped it about my neck and shoulders for a *comforter*, and it reminded me of that other time! Alas! one of the three is dead and sleeps among the clods of the valley, while the other two are clinging to a miserable existence, while there is

> " Charging of squadrons and rush of brigades,
> And wheeling of horses and doing of deeds!"

WILL. M. McLAIN,
32d Ohio Vol.

URBANA, Feb. 1865.

LETTER CCXX.

. ARMY OF THE POTOMAC,
Annapolis, 1864.

THE view across the river is very beautiful: the waving corn and fields of grain; the houses nestled in the woods and crowning the hills, combined with the sheen of the water, the craft, from the large steamer down to the little sail and row boat, which are continually plying upon its surface, form a very refreshing prospect upon a hot day.

The great event of the day was the raising of the flagpole. As the stars and stripes opened their folds to the breeze, the band struck up the "Star Spangled Banner," which was followed by prayer and singing. It began to rain before the speeches commenced, and we all adjourned to the chapel. The speakers were members of the Maryland Legislature, which meets here (at Annapolis). If one can judge by their "talk," they are very patriotic; but I would rather hear them "talk" through the muzzles of their guns. The time for talking is over, and has been for some time. Action is what we want.

BEFORE PETERSBURG.

A merry Christmas for all hands! We had roast turkey for dinner, cranberry sauce, and green peas. The churchbells are ringing for worship in Petersburg, the spires of which are in plain sight. Deserters are coming into our lines every night, and seem much pleased to find themselves safe and sound in the land of freedom.

WARD B. FROTHINGHAM,
Lieut. 59th Reg. Vet. Vols.

LETTER CCXXI.

LEE'S SURRENDER.

VIRGINIA,—CAMP IN A FIELD,
April 14th, 1865.

DEAR AUNT—We have had so much fighting to do that we have not had time for any thing else but sleeping, eating, and marching; all of which we did in the latest and most approved style. The Third Division of Cavalry, under command of General Sheridan and General Custer, started from Petersburg and marched to the right of the line and commenced the battle. General Custer drove the rebels from their position; and when we got them started we kept them going, but at night the rebels made a stand, and then we would flank them and drive them out, capture some prisoners, a battle-flag, or a battery, and then chase them again. But of all the battles that ever I was in, the fight of Harper's Farms was a little the hottest.

Our regiment was in advance. General Custer rode up, with his band playing "Hail Columbia," "Star Spangled Banner," and "Rally Round the Flag, Boys," and then the bugle sounded the charge. Away we went, with our sabres swinging at our wrists, ready to grasp at a moment's warning, and our carbines at an advance, ready for use. We had not gone more than forty rods, when the rebels opened fire upon us from three points, with grape and canister, solid shot, and shell, and musketry. We charged up to the face of the rebel batteries, under their fire; but we had to retreat. In the second charge, however, we captured their batteries and a number of prisoners.

The name of Sheridan will live always in the memory of the American people! It was glorious to see him seize the battle-flag, and ride to that part of the line where the fire was hottest and the fight the hardest. But the most glorious part of it all was Lee's surrender!

General Custer was riding at the head of our regiment when the flag of truce came out, but the general did not wish to halt—he wished to whip them completely; but we had to stop and wait the arrival of the flag of truce, and listen to the message from Lee. General Custer's reply was, "Tell your commander we are on his front, his flank, and rear. Our only conditions are his *surrender*." This message was sent at ten o'clock Sunday morning, April 9th, and Lee surrendered at 4 o'clock P. M.

It was, indeed, a glorious sight to see the rebels lay down their arms. I intended to send you some relic from the scene where the papers of capitulation were signed, but I have been ill and could not. We fired one hundred guns to-day, in honor of our flag being raised again over Sumter.

E. G. MARSH,
15th N. Y. Cavalry, General Custer's Div.

LETTER CCXXII.
Our Loss.

FORT LEAVENWORTH, Kansas,
April 16th, 1865.

THE vicissitudes of life are strange, and sometimes appalling in the intensity of their effects. Only a few days ago I thought of writing to you to tell how my heart leaped with joy; and thanksgiving filled my soul with sweet emotions that would speak forth to a grateful and patriotic nature, because of the great successes of the army of late.

My strength was well-nigh spent in the service of my country, but the glad news of victory seemed reward enough for me. But, merciful heavens! whose sagacity and precaution had prepared him to believe that the nineteenth century had concentrated enough guilt and fiendish courage in any one depraved mortal to assassinate President Lincoln?

It is thirty-six hours since I learned the facts, but my mind refuses to consider any other subject; and as the truth of this unparalleled murder comes home again and again, it seems more and more astounding! I search in vain for figures of speech to equal the awful deed. But why am I thus amazed?

This act belongs to the same category of crime that constitute the "bone and sinew," frame and finish of the slaveholding rebellion. I called this crime unparalleled. It is unparalleled. So are nearly all their deeds unequalled only by their own acts of kindred nature.

So kind-hearted, devoted, and forgiving a patriot as Abraham Lincoln *assassinated!* And by whom? By one of the villanous traitor-crew, for whom he was the only mediator that would voluntarily save their necks from the traitor's rope, that they most undeniably deserve. But they seem bound on ruin and murder.

I thought I was stern and unyielding to sorrow's throes, but the news of this sudden, terrible death of our beloved President makes the tears flow as though I had a woman's eyes and the tenderness of a child. But the nation is safe.

In the language of your lamented friend, S. A. Rollins, "I ever had faith in my country."

A ruler, whose rod was love, and whose punishment was forgiveness, is swept away by the assassin's hand, to be succeeded by one whose criterion is *the law*, and the law is, *death to traitors and assassins!* He who was more used to the kindliness of Christianized society, is followed by one who knows so well the purpose, intent, crime, and villany of rebels, that he cannot miss his mark.

I thought I had done my duty in the field. I am more broken down and worn out than I thought, but I contemplate returning to the army, to stay as long as treason shows her hydra head. I think the war will continue longer than if Lincoln had lived, but I have full faith that all is for the best, and that God will marvellously bring good out of apparent evil. My faith in Republicanism is strong, and much *increased* during the war.

Lieut. Dougal McCall,
66th U. S. Cavalry.

LETTER CCXXIII.

Joy and Grief.

Raleigh, N. C., April 20, 1865.

I do most heartily join you in congratulations over our recent victories. Yesterday Johnston surrendered the whole of the remaining Confederacy to our glorious Sherman! But our joy is dampened by the foul murder of the "good man"—our beloved President. I wish I could, in the least, give you an idea of the feeling in our army—it is awful! I never saw such a desperate set of men in my whole life, as I see in every company. Go where you will, nothing but the most fearful curses and cries for revenge can be heard.

As soon as the news reached General Sherman he moved all his army away from the vicinity of the city, fearing the men would break through all bounds and destroy the whole concern. It was a merciful thing, for the place is crowded with women and children. As it was, the utmost vigilance had to be used to prevent the guards themselves from firing the buildings. If Johnston had not given up as soon as he did, I actually think that our men would have attacked him without orders. Another fight would be a scene of horror. The men would not take a prisoner. You cannot begin to imagine the feeling—it is fearful. . . . . .

We left Goldsboro on the 10th, and just before starting from our bivouac, on the morning of the 12th, the dispatch, from Grant to Sherman, announcing the capitulation of Lee, was read. It created the wildest joy among the troops. They rushed about, shouting, tossing caps, firing guns, dancing, and, in fact, they went wild. Our only foe then was Johnston. He, they allowed, didn't amount to much any way; the different combinations, Thomas, Sheridan, Stoneman, and Kilpatrick, entirely hemming him in, so that escape was impossible, and to fight was suicide.

Now, when the war is so gloriously finished, to think that our President should be so foully murdered, is more than we can bear. Commencing with treachery and deceit, they finished their career with midnight assassination! A fit birth and death. If fighting had continued, no one knows how it would end. Apart from the closing of the war, it is a mercy few of us yet appreciate. The South would have been deluged with blood; fire and sword would have laid a heavy mark on this once fair land. Nothing would have been left.

If I should speak my real feelings, I should say that I am sorry the war is ended. Pray do not think me murderous. No; but all the punishment we could inflict on the rebels would not atone for one drop of the blood so cruelly spilled. I would exterminate them, root and branch. They have often said they preferred it before subjugation, and, with the good help of God, I would give it them. I am only saying what thousands say every day. Our army is sorry that they have done their work; they have a deep-seated love for Abraham Lincoln, and when they see no chance for further chastisement of our enemy, they give vent to their feelings in other ways. I do hope you won't think me violent. I cannot help it. You, at home, little know the trials and dangers we have passed through in four years of war. To bring our beloved country through the storm, we have endured, without a murmur, the severe hardships of campaign life and the danger of many a battle, all because we had faith in our cause and in our President. For four long years he has guided the ship through storms that would have appalled a less honest and patriotic heart. For four long years we have given our nation's honor to his keeping, knowing well that it would be kept without a stain, and returned to us more bright than ever. At last, when his pure patriotism, and our endeavors, were on the eve of being rewarded by seeing our country free, and again in peace, he, our pride and our nation's idol, is taken from us. Oh, with what joy could we commence our homeward march, if he were only there to receive us! As it is, we feel sad and dispirited. It is a triumph for our foe; they, despairing of victory in fair fight, must cloud our triumph with this pall of darkness. Surely there must be some punishment for such a deed. The more I think of it the worse I grow. I'll change the subject.

In all probability we will very soon be on our way to Washington. It is Sherman's design to march his army there, and then disband it. We all look forward to home by the "glorious Fourth." What a day that will be! It will be a fitting ending of the army to march through Washington.

Yesterday I saw what pleased me, and I know you would have felt pleasure in it too,—the review of the 10th A. C., composed principally of negroes. Actually I never saw a finer body of men in uniform than on that occasion. Every thing was in the best condition; clean clothes, bright buttons, guns in splendid order, first-rate marching, and, in fact, every thing tending to the appearance of good soldiers, including a certain proud and manly bearing, was there to be seen. I must not forget to mention their flags. They were in perfect shreds, torn in pieces, and one instance only the bare staff. A soldier always looks to the flag for evidence of service. The colored soldiers can bear theirs with pride. It must have been galling to the citizens of this place to see their former slaves proudly marching through their streets, conscious of their new position—they the masters! To-day our corps (23d) passed in review. I will not say much about it, only that they appeared as well as any other corps that has passed. It numbers 32,000 men—a large corps. All the army is to be reviewed by Sherman—one corps each day.

I am sincerely glad that the self-imposed labor to aid the soldier is soon to be finished. In a little while, only the poor fellows in hospitals will need our care. What a relief it will be to know that when one goes out no other will take his place. How many of our fine fellows are crippled for life! We have lost many of our friends, but the South has lost many, many more. Hardly a lady here but wears mourning. They have, in a great measure, come to the conclusion that they were very much in the wrong; it is an old saying, that "it is better late than never." In this case it hardly will apply, I think. We can see the effects of their repentance by going into the city. All the ladies are out walking, apparently not afraid of the "Yanks."

I wish with you, when you want to be in Charleston. It will be "the time of all times." Beecher will do the occasion full justice.

To-day's mail brings the name of the murderer of our President. What could have been the cause of his doing such a deed? As I write the "Sergeant's Call" has sounded—I hope, for the mail. How good it is to receive letters from home!

Oh, that 10th of April must have been a crazy time at home, surely. I can almost hear the joyous shouts and ringing of bells. Let them ring. They will be heard all over this earth, and be a voice of thunder to all the powers that would help on our destruction. "Uncle Sam" can take care of his own family affairs.

I'll send a genuine "Confederate bond" for $1,000. One man found an immense quantity of the stuff in the State Bank of Raleigh. It is not worth the paper it is printed upon. I wonder how much the people of England will realize from their investments in the loan?

The latest idea of our movements that I hear is, that the whole United States Army will be assembled at Hagerstown, Maryland, some time during the summer, and, after being reviewed by the President and Congress, will be dismissed to their own States. Rather a large force to bring together. If it is true, it will bring people from all parts of the world to see the display. Thus will end the great crusade against oppression, and so will perish forever the "slaveholders' rebellion."

T. R. KEENAN,
17th Mass. Vols.

"There surely never was," writes one to whom many of the soldiers' letters were addressed, "such a record as this in the annals of history! What army ever wrote such sublime, heroic sentences, such high-toned sentiments as will be found in the pages of this, our citizen-soldiers' record? Other armies have, like some vast machine, obeyed blindly the stern decrees of the leader—this band of crusaders against the Saracen hordes of slave-masters to rescue the Holy Sepulchre of liberty from their traitorous grasp, knew well for what cause they unsheathed the sword—knew it was life or death to the Republic — life or death to freedom throughout the world! Thank Heaven for this band of Heroes, more famous to be in song and story than those warriors of Greece and Rome, embalmed in Homer and Virgil's verse! Thank Heaven for the bright array of martyrs gone up from many battle-fields, dreary Southern prisons, and far-off hospitals, to stand before the 'great, white throne,' and give their testimony for Liberty! We shed bitter tears over our dead heroes, but they are the ministering spirits of our father-land, the saints in our calendar of freedom."

As the pages of this volume have been put to press, the last scenes of the terrible drama have been enacted—the conquering march of Sherman, the fall of Charleston, of Wilmington, the movements of the grand "Army of the Potomac," resulting in the evacuation of Richmond, and surrender of the insurgent leader Lee; and close upon it—bitter, relentless culmination of hate!—the Commander-in-chief, greatest, best, chief martyr in his country's cause, has joined the army of patriots gone up from camp and field, from river and mountain-pass, and cruel prisons; our President, honored, beloved, relied on, is taken away! Our Head, the wise, just, humble, thoughtful, reverent, tender-hearted man; our

Ruler, the enlightened, sagacious, magnanimous, disinterested patriot, is ruthlessly stricken down in the midst of labors, of sacrifices, with all his anguished longing and striving for the welfare and unity of the whole people beating true and warm in his loyal heart! A nation in tears, no figure of speech! Heaven help us! Help us to emulate his virtues, and enshrine his memory in our heart of hearts evermore, in equal veneration, gratitude, love, with him who stood hitherto alone, unapproachable. Washington and Lincoln—names not disjoined, immortal, undying!

www.ingramcontent.com/pod-product-compliance
Lightning Source LLC
Chambersburg PA
CBHW051858300426
44117CB00006B/447